WOMEN AND GENDER PERSPECTIVES IN THE MILITARY

WOMEN AND GENDER PERSPECTIVES IN THE MILITARY

AN INTERNATIONAL COMPARISON

Robert Egnell and Mayesha Alam, Editors

Foreword by Amb. Melanne Verveer

Georgetown University Press / Washington, DC

© 2019 Georgetown University Press. All rights reserved. No part of this book may be reproduced or utilized in any form or by any means, electronic or mechanical, including photocopying and recording, or by any information storage and retrieval system, without permission in writing from the publisher.

The publisher is not responsible for third-party websites or their content. URL links were active at time of publication.

Library of Congress Cataloging-in-Publication Data

Names: Egnell, Robert, editor. | Alam, Mayesha, 1988– editor.
Title: Women and gender perspectives in the military : an international comparison / Robert Egnell and Mayesha Alam, editors.
Description: Washington, D.C. : Georgetown University Press, 2019. | Includes bibliographical references and index.
Identifiers: LCCN 2018004910 (print) | LCCN 2018033463 (ebook) | ISBN 9781626166264 (pbk. : alk. paper) | ISBN 9781626166257 (hardcover : alk. paper) | ISBN 9781626166271 (ebook)
Subjects: LCSH: Women and the military. | Women soldiers. | Armed Forces—Social aspects. | Sociology, Military.
Classification: LCC U21.75 (ebook) | LCC U21.75 .W65 2019 (print) | DDC 355.0082—dc23
LC record available at https://lccn.loc.gov/2018004910

20 19   9 8 7 6 5 4 3 2   First printing

Cover design by Martyn Schmoll.

CONTENTS

Foreword by *Ambassador Melanne Verveer* — vii

Acknowledgments — xi

1 Introduction: Gender and Women in the Military—Setting the Stage — 1
Robert Egnell and Mayesha Alam

2 Women in UN Peacekeeping Operations — 23
Sabrina Karim

3 Sweden's Implementation of a Gender Perspective: Cutting Edge but Momentum Lost — 41
Robert Egnell

4 The Gender Perspective and Canada's Armed Forces: Internal and External Dimensions of Military Culture — 73
Stéfanie von Hlatky

5 The Role and Impact of Change Catalysts on the Netherlands Defense Organization: Integration of Women and Gender in Operations — 87
Yvette Langenhuizen

6 Women and Gender in the US Military: A Slow Process of Integration — 113
Brenda Oppermann

7 Women, Gender, and Close Combat Roles in the UK: "Sluts," "Bitches," and "Honorary Blokes" — 141
Anthony King

8 Are Women Really Equal in the People's Army? A Gender Perspective on the Israel Defense Forces — 153
Hanna Herzog

9	The Case of Australia: From "Culture" Reforms to a Culture of Rights *Susan Harris Rimmer*	173
10	Three Waves of Gender Integration: The Causes, Consequences, and Implications for the South African Armed Forces *Lindy Heinecken*	207
11	Integrating Gender Perspectives at NATO: Two Steps Forward, One Step Back *Charlotte Isaksson*	225
12	Conclusion: Lessons of Comparison and Limits of Generalization *Robert Egnell and Mayesha Alam*	253
	List of Contributors	267
	Index	271

FOREWORD

The prevention of conflict, the protection of human rights, and the promotion of peace and security worldwide cannot be achieved without the full and equal participation of women. Systems and processes—at international and national levels—must be adjusted to, at once, include women and, at the same time, take into account the roles and experiences of both men and women. This was the historic clarion call issued by the international community in October 2000, when the UN Security Council unanimously adopted Resolution 1325 on Women, Peace, and Security. Though much progress has been made globally, the promise and potential of UNSCR 1325 remains unfulfilled. This is especially true in the field of military operations, which remains a largely male-dominated arena that continues to be held back—in both effectiveness and equal opportunity—by cultural, bureaucratic, and resource barriers.

When the US National Action Plan (NAP) on Women, Peace, and Security was launched in December 2011, then–secretary of state Hillary Rodham Clinton emphasized the role of military institutions in bridging the gap between the security and agency of women and the peace and stability of nations. As the inaugural US ambassador for global women's issues, I was privileged to help lead the interagency effort that culminated in the NAP. I remember vividly the discussions and debates with colleagues in the White House and the Pentagon that surrounded the drafting of the sections on reforms to the US armed forces. We recognized early on that the US military—the most powerful in the world—had a significant role to play in international security and, thus, ought to set an example in the implementation of UNSCR 1325 and its successive resolutions. To underscore this point, the president issued an accompanying executive order to the NAP. As was true then and remains so today, the inclusion of women, and the integration of gender perspectives into military institutions, has implications for a range of operational objectives—from peacekeeping to national defense, from responding to terrorist attacks to preventing violent extremism, from managing transnational threats to growing peaceful and stable societies. The US Congress later recognized the importance of women's agency to peace and security when it adopted the Women, Peace, and Security Act of 2017, which is now law.

In recent years I have been serving as the special representative for gender for the Chairpersons in Office of the Organization for Security and Cooperation in Europe (OSCE), the largest regional security organization in the world. The OSCE has been increasingly focused on promoting women's participation in the security sector—in the military, policing, border security, and management as well as in conflict resolution—understanding that this is a matter of necessity, critical for operational effectiveness. So too the North Atlantic Treaty Organization (NATO) is committed to raising the profile of women at all levels of the alliance and ensuring women's participation in its training and operations.

This book had its beginnings in a symposium on "Bridging Theory and Practice" organized by the Georgetown University Institute for Women, Peace, and Security. It represents a very timely contribution to our collective understanding of women and gender in military operations. Robert Egnell and Mayesha Alam do a superb job as editors of the volume. Each of its highly informative chapters takes the reader on a journey through the history, politics, and evolution of the military institution in question. I would recommend this book as essential reading to students, scholars, practitioners, and policymakers alike. The case studies highlight opportunities, challenges, progress, and lessons that explain how, why, and to what extent military operations have adapted to and been shaped by women's increased participation as well as gender mainstreaming. Egnell and Alam draw our attention to the internal and external push and pull factors that brought about change in each context, pointing to noteworthy ideational, structural, and material factors. In doing so, they keep our focus on not only the normative but also strategic drivers at play.

At the same time, the edited volume is much more than the sum of its parts. As a collection of cross-regional country experiences, Egnell and Alam's book identifies catalysts for change at the national and international levels. The analyses here, particularly the chapters on UN and NATO, also reiterate how countries working together, beyond borders and in pursuit of common goals, can advance gender mainstreaming and women's participation. The obstacles for international cooperation may seem steep, but the stakes to do so efficiently are even higher. It is critical to close the gender gap in military operations.

I congratulate the editors and contributing authors of this publication for their efforts and commitment to deepening knowledge about women, peace, and security. The ambitious task they take on in this book offers insights about what has been achieved and what remains to be done in the cases covered and beyond.

Ever onward,

Melanne Verveer
US Ambassador for Global Women's Issues (2009–13)
Executive Director, Georgetown Institute for Women, Peace and Security
Washington, DC, January 2018

ACKNOWLEDGMENTS

This book, like any meaningful intellectual endeavor, would not have been possible without the support and commitment of a range of people and institutions. It is our privilege and responsibility to acknowledge their efforts.

The invigorating and informative discussions that served as the launching pad for this book are, first and foremost, thanks to the leadership of Ambassador Melanne Verveer and the Georgetown Institute for Women, Peace, and Security. We both had the honor of working with the institute from its founding, helping it to become a pioneering center for policy-oriented research, expertise, and networking. In June 2015 the institute convened a symposium as part of its Bridging Theory and Practice series that brought together an esteemed group of scholars, practitioners, and policymakers from around the world—including many of the contributors here—which gave inspiration for this volume. The Bridging Theory and Practice series, made possible thanks to the generosity of Nicolaus and Christiane Weickart, continues to gather international leaders to address a variety of critical challenges and brainstorm solutions in the field of women, peace, and security. This particular seminar, on gender and women in military operations, also benefited significantly from the generosity of the US Department of Defense, which provided invaluable funding.

Of course, we have a book only because of the sustained engagement of the contributing authors: Sabrina Karim, Stéfanie von Hlatky, Yvette Langenhuizen, Brenda Oppermann, Anthony King, Hanna Herzog, Susan Harris Rimmer, Lindy Heinecken, and Charlotte Isaksson. Thank you to each and every one of you for your time, labor, and dedication to seeing this project through to the end. Furthermore, along the way several dedicated people have been invaluable in research and editing assistance—Kristin Pettersen, Rachel Friedman, and Stephanie Young.

We are grateful to our editor, Donald Jacobs, for his patience and encouragement throughout the writing and editing process. We hope that Georgetown University Press will continue to invest in scholarship on gender and security.

Finally, we are ever indebted to our families for their unwavering love and affection.

1

Introduction

Gender and Women in the Military—Setting the Stage

Robert Egnell and Mayesha Alam

Whether fighting wars or pursuing diplomacy, devising military tactics or developing nuclear strategy, the arena of international security has traditionally been conceived—by both those on the inside and out—as the purview of men. Throughout virtually the entire world, the relationship between gender—as a social construct—and the military has been largely ignored. And yet conceptualizations of gender, of masculinity and femininity, of the roles appropriate for men versus women, matter in international security even if, for far too long, those in the highest echelons of power—whether government or military—have been reluctant to acknowledge this fact. Ideas shape values and judgments, they guide decisions, and they give life to interactions between people, between institutions, and between states. Beyond theory, gendered experiences of war and peace manifest differently for men and women, shaping their needs and abilities to both resolve and perpetuate armed conflicts.

It was not until the turn of the millennium, however, that the UN Security Council—the international body designated with the responsibility of maintaining peace and security—formally recognized that women, not just men, matter to the construction of a safe and stable world. The adoption of UN Security Council Resolution (UNSCR) 1325 in October 2000 brought unprecedented global attention to the plight of women during armed conflict as well as the need to ensure their participation in peace and security processes. UNSCR 1325—by its principles and scope—raised important questions that, in many ways, challenged traditional notions of security: Who is it for? How can it best be achieved?

Since then the UN Security Council has adopted a suite of resolutions that make up the international women, peace, and security agenda.[1] At the national level, some seventy countries have adopted national action plans (NAPs) that detail the priorities and approaches to implementing the framework of UNSCR 1325. Despite these important normative and policy developments, the chasm between vision and reality remains deep. The seminal 2015 Global Study, produced by UN Women to mark the fifteenth anniversary of UNSCR 1325, identifies inconsistent implementation and under-implementation as the most persistent and prevalent challenges. There are myriad explanations for the implementation gap, such as a shortage of political will, institutional paralysis, competition over limited resources, geopolitical realities, conceptual misunderstanding, and other factors, but one that is particularly relevant to this edited volume is the inadequate sharing of best practices and lessons learned between countries and regions.

Military operations—whether war fighting or peacekeeping—is, arguably, the sector in which the least amount of global progress has been made. This volume aims to fill a lacuna in scholarship by investigating, documenting, and analyzing the role of women and gender in military organizations and operations. The scope of the volume, therefore, encompasses (1) the opening up of national armed forces to women, (2) the integration of gender perspectives in military operations, and (3) the implementation of UNSCR 1325 in military organizations at national and international levels. Not all of these dimensions are necessarily addressed in each chapter, but all three are interconnected and important to consider in concert. By "integration of gender perspectives," we refer to the recognition, acknowledgment, and corresponding assessment of how structures, policies, mission mandates, and institutional culture affect men and women differently. This includes both within military organizations and in the field of operations. Our goal is to advance understanding among scholars and practitioners about the implementation of reforms in military organizations with respect to women and gender, including the inclusion of women and the implementation of gender perspectives at national and international levels. In doing so, we hope to add to the growing body of scholarship in the field pioneered by a range of scholars who have focused on related issues, such as the gendered nature of war fighting, the historical siloing of women to support roles in national militaries, and the sluggish and complicated ways in which considerations of gender have been operationalized in missions.[2]

To achieve our overarching aim, the book conducts a comparison of the integration processes in eight countries as well as in the UN and North Atlantic Treaty Organization (NATO). Not only are detailed analyses of the processes in each case provided, but the case studies also zoom in on several common research questions and variables. First, to provide analytical structure for the cases, we rely on a framework first developed by Louise Olsson in a 2008 study of the Nordic Battle Group's efforts to implement Resolution 1325. She structured her analysis into four different work areas in a classic 2 × 2 matrix that also applies very well to this book.[3] The framework is summarized in table 1.1 and captures these four aspects of the implementation of the resolution in two dimensions. The first part of the matrix captures the internal-external dimension, referring to how military organizations are organized internally and how they are externally working to obtain certain outputs in the field of operations. In essence, on the one hand, how the military is organized, and on the other hand, what they do and how they do it. The second part cuts across the first and covers representation-integration. This means looking at male and female participation on the one hand and the integration of the resolution and broader gender perspectives in the policies and operations of the organizations.[4]

Second, in accordance with that framework, the chapters here look more closely at a set of common research questions that are particularly relevant to specific country cases: Where did the pressure and the decisions to change come from? Who, or what department, was put in charge of the process? Was emphasis placed on the integration of women or gender perspectives, and in what ways? Who were the key agents of change? What were the biggest roadblocks? Which processes or decisions turned out to be essential or limiting? Was the aim of the process described as one of increased military effectiveness or gender equality? Were inside or outside change strategies used? How does the timing and tempo of change fit into a broader international normative and political context? The case study chapters address these questions and factors, allowing us to trace common themes and patterns, while at the same time being flexible enough to tell the unique stories of each case. Thus, the volume strikes a balance between structured comparison and coverage of a range of contextual considerations and challenges involved in the implementation of gender perspectives in military affairs.

To be clear, the ten cases included in this volume are noteworthy, but they are not necessarily representative of the experience of every country or region. A detailed global analysis is beyond the scope of our endeavor, but by tracing and comparing the processes in the selected cases, the book highlights some of the approaches adopted and adapted in furtherance of gender mainstreaming and balancing, as well as their limits.

The nature of, and approaches to, the implementation efforts have varied extensively within and across contexts. Some countries are focused on the integration of women throughout the organization, while others are emphasizing the importance of gender perspectives in operations—something that does

Table 1.1: Framework with Four Work Areas for the Implementation of UNSCR 1325

	Representation	Integration
Internal (i.e., the internal aspects of the military organization)	Mapping policies and equal opportunities: • Male and female personnel—all functions and levels • Work environment • Access to resources and material	Work structure of NATO missions and operations: • Training • Analysis • Planning • Reporting • Evaluation and policy development
External (i.e., how the military organization conducts operations and missions)	Liaison, intelligence, and support: • Interaction with local men and women • Cooperation with and promotion of local partners, including women's organizations	Mandate, interpretation, and execution: • How the main assignments are selected and prioritized • Execution of selected and prioritized assignments • Adaption to local developments

not necessarily require female participation. Some are justifying the process through rights-based arguments about the importance of women's empowerment and gender equality, while others stress operational effectiveness as the primary rationale for change. Some armed forces have been subjected to external pressure, while others change as the result of internal drivers. This variation in change processes has yet to be systematically studied and evaluated, meaning we know little about what works and what does not, or what kind of impact the change processes have on the organizations and their conduct in the field of operations. Is it already possible to find evidence that these implementation processes lead to higher numbers of women, an evolution of organizational cultures, or improved operational effectiveness? While effects may be difficult to measure or quantify, understanding not only why but also how change takes place within military organizations is crucial to creating and maintaining effective initiatives and optimizing interventions in future efforts.

As is apparent in the chapters that follow, many of the developments made to date—especially with respect to the opening up of militaries to women—happened before the adoption of UNSCR 1325. Instead, these processes were the result of broader societal changes that increased gender equality and women's rights. These changes were codified both internationally, with the 1979 Convention on the Elimination of All Forms of Discrimination against Women (CEDAW), and nationally with the Swedish Equality Act of 1980, the US Women's Armed Services Integration Act of 1948, or the Australian Sex Discrimination Act of 1984, as a few examples.

In the last fifteen years, there has been, however, growing recognition that implementation of the women, peace, and security agenda will require not only cooperation between states but also learning from each other and lesson sharing. Accordingly, the authors highlight prevalent organizational hurdles but also potential opportunities for collaboration between institutions and countries. The cases also shine a spotlight on the role and impact of individual change agents in leadership positions within organizations who devised strategies to promote equality and effectiveness and the obstacles they faced in instituting organizational change.

A comparative study, especially an edited volume, requires a framework for analysis to enable case comparison and to produce a coherent volume. To that end, we take an integrated approach to the analysis here by drawing on both feminist and military theories, which, taken together, provide the theoretical grounding for the volume.

Connecting Gender and Military Effectiveness

Gender and military effectiveness may at first glance seem like issues that are worlds apart. In reality, however, military effectiveness is a highly gendered area of research and practice. Feminist international scholarship has long been concerned with the hypermasculinized culture of military organizations and the ways in which war fighting intersects with patriarchy.[5] It is important to recognize that there are different and sometimes divergent schools of thought under the umbrella of feminist scholarship, just as with military studies. We believe it is important to distinguish between these different perspectives and refrain from painting them with a broad brush of generalizations. Some experts on military effectiveness, for example, may treat concerns related to the inclusion of women, the integration of gender perspectives, and the implementation of UNSCR 1325 as marginal at best and conducive to reducing fighting power at worst, whereas others may recognize this as an area of growth and evolution. Similarly, some feminist scholars may see no need to focus on the role of women and gender in military organizations because they disagree with the existence of militaries and violence as tools of order and stability altogether. Some may approach the set of questions we grapple with in this volume as primarily about rights and equality, while others may take an instrumentalist approach based on strategy and utility.

We argue that zero-sum views are both inaccurate in the research arena and unhelpful in the pursuit of international security and stability. For example, reducing the integration of women into armed forces or the operationalization of gender mainstreaming as little more than forms of affirmative action not only misrepresents the multidimensional vision of UNSCR 1325 but also provides little explanatory power in studying change. At the same time, feminist views that summarily vilify the military, abhor the inclusion of women in armed forces, or dismiss the mainstreaming of gender perspectives in military operations are reductive and unconstructive. In short, unchecked extreme positions—irrespective of their theoretical foundations—do not get us very far. The different sides have much to learn from each other, and there are plenty of synergies to be explored. Let us therefore explore how gender perspectives can enhance operational effectiveness and then look at how military organizations can support the implementation of gender perspectives, women's rights, and participation as prescribed in the suite of UN Security Council resolutions beginning with 1325 and the NAPs. First, however, it is important to consider what military effectiveness means in the contemporary strategic context and why it matters.

Military Effectiveness and Fighting Power in a Changing World

An effective military organization is one that succeeds in performing the core tasks that the political leadership asks of it.[6] During the twentieth century, this was generally equated with fighting and winning conventional wars—and thereby defending the nation (or a state's constitution). Thus, national armed forces have historically been organized, been trained, been equipped, and developed a certain professional culture and ethos with the intention of maximizing their effectiveness in performing precisely that fundamental duty. The extreme nature of the task, or what theorists of civil-military relations often refer to as the "functional imperative," also means that military organizations in many respects are entitled, and indeed need, to be different from broader society.[7] Discipline, loyalty, strength, obedience, "warrior mind-set," and unit cohesion are just some aspects of this ethos that may sound arcane or even troubling to some civilians, but from a professional military perspective, they are considered absolutely necessary for the effective application of violence in the midst of war.

The need to be different has also meant that certain developments in culture and civil society, such as increased individualism and the integration of racial, religious, and sexual minorities, are slow to be adopted. The same has, throughout much of the world, been true for the inclusion of women in national armed forces, and even today many militaries exclude women from combat roles. Oftentimes, the unwillingness of the armed forces to respond and adapt to shifts toward greater inclusion is entwined in questions about effectiveness. In the United States, for example, the desegregation of the armed forces became a hotly contested issue about operational effectiveness several decades ago in similar ways to questions more recently about whether allowing gay and transgender men and women to serve openly in uniform would harm the efficacy of the mission on the battlefield.[8] When it comes to the inclusion of women and the application of gender perspectives in mission planning and execution, debates within and outside militaries have centered on not only questions about rights and equal opportunities but also the potential impact on mission outcomes. At the same time, the types of wars and the nature of war fighting have also changed significantly since the turn of the century.

While Russia's illegal annexation of Crimea and the ongoing conflict in Ukraine is a glaring reminder that conventional interstate warfare still very much exists, it is nevertheless fair to say that in the contemporary context, different forms of small wars, counterinsurgency, low-intensity conflict, and complex stability and peace support operations are the most common military missions. The aims of such military operations have often changed from the pursuit of concrete military strategic objectives to the establishment of certain conditions from which political outcomes can be decided.[9] In this context, military activities often play a supporting role in so-called comprehensive, integrated, or whole-of-government approaches and operations that involve a large number of actors and activities aimed at achieving more far-reaching political goals of stabilization, democratization, economic growth, and the implementation and maintenance of respect for human rights and the rule of law. Key tasks of military organizations in this environment therefore include the protection of civilians—including against sexual and gender-based violence—humanitarian and diplomatic activities, and the establishment of order. The political objectives are indeed the most important, and military organizations must not only operate to provide the platform from which civilian actors can achieve these aims. They must also take great care not to violate the principles that tend to govern the larger endeavor: respect for human rights, ideals of democratic governance, and gender equality.

Nonetheless, military theorists often describe military capability as "combat power"—a combination of physical factors (the means—meaning the size and matériel of the organization), conceptual factors (doctrine or the way the means are employed), and moral factors (the will of the soldiers). Within the debates about fighting power, traditional theories about military capability and effectiveness have tended to overemphasize physical military factors, such as troop numbers and the quality of equipment, while paying lesser attention to the more intangible factors that influence a state's capacity to use its material resources effectively—like morale, culture, education, and doctrine.[10] However, the many cases in which the numerically and technologically inferior wins the battle and campaign suggest that such explanations of military capability are misleading—especially when they fail to acknowledge the importance of the policies for which the military instrument is used.[11]

Where do gender perspectives and the integration of female soldiers and officers enter this equation? While one should be careful about falling into the essentialist trap by assigning special capabilities to female soldiers and officers, the argument can be made that adding women to combat units and a gender perspective to military operations more generally has the potential to add new capabilities and thereby also improve the effectiveness of operations.[12]

To begin, women can play a role with regard to the *means*, the material factor. Including the large portion of women who are physically fit for military service in the armed forces allows societies to maximize the size of those forces. However, the emphasis on "lean and mean" organizations rather than mass in twenty-first century warfare means that the main potential contribution is more likely to lie in how and with what conviction armed forces conduct operations.

Adding a gender perspective has the potential to transform the traditional military paradigm by including and creating an increased understanding of the importance of nontraditional security issues. Looking at the strategic process without a sound understanding of all aspects of the conflict—such as the actors involved, the political climate, the local culture, and the economic situation on the ground—it is very difficult to establish what objectives the military and civilian organizations should pursue in the quest for the political aim.[13] A gender perspective casts a critical eye on an area of operations that involves the examination and understanding of social, economic, political, cultural, and religious practices, of how equality and inequality manifest themselves in the distribution of and access to resources, and of decision-making power not just between rich and poor but in all parts of society. Gendered dimensions of conflict can indeed be tremendously transformative by affecting both *what* the operation does and *how* it does it, in terms of its priorities and tactics. It affects the aims of operations and expands the range of violence that must be addressed (including sexual violence and other violence directed at the civilian population, not just the violence of traditional warfare). Gender perspectives can also affect tactical behavior by changing which patrol routes to use, which people within the community to consult, and what types of activities the local population should be protected from.

From a more essentialist (and therefore rather problematic) perspective, women are also portrayed as providing specific competencies and perspectives that improve the conduct of operations. Women in combat units, as well as the implementation of a gender perspective in operations, have the potential to increase the information gathering and analysis capability of units. Gaining access to local women not only allows a unit to develop a better understanding of local conditions and culture but can also improve the unit's relationship with the community and the perceived legitimacy and force protection of troops in the area of operations. The most obvious examples are female or mixed engagement teams, intelligence officers, cultural analysts, and interpreters who provide access to populations and areas that all-male units cannot engage or search in the same ways. These arguments are sometimes made with reference to women's ability to perform certain tasks by virtue of their biological sex and not because of certain female characteristics. The UN Department of Peacekeeping Operations rightly highlights that female soldiers and gender perspectives are absolutely essential for certain tasks in peace operations in which military and civilian aims and tasks overlap. As an example, they help address specific needs of female ex-combatants during the process of demobilization and reintegration into civilian life. They can interview survivors of gender-based violence, mentor female cadets at police and military academies, and interact with women in societies where women are prohibited from speaking to men.[14] Moreover, female soldiers can also serve as role models in the local environment by inspiring women and girls in often male-dominated societies to push for their own rights and for participation in formal and informal peace processes. While these competencies may be dismissed as unrelated to a traditional view of military fighting power, they may prove essential in the more common tasks of stability operations.

However, more essentialist arguments related to "female characteristics" are also common. An example comes from the difficulty in achieving civil-military coordination and cooperation in campaigns involving a broad set of actors. Male dominance of the military is pointed to as one of the cultural features that create friction between military and humanitarian organizations.[15] Female liaison officers could therefore potentially build bridges between the two sets of organizations. These more essentialist arguments are still important for military recruitment purposes as long as men and women continue to be socialized into rather fixed gender roles. This means that increased diversity through the recruitment and participation of women, as well as the integration of gender perspectives, can provide the military organization with certain competencies that would otherwise risk going untapped.

While the inclusion of female soldiers and civilian personnel in military organizations has the potential to reap an array of benefits, their mere presence should not be seen as a silver bullet or be overly exaggerated. The impact, as the chapters in this volume also show, is not going to be revolutionary, and without first changing the mind-set of commanders and planners, the importance of women's perspectives, information, and analyses is likely to be undervalued within a more traditional narrative. The impact is therefore likely to be limited until a more general mainstreaming of a gender perspective is achieved, and even at that time, it is still only one component of many others that determine the effectiveness of an operation.

Military Support of the Women, Peace, and Security Agenda

A closer look at UNSCR 1325 and many of the different NAPs on women, peace, and security reveals that they are intended to be strategic frameworks for conducting more effective and sustainable peace negotiations, peacekeeping missions, and conflict resolution interventions by the international community. These frameworks encompass a range of complex issues, including judicial and legal reform (as part of state building), security sector reform, formal and informal peace negotiations, peacekeeping, political participation, and protection from and responses to sexual violence in armed conflict. UNSCR 1325 and four subsequent resolutions also under the umbrella of the women, peace, and security agenda (UNSCR 1820, 1888, 1889, and 1960) thereby lay out actions to be taken by governments, the United Nations, and other international and domestic actors. Military organizations are at the very heart of this process. On the one hand, they are seen as the "problem" because they are perpetrators of violence (including against women and civilians more broadly) and maintainers of the patriarchal war system. On the other hand, they are also called on as protectors of women and civilians in violent conflicts. Nevertheless, there is plenty of potential for substantial military contribution to the implementation of the four main pillars of the resolutions on women, peace, and security.

Participation

This pillar emphasizes the importance of full participation and inclusion of women (including civil society actors) in the decision-making processes and execution of activities related to peacemaking, postconflict reconstruction, and prevention of conflict. Military organizations can support this process by working internally to ensure women's full participation within their own ranks, as well as to make sure that engagement with civil society and local leaders also includes and empowers women.

Protection

The protection of women and girls in armed conflict is an obvious military role that necessitates a deeper understanding of gender perspectives to be effective. Protection mandates profit from internal training of military personnel, including zero tolerance of sexual exploitation and abuse of local populations and assurance that gender will be an integral part of advising and assisting tasks, security sector reform (SSR), and disarmament, demobilization, and reintegration (DDR) processes. Military organizations thereby have an opportunity to engage in both short-term protection and long-term activities that deal with the underlying reasons for the violence.

Prevention

The prevention of conflict-related sexual violence is a complex but urgent matter that requires changing the behavior of perpetrators. This may involve a range of activities depending on the perpetrator and the reasons for the sexual violence. Preventing sexual violence, sometimes used strategically as a weapon of war and other times tolerated as an indiscretion, requires changing the cost-benefit calculations of the perpetrating units by using force or the threat of force to deter such behavior. While such deterrence is ideally conducted by legal systems holding perpetrators accountable for their actions, in the midst of conflict often only the military has the muscle to provide a convincing enough threat to change individual or group behavior. Addressing broader societal sexual violence requires ending impunity by strengthening judicial capacity and by changing cultural norms that tolerate such crimes.

Gender Mainstreaming

Gender mainstreaming is the process of taking into consideration the implications for women and men of any plans, policies, and activities and informing practice through this assessment and understanding. UNSCR 1325 calls for the systematic implementation of a gender perspective in peacekeeping and peace building by all member states, especially in the context of peace missions led by the UN.[16] The ultimate goal of mainstreaming is often described as achieving gender equality. This is somewhat problematic for military organizations that have other core tasks and that may not see gender equality as part of what they are responsible for. Again, military organizations emphasize the need to be different from other societal structures in order to ensure effectiveness in their core tasks. However, as described previously, mainstreaming gender throughout the organization also has significant positive potential in terms of supporting the analysis, planning, and execution of operations. The mainstreaming of gender perspective throughout military organizations, both at home and abroad, is likely to serve as an important signal to the broader society about military values and military missions. If women can make substantial contributions to what is surely the most masculine and patriarchal arena of all, there are few limits left in terms of women's participation and empowerment in other sectors of society.

In sum, there are several different ways that the inclusion of women or the implementation of gender perspectives has the potential not only to alleviate the negative impact of war for women and to improve women's participation and empowerment in society, but also to improve military effectiveness, primarily with regard to how force is applied to achieve political aims. There are also many potential benefits of a gender perspective that bear less relation to traditional views of military effectiveness but that may have an important impact on operations as a whole—such as by supporting women's participation and status in society and by building the foundation for representative governance and security structures. Let us therefore leave the question of *why* this should be done to instead focus on the equally challenging question of *how* this process can be undertaken—outlining a number of areas of contention and analysis in the case studies.

Approaches to the Implementation Process

The only realistic starting point when attempting to integrate gender perspectives in military organizations is to first understand that militaries tend to be deeply skeptical organizations resistant to change. However, experience in countries like Sweden and the Netherlands indicates that this is not an impossible sell if the process is introduced and managed in a way that speaks to the core tasks of military organizations.[17] This section discusses a number of tactical considerations in the implementation process and addresses a number of debates within feminist theory while doing so.

The most challenging task is to gain access to the organization, to begin the work. This is closely related to the issue of how the process and its aims are described and communicated. Feminist scholars typically use a rights-based approach when discussing the integration of women and gender perspectives in military organizations, or put another way, including women in the military is "the right thing to do." A rights-based process would focus on UNSCR 1325 and speak of increased women's participation and empowerment as inherently good pursuits. While such arguments and aims may sound compelling to a civilian audience, they often fall on deaf ears within military organizations. The functional imperative of fighting and winning wars in defense of the nation remains too strong, and while military leaders might very well support the general notion of increasing gender equality in their society, equality is simply not perceived as having anything to do with military operations. Thus, a first area of contention and analysis is that of the arguments used to "sell" gender mainstreaming and the participation of women in military organizations. Were rights-based arguments of gender equality used, or were more instrumental arguments of operational effectiveness stressed? What worked in what context?

A central issue for feminists studying or promoting change is the extent to which "inside" or "outside" strategies are the most appropriate or effective. Dianne Otto argues that the framework of UNSCR 1325 limits it to "inside" strategies—working within mainstream institutional structures rather than using activism and more radical work conducted outside the mainstream structures in a much more transformative or even revolutionary way.[18] Military organizations, as highlighted earlier, are not just potential protectors of women and civilians; they are also described as "the problem." Not only are military organizations often the perpetrators of some of the worst atrocities conducted in the midst of conflict,[19] but they also have more general problems, highlighted by the high occurrence of sexual harassment and assault within and around military garrisons in peacetime.[20] In other words, many feminists approach military organizations with uneasiness—sometimes even hostility—and they may doubt whether working within the existing institutional and cultural structures of the armed forces is sufficient or even appropriate; perhaps a more transformative, radical, activist agenda from the outside is necessary to successfully implement UNSCR 1325 and the NAPs. If so, what should this transformative agenda entail, and to what extent would it influence the effectiveness of the organization in pursuing its core tasks—employing organized violence? In any case, the debate between inside and outside strategies for organizational change is both interesting and pertinent and, therefore, a self-evident part of the analyses of this book.

Another tactical consideration is derived from the feminist debate whether "gender balancing" (increasing female recruitment and representation) or "gender mainstreaming" (achieving gender equality by assessing the implications for women and men of any planned action, including legislation, policies, and programs in all areas and at all levels) is the most effective and implementable approach to achieve organizational change. The most common assumption is that gender balancing is an easier and more implementable strategy than gender mainstreaming.[21] This is supported by the many cases of Western armed forces that have increased the representation of women in the armed forces but that at the same time struggle to implement a gender perspective. Interestingly, though, Annica Kronsell challenges this assumption by studying the cases of Sweden and the European Union. She notes that in those cases, mainstreaming has been easier than recruiting and promoting women.[22]

It is indeed important to stress that there is a difference between sex and gender and that women are not by definition gender aware, or necessarily promoters of gender equality. Indeed, few women join the military to become advocates of women's rights or gender equality. Instead, just as their male colleagues, women typically sign up because they believe in the cause of defending the nation, they seek the professional opportunities and rewards that a career in the armed forces may bring, and they are drawn to the culture of the military organization. As a consequence, to successfully promote gender perspectives within military organizations, a gender-aware man may sometimes be more effective than an unaware woman. In any case, an important question for the book is to investigate the correlation and possible causalities between the integration of gender perspective and the integration of women. Do the cases indicate that the integration of women in military organizations also leads to greater understanding and application of gender perspectives in operations or vice versa?

Another related debate is whether the implementation process should focus on specific gender-related functions or experts, such as gender advisors attached to regular units, or broader mainstreaming within the organization. The risk with specific functions or experts is, according to Dianne Otto, the "exile of inclusion." Not only are the specialists expected to conform to the existing culture and structure of the organization; they also risk becoming isolated within silos of preexisting organizations or in separate institutions. The organization is thereby more likely to remain oblivious or "blind" to gender issues when the experts are absent.[23] So what should we do? What do the cases indicate are the most useful strategies for change?

There are also interesting questions about more practical issues of implementation in the field of operations. What is the most useful makeup of military "engagement teams," which have purposes ranging from gathering intelligence from women and addressing broader security needs of local women and children to promoting gender equality through local development initiatives? Should they be all female or mixed? Can all-female engagement teams (FETs) obtain access to men in traditional societies as effectively as mixed engagement teams can? Does the gender of the interpreter matter when teams attempt to engage local men and women?

The number of interesting question and debates with which to study the individual cases of this book are both plentiful and wide ranging. Let us therefore take a closer look at how the book is organized in order to address these many questions.

Outline of the Book

In chapter 2 Sabrina Karim analyzes the experience of gender mainstreaming and gender balancing at the UN Department of Peacekeeping Operations (DPKO). Through UNSCR 1325 and subsequent related resolutions, the UN is the inspiration for many of the change processes in the different cases. However, DPKO has struggled to implement the resolution within its own planning and execution of operations. Chapter 2 is nevertheless an opportunity to increase our understanding of the thinking and processes behind the resolution, as well as the particular challenges an international organization faces in implementing values that many member states simply do not subscribe or give importance to. Not only does Karim study the attempts at change within DPKO headquarters in New York, she also examines how the resolution has affected the conduct of operations of UN peacekeeping contingents.

In chapter 3 Robert Egnell describes the experience of the Swedish armed forces to highlight a frontrunner country in UNSCR 1325 implementation. Despite considerable resistance from parts of the organization, the Swedish military has gone through an impressive process of change in the last decade that started with highly limited and isolated gender-related projects and that today involves an institutionalized gender organization that strives to mainstream a gender perspective, conduct training, and establish specific gender-related functions, such as gender field advisors and gender focal points. The gender field advisors have deployed with Swedish and international units in conflicts around the world as part of this process and have thereby gained useful experience and learned lessons that continue to help refine the Swedish approach to gender implementation in military operations. The latest development has been the establishment of the Nordic Centre for Gender in Military Operations, a NATO-appointed Centre of Excellence that aims to function as a platform for cooperation and continued implementation of a gender perspective in both Sweden and abroad. The chapter sets out to explain why this process happened, what the key factors for success were, and what lessons can be drawn.

In chapter 4 Stéfanie von Hlatky studies the Canadian case. The Canadian case zooms in on the strategic-level planning and execution of international operations within the Canadian armed forces. The gender perspective is comprehensive because it targets both intervening states and the societies in which the intervention takes place. The assumption is that military interventions affect women, men, girls, and boys differently. Therefore, failure to recognize this reality of conflict weakens states' ability to design successful intervention models. The chapter argues that, while Canada has been a pioneer in adopting gender-based reforms in the past, it is struggling with the implementation of the current gender-mainstreaming framework because it clashes with core features of the Canadian armed forces' military organizational culture.

Yvette Langenhuizen continues the story of small and middle powers with relatively ambitious agendas within this area by looking at the case of the Netherlands in chapter 5. She notes that women have been part of the Dutch armed forces since 1944 but mainly as a separate force. The process of real integration commenced in the late 1970s. With the transition from a conscription system to an all-volunteer force, and with a shift from a Cold War focus to peacekeeping and stabilization operations, efforts aimed at the recruitment and retention of women increased substantially during the 1980s and 1990s. Over the last decade, the integration of a gender perspective as a tool for operational effectiveness has become part of the Dutch military thinking, mainly linked to experiences of the Dutch armed forces in Afghanistan within the NATO-led International Security Assistance Force (ISAF) mission. The Dutch Ministry of Defense has developed its own action plan, in addition to the joint Netherlands Action Plan on UNSCR 1325, to ensure the implementation of UNSCR 1325 in all its military operations. In doing so, it has set an international example that, while not perfect, holds important lessons. The chapter sets out to increase understanding of the integration processes by studying obstacles, opportunities, and strategies in the trajectory of decisions and events.

Chapter 6 crosses the Atlantic again by studying the US case—a case that involves a superpower engaged in numerous conflicts throughout the period covered by this volume. Brenda Oppermann provides a critical perspective on the US military's implementation of gender perspectives and the way this experience is informed by and relates to the US National Action Plan on Women, Peace, and Security. Oppermann's chapter highlights limited successes, tremendous organizational resistance, and some possible ways ahead. It zooms in on the tactical level to increase our understanding of what happens when policy directives from Washington, DC, reach fighting units in the midst of war. More specifically, it studies the US Army Tenth Mountain Division's work as it took command in southern Afghanistan (Regional Command–South). The chapter thereby aims to add to our understanding of implementation processes at the tactical level in the operational theater. The division's experience shows what happens when good intentions are not enough and also indicates a number of the hurdles that the women, peace, and security agenda is facing within the organization. Oppermann offers invaluable insights and lessons for future implementation processes in both the US and abroad.

In chapter 7 Anthony King tackles the British case and makes the argument that the integration of women and gender perspectives in the British armed forces has been facilitated by the all-volunteer professional forces in which individuals are judged purely by competence. Female soldiers have been accepted in all military roles if they perform competently. There are serious limitations in the infantry, however, as only a small number of women pass the selection tests, and it is likely no more than 1 percent of the infantry is female at present. Moreover, masculine prejudices abound, and women are still the victims of discrimination, harassment, and abuse. The key test for integration is the factor of unit cohesion. What does the integration of women and gender perspectives do to this all-important factor for operational success? The chapter thereby aims to contribute to our understanding of the impact of these change processes by tackling a key concern for military effectiveness and the existing military establishment.

In chapter 8 Hanna Herzog provides a study of the interesting case of Israel. Israel is the only country that, since its establishment in 1948, has had compulsory military service for both women and men. The chapter argues that various intra- and inter-logics act simultaneously as formal and informal mechanisms of re-gendering and de-gendering the structure, organizational norms, and practices of the Israeli army. Up to the end of the 1980s, the encounter between these different logics reinforced the gendering of the army. From the 1990s onward, the intersections between the forces in the field have stimulated processes of de-gendering, although they do not form one clear, linear trend of development but rather a multitude of facets of gendering and de-gendering; these facets often exist simultaneously. The discussion of the chapter thereby points out central gendering logics, the relationships between them, and the way they have been challenged in the Israel Defense Forces over the years.

Susan Harris Rimmer studies the Australian case in chapter 9. She notes that the Australian Defence Force (ADF) has historically been, and in some aspects remains, a "hypermasculinist" institution, as the outgoing chief of army informed the United Nations in 2013. The ADF has been under significant pressure to reform since 2011, and in response to a series of high-profile scandals involving new technology, violations of human rights, and instances of sexual and gender-based violence, the ADF undertook a series of cultural reforms. As an example, the chief of defense has created more gender advisor positions within the ADF and has made several important appointments of women at senior levels. Australia also launched its National Action Plan on Women, Peace, and Security in 2012, whereby the ADF has key tasks to acquit by 2018. There are, however, also signs that point to an ADF culture that weathers storms but then reverts to previous habits and structural limitations when active, high-level leadership and public pressure decreases. The chapter critically engages with the ADF's various experiences of gender mainstreaming and gender balancing.

In chapter 10 Lindy Heinecken takes us through the South African experience of integrating gender perspectives and increasing women's participation in the armed forces. The South African armed forces have undergone three distinct phases of gender integration. The first phase was promoted by a shortage of qualified white males during the height of the Border War in the 1970s during the apartheid era. As the military organization's posture of the time was offensive, women were not permitted to serve in any combat and could serve only in the support branches. Gender equality was not the driver for gender integration. Women served in supportive roles to augment the capacity of men, were trained separately, and were encouraged to actively maintain their femininity on duty. The second wave commenced shortly after the formation of the South African National Defence Force (SANDF) in 1995 and was associated with the transition to democracy, the end of the Cold War, and the shift to a more defensive military posture. Unlike the first wave, the second was driven by an equal rights agenda stemming from the Constitution of the Republic of South Africa, which compelled the SANDF to open all positions, including combat roles, to women. A prominent affirmative action campaign was launched to address gender imbalances and to increase the number of women in the SANDF. This gave rise to tensions around equal opportunities and meritocracy associated with the impact of inclusion of women on military effectiveness. The third wave commenced around 2008 and was associated with UNSCR 1325, whereby the emphasis was placed on gender mainstreaming and a shift in defense priorities toward human security. This focus shifted away from a gender-neutral and equal rights position to recognizing gender differences and acknowledging that women possess certain qualities that are not only necessary but also crucial to security. However, as the SANDF still continues to train for war fighting, there has also been a gender backlash that Heinecken explains in the chapter. The SANDF is now at the crossroads of how to infuse a more gender-balanced approach to security, given the dominance of a military culture that remains steeped in the warrior ethos and hegemonic masculinities.

Chapter 11 leaves the country cases and returns to the arena of international organizations. Charlotte Isaksson provides a detailed study of NATO and the key achievements and challenges in the process of implementing gender perspective and UNSCR 1325 and related resolutions. She does this by taking a closer look at these processes within NATO's Allied Command Operations (ACO), which also encompasses NATO operations and missions. The approach to the internal implementation within ACO has been to transform and change the thinking, planning, and conduct from within by identifying the existing structures, systems, and processes and integrating UNSCR 1325 into them rather than creating something new and additional that is likely to create a stronger resistance to change. For ACO this meant a need to find and define internal stakeholders and actors who would assume responsibility for the change process and for reaching the desired end state. The chapter argues that the key remaining obstacles are not the need for additional policy frameworks or working mechanisms. Instead, they are proceeding with the implementation of the already adopted UNSCR 1325 and related policies in the entire organization—from the strategic to the tactical level. NATO is a large organization that, by its nature and mandate, presents unique challenges and opportunities. Understanding the change process within ACO is key to increased understanding of how such processes can be managed.

Finally, chapter 12 pulls together conclusions based on the data and experiences detailed throughout the book to provide a more comprehensive narrative of change processes. Important lessons, situated within policy and theory frames with an eye to future research and practice, emerge.

This volume demonstrates the difficult and inconsistent implementation of international and national commitments to advance women, peace, and security in military operations is the result of a variety of factors related to resources, leadership, bureaucracy, information, institutions, and mission mandates. No two contexts are identical, but patterns in gaps of implementation are traceable across cases. And yet some developments at both the national and international levels are encouraging, so it is important to recognize the emergence of innovative thinking and to take stock of approaches that have been brought to bear by well-meaning individual leaders, national militaries, and peace-support missions.

Notes

1. To date there have been eight Security Council resolutions on women, peace, and security: 1325 (2000), 1820 (2009), 1888 (2009), 1889 (2009), 1960 (2011), 2106 (2013), 2122 (2013), and 2242 (2015). "The Resolutions," Peace Women, accessed January 16, 2018, http://www.peacewomen.org/why-WPS/solutions/resolutions.
2. See, for example, Cynthia Cockburn, "Gender Relations as Causal in Militarization and War: A Feminist Standpoint," *International Feminist Journal of Politics* 12, no. 2 (2010): 139–57; Carol Cohn, ed., *Women and Wars: Contested Histories, Uncertain Futures*

(Cambridge: Polity Press, 2013); Joshua S. Goldstein, "War and Gender," in *Encyclopedia of Sex and Gender* (New York: Springer, 2003), 107–16; Valerie M. Hudson, Mary Caprioli, Bonnie Ballif-Spanvill, Rose McDermott, and Chad F. Emmett, "The Heart of the Matter: The Security of Women and the Security of States," *International Security* 33, no. 3 (2009): 7–45; Laura Sjoberg and Sandra Via, *Gender, War, and Militarism: Feminist Perspectives* (Santa Barbara, CA: Praeger, 2010); J. Ann Tickner, *Gender in International Relations: Feminist Perspectives on Achieving Global Security* (New York: Columbia University Press, 1992).

3. Louise Olsson, "Resolution 1325 och den Nordiska snabbinsatsstyrkan," in Anders W. Berggren, *Förutsättningar för att verka internationellt—Slutrapport från temaområdet Människan i NBF* [Prerequisites for working internationally—Final report from research project People in NBF] (Stockholm: Swedish Defence College, 2008).
4. Builds on ibid.
5. Tickner, *Gender in International Relations*.
6. This section draws on Robert Egnell, "Women in Battle: Gender Perspectives and Fighting," *Parameters* 43, no. 2 (Summer 2013): 33–41; Robert Egnell, Petter Hojem, and Hannes Berts, *Gender, Military Effectiveness, and Organizational Change: The Swedish Model* (London: Palgrave Macmillan, 2014).
7. Christopher Dandeker, "On the Need to Be Different: Military Uniqueness and Civil-Military Relations in Modern Society," *RUSI Journal* 146, no. 3 (June 2001): 4–9.
8. Aaron Belkin, "Don't Ask, Don't Tell: Is the Gay Ban Based on Military Necessity?," *Parameters* 33, no. 2 (Summer 2003): 108; Richard M. Dalfiume, *Desegregation of the US Armed Forces: Fighting on Two Fronts, 1939–1953* (Columbia: University of Missouri Press, 1969).
9. Rupert Smith, *The Utility of Force: The Art of War in the Modern World* (London: Allen Lane, 2005), 269.
10. For a useful summary, see ibid., 240–43.
11. Risa A. Brooks, "Making Military Might: Why Do States Fail and Succeed?," *International Security* 28, no. 2 (Fall 2003): 149–91; Stephen Biddle, *Military Power: Explaining Victory and Defeat in Modern Battle* (Princeton, NJ: Princeton University Press, 2004).
12. For a useful discussion of the positive impact of women and gender perspectives, see Sahana Dharmapuri, "Just Add Women and Stir," *Parameters* 41, no. 1 (Spring 2011): 56–70.
13. Smith, *Utility of Force*, 374.
14. United Nations, "Women in Peacekeeping," https://peacekeeping.un.org/en/women-peacekeeping.
15. Donna Winslow, "Strange Bedfellows in Humanitarian Crisis: NGOs and the Military," in *Twisting Arms and Flexing Muscles: Humanitarian Intervention and Peacebuilding in Perspective*, eds. N. Mychajlyszyn and T. D. Shaw (Aldershot: Ashgate, 2005), 116.
16. Definition from the UN Economic and Social Council (ECOSOC), adopted on July 18, 1997.
17. Egnell, Hojem, and Berts, *Gender*.
18. Dianne Otto, "The Exile of Inclusion: Reflections on Gender Issues in International Law over the Last Decade," *Melbourne Journal of International Law* 10, no. 1 (2009), https://papers.ssrn.com/sol3/papers.cfm?abstract_id=1508067.
19. Kathleen Kuehnast, Chantal de Jonge Oodrat, and Helge Hernes, eds., *Women and War: Power and Protection in the 21st Century* (Washington, DC: US Institute of Peace Press,

2011); Maria Eriksson Baaz and Maria Stern, *Sexual Violence as a Weapon of War?* (New York: Palgrave Macmillan, 2013).
20. David S. Cloud, "Military Is on the Spot over Sexual Assaults," *Los Angeles Times*, June 5, 2013, http://articles.latimes.com/2013/jun/05/nation/la-na-rape-military-20130605; Office of the Secretary of Defense, *Fiscal Year 2009 Annual Report on Sexual Assault in the Military* (Arlington, VA: Sexual Assault Prevention and Response Office, 2010); Ann W. Burgess, Donna M. Slattery, and Patricia A. Herlihy, "Military Sexual Trauma: A Silent Syndrome," *Journal of Psychosocial Nursing and Mental Health Services* 51, no. 2 (February 2013): 20–26.
21. Annica Kronsell, *Gender, Sex, and the Postnational Defense* (Oxford: Oxford University Press, 2012), 135–36; See also Egnell, Hojem, and Berts, *Gender*.
22. Kronsell, *Gender, Sex*, 135–36.
23. Otto, "Exile of Inclusion."

2

Women in UN Peacekeeping Operations

Sabrina Karim

Since the formation of peacekeeping operations in 1948, when the Security Council authorized the deployment of UN military observers to the Middle East, there has been consensus on several points. First, peacekeeping missions contribute to longer-term peace.[1] Second, peacekeeping may reduce levels of one-sided violence and battlefield fatalities.[2] Third, peacekeeping may mitigate the potential for conflict to spread from one state to the next.[3] Fourth, peacekeeping can reduce the geographic scope of violence.[4] Finally, peacekeeping missions with a mandate for humanitarian assistance and with mediation mandates may improve human rights.[5] While peacekeeping missions are vital for ensuring a durable and quality peace, the adoption of a gender perspective in UN peacekeeping operations is a relatively new innovation that came to fruition in the 2000s. Despite the novelty of a gender perspective in UN peacekeeping missions in the 2000s, the UN Department of Peacekeeping Operations (DPKO) was the first military organization to adopt this perspective. Thus, given that the UN was the starting point for this agenda, there is much to be learned from how it has implemented a gender perspective in UN peacekeeping operations.

This chapter explores the UN's implementation of a gender perspective by asking three main questions. First, why were decisions made in the UN to include a gender perspective in peacekeeping operations? And who were the key decision makers in making changes in missions? Here the key insight is that attempts to bring attention to the women, peace, and security (WPS) agenda started in the 1990s, but the adoption of UN Security Council Resolution (UNSCR) 1325 in 2000 set the stage for UN peacekeeping operations to ensure a gender perspective in all peacekeeping missions. Next, what does the integration of women and gender perspectives look like when it is operationalized in peacekeeping missions? DPKO has implemented UNSCR 1325 mainly through two mechanisms: gender balancing and gender mainstreaming. While gender mainstreaming may be a more holistic way to ensure that missions adopt a gender perspective, gender balancing has been a more popular route owing to expedience. Nevertheless, there are drawbacks to this approach, mainly that female peacekeepers are not able to reach their full potential because of the gendered structures that exist both in contributing country militaries and within the peacekeeping mission. While gender mainstreaming is perhaps a preferable tool, it suffers from inadequate conceptualization and has not been effective because of a pervasive male dominance within peacekeeping culture.

Moving forward, an assessment of DPKO's past strategy, achievements, and shortcomings is necessary to evaluate the potential for peacekeeping missions to lead in promoting gender issues globally. Because of its comparative advantage in implementing a gender perspective, the UN is regarded as a model for WPS efforts in the militaries of individual countries. Thus, to understand how the UN has implemented a gender perspective and the effects of such implementation, this chapter first explores the evolution of integrating a gender perspective into peacekeeping operations and provides an understanding of why decisions were made to include a gender perspective in peacekeeping operations in the 2000s. This historical tracing helps us understand how gender perspectives might be brought to national militaries. The chapter then demonstrates that the UN, policymakers, and some scholars opted to take an instrumentalist approach in justifying why a gendered approach was necessary. The next part of the chapter highlights how implementation occurred; the UN implemented both gender balancing and gender mainstreaming but has perhaps prioritized gender balancing because it is easier to measure. The chapter concludes with some of the existing challenges that remain to more fully integrate a gender perspective in peacekeeping operations.

The Evolution of a Gendered Approach in Peacekeeping Missions

United Nations peacekeeping operations began during the Cold War, when most missions comprised military personnel observing compliance with cease-fires and settlements. In the 1990s peacekeeping operations began to take a more multidimensional approach, and with the Brahimi Report issued in 2000, most peacekeeping missions expanded their mandates to include peacebuilding activities, such as organizing elections; disarming, demobilizing, and reintegrating solders; promoting security sector reform; establishing rule of law; and promoting good governance and human rights. Yet although conflict has always been a gendered experience, and despite a growing movement toward a WPS agenda in the 1990s, issues pertaining to gender were not a part of the Brahimi Report, and a gender perspective was not included in peacekeeping operations until later in the 2000s. Not until a larger global movement institutionalized the WPS agenda did gender perspective become an important component of peacekeeping missions.

The WPS agenda first appeared in the 1995 Beijing Platform for Action, which contained an entire chapter focused on women, peace, and security. During the 1990s the nongovernmental organization (NGO) community was increasingly concerned about the negative impacts of war on women, particularly widespread sexual violence seen in civil wars in Bosnia and Rwanda. Activists were also upset that women faced significant barriers to entering peace talks and myriad negative impacts post-conflict. The Beijing Conference's fifth anniversary (Beijing+5) provided critical momentum for progress on WPS issues at the UN and paved the way for the UNSCR 1325 movement.

The first major document regarding the WPS agenda and peacekeeping missions was the Windhoek Declaration and the Namibia Plan of Action on Mainstreaming a Gender Perspective in Multidimensional Peace Support Operations, which stressed the importance of gender mainstreaming and gender balancing in UN peace operations. The declaration and accompanying plan of action were based on a comprehensive study of peacekeeping missions in Bosnia, Cambodia, El Salvador, Namibia, and South Africa conducted by DPKO in cooperation with the Division for the Advancement of Women titled "Mainstreaming a Gender Perspective in Multidimensional Peace Support Operations." The study concluded, "Women's presence improves access and support for local women; it makes men peacekeepers more reflective and responsible; and it broadens the repertoire of skills and styles available within the mission, often with the effect of reducing conflict and confrontation." These justifications for increasing the representation of women in peacekeeping missions are still used today.[6]

The WPS agenda has been an integral part of DPKO since the October 2000 adoption of UNSCR 1325, which legally mandated that peacekeeping operations include women in decision-making roles in all aspects of the peacekeeping and peacebuilding process. UNSCR 1325 was the product of a broad coalition of NGOs, social movements, and states that worked together to convince member states that "women as victims of war" and "women as creators of peace" should be systematically involved in peacekeeping and peacebuilding operations.[7] The resolution's adoption is considered by many to be a historic milestone since it marked the first time that the UN Security Council dealt specifically with gender issues and women's experiences in conflict and post-conflict situations and recognized women's contribution to conflict resolution and prevention.[8] UNSCR 1325 mentions the incorporation of a gender perspective in peacekeeping operations several times. It highlights

- "the urgent need to mainstream a gender perspective into peacekeeping operations";
- the "need for specialized training for all peacekeeping personnel on the protection, special needs and human rights of women and children in conflict situations"; and
- the "willingness to incorporate a gender perspective into peacekeeping operations."

The resolution also

- urges "the Secretary-General to ensure that, where appropriate, field operations include a gender component";
- "requests the Secretary-General to provide to Member States training guidelines and materials on the protection, rights and the particular needs of women, as well as on the importance of involving women in all peacekeeping and peacebuilding measures";
- "invites Member States to incorporate these elements as well as HIV/AIDS awareness training into their national training programmes for military and civilian police personnel in preparation for deployment"; and
- "further requests the Secretary-General to ensure that civilian personnel of peacekeeping operations receive similar training."

Subsequent resolutions since UNSCR 1325, such as UNSCR 1820 (2008), 1888 (2009), 1889 (2009), 1960 (2010), 2106 (2013), 2122 (2013), and 2242 (2015), also affirm that gender should be an integral part of peacekeeping operations globally.

Because of UNSCR 1325 and the subsequent resolutions, gender is now mentioned in almost every mandate authorizing peacekeeping missions.[9] However, the mandates vary in their scope of mentioning gender. Some only prohibit the sexual exploitation and abuse (SEA) by peacekeepers, while others mention specific objectives, such as promoting women's participation in politics or protecting women from sexual violence. DPKO points to several successes since UNSCR 1325 in gender balancing and gender mainstreaming. According to the "Ten-Year Impact Study on Implementation of UN Security Council Resolution 1325 (2000) on Women, Peace and Security in Peacekeeping," peacekeeping missions are helping to implement policies on the ground that promote the UNSCR 1325 agenda, and when it comes to implementing UNSCR 1325 within peacekeeping missions, gender focal points and gender units have been established to help guide members of the military and police. In 2014 the UN deployed its first female force commander to the UN Peacekeeping Force in Cyprus (UNFICYP). Additionally, women's protection advisors (WPAs), mandated by the Security Council in 2009, have been deployed to countries with evidence of conflict-related sexual violence (CRSV). Nevertheless, DPKO, especially the gender unit, which is the main implementer of UNSCR 1325 in peacekeeping operations, faces numerous challenges ensuring that peacekeeping missions fulfill the resolution's mandate, including the implementation of gender balancing and gender mainstreaming in peacekeeping operations.

Why Take a Gendered Approach in Peacekeeping?

While the institutionalization of the WPS movement through UNSCR 1325 provided a legal, albeit nonbinding, framework for including a gender perspective in peacekeeping operations, the actual implementation of the gender perspective relied on instrumental justifications for women's inclusion. The justification is important to understand because it demonstrates one particular pathway by which other military institutions might adopt a gender perspective and it demonstrates the drawback from this approach.

Starting with the Windhoek Declaration and the Namibia Plan of Action on Mainstreaming a Gender Perspective, the UN has used a variety of justifications that mainly focus on military (or peacekeeping) effectiveness rather than on a rights-based approach. The UN argument is that "female peacekeepers act as role models in the local environment, inspiring women and girls in often male-dominated societies to push for their own rights and for participation in peace processes." Further, "the increased recruitment of women is critical for: empowering women in the host community; addressing specific needs of female ex-combatants during the process of demobilizing and reintegration into civilian life; helping make the peacekeeping force approachable to women in the community; interviewing survivors of gender-based violence; mentoring female cadets at police and military academies; interacting with women in societies where women are prohibited from speaking to men." Finally, "the presence of women peacekeepers can also: help to reduce conflict and confrontation; improve access and support for local women; provide role models for women in the community; provide a greater sense of security to local populations, including women and children; and broaden the skill set available within a peacekeeping mission."[10] Even recent documents, such as "Forward Looking Gender Strategy (2014–2018)" issued by DPKO and the Department of Field Support (DFS), incorporate sections on the "comparative advantages of gender and peacekeeping," in which they argue, "The focus on gender equality during the last decade in . . . policies, guidance notes, guidelines and peacekeeping strategies has increased awareness, skills and personnel and institutional capacity to recognise the specific needs, contributions, roles and abilities of women and girls and include them as key partners in peacekeeping work."

Scholars have echoed policymakers in suggesting that women bring particular advantages to peacekeeping operations. Bridges and Horsfall argue that increasing the representation of women will help combat sexual misconduct perpetrated by some male soldiers and will engender trust and improve the reputation of peacekeepers among local populations.[11] In general, these claims are more instrumental in nature—female peacekeepers provide a service to missions that may not be possible without men. The justifications focus on how women improve peacekeeping missions and not on the fact that increasing representation is important as a right more broadly.

While an instrumental approach is helpful because it allows those in the militarized organization to understand why women might be important, there might be drawbacks in using this approach. Karim and Beardsley outline several concerns with using an instrumental approach to justify, in particular, gender balancing.[12] They note that justifying women's representation in terms of added value places a burden on women to succeed in order to be accepted. The burden of making the mission more effective is disproportionally placed on women as men's representation does not have to be justified. Moreover, as we shall see later, female peacekeepers work in the context of a highly male-dominated institution, which inhibits their ability to reach their full potential. Thus, the instrumental value that women bring to a mission may not be achieved unless there is also transformative cultural change within the mission. Regardless of the potential danger in using an instrumental approach, this approach has been adopted by the UN and is likely to be used by other military organizations.

Gender Balancing versus Gender Mainstreaming in Peacekeeping Operations

Implementation of a gender perspective in peacekeeping operations has included both gender balancing and gender mainstreaming. According to the July 2000 UN document "Mainstreaming a Gender Perspective in Multidimensional Peace Operations," both gender balancing and gender mainstreaming are important principles for peacekeeping missions. UNSCR 1325 reifies this statement. Yet gender balancing and gender mainstreaming are different ways to adopt a "gendered approach" to peacekeeping. Gender balancing is "the degree to which men and women hold the full range of positions in a society or organization."[13] The goal is to increase women's representation in peacekeeping missions. As mentioned previously, the UN has described the benefits of gender balancing using an instrumental lens. This lens suggests that the addition of female bodies to peacekeeping missions is expected to have a transformational effect on an operation. As we shall see later, however, these expectations are not well founded, because they ignore the fact that female peacekeepers operate in a male-dominated organization, which prevents them from reaching their full potential.[14]

Gender mainstreaming, in contrast, is "the process of assessing the implications for men and for women of any planned action, including legislation, policies or programmes, in all areas and at all levels" and "a strategy for making women's as well as men's concerns and experiences an integral dimension of the design, implementation, monitoring and evaluation of policies and programmes in all political, economic and societal spheres so that women and men benefit equally and inequality is not perpetuated."[15] The goal is to change mission culture so that it is not dominated by male-centric beliefs, opinions, and actions. Gender mainstreaming does not require increased female representation. Scholars have argued that gender mainstreaming might be more effective than gender balancing in addressing mission needs because it not only allows women who are in the mission more authority but also ensures that the responsibility of the WPS agenda falls on both men and women.[16] Moreover, gender mainstreaming may ensure that gender balancing occurs without the use of an instrumental justification for women's inclusion. As we shall see later, however, gender mainstreaming is not fully implemented in missions because of entrenched organizational culture and ambiguity about how to implement mainstreaming. In general, peacekeeping missions have attempted to implement both balancing and mainstreaming but have been more successful in gender balancing because it is easier to implement. This is despite the fact that gender mainstreaming and the promotion of gender equality through mission culture are perhaps more successful in enhancing the operational effectiveness of missions.[17]

Since 2000 there have been numerous UN documents that develop the concepts of gender balancing, gender mainstreaming, and their operationalization in the field. In 2010 DPKO and DFS issued "Integrating a Gender Perspective into the Work for the United Nations Military in Peacekeeping Operations," which provides guidelines at the strategic, operational, and tactical levels for gender mainstreaming in missions. More recently, "Forward Looking Gender

Strategy (2014–2018)" has highlighted the links among women, peace, and security and reaffirmed the DPKO/DFS commitment to work effectively at all levels to promote and achieve gender mainstreaming in peacekeeping.

The DPKO/DFS gender strategy builds on results, best practices, and lessons from peacekeeping operations and addresses critical gaps in institutionalizing gender work in the departments; rearticulates the gender architecture in peacekeeping operations in a changed and further evolving landscape; refocuses how gender equality work in peacekeeping is conducted, with emphasis on gender mainstreaming within the mission (as opposed to the provision of direct support to national partners); clarifies and reinforces roles and accountability for all categories and levels of peacekeeping staff and provides guidance for their activities in implementing the WPS resolutions; considers the important roles that UN Women and the Office of the Special Representative for the Secretary General for Sexual Violence in Conflict (SRSG-SVC) play in implementing the WPS agenda and promotes synergy, including through the UN's coordination network for WPS-related issues; and promotes improved data collection, analysis, reporting, and dissemination of progress and impact results.

Moreover, *Preventing Conflict, Transforming Justice, Securing the Peace: A Global Study on the Implementation of United Nations Security Council Resolution 1325*, issued by UN Women in 2015, highlights the importance of both gender mainstreaming and gender balancing. It uses the language of instrumentalism to highlight the importance of gender balancing: "Pursuing the goal of 'gender balance' as suggested in the Beijing Platform for Action, can encourage transformational change in institutions and has been found to lead to different choices in social spending."[18] The study also suggests that gender mainstreaming is only possible with the inclusion of a gender unit. For example, "while in-mission capacity is crucial across peace operations missions, equally critical is the dedicated capacity at headquarters level, where staffing is necessary for comprehensive gender mainstreaming across the range of work of both DPKO and DPA [Department of Political Affairs]. Gender units with senior leads and sufficient staffing should be institutionalized within the regular budget envelope of both DPA and DPKO/DFS."[19]

As suggested by the 2015 study, one of the main ways that gender has been mainstreamed in peacekeeping missions is through the appointment of gender advisors and the establishment of gender units. Gender advisors and gender units aim to ensure a broad range of activities on gender, both within the mission and in host populations. Within the mission these include systematic training of all peacekeeping personnel on the gender dimensions of their operations, the integration of gender perspectives in all standard operating procedures, and the planning, implementation, and evaluation of gender activities in all functional areas. In 2010 there were gender advisors in ten multidimensional peacekeeping missions and gender focal points—that is, key personnel in the military and police part of missions designated as responsible for gender issues—in six traditional peacekeeping missions. However, *Global Study* notes that gender units in missions are generally understaffed and under-resourced relative to the tasks they are expected to accomplish.

Another way gender has been mainstreamed is through WPAs, which have roles complementary to those of the gender advisors. WPAs focus specifically on the integration of CRSV considerations in the activities of the mission, including monitoring, analysis, and reporting on sexual violence and advocating and engaging with parties to the conflict with regard to their obligations to prevent and address CRSV.

Despite gender mainstreaming efforts, including the appointment of focal points, gender advisors, and WPAs, more attention has been placed on gender balancing in peacekeeping operations. In 2007 the UN hailed the first all-female police unit deployment from India to Liberia. Another unit was deployed in 2010 from Bangladesh to Haiti. UN Secretary General Ban Ki-moon has emphasized increasing the representation of women in peacekeeping missions but has not placed as much emphasis on gender mainstreaming. For example, in 2009 he launched a campaign to increase the share of female peacekeepers to 10 percent in military units and 20 percent in police units by 2014—a goal that was not met. With the passing of UNSCR 2242 (2015), the UN set an ambitious new target to double the number of women in peacekeeping over five years. The increased focus on and implementation of gender balancing may be because the results are easier to measure than they are for gender mainstreaming. Gender balancing requires counting the number of women in missions, whereas gender mainstreaming is a more complex concept, and policymakers and scholars have struggled with how to implement and measure it.

Evaluating DPKO's Gendered Approach

Both gender balancing and gender mainstreaming have had successes, but challenges remain. These successes and challenges are evaluated in depth in turn.

Gender Balancing: Has the Representation of Female Peacekeepers Increased?

In anticipation of UNSCR 1325's tenth anniversary, UN Secretary General Ban Ki-moon launched a campaign in 2009 to increase the share of female peacekeepers to 10 percent in military units and 20 percent in police units by 2014. The UN missions did not meet the deadline. Yet women's representation in UN peacekeeping operations has increased since the passage of UNSCR 1325. The UN reports that in 1993, women made up 1 percent of deployed uniformed personnel. It started disaggregating data on peacekeeping deployments for military personnel in 2006 and police in 2009. While the overall proportions of female peacekeepers are still quite low presently, there is a positive trend in female peacekeeping for both military and police contributions, and it is rare for missions to not have any female peacekeepers at all. Since December 2006 the proportion of female troops has doubled, although it remains low at less than 3 percent of the total troop contingents. During this same period, the proportion of women in an individual police role nearly doubled and is higher than the proportion of female troops, although the upward trajectory has attenuated. From the end of 2010 to present, there has been non-trending fluctuation in the proportions of women, between 12 and 16 percent in all missions.[20]

Peacekeeping operations are unique in that variation in female peacekeeping contributions depends on contributing country incentives. The UN may mandate that contributing countries send higher proportions of women, but ultimately, the contributing country is the one that decides its numbers. Crawford, Lebovic, and Macdonald find that gender diversity is not a primary goal of most contributors and is largely a by-product of force sizes.[21] Other scholars suggest that two incentives may guide the variation in female peacekeeping contributions: the availability of female personnel and gender equality within the contributing countries. Karim and Beardsley find that when countries have higher numbers of women in their national militaries, they are more likely to send female peacekeepers.[22] The authors also find that when contributing countries have better records of gender equality, they are more likely to send female soldiers to peacekeeping missions. This is because gender-equal norms in society are reflected in the military, and thus, some norms that might keep militaries from deploying women to dangerous locations, such as norms of a need to protect women, are less. This means that countries that promote gender equality well in their *national* militaries may be more likely to send female peacekeepers to missions and therefore improve gender balancing in peacekeeping missions.

However, Karim and Beardsley find that female military peacekeepers actually end up in the safest missions, or missions in which fewer peacekeepers die and the host country has a higher gross domestic product.[23] This suggests that even though representation may be increasing, women may not be deploying to missions evenly or where they may be most needed. Indeed, high-ranking officials in the Bangladeshi military—Bangladesh is one of the top-contributing countries to peacekeeping missions—said that Bangladesh is careful about where it sends its female soldiers. Additionally, female soldiers who deploy on missions are typically doctors, nurses, or administrative staff, and not necessarily frontline soldiers or those doing the actual peace building.[24] Thus, one of the main challenges for gender balancing in peace operations is compliance from member states to send women to different types of missions.

Moreover, women are not represented in all parts of the peacekeeping operations. While UNFICYP installed its first female force commander in 2014, no other mission has a female force commander, and Cyprus is one of the safest missions (with respect to peacekeeping deaths). Women are not likely to be appointed to higher positions in other missions, because there are few women of rank in the first place. In a 2012 survey of female peacekeepers in the UN Mission in Liberia (UNMIL), women complained that they were not allowed to leave their bases and interact with other women from other contingents, were not allowed to interact with the host population, and experienced high levels of discrimination in their job.[25] Male peacekeepers did not make similar claims. Female peacekeepers also complained of problems of sexual harassment within the mission. This means that female peacekeepers, despite their increases in number, are not allowed to reach their full potential when in the mission.[26]

Nevertheless, some evidence indicates that female peacekeepers do make a difference on the ground and consequently that gender-balancing policies might improve mission effectiveness. In particular, female peacekeepers have been primary drivers of gender-equality policies in host countries. For example, in UNMIL female peacekeepers helped establish a sexual harassment policy for the Liberian National Police, implement gender quotas for the Liberian National Police, and establish laws and policies around sexual violence.[27] As mentioned, however, the problem is that women do not deploy to all missions equally, and even when women are deployed to peacekeeping operations, they often do not interact with locals or local women, which means that the benefits of having female peacekeepers present in missions is not being fully realized.

Gender Mainstreaming: Has the Culture of the Organization Changed?

The justification that the UN uses for gender balancing and gender mainstreaming suggests that implementation of such policies may lead to a cultural shift in peacekeeping operations and reduce male dominance and patriarchy within the institution. A cultural shift in UN peacekeeping operations would mean a fundamental shift in gender equality within missions; female peacekeepers and local women would be perceived and treated differently by male peacekeepers.

Not only would there be representation of women at a higher level (10 percent in the military and 20 percent in the police), but women would be represented in all spheres of decision making and included in a variety of roles. There would be few reports of SEA in missions and fewer instances of transactional sex between peacekeepers and locals. Additionally, women would not be discriminated against in peacekeeping missions. Finally, when peacekeepers are deployed, they would engage in activities in the field with a gender perspective. In other words, if the gender advisors and focal points are working, then a gender perspective should permeate into the work of all soldiers and police officers.

Some evidence suggests that adopting a gender perspective may help to achieve mission goals. If both male and female peacekeepers are trained to incorporate a gender perspective, peacekeeping missions may be better vehicles for promoting human rights, gender equality, and good governance. While a comprehensive study about whether gender training, gender focal points, and gender advisors help with these goals has not been conducted, some anecdotal evidence indicates that gender mainstreaming may be important for achieving parts of peacekeeping mandates. Using evidence from the UN Mission in Timor-Leste (UNMIT) in 1999–2006, Olsson finds that peacekeeping missions may change gender power relations in the host country.[28] In their edited volume, Olsson and Truggestad find that peacekeeping operations benefit when gender mainstreaming is conducted.[29] Additionally, there is some evidence that peacekeeping missions help promote gender equality in the host country. When peacekeeping missions are present, host countries are more likely to adopt gender-balancing policies and UNSCR 1325 national action plans.[30] Thus, peacekeeping missions may be important vehicles for promoting gender equality in host countries, but the extent to which gender mainstreaming within peacekeeping operations helps with this process is still unclear.

Despite the potential successes that gender mainstreaming has brought to missions, the evidence suggests that there has been minimal cultural change within peacekeeping operations when it comes to gender. Carreiras argues that because peacekeeping missions draw from military and police institutions that are highly gendered organizations, missions themselves are highly gendered spaces.[31] Indeed, peacekeeping missions continue to be dominated by men in terms of numbers, which reinforces masculine imagery. Even the recent efforts to increase the numbers of women, especially in the UN Police (UNPOL), have not had too much of an effect on the culture of peacekeeping operations.

Additionally, studies reveal that SEA continues to be a major problem in peacekeeping missions, even though conduct and discipline teams (CDT) were established in all peacekeeping missions in response to a large number of SEA cases by UN and related personnel in the late 1990s and early 2000s.[32]

Nevertheless, in Liberia, for example, a study estimates that about 58,000 women age 18–30 have engaged in transactional sex with UN personnel at some point since the mission's inception in 2003.[33]

Many authors argue that it is unrealistic for female peacekeepers to change the culture of peacekeeping operations. Nevertheless, gender mainstreaming may help mitigate some of the pernicious effects of male dominance in peacekeeping operations. Karim and Beardsley find that if peacekeeping missions are composed of countries that do well on gender equality, those missions are likely to have fewer counts of SEA.[34] This suggests that to fight patriarchy in peacekeeping operations, the focus should be on improving the quality of individuals in missions by setting standards for recruitment of personnel based on individual beliefs about gender equality and by bettering training of personnel. Again, gender equality in national militaries seems to be the key for gender mainstreaming in peacekeeping operations.

Despite minimal cultural changes within missions, some authors have argued that peacekeeping missions challenge what it fundamentally means to be a soldier and that this may lead to changes in culture for national militaries.[35] The authors argue that involvement in peacekeeping missions affects military identity as the goals and objectives of missions challenge gendered ideas of protection. The challenges to the soldier's identity are reflected in a famous quote by former UN Secretary General Dag Hammarskjöld: "Peacekeeping is not a soldier's job, but only soldiers can do it." The quote reflects the idea that peacekeeping asks soldiers to do work that might be normally done by civilians, such as promoting human rights and organizing elections, in a post-conflict setting that may be relatively unsafe. That soldiers are expected to do what they might consider to be more "feminine" work—in contrast to combat—may lead to some problems in missions. Some scholars have blamed such "identity crises" for some of the SEA that occurs in missions.[36] Other scholars suggest that peacekeeping missions have led states to redefine the objectives of their own national militaries to be more oriented toward a "post-national defense."[37] In this way, peacekeeping missions may change the cultures of national militaries, but these missions continue to be a place of entrenched patriarchy.

While the main challenge to increasing women's representation in peacekeeping missions is incentivizing contributing countries to send more women, there are numerous challenges to effectively mainstreaming gender in peacekeeping missions. For one, the task of gender mainstreaming is difficult because it involves changing an entrenched institutional culture. Many of the masculine-oriented rules, norms, identities, and ideas that make up the culture of peacekeeping missions cannot be changed overnight. Moreover, some of the challenges for gender mainstreaming stem from a lack of proper understanding of what mainstreaming means and from the difficulty of measuring implementation of gender mainstreaming. How do individuals know whether they have mainstreamed gender into their programs? How do you measure gender mainstreaming? The 2015 *Global Study* and the gender strategy suggest creating gender units to help mainstream. But these questions still plague peacekeeping personnel even as gender focal points and gender advisors exist to answer them. The problem is that civilian gender focal points and gender units are not embedded with military personnel and do not meet with them often. In most missions they meet with military and police personnel only to train them on UNSCR 1325. These trainings do not necessarily focus on how UNSCR 1325 may be useful for peacekeeping effectiveness and rather address definitions and the specifics of the mandate.[38]

The lack of understanding is further compounded by the fact that peacekeeping operations comprise soldiers from many different countries. Within the mission individuals have varying degrees of knowledge and understanding about not only the mechanics of their jobs but also gender perspectives. Coordinating among individuals with differing understanding and skills is a challenge for peacekeeping missions in general, but it is also challenging for gender advisors and focal points that must work around different cultural understandings of gender. Moreover, there is no consensus on how to measure gender mainstreaming in the academic arena, let alone in the policymaking world. The lack of understanding of how to mainstream and how to measure mainstreaming is a barrier that missions must overcome in order to more effectively adopt a gender perspective in missions.

Conclusion

With the adoption of UNSCR 1325, considerable progress has been made in incorporating a gender perspective in peacekeeping operations, specifically in improving gender balancing and mainstreaming. Before the resolution's adoption, a gendered approach to peacekeeping was conducted ad hoc. UNSCR 1325 institutionalized gender balancing and mainstreaming within peacekeeping missions, and now nearly all missions include in their mandate references to gender. Peacekeeping operations have increased the number of women in both the military and police contributions and included gender advisors, focal points, and units as ways to mainstream gender. Yet there is still room for improved planning and implementation. Peacekeeping operations are still dominated by men, and female peacekeepers still feel discrimination and even experience harassment. SEA is still a major problem in missions. Notwithstanding UN attempts to increase the number of women, there are still few women in operations, and the evidence suggests that women are more likely to be deployed to the safest missions. Thus, there is still a long way to go before peacekeeping missions achieve true parity between the sexes in missions.

Achieving gender balancing and mainstreaming is still a problem even though the UN has used language of instrumentalism to recruit more women. The UN and even scholars have suggested that women bring unique traits and skills to missions: specifically their ability to inspire local women to join the security forces and to help normalize the role of women in the security sector. However, unlike national militaries, peacekeeping operations rely on member states' contributing troops and police officers. This means that contributing country incentives determine whether women will be sent to peacekeeping operations. Saying that women are helpful for achieving peacekeeping goals and objectives is unlikely to sway member countries to send more women. Instead, the UN should provide extra incentives for member states to deploy women and should make it easier for countries to do so. For example, female peacekeepers who have already deployed can help the UN recruit women in the host country. The UN can provide extra monetary compensation when member countries deploy women. Additionally, the UN can help member countries recruit more women into their national militaries and help train women who are in the national militaries so that they meet UN requirements for deployment (such as driving tests and computer skills).

When it comes to gender mainstreaming, the major barrier is a lack of understanding of how to implement mainstreaming. The problem is exacerbated by the fact that peacekeeping operations are composed of soldiers from many different countries. Standardization of practices is difficult because individuals have different skills, knowledge, and beliefs related to gender. Thus, the UN should issue not only standardized definitions of gender mainstreaming but also clear guidelines about how to mainstream and how to measure it, not just in work with local communities but also within missions. Additionally, gender focal points, advisors, and units are useful for training and policy implementation in the host country, but they may be better served if they are actually themselves mainstreamed into mission operations. In other words, instead of having civilian units that do training, it may be better if members of the military and police, preferably higher-ranking members, conducted the training.[39] Leadership in missions is also crucial for gender mainstreaming. The force commander and other high-ranking officials must make gender a priority in missions. Another way to ensure mainstreaming is to recruit peacekeepers who perform well when it comes to gender awareness. One criteria for recruitment could be based on beliefs about gender equality. Related to this, some mission awards could be dedicated to improving gender equality within the mission. In medal parades the force commander could issue an award for gender mainstreaming. Thus, individuals would have an incentive to mainstream gender into their work.

Despite the challenges, there is room for optimism. Recent documents and guidelines for gender balancing and mainstreaming suggest that the UN is interested in improving its record on gender in peacekeeping operations. The 2015 High-Level Independent Panel on Peace Operations and 2015 "Global Study on UNSC Resolution 1325" devote considerable space to demonstrating the importance of adopting a gender perspective in peacekeeping operations. They also make recommendations, such as the ones mentioned previously about how to achieve both gender balancing and gender mainstreaming, marking a significant improvement over previous reports, such as the 2000 Brahimi Report, which did not mention gender at all. Thus, what remains to be seen is whether future peacekeeping operations heed the suggestions made by these reports.

Notes

1. Virginia Page Fortna, *Does Peacekeeping Work? Shaping Belligerents' Choices after Civil War* (Princeton, NJ: Princeton University Press, 2008); Michael J. Gilligan and Ernest Sergenti, "Do UN Interventions Cause Peace? Using Matching to Improve Causal Inference," *Quarterly Journal of Political Science* 3, no. 2 (July 2008): 89–122.
2. Lisa Hultman, Jacob Kathman, and Megan Shannon, "United Nations Peacekeeping and Civilian Protection in Civil War," *American Journal of Political Science* 57, no. 4 (October 2013): 875–91.
3. Kyle Beardsley, "Peacekeeping and the Contagion of Armed Conflict," *Journal of Politics* 73, no. 4 (October 2011): 1051–64.
4. Kyle Beardsley and Kristian Skrede Gleditsch, "Peacekeeping as Conflict Containment," *International Studies Review* 17, no. 1 (March 2015): 67–89.
5. Amanda Murdie and David R. Davis, "Problematic Potential: The Human Rights Consequences of Peacekeeping Interventions in Civil Wars," *Human Rights Quarterly* 32, no. 1 (February 2010): 49–72.
6. UN Department of Peacekeeping Operations, *Mainstreaming a Gender Perspective in Multidimensional Peace Operations*, July 2000, http://www.peacewomen.org/assets/file/Resources/UN/dpko_mainstreaminggenderperspective_2000.pdf.
7. For an evolution and evaluation of UNSCR 1325, see Louise Olsson and Theodora-Ismene Gizelis, "An Introduction to UNSCR 1325," *International Interactions* 39, no. 4 (May 2013): 425–34; Louise Olsson and Theodora-Ismene Gizelis, eds., *Gender, Peace and Security: Implementing UNSCR 1325* (New York: Routledge, 2015); Nicola Pratt and Sophie Richter-Devroe, "Critically Examining UNSCR 1325 on Women, Peace and Security," *International Feminist Journal of Politics* 13, no. 4 (December 2011): 489–503; Laura J. Shepherd, "Power and Authority in the Production of United Nations

Security Council Resolution 1325," *International Studies Quarterly* 52, no. 2 (June 2008): 383–404.
8. Previous UN resolutions had treated women as victims of war, in need of protection. However, 1325 also recognized women as agents in building peace and guaranteeing security. See Pratt and Richter-Devroe, "Critically Examining UNSCR 1325," 489–503.
9. Sabrina Karim and Kyle Beardsley, "Female Peacekeepers and Gender Balancing: Token Gestures or Informed Policymaking?," *International Interactions* 39, no. 4 (June 2013): 461–88.
10. See Sabrina Karim and Kyle Beardsley, *Equal Opportunity Peacekeeping* (Oxford: Oxford University Press, 2017), 46–48.
11. Donna Bridges and Debbie Horsfall, "Increasing Operational Effectiveness in UN Peacekeeping," *Armed Forces and Society* 36, no. 1 (May 2009): 120.
12. Karim and Beardsley, *Equal Opportunity Peacekeeping*.
13. UN Department of Peacekeeping Operations, *Mainstreaming*, 6.
14. Sabrina Karim and Kyle Beardsley, "Explaining Sexual Exploitation and Abuse in Peacekeeping Missions: The Role of Female Peacekeepers and Gender Equality in Contributing Countries," *Journal of Peace Research* 53, no. 1 (January 2016): 100–115.
15. Ibid.
16. Karim and Beardsley, *Equal Opportunity Peacekeeping*.
17. Ibid.
18. UN Women, *Preventing Conflict, Transforming Justice, Securing the Peace: A Global Study on the Implementation of United Nations Security Council Resolution 1325*, 2015, http://www.peacewomen.org/sites/default/files/UNW-GLOBAL-STUDY-1325-2015%20(1).pdf, 174.
19. Ibid., 279.
20. Karim and Beardsley, *Equal Opportunity Peacekeeping*.
21. Kerry F. Crawford, James H. Lebovic, and Julia M. Macdonald, "Explaining the Variation in Gender Composition of Personnel Contributions to UN Peacekeeping Operation," *Armed Forces and Society* 41, no. 2 (March 2014): 257–81.
22. Sabrina Karim and Kyle Beardsley, "Ladies Last: Peacekeeping and Gendered Protection," in *A Systematic Understanding of Gender, Peace, and Security: Implementing UNSC 1325*, ed. Ismene Gizelis and Louise Olsson (London: Routledge, 2015).
23. Karim and Beardsley, "Female Peacekeepers," 461–88; Karim and Beardsley, "Ladies Last"; Karim and Beardsley, *Equal Opportunity Peacekeeping*.
24. Karim and Beardsley, *Equal Opportunity Peacekeeping*.
25. Ibid.
26. Sabrina Karim, "Re-Evaluating Peacekeeping Effectiveness: Does Gender Neutrality Inhibit Progress?," *International Interactions* 43, no. 5 (2017): 822–47.
27. Karim and Beardsley, *Equal Opportunity Peacekeeping*.
28. Louise Olsson, *Gender Equality and United Nations Peace Operations in Timor Leste* (Boston: Brill, 2009).
29. Louise Olsson and Torrun L. Truggestad, eds., *Women and International Peacekeeping* (New York: Routledge, 2001).
30. Karim and Beardsley, *Equal Opportunity Peacekeeping*.
31. Helena Carreiras, "Gendered Culture in Peacekeeping Operations," *International Peacekeeping* 17, no. 4 (October 2010): 471–85.

32. Karim and Beardsley, "Explaining Sexual Exploitation," 100–115; Ragnhild Nordås and Siri C. A. Rustad, "Sexual Exploitation and Abuse by Peacekeepers: Understanding Variation," *International Interactions* 39, no. 4 (May 2013): 511–34.
33. Bernd Beber, Michael Gilligan, Jenny Guardado Rodriguez, and Sabrina Karim, "Peacekeeping, International Norms, and Transactional Sex in Monrovia, Liberia," *International Organization* 71, no. 1 (Winter 2017): 1–30.
34. Karim and Beardsley, "Explaining Sexual Exploitation," 100–115.
35. Carreiras, "Gendered Culture," 471–85; Sandra Whitworth, *Men, Militarism, and UN Peacekeeping: A Gendered Analysis* (Boulder, CO: Lynne Rienner, 2007); Laura L. Miller and Charles Moskos, "Humanitarians or Warriors? Race, Gender, and Combat Status in Operation Restore Hope," *Armed Forces and Society* 21, no. 4 (1995): 615–37.
36. Carreiras, "Gendered Culture," 471–85.
37. Annica Kronsell, *Gender, Sex and the Postnational Defense: Militarism and Peacekeeping* (Oxford: Oxford University Press, 2012).
38. These are observations from attending training sessions in the UNMIL in 2012.
39. This may be particularly important for standardization of practices across various contingents because the military in all countries is hierarchical and understands rank.

3

Sweden's Implementation of a Gender Perspective
Cutting Edge but Momentum Lost

Robert Egnell

The Swedish Armed Forces have been among the forerunners in implementing a gender perspective in military organizations and operations. Despite considerable resistance from parts of the organization, the Swedish military has during the last decade gone through an impressive process of change, beginning with limited and isolated gender-related projects and today involving an institutionalized gender organization that has worked to mainstream a gender perspective, conduct training, and establish specific gender-related functions, such as gender field advisors (GFAs) and gender focal points. GFAs have deployed with Swedish and international units in conflicts around the world during this process and have thereby gained important experience and continued to refine the Swedish approach to gender implementation in military operations. The pinnacle of this development has been the establishment of the Nordic Centre for Gender in Military Operations, a North Atlantic Treaty Organization (NATO) department head that aims to function as a platform for continued implementation of a gender perspective in Sweden and abroad. At the same time, Sweden has struggled to recruit women. With about 6 percent women, the Swedish Armed Forces are among the worst in the Organization for Economic Co-operation and Development (OECD) comparison. This raises many questions.

This chapter, based on research conducted for a book on the topic, aims to increase understanding about these organizational adaptations and change processes.[1] It does so by initially describing the broader background of the change processes and then studying the change process in the Swedish Armed

Forces specifically. The research is based on about forty interviews with key stakeholders, GFAs, and commanders with experience working with GFAs. The main argument is that the relatively impressive change process can be explained by a combination of normative change, tactical adaptation, and an unusually well-managed organizational change process.

The chapter tells two interestingly separate stories. The first story describes and seeks to explain the relatively successful process of organizational change to implement gender perspective for operational effectiveness. The second story is of the rather failed process of recruiting and integrating women into the armed forces. This means that while Sweden is one of the most gender-equal societies in world, and while the armed forces have done a good job of implementing UN Security Council Resolution (UNSCR) 1325 in terms of policies and operational approaches, the Swedish case is still one of failed integration of women. Even with a relatively early start and the removal of all formal obstacles to full integration, the number of women in the Swedish Armed Forces remains very low, and despite efforts to increase the numbers, progress is slow. Thus, an important finding of the chapter is that gender sensitivity does not necessarily lead to increased recruitment of women. Finally, as the strategic context is worsening around the Baltic Sea owing to Russia's increasingly hostile behavior, the focus of the Swedish Armed Forces has shifted from expeditionary operations to national defense. This has meant a loss of momentum and potential marginalization for issues of gender mainstreaming and equality.

Application of Gender Perspectives in Military Operations

While the Swedish social context can be described as one of strong societal support for women's rights and gender sensitivity, the first formal impetus for introducing gender perspectives in military operations was external and consisted of the international process of writing and passing the landmark UNSCR 1325 on women, peace, and security.[2]

In general terms, UNSCR 1325 not only addresses the unique and disproportionate impact that armed conflict has on women but also recognizes the undervalued and underutilized contributions women make to conflict prevention and resolution, peacekeeping, and peace building. The resolution moves beyond the traditional protection of women as victims or noncombatants and stresses the importance of women's full and equal participation as active agents in peace and security organizations.

Since UNSCR 1325 was passed, the Swedish Armed Forces have reported on the organization's work to combat discrimination, including discrimination related to gender or sexual orientation. In early 2003 the third attachment (regarding personnel issues) of the Swedish Armed Forces' report for 2002 stated that, as part of its equality work, the armed forces had been directed by the Ministry of Defence to arrange a national knowledge-building and competence surveying seminar regarding UNSCR 1325/2000 (referring to the resolution number and year). This was the start of the Swedish Armed Forces' effort to implement the UN resolution in its work, and during 2002, Task Group 1325/2000 was established to contribute to this development.[3]

The 2004 government appropriation directive required the armed forces to report on their continuing work for increased awareness concerning UNSCR 1325.[4] The following year the same requirement was repeated, and the government added that education should continue to be developed "so that personnel [who will participate in international crisis management] will have a sound understanding of how they should act according to [UNSCR 1325] in the area of operations."[5]

In the end the formal paper trail for the implementation of UNSCR 1325 in the Swedish Armed Forces is something of a facade. The government was neither entirely clear about the tasks entailed in UNSCR 1325 implementation nor very supportive of the processes that the armed forces initiated. Most of the work that was conducted therefore resulted from the actions of various change agents who devised their own activities and solutions and who thereby dragged both the political leadership and the armed forces along with them.

The first serious change process was that of "Genderforce"—an interagency project on gender involving a number of key government agencies, but also civil society groups like Kvinna till Kvinna.[6] The project was limited in scope, but two important developments took hold: (1) the GFA concept and training course and (2) the gender coach program. Despite positive evaluations and a request to continue the project, Genderforce was discontinued on December 31, 2007, largely because the partner agencies declined to finance the project.[7]

However, the Swedish Armed Forces continued their work, and most important, the recommendation from Genderforce to establish a full-time position for implementing a gender perspective was enacted. In 2016 Genderforce was again resurrected to implement the third edition of the Swedish national action plan on the implementation of UNSCR 1325.

Gaining Momentum in Afghanistan

Toward the end of the Genderforce project, the Swedish Armed Forces took over the British provincial reconstruction team (PRT) in Mazar-e-Sharif in northern Afghanistan. A Swedish contingent was at the same time deployed with the European Union Mission in the Congo (EUFOR RD Congo) in the eastern Democratic Republic of the Congo (DRC). The Swedish Armed Forces were, in other words, facing serious challenges in the field of operations—something that intuitively for a military organization could signal a moment to disregard gender and women altogether to focus on the "more serious," or kinetic, issues. The opposite happened, however.

In 2006–7 the security situations in Afghanistan and Iraq were deteriorating dramatically, signaling a failure of the international community to understand the problems and the best ways to deal with them. The strategic buzzword of the day became "counterinsurgency"—a concept that emphasized winning the hearts and minds of the local population and recognizing the importance of civil-military cooperation and cultural understanding. The US Army/Marine Corps Counterinsurgency Field Manual (FM 3-24) describes the first historical principle of such operations as "legitimacy is the main objective," that is, "to foster development of effective governance by a legitimate government."[8] Lessons from both Iraq and Afghanistan clearly highlighted a need to engage better with the local population—including women.

Military deployments in conflict and crisis situations are often considered vital to establish the necessary level of security. However, military activity can work only in a support function to the civilian activities of political and economic reform.[9] As an example, the commander of International Security Assistance Force (ISAF) in Afghanistan accurately noted that the Afghan people will decide who wins. The government of Afghanistan and ISAF are therefore involved in a struggle for the support of the local population.[10] Garfield stresses this point by arguing that defeating the political subversion of insurgencies requires making a difference in the lives of the local population as early as possible. This involves efforts to ensure fair treatment, the creation of jobs, improvements in education and medical services, a bearable standard of living, basic personal security, and some form of legitimate representative governance.[11]

This was a serious diversion for more conventionally focused military organizations like the US Army. For the Swedish Armed Forces, which have a history of involvement in peacekeeping, these concepts seemed rather natural, whereas the kinetic aspects of counterinsurgency operations, the clear-hold-build tactics, proved to be more of a challenge. While the hearts-and-minds aspects of counterinsurgency seemed intuitive to the Swedish contingent, having to approach the Afghan population in general, and women in particular, revealed a gap in competence and capability. The response to this challenge was to deploy GFAs to the PRT in Afghanistan—a concept tested in the DRC for the first time in 2006.

The main effort of implementing UNSCR 1325 was in Sweden early on invested in developing the GFA concept and deploying these advisors abroad. Describing the work of the GFAs in generic terms is difficult, as the position has constantly evolved over the years in Afghanistan. This process of change has been based on lessons learned, changed policies, and the personalities and preferences of the GFAs and their commanding officers. Making the GFA role as effective as possible is an entirely new and untested process that has necessitated experimentation and innovation to overcome challenges and to improve what was already working. Each individual GFA has contributed to this process by introducing and testing new routines and instructions for themselves and their successors. Many of the challenges faced in early deployments have therefore been dealt with and sometimes solved.

Nonetheless, according to the Swedish Armed Forces, GFAs are responsible for the implementation of UNSCR 1325 and UNSCR 1820 to mainstream gender issues at all levels of the military's work. Their tasks and roles nevertheless vary depending on the size and type of the operation, the mandate, the operational area, and the reinforcing or deterring structures in the operational area. During the mission the GFA supports the commanding officer in operational planning and is responsible for the overall implementation and mainstreaming of the gender efforts in the mission. During his or her time abroad, the GFA should also be an asset from a security perspective (force protection through good relations with the citizens of the area of responsibility [AOR]) and a liaison with the task of providing a link to important civilian elements in the local community. Other tasks include directly supporting the commander in the planning, conduct, and evaluation of operations; educating, monitoring, and supporting the gender focal points; and presenting a gender analysis related to the operational work in the AOR.[12] Several interviewees have nevertheless reported that the GFA's function was often very unclear, both to the GFAs and to their commanders and colleagues.[13]

While supposedly generic, the GFA concept has to a large extent been developed within the specific context of the Swedish contribution to the ISAF in Afghanistan. GFA standard operating procedures (SOPs) were originally based on guidance documents from the EUFOR RD Congo and EUFOR Tchad/RCA gender advisors (i.e., the advisor for the European Union missions in both DRC and in Chad and the Central African Republic). Both sets of documents had been developed by the gender advisors themselves.

GFAs have been appointed by the commanding officer in close cooperation with the senior gender advisor at Swedish Armed Forces Headquarters. They serve six months in Afghanistan and follow the same rotation as the armed forces in general—as opposed to political and development advisors who serve for twelve months and are appointed by the Swedish Ministry of Foreign Affairs and the Swedish International Development Agency (Sida). They have been recruited from both military and nonmilitary positions and possess varying backgrounds and education. Only two have been civilians, and it has been a conscious decision to focus on recruiting military personnel to ensure sufficient organizational knowledge and understanding. Some interviewees said that they were recruited at a relatively late point in time and thus did not take part in all the pre-deployment training that the rest of the unit received, including team-building activities.[14]

The first gender advisors were deployed without much preparation or instructions because there was inadequate time available for developing training modules or structures to prepare individuals for their specific functions in the field of operations. However, gender advisors could always turn to a contact person (most often the senior gender advisor) at Swedish Armed Forces Headquarters for advice and guidance during the mission.

Relatively quickly after the earliest deployments, a structure was nevertheless put in place with mandatory pre-deployment training and preparations for the GFAs. This has included attending the GFA course (in recent years conducted at the Nordic Centre for Gender in Military Operations) and participating as gender advisor in an international staff exercise, such as the Combined Joint Staff Exercise (CJSE). Finally, all GFAs undergo a one-day qualitative psychological evaluation, equivalent to the evaluation for aspiring colonels, and also receive a brief by the senior gender advisor at headquarters.

Over time a gender annex to the operational plan (OPLAN) for the Swedish ISAF PRT was also developed and revised. The original version was less specific and gave significant freedom to the GFAs themselves to prioritize and structure their work. This was a hard task to perform if the unit was not "culturally ready" for some aspects of implementing a gender perspective. As an example, during these early stages, different GFAs would prioritize the various tasks, such as supporting staff work or coordinating with external actors, differently. A standardized prioritization of the tasks was developed. For example, taking an active part in the planning process was deemed to be one of the most important tasks, while coordinating with external actors, such as nongovernmental organizations (NGOs), was one of the least important.

The commander's use of the GFAs is an important aspect of the program. Through his or her participation in the Command Group, the GFA has direct access to the commanding officer.[15] Active support from the commanding officers has been crucial for the GFAs to successfully complete their tasks, although such support has varied substantially. Some commanding officers have expressed public support and priority for the implementation of a gender perspective but have in practice showed little interest in it.[16] According to a former gender advisor, while her commanding officer made decisions that she suggested, as gender advisor she was responsible for ensuring those decisions were implemented.[17] One commanding officer had previously participated in the Genderforce project and thus had knowledge of what implementing a gender perspective entailed and what the role of a GFA was.[18] Such knowledge and understanding resulted in greater support for the GFA's work.

The deployment of Swedish gender advisors—first to the DRC and then later in greater numbers to Afghanistan—clearly began in an unstructured and unprepared manner, but the program has continuously evolved and improved over time thanks to persistence, learning, and leadership. The senior gender advisor made a conscious decision early on to start deploying gender advisors before the armed forces were ready and before all the necessary structures, instructions, concepts, and training were developed. By learning from practice rather than theoretically perfecting the function at home, the gender advisors have made much quicker progress in implementing a gender perspective—something that is obvious in the advantage that Sweden holds compared to most other nations. Waiting for the bureaucratic processes to develop before acting would have taken much longer, especially in an organizational culture so resistant to change. The deployment of gender advisors can therefore be viewed as a long organizational learning and development process. The organization improves with each new set of lessons. The experience of the Swedish Armed Forces highlights that given the many external factors that shape the circumstances and possibilities for a gender advisor to succeed in his or her work, when things do not go as planned, the individual advisors cannot be held responsible for the lack of implementation of a gender perspective.[19]

Consolidation: Institutionalization and Norm Diffusion

As illustrated in the previous sections, the early years of project-based work on gender issues saw an increasing number of gender directives in formal Swedish Armed Forces documents as well as from the political leadership. This early work also produced a growing pool of people with some expertise in gender-related areas of work, thanks to courses, seminars, gender coaches, and deployments as gender advisors. The final phase of this work to date involves the consolidation and institutionalization of these achievements—a process taking place partly because of operations in Afghanistan.[20]

Nordic Centre for Gender in Military Operations

The Nordic Centre for Gender in Military Operations merits particular attention, as it provides the first example of a truly institutionalized gender organization within the military—the bricks and mortar of the achievements to date. Efforts to establish the center commenced in the summer of 2008, when the idea for a center was first proposed by the Norwegian and Swedish Armed Forces. Previously, the Nordic countries had co-established a mixed-gender military observation team (MOT), following the all-female MOT Juliette, but the mixed MOT project was eventually abandoned. Despite the abandonment of the mixed MOT, the Nordic countries knew they still needed to raise awareness and competence with respect to implementing a gender perspective in military operations, and the idea of establishing the Nordic Centre was aired. The Swedish senior gender advisor and others did extensive preparatory work over the next two years, and in 2010 a Nordic Defence Cooperation (NORDEFCO) report recommended the establishment of a common center for gender in military operations.[21] The center was inaugurated on January 24, 2012. Gathering lessons learned and institutionalizing the training of gender advisors in Afghanistan were key components in the creation of the center.

The center, together with the Swedish International Unit (SWEDINT), is located just outside Stockholm, Sweden. The staff includes instructors, analysts, and people responsible for cooperation and development. As already noted, the center plays a key role in supporting further efforts to strengthen the armed forces' implementation of a gender perspective and in supporting similar implementation developments in other countries. In that spirit, on February 22, 2013, the Swedish Armed Forces signed a memorandum of understanding with Headquarters, Supreme Allied Command Transformation (HQ SACT), and Supreme Headquarters Allied Powers Europe (SHAPE) that formalized Sweden's Nordic Centre for Gender in Military Operations as the lead for gender education and training by designating it as the department head for all NATO-led curricula concerning gender. The center is thereby in a unique position to capture and disseminate the lessons of the Swedish experience, as well as the experiences of NATO partners and even those of the other countries' militaries.

Gender Focal Points

To support the work of GFAs, who still often have a difficult time influencing the conduct of operations and therefore institutionalizing the mainstreaming of gender perspectives, gender focal points were appointed within specific units. According to the Swedish Armed Forces information folders, having gender focal points appointed within the respective units "is a well-tried method for integrating a gender perspective into the different branches and units. Gender Focal Points are appointed by their superiors and allocate approximately 5 percent of their working time to the task of implementing gender measures in the field."[22] The focal point is also expected to assist the commander in implementing procedures dealing with gender issues, inform and train troops on gender issues in operations, receive reports from witnesses on gender-related problems, collect lessons regarding gender issues related to operational work, stay in regular contact with the GFA, and report to the GFA every two weeks or as soon as possible on matters of urgency.[23]

Beginning around 2008, all rotations in Afghanistan had designated gender focal points in every platoon and section of the staff before deployment. They have generally been described as important assets for gender advisors and GFAs, although they have clearly been used to varying degrees.[24] In general, the gender focal point's usefulness to the gender advisor or GFA has probably been the result not only of the gender focal point's personal motivation but, more important, of his or her commander's commitment to implementing a gender perspective.[25]

Mixed and Female Engagement Teams

In addition to GFAs and gender focal points, other organizational innovations have been employed to improve the implementation of a gender perspective. Notably, the Swedish Armed Forces have experimented with various female and mixed-gender engagement teams (FETs and METs), as well as MOTs that have been dedicated to working on this issue.[26]

In 2006, before a GFA was deployed to the Swedish PRT, an all-female team called MOT Juliette was established. This was an experiment with an all-female MOT that consisted of only three female officers (there were no more) and therefore lacked the capabilities of a normal MOT, which typically includes six people. None of the female officers had any previous operational experience, and their task was poorly defined. The only direction given was to act as a "tentacle" among the local female population. The women were supposed to build networks, support local women, and provide security to the local community. While the officers reported positive experiences overall in MOT Juliette, they also said they faced obstacles, such as a lack of transportation, support, and understanding from other mission members.[27]

While MOT Juliette was in many ways a good idea, it lacked several fundamental prerequisites for success.[28] Made up of only three people, MOT Juliette needed support from extra soldiers for force protection. Since the other units were reluctant to give up their own resources to provide that support,

MOT Juliette's mobility outside the camp was often limited. Nonetheless, the three women who took part in MOT Juliette reported that it was an interesting time and that they achieved some small successes—not least a feeling that they became role models for local women simply by being there, driving the vehicles, and participating in meetings with local residents and leaders.[29] The challenges of MOT Juliette in the end led leaders of the Swedish Armed Forces to conclude that they should use mixed teams, rather than all-female teams, in a prepared and structured way. Therefore, MOT Juliette was not succeeded by any similar all-female teams in subsequent rotations.

A second attempt at a gender-focused MOT was a Nordic cooperation project. The Swedish Armed Forces were tasked with establishing MOT 1325 in 2009.[30] For unknown reasons this was not realized, and instead of Nordic MOT 1325, the Swedish contingent commander established a Swedish MOT Y. The leader of MOT Y was a male captain recruited because he was highly respected by colleagues and was thought to have the proper disposition for understanding the importance of implementing a gender perspective. The captain was allowed to recruit his own team members, but his second in command had to be a woman, and both sexes had to be equally represented within the MOT. The MOT members were given supplemental education and training, in addition to the regular training package given to all MOTs. Although the senior gender advisor had initially opposed the establishment of MOT Y as a substitute for MOT 1325, the mixed-gender MOT was reportedly a successful initiative in terms of creating a functioning unit delivering both internal support and external results.[31]

The challenges faced when a team leader attempts to set up an MET are some of the more striking examples of the organization's resistance to gender-related work. The chief of joint operations issued a directive to create METs in all Swedish units in Afghanistan. However, some officers in leading positions resisted this directive and refused to recruit enough women to establish effective METs. In one instance, it took additional pressure, in the form of a personal meeting with the chief of joint operations, to move matters forward. Several women were eventually recruited, but with very short notice before the unit's departure to Afghanistan. This, in turn, made the women's integration into the units difficult.[32]

Some evidence indicates that using METs increased operational effectiveness. In one case the Swedish Armed Forces conducted patrols in southwestern parts of their area of operations where ISAF had not operated previously. The Swedes needed to inform the local population of their mission. Because they had chosen to conduct the patrol with an MET, they were able to communicate with all elements of the local community, including the women.[33] The impact of this is impossible to fully assess, but there are clearly potential benefits from such "complete social engagement." In another case, female members of an MET received information about a Taliban commander unlawfully collecting taxes in the area when they visited a school that men were not allowed to access. Thanks to this information, the male members of the team, working with the Afghan National Police, were able to arrest the Taliban commander, thereby freeing the area of the unwanted taxation.[34]

Several interviewees said that mixed teams were able to communicate with a broader array of people, which thereby increased operational effectiveness. Heterogeneous units, by counteracting groupthink, considered more perspectives, in turn creating an organizational culture better suited to the different forms of complex peace operations and counterinsurgency. For example, according to a former commanding officer, men and women look for different things when searching houses, thereby contributing to a broader intelligence picture.[35] Furthermore, the mixing of genders helped moderate an overly masculine tone of communication within the unit. One GFA said that all-male patrols were met with more hostility and aggression than mixed teams in the area of operations.[36] The general MOT structure (not just the gender-focused MOTs) was eventually abandoned because of the worsening security situation in Afghanistan. Having small units in soft-skin vehicles patrolling far from the home base was simply too dangerous.

The shortage of female soldiers and officers has circumscribed the Swedish capability to establish mixed teams, including METs. There have been initiatives to increase the number of women in the Swedish mission in Afghanistan. The chief of joint operations authored a directive stating that the proportion of women in MOTs and provincial offices (POs) should increase noticeably from late 2007 and forward. Despite this, little progress has been made, and in late 2011 approximately fifty women could be found among the roughly five hundred members of the unit—that is, only approximately 10 percent.[37]

Apart from female soldiers and officers, an asset considered critical to successful work with local women is the availability and use of female interpreters by the Swedish Armed Forces. Because the Swedish Armed Forces lack female military interpreters, they have depended on hiring local women as interpreters to carry out their mandate. In general, this has been challenging because Afghan culture often precludes women from working outside the home. The Swedish Armed Forces have been forced to seek the permission of close male family members of the potential female employee. Furthermore, local female interpreters have been constrained in their work because they are usually not allowed to travel during the night; in some cases, chaperones have been used to allow female interpreters to participate in operations.

Swedish Process of Implementation

The process of implementing a gender perspective in the Swedish Armed Forces has been relatively successful, leading to substantial institutional innovations and changes in operational and tactical planning and conduct in the field of operations. Three factors help explain this success: the work and support of a number of key change agents; the limited initial approach that focused on military effectiveness rather than on women's rights; and the organizational placement of the senior gender advisor in the Swedish Armed Forces Headquarters, directly under the chief of joint operations (rather than in the policy or human resources departments).

First, a very small number of key actors, or agents of change, effectively managed the change process. It is difficult to overstate the importance of Charlotte Isaksson, in particular, who was the architect of the entire process until she left for a similar position with NATO. In the Swedish military, she created and held the position of the first Swedish Armed Forces senior gender advisor and built an entire organization of gender experts and advisors around her. However, the significant impact of this single actor would not have been possible without support from several people surrounding her—not least because she, as a civilian, lacked the authority that accompanies being an officer in an organization structured around formal hierarchies.

Second, the change agents in the Swedish Armed Forces made a strategic decision to approach the implementation of a gender perspective in the organization as *an issue of operational effectiveness*—as opposed to one "merely" of gender equality, women's rights, or human resources. The basis of this decision was the reasonable assumption that the introduction and implementation of a gender perspective was likely to face strong resistance within the male-dominated organizational culture of the Swedish Armed Forces. This limited tactic never reflected the more ambitious aims of the implementation process as envisaged by the key agents of change, or the more ambitious agenda entailed in Resolution 1325. However, the decision makers hoped that this limited "inside" approach would be a useful way to gain entry to the organization and to build a platform from which to pursue a more ambitious long-term agenda.

Third, the relative success of the Swedish experience in developing a framework for implementing a gender perspective can also be partly explained by the way the senior gender advisor managed the process and by the receptiveness of the chiefs of joint operations who served during this period of change. A key decision was to strategically place the senior gender advisor directly under the chief of joint operations in order to maximize the credibility and centrality of the senior gender advisor position. This was in contrast with other countries that have tended to organize the units responsible for implementing a gender perspective within their policy planning processes or human resources departments, thereby effectively sidelining gender advisors and diminishing the importance of implementing a gender perspective as crucial to the core tasks of the organization.

In contrast, the benefit of the Swedish structure is that it considered a gender perspective to be an issue of operational effectiveness rather than solely a largely politically laden human resources issue of women's rights and participation. The core task of military organization is to fight and win the nation's wars or to apply organized violence, or the threat of such violence, in pursuit of the national leadership's political aims. This is what these organizations are structured, trained, and equipped to do, which means that arguments about equal women's rights and gender balancing simply do not generate adequate interest to effect change. In other words, a gender perspective focused on operational effectiveness is seen as more relevant within the military organization. The strategic placement of the gender advisor and the focus on operational effectiveness not only amplified the implementation of a gender perspective in the Swedish Armed Forces as a core issue of output in terms of operations, but also sent a strong signal to the organization regarding the importance of a gender perspective in the conduct of military affairs. When presenting a gender perspective as an issue of operational effectiveness, the change agents not only addressed the core task of the organization but also used language that military commanders were more comfortable and familiar with.

The Swedish process addresses three debates on the practical implementation of a gender perspective in military organizations. One is whether gender balancing (increased recruitment and promotion of women) or gender mainstreaming (implementing a gender perspective throughout the organization) is more effective. The other debate is whether these processes should be approached tactically or instrumentally as an issue of women's rights or as an issue of military effectiveness. Do we pursue change because it is the right thing to do or because it is the smart thing to do? If the change process is approached in an instrumental fashion, what are the risks of linking the integration of women or a gender perspective to operational effectiveness? The third debate is about the effectiveness of "inside" strategies (working from within the organization) versus "outside" pressure and activist approaches. While the most appropriate strategies will clearly vary somewhat from case to case, this study of the Swedish Armed Forces highlights the positive effects of working from within the organization, with a narrow approach that cuts to the core of the organization's main tasks—that is, operational effectiveness—and that initially focuses on gender mainstreaming rather than on recruitment of women.

The strategic approach chosen by Sweden has worked well. While there is no way to know exactly what the impact of alternative approaches might have been, the senior gender advisor in the Armed Forces Headquarters and the larger GFA organization have fought a successful intra-organizational "insurgency" that has made a gender perspective a real and permanent feature of Swedish contributions to international operations. However, by adopting this narrow focus, other issues, perhaps equally if not more important in terms of implementing UNSCR 1325, have yet to be adequately addressed. Most important, the more transformative potential of a gender perspective, in terms of fundamentally changing the armed forces, has not yet been adequately explored (discussed later).

This study's detailed analysis of the Swedish implementation of a gender perspective in the field of operations has also provided a first attempt at addressing the impact of these activities in the field. To what extent do they improve the military organization's general performance and, more specifically, its ability to protect and empower women and promote stability and respect for human rights? While the findings are far from conclusive—mostly owing to the lack of clear measures and hard data on "effectiveness" in terms of outcomes and effects at different levels—the study found that many commanding officers found the GFA function to be a useful tool that assisted them in intelligence gathering, analysis and understanding of situations, and the planning of operations. This also meant that the military units became better at addressing women's needs and concerns in the area of operations. Apart from that general sense of utility, plenty more anecdotal evidence suggests the positive tactical impact of the activities and approaches suggested by the field advisors—both for local women and for the Swedish unit itself.

As many countries are currently going through similar processes of implementing a gender perspective in the field of operations, some common debates regarding field activities may be informed by the findings of this study. The first debate is about the most useful makeup of engagement teams, which are tasked with meeting and addressing local women and children. Should these teams be all female or mixed? Can FETs obtain access to men in traditional societies as effectively as METs can? Does the sex of the interpreter matter when a team is attempting to engage local men and women? FETs, which have been used more extensively by the United States, have been the focus of much attention and discussion. In the Swedish case, the lessons from Afghanistan point toward the use of mixed teams as preferential to FETs. One reason METs work for Sweden is that the numbers of female officers and soldiers remain low, and those available should therefore be used to form flexible engagement teams that can interact more effectively with both local women and men. Moreover, a fully developed gender perspective should equally include male perspectives, which risk becoming lost in the FET concept, just as women's perspectives are often lost in male-dominated organizations. Either way, this means that more women must be recruited to the armed forces in general and to frontline combat units in particular.

The second debate regarding the implementation of a gender perspective in the field of operations is about what the operational emphasis of the GFAs' and engagement teams' activities and operations should be. The two options seem to be an emphasis on the role of internal advisors and facilitators in the unit and staff or on the role of an "operator" in the field of women's rights, often engaging in local projects to support women. This study finds that the work of GFAs within the military unit and staff, and in the planning process in particular, is much more effective than external women's development and empowerment activities. There are several reasons for this. Most important, external projects performed by military units have seldom improved women's conditions in the area of operations or won the hearts and minds of the local population. Even if external projects may at times produce small measurable improvements in women's rights or local support, the limited nature of such results must be measured against the potential to increase military effectiveness by helping the rest of the unit conduct operations, win local legitimacy, and increase its cultural understanding of the local context through the implementation of a gender perspective. In other words, the GFA should be a facilitator of a gender perspective implemented by the units in the field.

Another reason for avoiding project-based work within the areas of development and humanitarian affairs is that, while external projects may yield positive results for the women involved, ideally NGOs rather than military forces should run such projects. The military is a less competent and cost-efficient tool for such projects, compared to humanitarian and development actors. Furthermore, NGOs are often present in areas for a longer period and are thereby able to provide a more sustainable form of assistance to the local community.

Integration of Women in the Swedish Armed Forces

Given all this gender mainstreaming within the Swedish Armed Forces, what is happening with the recruitment of women?[38] This section describes some important features of the process to integrate women into the Swedish Armed

Forces. It also explains why Sweden, despite being a gender-equal society, and despite having armed forces that are effectively implementing UNSCR 1325 and gender perspectives in operations, is still struggling to integrate women in its armed forces.

The year 1980 saw the enactment of the Swedish Equality Act and also the first women allowed to enter officer positions in the Swedish military. Thirty-seven years later women make up only about 6 percent of the Swedish Armed Forces' officer corps. The Swedish Armed Forces assert that they are actively striving to construct an equitable and gender-equal organization in which all members are respected for their expertise and knowledge and in which gender-related factors are irrelevant in the way members are treated and viewed. The official policy is that the Swedish Armed Forces will be a more effective organization as a result of achieving a better gender (and ethnic) balance: "The goal is for the Swedish Armed Forces to improve, become more effective and even more credible in its task to defend democratic values and human rights, both nationally and internationally."[39] The official policy also cites research showing that sexual harassment and other forms of discrimination for gender-related factors occur less frequently in gender-balanced settings and workplaces. The internal directives regarding these issues therefore stress the importance of an organization that reflects the diversity of society at large and includes an ambition to increase the number of female soldiers and officers.

Directives and Guidelines

The gender equality and internal antidiscrimination work of the Swedish Armed Forces is guided by the Equality and Gender Equality Directive. The latest iteration of this document, valid from 2016 to 2018, was produced by a working group that included representatives from the Swedish military labor unions and several parts of the armed forces—the navy, army, and air force as well as the personnel department, Human Resources Centre, and Joint Forces Command (represented by the senior gender advisor).[40] The document shows "the direction and focus areas for units, schools and centers in the development of local action plans."[41] It also details responsibilities for various parts of the organization and highlights organizational objectives and actions to be taken within the following areas: general working conditions, parenthood and work, harassment prevention, recruitment, and international operations. Among the activities specified, we find ensuring that recruitment for operations is in line with Resolution 1325, that integration of a gender perspective takes place at the operational and tactical levels, that all contingents have plans of action for implementing Resolution 1325, that commanders in the organization undertake the necessary training for including a gender perspective in their work, and that gender focal points are appointed in the organization and given the necessary capacity-building training to provide support.[42]

While there have been directives on effecting gender equality since 2003, this new steering document broke with tradition in 2014 by combining what were previously two distinct documents: the Equality Guidance Document and the Gender Equality Plan. The joint document thereby highlights a new and more holistic approach to equality issues within the organization, one that brings together equality and discrimination issues of gender, race, and LGBT rights.[43]

The aims of the Swedish Armed Forces in terms of fostering equality and gender equality for 2016–18 are specified in several key priorities. The first is to, as far as possible, integrate and thereby mainstream gender equality perspectives in all directives of the armed forces. The second priority is to achieve "correct" physical standards and tests, meaning that they should be based on objective analysis of the actual job tasks and not based on traditional gender biases or contrived views of the job requirements. The third priority emphasizes the work environment and equipment. "As far as technically possible and reasonable in relation to the nature of the task," there must be equipment and supplies for both women and men. A gender perspective should therefore be applied to all new purchases of supplies and equipment. The final aim is to increase the number of female recruits and officers at all levels. Specific further aims have in the past included having everyone in senior leadership positions complete Course B724: Gender Mainstreaming. The aim is also to put all the top leadership of the Swedish Armed Forces through the resurrected gender coach program. Finally, national and international operations should be planned, conducted, and evaluated in accordance with UNSCR 1325, its follow-up resolutions, and the government's national action plan.[44]

The equality plan also highlights several areas within which the organization should focus its efforts. One area, directly related to gender equality and equal opportunity, is the possibility for both women and men to foster a better work-life balance by permitting and supporting extended parental leave. The policy is that parenthood and parental leave should not obstruct the development of skills or careers. Paid parental leave is, however, not a specific benefit within the armed forces but a contractual benefit of all federal employees in Sweden—men and women.[45] Thus, the policy to support extended parental leave is one of promoting a culture in which parental leave for men or women is not frowned on and in which it does not have an impact on the career.

These aims and areas of focus are a rather tall order in an organization with so much ingrained resistance, and the practical impact of these directives remains to be seen. Concerned interviewees stressed the fact that this document is most often not seen as central within the organization and that implementation, when it happens, is often based on the initiative and leadership of certain commanders who are interested in these issues, rather than on a sense of mandatory obligation to implement the directive. However, where interest does exist, the directive has proved to be an important guide for work within this area.[46] The peripheral status of the document is also unsurprising given that there are countless directives with different purposes within the Swedish Armed Forces. The aims of this document are often treated as somewhat trivial concerns, and many other directives are considered more important to the core activities of military organizations. As an example, the Supreme Commander's Directive for the same period, a document higher up in the bureaucratic pecking order, has left out the equality directive's target quotas for women at different levels of command—something that could send a signal about the perceived limited importance of those particular aims throughout the organization.[47] More focus areas from the document are discussed in greater detail in the following sections.

Recruitment

Recruitment is a central area in the Swedish Armed Forces' attempts to implement a gender perspective and to achieve gender equality. The general aim of the organization is to be perceived as an attractive employer for both men and women—something that the armed forces acknowledge will require clarity about their core tasks and recognition that their core tasks are based on democratic principles among which gender equality is an important component. The armed forces also highlight that they value members' skills and abilities regardless of gender, ethnicity, or religious background, and they make efforts to convey that message to attract, recruit, and retain the right people with the right skills.[48]

Today recruitment is formally gender-neutral, with women and men applying on equal terms to all parts of the organization. The physical standards—both the general and the job-specific ones—are also gender-neutral.[49] The Swedish Armed Forces argue that "a prerequisite for being able to attract, recruit and retain people with the right skills is that everyone, regardless of gender, sexual orientation, or ethnicity is assessed based on their personal characteristics and capabilities."[50] The Swedish Armed Forces is nevertheless traditionally a completely male-dominated organization, and the degree of actual implementation of these policies varies. The messaging is not having the intended impact of increasing numbers of women.

As already noted, an important goal in the previously mentioned directive on gender equality is that the proportion of women should increase at all levels. The equality directive for 2012–14 for the first time included a target quota for the number of women to be recruited and promoted at different levels. The goals included increasing recruitment of women to a level that achieves a quota of 20 percent women among soldiers and sailors. At higher levels of command, the aim was limited to 10 percent by 2014. The target quotas for female recruitment have since been criticized for being "pulled out of a hat" rather than being the outcome of a discussion with commanders at different levels about what is feasible and practical.[51] There are also serious doubts about the possibility of achieving the aims—especially the 10 percent quota at higher levels of command.

As Sweden moved from conscription for men to an all-volunteer force, and in that process also emphasized female recruitment, the figure briefly went up to a historically high 15 percent of recruited soldiers and sailors. However, after the initial surge, these figured have begun to drop again. Moreover, retaining women has proved even more difficult than recruiting them, perhaps also indicating that the Swedish Armed Forces are not a particularly welcoming environment for women. These challenges have historical precedents. Annica Kronsell notes that while there have been no previous target quotas for the organization as a whole, there have been occasional informal target quotas in the previous directives on gender equality. One example was an aim to recruit 20 percent women for the Nordic Battle Group in 2008. The actual outcome was only 5 percent, highlighting that aims and good intentions alone are insufficient for organizational changes of this scale and nature.[52]

The number of women deployed in Swedish military operations abroad is on average 10 percent, but this percentage varies considerably between missions. For example, the Swedish battalions to the UN Mission in Liberia consisted of 4.8 percent women, while the contributions to NATO operations in Kosovo had 11.4 percent.[53]

Thus, putting politically correct words and ambitions aside, the Swedish Armed Forces have struggled to recruit and promote not only women but also people of different ethnic backgrounds and sexual orientations. Despite its aspirations, Sweden remains at a level of about 6 percent women in the armed forces, while most other Western armed forces have successfully increased female participation at all levels.[54] As examples, the US and France can be mentioned—both with around 15 percent women in the armed forces.

The armed forces have struggled not only to recruit new female soldiers and officers but also to promote women to senior positions. There are very few women in visible positions of authority in the Swedish Armed Forces today and therefore very few role models. Two female brigadier generals have nevertheless been appointed in the last two years—one in the air force and one in the navy. Five more top women have served as the general director of the Swedish Armed Forces, the general-level physician (the highest-ranking doctor within the organization), the finance director, the chief legal advisor and director of legal staff, and finally the director of communications.[55] It is notable that the five women in the top leadership of the organization have been civilians rather than women rising through the ranks of the military hierarchy. There is also no generation waiting to crash the glass ceiling. In 2016 no military women applied or were nominated for promotion to the selection group that will be appointed colonels. The general lack of senior female officers has also been identified as a problem that needs to be addressed. According to one interviewee, one reason for this is that very few women have reached a high enough rank to be promoted to general—a critical factor needed to justify promotion to the next level.[56]

The challenges to recruiting and promoting women within the Swedish Armed Forces tend to surprise an international audience that has rightly come to expect better from a country with such a good reputation regarding women's issues. Why have the armed forces failed to live up to these expectations? The biggest challenge has been the system of universal male conscription. Until 1980 women were not allowed in the military, apart from certain unarmed volunteer defense organizations. In 1980 certain positions were opened, but the system of conscription for military service still provided a number of tremendous obstacles. First, to be eligible to apply for the officer's academy, national service had to be completed. To go through the national service, women had to individually contact the conscription agency and sign up for a physical, mental, and psychological evaluation. However, before they were allowed to apply to become a cadet in the officer academy, they would have to go through fifteen months of military service (with good enough evaluations), most often as one of very few women in a culture based on male heterosexuality and homosociality.[57] Thus, while all young men by default were conscripted and had an opportunity to try military life for a year, women were excluded except in cases in which individual women with a great deal of initiative actively sought a military career. During the era of national military service, or the "duty to protect" as it is called in Swedish, all efforts to recruit women in larger numbers, albeit rather limited, seem to have been in vain.

However, on July 1, 2010, an all-volunteer force replaced national conscription for men. This has radically changed the recruitment of women, and the number of female military personnel is now rapidly increasing. Potential recruits can now apply for basic military training (Grundläggande Militär

Utbildning, or GMU), which lasts for three months. Following this, a complementary military training (Kompletterande Militär Utbildning, or KMU) can be completed to qualify for employment as a soldier or sailor or to become eligible for further education and training as an officer or a specialist (which is the equivalent of a noncommissioned officer in most other countries).

The Swedish government and the Swedish Armed Forces expressed hopes that the new system of voluntary recruitment would help raise the proportion of female recruits and officers.[58] The first numbers were encouraging. In spring 2011 the proportion of female recruits was approximately 10–12 percent, only marginally higher than during the period when conscription was in effect. By May 2013 the numbers had risen significantly with a record year of 24.4 percent female recruits at the basic training level, 11 percent women employed as soldiers and sailors, 16.2 percent women in the officer's academy, and 10 percent female specialists. However, change takes time, which is obvious in the number of currently employed female officers, which has marginally increased to 5.4 percent.[59] As already mentioned, the numbers of female recruits and employed soldiers and sailors have since dropped substantially again. The Swedish Armed Forces are nevertheless also practicing affirmative action, with the hope of slightly raising women's overall representation among recruits; all women who have met minimum requirements are being recruited.[60]

An interesting special effort to increase recruitment started in 2009–10, the last year before the switch to an all-volunteer force. To create a more welcoming environment for young women, and to make sure that there were female role models around, the Swedish Armed Forces concentrated female officers and recruits to three regiments. This was a deliberate attempt to create a "critical mass" of women in order to avoid the perception that they were outliers in an otherwise all-male environment. The outcome of this project was interesting. In the summer of 2009, 16 percent or 73 out of the 461 new conscripts at the Command Regiment in Enköping were women. In 2012 the same regiment recruited 17 men and 17 women to basic military training of the all-volunteer force. Apart from the remarkable equality in recruitment, the numbers are interesting because the regiment was hoping for 60 recruits and received only 34, which means that they accepted all who met the formal criteria. We therefore cannot explain this through affirmative action but rather equal interest from men and women.[61]

To attract recruits, the armed forces have also conducted several advertising campaigns. Some of these advertisements have been criticized for being biased toward media outlets that are read by a larger proportion of men than women.[62] They have also been described as portraying an action-oriented stereotype of military service that caters to male interests rather than to female ones. An example was a TV commercial that showed a squad of camouflage-painted and very "warrior-looking" soldiers in a high-speed chase of Somali pirates in the Gulf of Aden. The question at the end of the commercial was, "Do you have what it takes?" The commercial was criticized for not reflecting the actual work of Swedish units in that particular international operation, for using boats that do not exist in the Swedish Navy, and for using as "actors" South African security contractors dressed in Swedish uniforms. However, in 2012 the armed forces also started developing advertisements specifically tailored to women.[63] Efforts are, for example, made to always include women on posters and in TV commercials. It should be noted that all of this—advertising campaigns, recruitment quotas—is unchartered territory for an organization that has historically relied on conscription.

Further changes have involved studying and reconsidering the physical standards required to be employed and to work in certain positions and units. Since 2010 these standards are completely gender neutral and have also been adapted to avoid traditional male strengths, such as upper body strength tests, that women perform comparatively poorly in and that do not necessarily reflect the demands of the job of a deployed soldier.[64] Another focus area involves studies to understand and potentially rectify the problem of higher levels of injury to female recruits in training. As is the case internationally, injury is a bigger problem in training than it is during deployment, and a challenge will be to reconsider the nature of physical training during the short initial period of basic training. As an interviewee accurately highlighted, the armed forces previously had seven months to slowly build up the recruits' physiques. Initial basic training is now limited to three months. Adding to the challenge is the fact that recruits have lower and lower physical standards when they join—a consequence of the changes in lifestyles in the last twenty years prompted by the IT revolution.[65]

The all-volunteer force experiment did not last long, however. The Swedish Armed Forces never succeeded to fill all positions on a voluntary basis, and in March 2017 the Swedish government decided to reintroduce conscription as a complement to voluntary recruitment. The reintroduced conscription nevertheless included one important difference: this time it is gender neutral. The first gender-neutral recruits entered training in 2018, and the consequences for integration of women remains to be seen.

Antidiscrimination and Equal Opportunities

The Swedish Armed Forces have in the recent past used specialized functions to counteract discrimination. Following the end of Genderforce, four people were hired to be responsible for fighting different aspects of discrimination.⁶⁶ Later, in 2009, the armed forces underwent a so-called human resources transformation, and the Human Resources Centre (HR Centre) was established. The HR Centre has direct contact with soldiers and officers and includes on its staff the equal opportunity advisor to the director of human resources, who is responsible for the strategic implementation of antidiscrimination and equal opportunity guidance documents. The first senior gender advisor in the Swedish Armed Forces worked as an equal opportunity advisor to the director of human resources before she transferred to the chief of joint operations staff in 2006.⁶⁷

The Swedish Armed Forces stress that all personnel have a responsibility to contribute to a more gender-equal organization. However, they concurrently acknowledge that in organizational change and development processes, commanders have a special responsibility as leaders. That responsibility is one reason the gender coach program has been resurrected; commanders at different levels are now required to go through training on gender issues. These efforts are part of a gender-mainstreaming effort that is currently the prioritized strategy for equality-related work in the Swedish Armed Forces. This mainstreaming means that a gender perspective should be incorporated in all policies at all levels and at all stages of planning processes in order to address how decisions and activities affect women and men—at home and abroad in the field of operations. Again, an operational effectiveness approach has been part of the rationale for gender mainstreaming in Sweden. In this case, advocates argue that implementation of gender mainstreaming in the planning, conduct, and evaluation of operations increases the operational effectiveness in the area of operations and contributes to the protection of human rights—something that is often part of the operational aims of contemporary peace operations (discussed later).⁶⁸

The main challenge when it comes to equal opportunity and discrimination has been glass ceilings created by what interviewees refer to as "subjective standards and criteria in evaluation processes."⁶⁹ Until recently, one of the more important evaluation criteria in the yearly assessment reports was called "suitability for next school step." Until very recently, the Swedish promotion system was completely based on school steps during the career. The importance of attending a school, rather than being appointed to a certain position that led to promotion, meant that nomination and acceptance to these schools became essential career-wise. However, the criterion of "suitability for next school step" was not specified, and its meaning was therefore unclear and almost entirely subjective. Officers have been completely subjected to commanders' individual judgment.

This subjectivity has in the past hurt all people who were "different" in one way or another, especially women who have completely stood out in what has traditionally been an all-male institution. Interviewees in the personnel staff of the Swedish Armed Forces Headquarters speak of a glass ceiling for women at the level of major.[70] At that level the already limited remaining women in the Swedish Armed Forces tend to "level out" in their careers or leave for alternative careers. This challenge festers within the organization as it in turn limits the number of women eligible for higher command. Although the Swedish Armed Forces openly practice affirmative action, this practice becomes very sensitive when there is only one female candidate among many men.

Another challenge for equal opportunity measures was the nature and structure of the process of nomination to schools and command posts. This process traditionally lacked transparency because it was conducted by small nomination boards within the different regiments around the country. The hopefuls had no idea what was said during nomination board meetings and at central command, and schools received only a nomination list, not commentary about people not on the list. Thus, people were blocked from nominations within their units and were therefore never considered for positions or schools.

This challenge has recently been rectified through many activities at different levels. Yearly assessment reports have been replaced by yearly individual development activities. These activities involve new criteria for individual performance assessment that strive to increase gender awareness by including gender and equality considerations. One of the gender-aware negative criteria is "unwanted behavior," which is determined using seven detailed questions designed to reveal behavior that does not match the armed forces' values. The transparency of the nomination boards throughout the organization is now being regulated with directives regarding the makeup of the board, the criteria to be used, and demands to exercise positive discrimination by always nominating at least one man or one woman. A central nomination board within the military headquarters has also been established as an oversight mechanism and as an extra opportunity to meet problematic minority recruitment and nomination quotas. The central nomination board can force reconsiderations or request extra information from the regimental boards on those nominated as well as those not nominated. A request for further information has already been exercised in cases in which no women were nominated from a unit. This request also led to subsequent revisions of the nomination lists and acceptance to the school.[71]

Sexual Harassment and Assault

The prevalence of sexual harassment and assault within military organizations is a salient issue, as illustrated by the discouraging statistics about these matters that have begun to emerge from around the world. In the US context, the issue has taken political center stage, with extensive media coverage, congressional hearings, and delayed promotions of senior officers.[72] Senator John McCain's comment on the issue is typical: "I cannot overstate my disgust and disappointment over continued reports of sexual misconduct in our military. We've been talking about the issue for years, and talk is insufficient."[73]

While sexual harassment and assault are problems occurring in the Swedish Armed Forces as well, they seem to happen on a more limited basis. As an example, few incidents of rape have been reported within the organization for several years—although the number of reported cases might not reflect the actual prevalence of the problem.[74] The high number of unreported cases of harassment that turn up in anonymous surveys indicates this risk. While official statistics are scarce, the Swedish Armed Forces also report a slight decrease of reported cases of harassment and abuse throughout the organization—despite, or perhaps thanks to, increasing numbers of female recruits over the past few years.[75] The Swedish Armed Forces also categorically state in the Directive on Equality and Gender Equality that they do not tolerate the abuse of power that harassment involves and that the prevention of such behavior is therefore an area of enhanced focus.

That statistics mean little and that abuse is prevalent in the Swedish Armed Forces just as it is in all sectors of society became obvious in the fall of 2017 as the #MeToo movement swept across the globe. In Sweden separate petition campaigns detailing horrific accounts of abuse, each signed by thousands of women, were organized within many professions and work sectors. Sweden's biggest daily newspaper, *Dagens Nyheter*, published an armed forces appeal signed by 1,768 women, and the anonymous accounts of abuse included everything from rape to harassment and toxic leadership.[76] The top leadership reacted quickly and strongly to the appeal, but the extent to which it will have a lasting impact on the organization's culture or behavior remains to be seen.

The Swedish Armed Forces does not have its own laws, courts, or regulation, and these matters are therefore formally dealt with as they are in any other government agency or workplace in Sweden. The Directive on Equality and Gender Equality notes that, while the victim's sense of vulnerability is always extant, the law regulates what counts as harassment and discrimination: "Sexual harassment means that someone behaves with sexual undertones in a way that violates your or someone else's dignity. Serious forms of sexual harassment or different forms of sexual violence and coercion is criminal and must be reported to the police."[77] The armed forces also seek to protect the victims or witnesses and argue that military employees who are the victims of, or who report, harassment in any form must not be subject to reprisals. Neither should those who have participated in an investigation or who have in other ways been supporting the prosecution in a harassment case.[78]

Conceptually, the HR Centre leads the work to further limit the prevalence of harassment within the armed forces, although the center stresses that the units and commanders at different levels of the organization have to implement measures relevant to this aim by following directives, procedures, and the law.[79] In a broader sense, the focus is currently on mitigating harassment by mainstreaming an understanding and appreciation of gender issues and equality throughout the organization. The goal is to instill the proper values in soldiers and officers early in their careers, in part by doing the work of mainstreaming in military schools and training centers for young recruits and cadets. The armed forces' value system is also currently operationalized in codes of conduct that serve as guides for appropriate behavior and in step-by-step manuals for those reporting or investigating complaints.[80] Through the combination of mainstreaming and practical implementation efforts in manuals and codes of conduct, this work is becoming increasingly institutionalized within the organization, becoming a more natural part of daily activities.

Back to the Future—Dismantle, Maintain, or Expand?

The fact that the operations in Afghanistan have been instrumental in promoting and developing gender perspective within the Swedish Armed Forces raises interesting questions about the future. The Swedish military has more or less withdrawn from Afghanistan, and with the increasingly hostile behavior of Russia, its focus is quickly switching from international operations to territorial defense and security in the Baltic region. This shift could undo the relatively fragile change process. The argument can be made that while gender perspective has a place in peacekeeping and counterinsurgency operations, it does not have a place in conventional military operations. The risk that this argument gains a foothold increases by the fact that it correlates with the general organizational culture of all military organizations—a preference for interstate conventional warfare. As the armed forces reorganize for national defense under the constraints of limited defense budgets, the Nordic Centre for Gender in Military Operations, the active focus on gender advisors and focal points, and the cultural adaptation that is an ongoing process could be lost with the assertion that there are more important priorities.

There is some logic in these arguments, but given the type of warfare we are likely to expect in the contemporary era, abandoning efforts to develop gender perspective may still be a big mistake. Even wars involving the great powers have been hybrid wars—including both conventional and unconventional aspects. Not least, the conflict in eastern Ukraine shows the complexity of operations and the prevalence of irregular forces and propaganda. Understanding the local context, winning the support of the population, and achieving legitimacy in the eyes of the local and global communities are still of great relevance, which means that gender perspectives are still of great utility. All countries seem to need a reminder that UNSCR 1325 must be implemented also in case of a war on their own territory.

The armed forces' gender efforts are comparatively inexpensive, while the potential benefits may in some cases be great. Throwing the progress made on the dust piles of history would therefore prove a big mistake. The Swedish Armed Forces have experience dismantling organizational competence and trying to retrieve that competence during force downsizing after the Cold War. It would be a shame to make the same mistake again.

Further, despite the successes, the work to implement Resolution 1325 still faces considerable resistance from within the military establishment. There is plenty of room for continued implementation of gender perspective. Should the armed forces choose to expand this work over the coming years, they should both take new, bold steps and seek some form of consolidation by continuously wearing down the resistance. Not least, the argument must be made that developing gender perspectives is an important aspect not just of expeditionary international operations but also of national defense and regional stability.

Steps to continue the work include broadening understanding. Increasing the importance and status of gender issues requires reaching more layers of the organization with gender mainstreaming training, officer education, and field exercises. This work needs more resources, political backing, and command authority within the organization. These changes risk increasing resistance as they inevitably challenge existing power structures, standard operating procedures, and cultural preferences. Finding a balance between consolidation and change is imperative.

Notes

1. Robert Egnell, Petter Hojem, and Hannes Berts, *Gender, Military Effectiveness, and Organizational Change: The Swedish Model* (London: Palgrave Macmillan, 2014).
2. Charlotte Isaksson, interview by the author, April 4, 2011.
3. Swedish Armed Forces, *Försvarsmaktens* årsredovisning *2002: Bilaga 3: Personalberättelse* [Swedish Armed Forces' Annual Report 2002: Annex 3: Personnel] (Stockholm: Swedish Armed Forces, 2003), 28.

4. Swedish Government, *Regleringsbrev för budgetåret 2004 avseende Försvarsmakten* [Appropriation direction for the Swedish Armed Forces 2004] (Stockholm: Regeringskansliet, 2004).
5. Swedish Government, *Regleringsbrev för budgetåret 2005 avseende Försvarsmakten* [Appropriation direction for the Swedish Armed Forces 2005] (Stockholm: Regeringskansliet, 2005).
6. Swedish Armed Forces, "Sammanfattning, slutredovisning och rekommendationer avseende projektet Genderforce" [Conclusion, final report, and recommendations regarding project Genderforce] (Swedish Armed Forces internal report, November 19, 2007), 1.
7. Isaksson, interview.
8. US Army and US Marine Corps, *Counterinsurgency Field Manual* (Chicago: University of Chicago Press, 2006), 37.
9. Ibid.
10. "ISAF Commander's Counterinsurgency Guidance," Headquarters, International Security Assistance Force, Kabul, Afghanistan, issued August 2009, accessed September 18, 2009, https://www.nato.int/isaf/docu/official_texts/counterinsurgency_guidance.pdf.
11. Andrew Garfield, *Succeeding in Phase IV: British Perspectives on the U.S. to Stabilize and Reconstruct Iraq* (Philadelphia: Foreign Policy Research Institute, 2006), 16.
12. Swedish Armed Forces, "Gender and Operational Effect: The Gender Field Advisor Function in the Swedish Armed Forces" (Swedish Armed Forces internal report, undated), 3.
13. Author interview with GFA, June 17, 2011; author interview with GFA, June 9, 2011; author interview with commanding officer, June 29, 2011.
14. Author interview with GFA, June 17, 2011.
15. Author interview with commanding officer, June 28, 2011.
16. Author interview with GFA, June 9, 2011; author interview with GFA, June 17, 2011; author interview with GFA, June 29, 2011.
17. Susanne Axmacher, "Vikten av tidig integration av genusperspektiv i insatser" [The importance of early integration of gender perspectives in operations] (Swedish Armed Forces internal report, 2008).
18. Author interview with GFA, June 13, 2011.
19. Ibid.
20. Egnell, Hojem, and Berts, *Gender.*
21. Susanne Axmacher, interview by the author, February 8, 2012.
22. Swedish Armed Forces, "Gender and Operational Effect," 3.
23. Ibid.
24. Ibid.
25. Author interview with GFA, November 16, 2011.
26. Egnell, Hojem, and Berts, *Gender.*
27. Louise Burenius, *Kvinnor i internationella insatser? En undersökning om hur kvinnligt deltagande kan påverka internationella insatser* [Women in international operations? An investigation of the effects of female participation in international operations] (Stockholm: Swedish National Defence College, 2009); Sophia Ivarsson and Lina Edmark, *Utlandsstyrkans internationella insatser ur ett genusperspektiv: Hinder och möjligheter för implementering av FN resolution 1325* [A gender perspective on the operations of the international units: Obstacles and opportunities for the implementation of UNSCR 1325] (Stockholm: Swedish National Defence College, 2007).

28. Axmacher, interview.
29. Swedish Armed Forces, *MOT Juliette: Sveriges första kvinnliga observatörsteam* [MOT Juliette: The first Swedish all-female observation team], https://www.forsvarsmakten.se/sv/information-och-fakta/var-historia/artiklar/mot-juliette/.
30. Swedish Armed Forces, *Verksamhetsuppdrag för 2009 och (prel) 2010 samt inriktning av verksamheten 2011* [Operational assignments for 2009 and (preliminary) 2010 as well as focus on operations 2011] (Stockholm: Swedish Armed Forces, 2009), 6.
31. Author interview with commanding officer, June 29, 2011.
32. Axmacher, interview.
33. Author interview with commanding officer, November 9, 2011.
34. Geneva Centre for the Democratic Control of Armed Forces, *Gender and Defence Transformation: Transforming National Structures, Sustaining International Operations* (Geneva: DCAF, 2011), 8.
35. Karl Engelbrektson, "Resolution 1325 Increases Efficiency," in *Good and Bad Examples: Lessons Learned from Working with United Nations Resolution 1325 in International Missions*, ed. Åsa Nyqvist (Stockholm: Genderforce, Swedish Armed Forces, 2007), 22.
36. Charlotte Isaksson, "Final Report on Gender Work inside EUFOR RD Congo" (Swedish Armed Forces internal report, December 15, 2006), 5.
37. Author interview with GFA, November 11, 2011.
38. This section builds on Egnell, Hojem, and Berts, *Gender*, chapter 5.
39. Swedish Armed Forces, "Försvarsmaktens jämställdhets- och jämlikhetsarbete" [The Swedish Armed Forces' work for equality and gender equality], https://www.forsvarsmakten.se/sv/om-myndigheten/vara-varderingar/jamstalldhet-och-jamlikhet/.
40. Susanne Axmacher, email correspondence with the author, November 19, 2011.
41. Swedish Armed Forces, "Försvarsmaktens styrdokument för Jämlikhet, 2009–2011" [Swedish Armed Forces steering documents for gender equality 2009–2011] (May 8, 2009), https://www.yumpu.com/sv/document/view/10615755/2011-02-15-forsvarsmaktens-styrdokument-for-jamlikhet-20094; Swedish Armed Forces, "Försvarsmaktens jämställdhetsplan, 2009–2011" [Swedish Armed Forces gender equality plan 2009–2011] (May 8, 2009), http://jamda.ub.gu.se/bitstream/1/298/1/forsvarsmakten.pdf, 4.
42. Swedish Armed Forces, "Försvarsmaktens Styrdokument för jämställdhet och jämlikhet 2012–2014" [The Swedish Armed Forces Directive for Equality and Gender Equality 2012–2014] (March 16, 2012), 4, https://www.forsvarsmakten.se/siteassets/4-om-myndigheten/vara-varderingar/hkv-2012-03-16_16-100--54891-styrdokument-for-jamstalldhet-och-jamlikhet.pdf.
43. Matilda Lidström Dougnac, interview by the author, June 24, 2013.
44. Swedish Armed Forces, "Försvarsmaktens Jämställdhets- och jämlikhetsplan 2016–2018" [The Armed Forces Equality and Gender Equality Plan 2016–2018] (February 28, 2016), https://www.forsvarsmakten.se/siteassets/4-om-myndigheten/dokumentfiler/jamlikhet/fm2015-7991.20-underbilaga-3.1-fmvp-16.pdf.
45. Ibid., 5.
46. Dougnac, interview.
47. Ibid.
48. Swedish Armed Forces, "Jämställdhet och jämlikhet 2012–2014," 6.
49. Peter Öberg, interview by the author, July 3, 2013.
50. Swedish Armed Forces, "Försvarsmaktens jämställdhets- och jämlikhetsarbete."
51. Dougnac, interview.

52. Annica Kronsell, *Gender, Sex, and the Postnational Defense: Militarism and Peacekeeping* (Oxford: Oxford University Press, 2012), 65, 117.
53. Ibid., 110, 117.
54. Ibid.
55. Öberg, interview.
56. Author interview with senior officer, Swedish Armed Forces Headquarters, November 1, 2011.
57. These two concepts have been described as the foundation of traditional unit cohesion. Kronsell, *Gender, Sex, and Postnational Defense*, 68.
58. Sten Tolgfors, "Mångdubbelt fler kvinnor i försvaret" [Manifold more women in the Swedish Armed Forces], *Svenska Dagbladet*, May 19, 2010, https://www.svd.se/opinion/brannpunkt/mangdubbelt-fler-kvinnor-i-forsvaret_4737281.svd; Öberg, interview.
59. Swedish Armed Forces, "Personalläget i Försvarsmakten maj 2013 enligt LEDS direktiv SC 202/16" [The personnel situation in the Swedish Armed Forces] (Swedish Armed Forces internal report, June 13, 2013).
60. Author interview with senior officer, Swedish Armed Forces Headquarters, September 13, 2011.
61. Lotta Lille, "Försvaret vill rekrytera fler kvinnor" [The armed forces wants to recruit more women], *UNT*, February 2, 2013, http://www.unt.se/enkoping/forsvaret-vill-rekrytera-fler-kvinnor-2254625.aspx.
62. Author interview with GFA, October 20, 2011.
63. Swedish Armed Forces, "Försvarsmaktens utvecklingsplan 2012–2021 (FMUP 12)" [The Swedish Armed Forces development plan 2012–2021] (Swedish Armed Forces internal report, February 4, 2011), 127.
64. Öberg, interview.
65. Ibid.
66. These included (1) gender, (2) sexual orientation and gender identity (LGBT), (3) ethnicity and religion, and (4) age and disabilities.
67. Susanne Axmacher, email correspondence with the author, December 19, 2011.
68. Swedish Armed Forces Headquarters, "Jämställdhet och jämlikhet 2012–2014," 6.
69. Charlotte Isaksson, interview by the author, February 10, 2013.
70. Dougnac, interview.
71. Öberg, interview.
72. See Craig Whitlock, "Lawmakers Demand Crackdown on Sex Assault in Military," *Washington Post*, June 4, 2013; Donna Cassata, "Claire McCaskill Puts Hold on Susan Helms Nomination over Overturned Conviction," *Huffington Post*, April 25, 2013, http://www.huffingtonpost.com/2013/04/25/claire-mccaskill-susan-helms_n_3157084.html.
73. Cited in Ed O'Keefe, "Why Congress Likely Will Move Quickly to Curb Sex Assaults in the Military," *Washington Post*, June 5, 2013.
74. Helena Hoffman, Swedish Armed Forces Human Resources Centre, interview by the author, June 27, 2013.
75. Ibid.
76. "1 768 kvinnor i försvaret: 'Alla anmälningar måste tas på allvar'" [1768 women in the Swedish Armed Forces: "All reports have to be taken seriously"], *Dagens Nyheter*, November 29, 2017, https://www.dn.se/debatt/1768-kvinnor-i-forsvaret-alla-anmalningar-maste-tas-pa-allvar/.
77. Ibid.

78. Swedish Armed Forces Headquarters, "Jämställdhet och jämlikhet 2012–2014," 5.
79. Hoffman, interview.
80. Swedish Armed Forces, "Vad händer nu? Information till all personal om diskriminering, trakasserier samt kränkande särbehandling" [What happens now? Information on discrimination and harassment] (Swedish Armed Forces internal report, undated).

4

The Gender Perspective and Canada's Armed Forces

Internal and External Dimensions of Military Culture

Stéfanie von Hlatky

On April 30, 2015, the Canadian Department of National Defence (DND) released an external review on sexual misconduct in the Canadian Armed Forces (CAF) drafted by former Supreme Court Justice Marie Deschamps. Deschamps's findings were unequivocal: the CAF's culture is hostile to women and has led to a permissive environment for sexual harassment. The review called for comprehensive cultural reform in the CAF. The Deschamps report illustrates that the issue of sexual misconduct, despite how it is treated in many security organizations, is not separate from the question of professional organizational culture. Considering this report, the Canadian public might find it ironic that the CAF are frequently deployed abroad to protect women's rights but are unable to provide a safe environment for women in their own ranks.

In this chapter I argue that understanding the role of gender in the CAF requires both an internal and external perspective. The internal dimension includes an organization's own policies toward personnel and the way its daily work is carried out at home. The external dimension, by contrast, includes exploring the gender perspective as part of the CAF's operations abroad. Studying both dimensions yields important findings as it more clearly identifies gaps in the implementation of gender balancing and gender mainstreaming goals in the military. Moreover, a two-dimensional study demonstrates that the phenomenon of sexual misconduct is more pervasive than national investigations—that tend to ignore the external dimension—suggest.

This chapter is organized as follows: the first section offers background on the integration of women in the CAF since World War II; the second section describes the analytical framework used and specifies the key definitions and concepts; the third section provides the empirical analysis of CAF policies and operations using a gendered lens; and finally, the chapter offers a conclusion that includes some policy recommendations.

Background and Chronology

Women have been part of the regular forces since 1906 but part of Canadian military history since 1885, when female nurses participated in the Northwest Rebellion. In Canada, as in many other countries, the two world wars saw significant shifts in women's involvement in the military, with more than 2,800 nurses serving between 1914 and 1918 and approximately 5,000 nurses serving between 1939 and 1945. By 1941, with more than 45,000 women enlisted as volunteers in full-time service, women's roles in the CAF broadened to include trades such as drivers, cooks, and mechanics. Up to that point, the push for the recruitment of women in the CAF was one of necessity; the military relied on the female volunteers to meet its needs. The situation was no different during the Korean War, but then, in 1965, the government of Canada instituted a cap of 1,500 female service members.

The turning point for the history of women in the CAF came in 1970 with the Royal Commission on the Status of Women, which resulted in five core recommendations to promote equal opportunity for women in the armed forces: "(1) standardization of enrolment criteria; (2) equal pension benefits for women and men; (3) opportunity for women to attend Canadian military colleges; (4) opening of all trades and officer classifications to women; and, (5) termination of regulations prohibiting enrolment of married women and requiring release of servicewomen upon the birth of a child."[1] Most of these recommendations took many years to be implemented. For example, women only gained access to military colleges in 1979. Moreover, senior military leadership actively resisted some of these changes. In the 1980s the Servicewomen in Non-Traditional Environments and Roles (SWINTER) project and the Combat Related Employment of Women (CREW) trials were intended to test whether women possessed the necessary physical abilities to access all trades and officer classifications. This kind of organizational stalling became less acceptable after the adoption in 1982 of the Canadian Charter of Rights and Freedoms, which prohibited, among other things, sex-based discrimination.

In the late 1980s, programs like SWINTER and CREW were dealt a decisive blow following a complaint with the Canadian Human Rights Tribunal about the CAF's discriminatory employment practices. The complaint led to several major changes, such as an order for the CAF to prepare for the full integration of women, across occupations, and to remove existing employment restrictions. This new mandate for the CAF was achieved in 1989, and the only remaining employment restriction—submarine service—was lifted in 2001. Despite the achievement of individual women in the CAF in the 1990s and 2000s, Canada's overarching policies toward female service members stagnated. The CAF adopted the mantra of gender neutrality, sometimes critically referred to as gender blindness.[2] Once the CAF had achieved the inclusion of women in a formal sense, military leaders did not go much further to consider the full integration of these women within the organization. In other words, including more women was considered a success in itself, and little thought was given to how new gender dynamics would play out. Problems began to emerge in the form of poor retention rates and several sexual misconduct scandals, like those reported in 2014 in a high-profile *Maclean's* investigation and resulting in the external review by Deschamps.[3] The chief of the defense staff, Tom Lawson, appointed a task force led by Lt. Gen. Chris Whitecross to propose an action plan based on the Deschamps review's recommendations. The appointment of the task force represented a wake-up call for the CAF; many were surprised at the lack of progress the military had made despite its having opened up trades to women. The rest of this chapter offers a gendered analysis of what can arguably be referred to as the stunted progress of women's integration in the CAF.

Analytical Framework: The Internal and External Dimensions of Military Culture

The driving concepts of this analysis are gender balancing and gender mainstreaming. While both concepts correspond to distinct approaches that are relevant for facilitating the integration of women, they are best understood as complementary. Gender balancing is focused on the achievement of a gender-diverse workforce; it is the attainment of strict equality goals through the inclusion and retention of women. Gender mainstreaming is about integrating gender-based analysis as part of policymaking and operational design at every stage of the process.[4] According to this approach, the aim is for gender to become mainstream by "making visible the gendered nature of assumptions,

Table 4.1: Analytical Framework and Examples

	Internal	External
Gender balancing	Recruitment campaign aimed to increase the proportion of female service members	Percentage of women deployed in military operations
Gender mainstreaming	Integration of gender-based analysis as part of personnel training	Integration of the gender perspective in operations

processes, and outcomes."[5] Just as it has become intuitive to consider risk analysis in policymaking frameworks, for instance, gender is increasingly being recognized as a necessary factor to consider, hence the term "gender mainstreaming."

I will make a distinction between the internal and external dimension of objectives for both concepts in the context of the CAF. The internal dimension is limited to policies that regulate the CAF as an organization. The external dimension includes the interactions and activities the CAF conduct abroad. Table 4.1 summarizes the analytical framework and illustrates how gender balancing and mainstreaming are operationalized in the context of the CAF's internal and external activities.

A relatively recent example of internal gender balancing is the CAF recruitment campaign targeting women. The goal of the campaign was to increase the number of female recruits. The campaign featured videos posted on the government's website, including one in which *Canadian Idol* alumna Tara Oram interacts with Lt. (Navy) Michelle Baranowski. As Oram spends the day with Baranowski, she "pushes her limits" through physical training and bonds with her military friend, all the while debunking "misconceptions" about life in the CAF. External gender balancing, by contrast, would instead refer to the percentage of women deployed in operations. Canada is asked to submit this data to the North Atlantic Treaty Organization (NATO) Committee on Gender Perspectives to allow the systematic comparison and benchmarking of gender-balancing policies and practices across the twenty-nine member states.

Gender mainstreaming (discussed in the next section) is more salient in the context of operations than it is in the CAF's internal practices. Internally, gender mainstreaming is the application of gender-based analysis to training approaches, as evidenced in the curriculum of military academies, or to strategic analysis conducted by doctrine and joint operations centers, for example. Since gender mainstreaming, as an analytical approach, is predicated on recognizing that men and women may have different types of experiences, it is somewhat at odds with Canadian military organizational culture, which—until the Deschamps report's recommendations—was strongly gender neutral, meaning all soldiers were considered equal, regardless of gender. Gender-mainstreaming strategies have, however, been integrated as part of operational planning and execution, especially during Canada's mission in Afghanistan. In Afghanistan, gender segregation was embedded in local cultural practices, and intelligence collection and community outreach required an understanding of gender-based power dynamics to gain access to Afghan women as collaborators and to gain a fuller operational picture.

The Female Experience in the Canadian Armed Forces

This section applies the analytical framework to better understand DND policies toward women in the military and female experiences in CAF operations.

Internal Balancing

The best source of information on the proportion of women in the CAF can be found, surprisingly, in a repository external to the government of Canada. DND submits annual reports called *Canadian Forces National Report to the Committee for Women in NATO Forces* to NATO. These reports from member states can be found directly on the NATO website and include information on policies related to the recruitment and retention of women in the armed forces and what is referred to as "women-friendly" policies. In the Canadian case, the report summarizes the legal basis for women's integration into the armed forces, the main policies for implementing gender mainstreaming, and basic data on the presence of women in the military, including figures for each service.[6]

While major strides were made following the removal of barriers to women's participation across trades in 1989, there has been no significant improvement in those numbers in the last decade. From 2002 to 2014, the percentage of women in the regular forces has only grown from 12 percent to 14.7 percent despite all trades being open to women. That percentage has hardly budged since, hovering around 15 percent. Nondiscriminatory policies regarding occupational requirement standards, therefore, are insufficient to reach targets of 20–25 percent women in the force, let alone a gender balance reflecting that found in the civilian labor force (though there are gender imbalances in many civilian fields).[7] This slow progress may have more to do with integration policies (or a lack thereof) than with formal entry barriers. Female CAF members have described their experience of joining the military as "assimilation" rather than as "integration," meaning that they had to conform to a male warrior culture or face professional and social exclusion.[8]

Moreover, the question of integration has been treated entirely separately from the problem of sexual misconduct toward women in the CAF. The latest external investigation into sexual misconduct, by former Supreme Court justice Marie Deschamps, questioned this separation. In *External Review into Sexual Misconduct and Sexual Harassment in the Canadian Forces*, Deschamps explicitly connects instances of sexual misconduct with the CAF's organizational culture. The report states:

> One of the key findings of the External Review Authority (the ERA) is that there is an underlying sexualized culture in the CAF that is hostile to women and LGBTQ members, and conducive to more serious incidents of sexual harassment and assault. *Cultural change is therefore key*. It is not enough to simply revise policies or to repeat the mantra of "zero tolerance." Leaders must acknowledge that sexual misconduct is a real and serious problem for the organization, one that requires their own direct and sustained attention.[9]

While it is too early to comment on the consequences of the Deschamps report, the report findings underscore the need to go beyond gender-balancing goals to make progress on the integration of women in the armed forces. Moreover, a key recommendation Deschamps made is to engage in benchmarking with close allies and partners. To this end, members of the CAF task force mandated with the implementation of an action plan on sexual misconduct visited the United States, Australia, France, and the UK to share best practices for the eradication of sexual misconduct in the military and for the inclusion of women more broadly.

External Balancing

External balancing is the goal of women's integration in the CAF through activities undertaken outside Canada. Included in this category are benchmarking exercises with other allies and, more significant, the participation of women in deployments.

Canada's annual reports to NATO (mentioned previously) detail the CAF recruitment, training, and retention policies targeting women. What stands out in Canada's earlier reporting is the lack of data on the proportion of female service members who are deployed (other countries, for example, the United States, include this data). The Canadian report from 2009 provides an interesting example. In a table titled "Representation of Women in the Canadian Forces," the column for the percentage of female service members deployed in operations is left blank, with the following explanation: "The percentage of women deployed on CF operations normally corresponds with the percentages displayed in the columns to the left as *gender is not a factor in selection for deployment*. However, *the percentage of CF women deployed to combat operations such as in Afghanistan is in the range of 8%.*"[10] This note demonstrates a hesitation on the part of DND and the CAF to systematically track and assess the progress of external gender-balancing policies publicly, though this is changing. The lack of publicly available data is a hindrance for external evaluation and oversight of the organization's progress on the inclusion and retention of women in the CAF.

Practices have improved somewhat over time. Canada's national reports for its United Nations Security Council Resolution (UNSCR) 1325 National Action Plan are more explicit. In the 2013 report, DND disclosed, "As of March 31, 2013, 145 of 1142 (10%) deployed CAF personnel on international operations were women. During the reporting year, 11 of 46 (24%) civilian employees deployed in support of CAF designated international operations were women."[11] With Canada's appointment of gender advisors in 2016, the number of women on CAF operations is more closely tracked, though not made readily available. Researchers will continue to have difficulty getting a complete picture of female participation in the CAF until DND starts systematically collecting and publishing data relevant to the assessment of its gender integration policies. Looking back on operations like Afghanistan, how are we to evaluate the role played by women? Mainstream media outlets like *FrontLine* magazine have reported on this issue: "As yet, either nobody knows, or they aren't talking. DND insists it has not collected information specifically about women's combat experience in Afghanistan, and has no definite plans to do so."[12]

Canada's allies have echoed these sentiments. A 2009 report published by the British Ministry of Defence noted, "As the CF has not applied any gender-based restrictions on employment since 1989, from a policy perspective the integration of women into the combat arms is now considered a *fait accompli*. Thus, they consider that there is no formal requirement to continue monitoring the effects of gender integration on operational performance or team cohesion."[13] While a lack of systematic data collection is problematic, several accounts and studies on the role of Canadian women in combat are available for helping one understand the practical implications of the gender turn in military operations.

While some numbers are available on the proportion of women in operations, DND data on the percentage of women deployed in combat operations specifically is patchier still. Even if DND does not disclose the number of women who volunteered and were deployed in combat roles during Afghanistan, Krystel Chapman (née Carrier-Sabourin) has analyzed and reported raw data from Access to Information Act requests. She found that between 2001 and 2011, 310 women occupied combat positions.[14] This means that during that period women held 8.3 percent of combat positions within the CAF.[15] The breakdown provided is as follows: 83 women in the infantry, 58 in field artillery, 34 combat engineers, 20 pilots, and 9 in armor.

While Chapman's study stated that women's participation in combat increased threefold as compared to the 1990s, this is a difficult comparison to make given that Canadian interventions in the 1990s did not include a combat component across services. Therefore, women (in the army most of all) did not volunteer to participate in offensive combat missions as they did in Afghanistan. In the air force, there are published accounts of female tactical helicopter pilots participating in peacekeeping operations in Haiti and Somalia but very few personal accounts published by Canadian women who participated in combat operations during the war in Afghanistan, with the exception of excerpts from Nichola Goddard's personal correspondence.[16] Goddard was killed in action in 2006.

At the NATO level, no records of the gender composition of International Security and Assistance Force (ISAF) personnel were available; there were only vague estimates that between 7 and 15 percent of ISAF personnel were female. A report commissioned by the NATO Secretary General's Special Representation for Women, Peace, and Security noted that there were no women at ISAF headquarters with a rank higher than colonel, which means that no women participated in the high-level decision-making meetings.[17] NATO should more closely monitor disaggregated data on gender within its own operations. Monitoring this data would serve to validate the information provided by (or missing from) individual member states and partners. Of course, NATO would then need all contributing member states to provide this information for every deployment cycle.

Internal Gender Mainstreaming

The main source of data on internal gender mainstreaming within the CAF is Global Affairs Canada (GAC), which tracks how Canada's commitments to UNSCR 1325 and the NATO Women, Peace, and Security (WPS) initiative are implemented within various government security organizations. The GAC reporting mechanism is the purview of the Peace and Stabilization Operations Program (PSOPs) and is called *National Action Plan for the Implementation of UNSCR Resolutions on WPS*. Although reporting is done through PSOPs, it is a multiagency process; the activities of GAC (the amalgamation of Foreign Affairs, International Trade, and International Development) and other relevant departments and agencies are described in the reports. The reports are typically self-assessments by the individual agencies based on comparable indicators. For example, for DND, key indicators include training (internal gender mainstreaming), the extent to which gender-based analysis is used in the organization's work abroad (external gender mainstreaming), and finally, gender-disaggregated data about deployment (external gender balancing).

These reports highlight stark differences among the internal gender-mainstreaming activities of the different security organizations. While GAC and the Royal Canadian Mounted Police (RCMP) have adopted gender-based analysis as part of their policy and training approaches as evidenced by various ongoing initiatives, DND is only beginning to do so. In the CAF the gender-mainstreaming offerings are slim, especially when it comes to training. Service members are essentially referred to the government's online gender-based analysis tool called GBA+. The CAF are working on tailoring GBA+ guidelines to their own purposes, an effort led by its Gender Advisors (GENADs). There are more specific examples, like the Peace Support Training Centre offering a Women and Conflict presentation as part of the Military Observer Course, which discusses the greater vulnerability of women in conflict situations. The CAF also offer broader diversity training for all personnel, but it is embedded in a session about human rights and not labeled as gender training. CAF training on sexual harassment is likely to be overhauled in the aftermath of the Deschamps report, which highlighted the shortcomings of the existing training approaches, which were widely derided as useless.[18]

External Mainstreaming

Canada's military intervention in Afghanistan between 2001 and 2014 provided the ideal testing ground for an assessment of gender mainstreaming as part of military operations abroad. While the ISAF Operational Plan included a gender annex, the interviews conducted in the research leading up to the NATO-commissioned report showed that gender awareness within ISAF was low, with the exception of the specially trained gender advisory team. GENADs were tasked with offering gender-awareness briefings to military personnel and were supported by the ISAF headquarters military leadership, including the commander of ISAF and the chief of staff. But implementing even the briefing requirements was difficult because many GENAD positions were left vacant.[19]

Gender focal points within DND (policy) and the CAF were similarly undersupported.[20] Awareness of those positions is generally low, and appointments to gender focal point positions are not always made on the basis of gender expertise. The practice seems to be that women are appointed to gender focal point or gender advisor roles because they are female. The professional burden of implementing gender-based reform has primarily been imposed on the organization's female members, although more men are now being tapped on the shoulder to fulfill these roles. Still, since the first three GENAD positions were created in 2016 to assist the chief of the defense staff, Canadian Special Operations Forces, and Canadian Joint Operations Centre, more women than men have served in those roles.

For Canada, gender work in ISAF thus strongly relied on the personal commitments of individuals rather than on the product of gender mainstreaming in any institutionalized sense. As should be clear from this volume, while gender mainstreaming is present in NATO's key documents (like Bi-Strategic Command Directive 40-1, which specifies gender guidance for military organizations), implementation is only partial and varies across NATO's membership. Canadian allies have realized more concrete achievements through the deployment of female engagement teams, mixed engagement teams, mixed civil-military cooperation teams, and cultural support teams, but results have been mixed. The concept for these teams was that including more women could produce operational gains because female service members could interact with previously inaccessible Afghan women who could supply additional intelligence. For Canada, the availability of female military personnel limited the feasibility of female-engagement teams. Canada's provincial reconstruction team in Kandahar incorporated gender-mainstreaming strategies as part of its female intelligence officers' work, but the reporting was anecdotal and the program's metrics are hard to assess since they were implemented and monitored in an ad hoc manner.

For the CAF in Afghanistan, gender awareness appeared to operate through more informal channels. Indeed, gender analysis is mentioned as an important factor in the development of ISAF's counterinsurgency strategy because of the hierarchical relations between men and women in Afghanistan. Because the operation was population-centric, Canadian military planners eventually incorporated gender and cultural factors into their analysis. To the extent that the CAF used a gendered lens, it was predominantly focused on the Afghan population through the prism of cultural awareness. This experience may have deeper implications for the role of women in the military. Indeed, the *type* of conflict that women participate in as soldiers—counterinsurgency operations in this case—may influence how successful their participation is perceived to be by their peers, by government, and by society in general.[21]

Even if it was not systematically monitored, female engagement with Afghan communities was perceived favorably. This "successful" experience contributed to changing negative attitudes toward the full integration of women in the military. As Karen Davis notes, "In Missions like in Congo or even Afghanistan, where women's rights issues are really at the forefront, it's important for the civilian population to see women, to have interactions with them."[22] The realization of this "comparative advantage" might be one of the mechanisms through which perceptions and attitudes begin to shift.

Another lesson from the Afghanistan experience is that women who were deployed faced more than just battlefield stress. Generally speaking, women and men have different experiences in the military.[23] Women are more often exposed to cumulative stressors, which include high-intensity combat experiences, military sexual trauma, and separation from family.[24] This was the case during Operation Enduring Freedom (OEF) and ISAF, when in addition to post-traumatic stress disorder (PTSD) from combat, there have been several reports of sexual assault cases on bases, especially at the Kandahar Airfield. Whether one looks at Canada, which lifted barriers for full female participation in the military more than a decade ago, or the US, which opened combat military occupations to women in 2016 (following the 2013 decision), defense officials have failed to thoroughly study and address some of the underlying problems that women face in the military, whether at home or abroad: "(1) ensuring physical and occupational competency, (2) eradicating sexual harassment and assault, or (3) realistically promoting the full acceptance of females as military leaders and, ultimately, as warriors."[25] Despite a respectable record in terms of gender-related policies, the CAF still suffered major scandals of sexual misconduct in the late 1990s and more recently in 2014. While the issue of sexual misconduct has been addressed as part of the Deschamps report, it has not been thoroughly investigated in the context of operations, in which servicewomen have experienced sexual assault by their own troops and allied troops.[26]

Conclusions and Policy Recommendations

This chapter has focused on the inclusion of a gender perspective in the CAF's internal policies and in Canada's military interventions. One of the key lessons from this exercise is that future research *and* policy in this field will depend on better data collection. Existing research on recruitment, retention, and selection for deployment is extremely hard to come by, and the challenge is even greater for gender-based research.[27] Compounding the problem is the fact that DND had previously not compiled gender-specific data on the CAF, claiming that it saw no need to do so given that gender *is not an issue* in the Canadian military. While there is an emerging literature on why fewer women than men join and stay in the military, researchers in this field have to draw on international sources of data.²⁸ Indeed, European and American scholars are leading the way.²⁹ Gender-specific data is important for learning more about how the integration of women in the armed forces is progressing. The CAF are only beginning to realize this.

The few Canadian studies that have been published are based on interviews with and exit surveys of female military personnel and are consistent with cross-national trends. They identify professional challenges specific to women who have reported that they never felt fully integrated into the military and that their ability to be promoted while in the military or their ability to find good jobs after leaving was hindered by the lack of experience brought on by exclusion.³⁰ In terms of Canada's military organizational culture, fear of saying something offensive has gotten in the way of a thorough evaluation of the consequences of female integration into the military and of the remaining barriers for their full participation, during peacetime and during deployments. As Kingsley Browne mentions, "Sensitivity about 'gender issues' has resulted in a system of double standards and a climate of political correctness ... [which] is so strong that revealing reservations about the performance of women in the military is likely to be a career-terminating event."³¹

It is clear from the analysis presented in this chapter that Canada's progress has been uneven to date. By drawing from a typology on gender balancing and mainstreaming in CAF policies (internal dimension) and operations (external dimension), this chapter contributes to identifying key gaps in the implementation of better gender integration in the Canadian military.

Notes

1. Canadian Department of National Defence, "Canadian Armed Forces: Historical Milestones for Women," last modified March 6, 2014, http://www.forces.gc.ca/en/news/article.page?doc=canadian-armed-forces-historical-milestones-of-women/hie8w7rl.
2. Stéfanie von Hlatky, "The Canadian Forces Can't Be Gender Blind," *Ottawa Citizen*, July 18, 2014, http://ottawacitizen.com/news/national/the-canadian-forces-cant-be-gender-blind.
3. *Maclean's* is a weekly Canadian magazine focused on political and economic affairs.
4. Maja Catic and Stéfanie von Hlatky, "Women, Gender and International Security," *International Journal* 69, no. 4 (2014): 570–73.
5. Sylvia Walby, "Gender Mainstreaming: Productive Tensions in Theory and Practice," *Social Politics* 12, no. 3 (2005): 321.
6. Differences across countries in reporting are noticeable when one reads all available reports since 2008. Member states do not follow the template consistently.
7. Women make up about 47 percent of the total labor force in Canada.

8. Author interview with a female CAF officer, May 2015 (not for attribution). Consistent with the interviews conducted by Marie Deschamps in the external review on sexual misconduct.
9. The report was made public on April 30, 2015, and was followed by the Action Plan on Inappropriate Sexual Behaviour, led by the CAF Strategic Response Team on Sexual Misconduct, whose work is still ongoing. For the original external review, see Marie Deschamps, *External Review into Sexual Misconduct and Sexual Harassment in the Canadian Armed Forces* (Ottawa: Department of National Defence, 2015), i, http://www.forces.gc.ca/assets/FORCES_Internet/docs/en/caf-community-support-services-harassment/era-final-report-(april-20-2015)-eng.pdf. Author's emphasis.
10. NATO, "Canadian Forces 2009 National Report to the Committee for Women in NATO Forces," (2009): 1–7, www.nato.int/issues/women_nato/meeting-records/2009/national-reports/canada-national-report-2009.pdf. Author's emphasis.
11. Department of Foreign Affairs, Trade and Development, "2012–2013 Progress Report: Canada's Action Plan for the Implementation of United Nations Security Council Resolutions on Women, Peace and Security," March 13, 2014, http://international.gc.ca/world-monde/issues_development-enjeux_developpement/gender_equality-egalite_sexes/women_report-rapport_femmes-2012-2013.aspx?lang=eng.
12. Richard Bray and Chris MacLean, "Infantry Women," *FrontLine Defence* 9, no. 5 (2012): 24–26, http://defence.frontline.online/article/2012/5/1200-Infantry-Women.
13. As mentioned earlier, the gender-based restriction on submarine service was not repealed until 2001. Paul Cawkill, Alison Rogers, Sarah Knight, and Laura Spear, "Women in Ground Close Combat Roles: The Experiences of Other Nations and a Review of the Academic Literature," United Kingdom Ministry of Defence, September 29, 2009, 20, https://www.gov.uk/government/uploads/system/uploads/attachment_data/file/27406/women_combat_experiences_literature.pdf.
14. Krystel Carrier-Sabourin, "Sisters in Arms: The Extent of Female Canadian Forces Members' Involvement in Combat" (paper presented at the Women in International Security Canada Workshop, Montreal, May 25–26, 2012).
15. Stewart Bell, "Women Filled 8.3% of Canada's Combat Positions in Afghanistan: Study," *National Post*, October 25, 2011, http://news.nationalpost.com/2011/10/25/women-filled-8-3-of-canadas-combat-positions-in-afghanistan-study/.
16. Claire Turenne-Sjolander and Kathryn Trevenen, "Constructions of Nation, Construction of War: Media Representation of Captain Nichola Goddard," in *Canadian Security into the 21st Century: (Re)Articulations of Security in the Post-9/11 World*, ed. Bruno Charbonneau and Wayne S. Cox (Vancouver: University of British Columbia Press, 2010), 126–49.
17. Helene Lackenbauer and Richard Langlais, eds., *Review of the Practical Implications of UNSCR 1325 for the Conduct of NATO-Led Operations and Missions* (Brussels: NATO, 2013).
18. Stéfanie von Hlatky, "Crisis at Home for Canada's Armed Force," *OpenCanada.org*, May 28, 2015, http://opencanada.org/features/crisis-at-home-for-canadas-armed-forces%E2%80%A8/.
19. Lackenbauer and Langlais, *Review*.
20. Stéfanie von Hlatky, "The Gender Turn in Canadian Military Interventions," in *Canada among Nations*, ed. Osler Hampson and Stephen M. Saideman (Waterloo, ON: Centre for International Governance Innovation Press, 2015).

21. G. J. De Groot, "A Few Good Women: Gender Stereotypes, the Military and Peacekeeping," *International Peacekeeping* 8, no. 2 (2001): 23–38.
22. Cited in Bell, "Women."
23. Carol Cohn, ed., *Women and Wars* (Malden, MA: Polity Press, 2013); Laura Sjoberg, *Gender, War and Conflict* (Malden, MA: Polity Press, 2014).
24. Amy E. Street, Dawne Vogt, and Lissa Dutra, "A New Generation of Women Veterans: Stressors Faced by Women Deployed to Iraq and Afghanistan," *Clinical Psychology Review* 29, no. 8 (2009): 685–94.
25. Connie Brownson, "The Battle for Equivalency: Female US Marines Discuss Sexuality, Physical Fitness, and Military Leadership," *Armed Forces and Society* 40, no. 4 (2014): 766.
26. von Hlatky, "Crisis at Home."
27. Paul Richard Higate, "Theorizing Continuity: From Military to Civilian Life," *Armed Forces and Society* 27, no. 3 (2001): 443–60.
28. Mady Wechsler Segal, "Women's Military Roles Cross-Nationally: Past, Present, and Future," *Gender and Society* 9, no. 6 (1995): 757–75.
29. Teresa Rees, "Reflections on the Uneven Development of Gender Mainstreaming in Europe," *International Feminist Journal of Politics* 7, no. 4 (2005): 555–74; Kristin M. Mattox, Sally G. Haskell, Erin E. Krebs, Amy C. Justice, Elizabeth M. Yano, and Cynthia Brandt, "Women at War: Understanding How Women Veterans Cope with Combat and Military Sexual Trauma," *Social Science and Medicine* 74, no. 4 (2012): 537–45.
30. Donna Winslow and Jason Dunn, "Women in the Canadian Forces: Between Legal and Social Integration," *Current Sociology* 50, no. 5 (2002): 641–67; Nancy Taber, "Learning How to Be a Woman in the Canadian Forces / Unlearning It through Feminism: An Autoethnography of My Learning Journey," *Studies in Continuing Education* 27, no. 3 (2005): 289–301; Canadian Defence Academy, *Women and Leadership in the Canadian Forces: Perspectives and Experience* (Winnipeg: Canadian Defence Academy Press, 2007).
31. Kingsley Browne, *Co-ed Combat: The New Evidence That Women Shouldn't Fight the Nation's Wars* (New York: Sentinel, 2007), 182.

5

The Role and Impact of Change Catalysts on the Netherlands Defense Organization

Integration of Women and Gender in Operations

Yvette Langenhuizen

In November 2014 the Dutch minister of defense, Jeanine Hennis-Plasschaert, replied to questions from Parliament regarding her ambitions on "gender and the armed forces." She stated that her vision was for the Dutch armed forces to remain, or to become, one of the highest-achieving nations globally in this particular field.[1]

This chapter explores the extent to which the Netherlands has realized its ambitions in the sphere of gender and the armed forces and aims to identify key change catalysts in the implementation of two specific agendas, namely, the integration of women in the Dutch armed forces (better gender balancing) and the integration of a gender perspective, also known as gender mainstreaming, in operations. This analysis uses the NATO-agreed definition for "integrating gender perspective," which includes a clear reference to United Nations Security Council Resolution (UNSCR) 1325.[2]

First, the chapter describes what has been achieved over the last couple of decades regarding the integration of women in the armed forces, and second, it assesses progress in the structural approaches to integrating a gender perspective into military operations. The analysis here focuses on what or who drove certain change processes in the Dutch context regarding these two objectives. The chapter also examines the extent to which the success of one of these change processes shaped the other, and touches on pushback and remaining challenges for the improvement of gender balance among personnel and gender mainstreaming in the operational context. Studying the Dutch context may hold relevance and offer lessons about change catalysts in other national or organizational experiences.

Integration of Women in the Netherlands Armed Forces

This chapter first focuses on the integration of women in the Netherlands armed forces, with the initial steps toward women's involvement dating back over seventy years ago.

First Female Military Corps

Discussions about opening certain military support roles to women took place on a small scale before and during World War I, during which the Netherlands remained neutral.[3] It was, however, not until World War II that the first female corps with military status was established. In December 1943 the Women Auxiliary Corps (Vrijwillig Vrouwen Hulpkorps, VVHK), an initiative driven by the Dutch Committee of the Red Cross in London and the Dutch minister of war, was established. The VVHK (later named Vrouwen Hulpkorps, VHK) was placed under the army and gained military status in 1944. The involvement of British women in the war effort is widely believed to have inspired the establishment of the first Dutch female military corps.[4]

The corps comprised a few hundred Dutch women who fled the Netherlands during the war and subsequently volunteered for service.[5] Their core task was the provision of medical support. Women in the VHK, however, received not only the standard Red Cross medical training but also basic training in military skills.[6] In October 1944, after parts of the southern Netherlands were liberated, a female volunteer corps (Marine Vrouwenafdeling, or MARVA) within the Dutch navy was established by royal decree. Queen Wilhelmina was initially not enthusiastic about the idea of establishing the MARVA but, reportedly, changed her mind after she received a letter accompanied by twelve signatures from women eager to serve.[7] After the war Dutch society remained suspicious of women joining the military, with the church and even the Dutch Women's Committee (Nederlands Vrouwen Comité) also openly questioning the desirability of the women's corps.[8]

In 1946 a partly external selection committee was established. It "supervised" whether women had the "right moral and personality traits" for joining the armed forces. Tasks of the female corps within the different branches of the armed forces were still very much in the support sector, but focus did diversify beyond purely medical tasks. Nonetheless, career opportunities were limited, and all branches had limitations on positions that could be taken up by women.[9] For example, functions aboard ships, pilot positions, and most of the army jobs remained off limits to women. The Netherlands government would later assess that the acceptance of women in the armed forces did not pose "problems" at the time because of the many restrictions on their presence and their separate and limited career tracks.[10]

Socioeconomic developments in the 1950s and 1960s led to increasingly critical reflections on traditional gender roles, including with regard to access to work. In 1956 the Dutch law on legal incompetency was amended so that married women became legally competent and also could no longer be legally forced out of civil service jobs upon getting married. Before this change in the law, marriage by default meant the end of a woman's career in the armed forces. In 1953 the Convention on the Political Rights of Women, which gave women the right to hold public office and exercise all public functions on equal terms with men without discrimination, was introduced. The Netherlands did not become a party to the convention until 1968 and ratified it in 1971.

Toward Real Integration

The second feminist wave in the Netherlands started in the mid to late 1960s and changed women's outlook on issues such as birth control and working outside the home. When the Netherlands became party to the Convention on the Political Rights of Women in 1968, it did so, unlike many other nations, including Germany, Denmark, and the UK, without introducing any formal reservations regarding women's participation in the armed forces. Several years after the ratification of the convention, a formal working group on the integration of women in the armed forces was established. The schools for officers and noncommissioned officers opened to female recruits in 1978.

In 1979, the same year the UN Convention on the Elimination of All Forms of Discrimination against Women (CEDAW) was adopted, the integration of women within the armed forces commenced when personnel from the separate female corps started to be assigned to the various branches of the army, navy, and air force. In the following year, Dutch legislation was introduced to implement European Economic Community (EEC) guidelines on the equal treatment of men and women with a specific focus on equal pay, equal treatment in the labor process, and equal standards for social security. The Netherlands decided to put commitments further into practice by launching a pilot project in February 1981 allowing the first women to sail aboard a navy supply ship.

A few years later, positions aboard combat ships also opened to women, making the Netherlands a global front-runner in eradicating restrictions on women's participation in the armed forces. The year 1982 saw the separate female corps fully disbanded and women serving were integrated into the armed forces. Women gained access to nearly all roles, including all pilot specialties. Only the marine corps and submarines remained formally closed to women. Conscription, however, remained applicable only to men. Experts argued that opening conscription would exacerbate discrimination against women since it would hamper their ability to engage in other career fields.[11]

Opening the armed forces to women brought both external and internal pushback and skepticism. The navy supply ship pilot project, for instance, was the subject of a range of negative comments in the media, including from military unions.[12] In 1986 a group of military spouses established the Committee of Women against Mixed Sailing. The Officers' Association also spoke out against the "rushed process" of integration, quoting political pressure and claiming that the Dutch public did not want a voluntary force (conscription still existed) and that women could not be rushed into responsibilities.[13] Discussions in Parliament focused on pushing forward the women's empowerment agenda, but at the same time, there were concerns about whether integration would jeopardize operational effectiveness and mission readiness.

Although all branches had formally opened, women did not flood the armed forces to the extent some had expected; their level of participation remained at a meager 3–4 percent of the total force in the early and mid-1980s. The government decided a push was needed, and the first defense-specific empowerment (*emancipatie* in Dutch) policy came into effect in 1989.[14] The plan set a target of achieving 5 percent women's participation for the end of the year and an increase to 8 percent by the end of 1993. The budget for child care was increased, female instructors were placed at training institutes, specific recruitment material was developed to appeal to women, and options for part-time work were explored. Despite all this the number of women joining the armed forces in the late 1980s somewhat stalled, and the 8 percent target was not reached by 1993. According to a Ministry of Social Affairs and Employment evaluation put forward to Parliament, this shortfall was due to low interest among women to join the armed forces despite measures designed to boost the organization's appeal. Women, reportedly, still considered a military occupation something for men, and the armed forces were still seen as a male bastion with very little space for women.[15]

The defense organization focused on attracting personnel for technical positions; this segment of the labor market was still dominated by male experts.

Many women who opted to join the armed forces went for short-term contracts that were specifically created to accommodate their inflow. These contracts, however, did not make promotion to higher ranks easy, because the career paths linked to short-term contracts usually failed to satisfy promotion requirements.[16]

The evaluation concluded, "The process of women taking up a representative place in the organization will be a long one." However, according to the Ministry of Social Affairs and Employment, the empowerment measures would boost the participation of women, including in the higher ranks, in "the longer run."[17]

From Conscription to a Voluntary Force: Meeting Recruitment Targets

The 1990s saw a continuation of empowerment policies without many new approaches, although efforts were often politically presented as fresh ideas. There was only a limited increase in the share of female staff. This despite a major change in the defense organization's recruitment policies and organization following the 1993 decision to suspend conscription. As of August 1996, the Dutch armed forces are exclusively volunteer forces. The shift from a conscription-based model to a voluntary force not only accentuated the civilianization trend (more civilian functions were created), it also meant the defense organization needed to attract women to meet recruitment targets.[18]

The Ministry of Defense launched a policy directive in 1997 aimed at giving "new impulses" to the gender-balancing agenda within the defense organization.[19] The policy document made clear that using women's work skills and potential was necessary to fill posts falling vacant in the shift from conscription to a voluntary force. It highlighted the defense organization's "self-interest" in investing in women but more so in terms of staffing levels than in terms of highlighting the benefits a more diverse workforce could bring to the organization's work and outputs.

In 1999 the armed forces' inspector general in his annual report noted that female military personnel were suffering from sexual intimidation and a lack of respect from their male colleagues. The Defense Women's Network (Defensie Vrouwen Netwerk, DVN) held a consultation and presented, in November 2000, a document titled "Solutions to Barriers to the Empowerment Policy of the Defense Organization."[20] The DVN clustered barriers into four subcategories: the organization (including lack of data on women leaving the organization, lack of women in top-level positions, lack of action taken against superiors that exhibited indecent behavior); the culture of the organization (including lack of mentoring of young women early in their career, an existing "macho culture," internal obstructions to part-time work possibilities); women themselves (including young women overcompensating and overburdening themselves physically, the decision of women in military couples to leave the organization instead of their male partner); and societal developments (including the defense organization's being an unknown or underrecognized employer for women on the labor market).

Some of the measures the DVN proposed to attract and retain more women included appointing high-level gender champions, appointing women in visible positions, instructing commanders to report to an independent commission biannually on progress in implementing empowerment policies, rapidly carrying out an independent investigation on misconduct and indecent behavior, and investing in mentoring, especially for young women who joined the armed forces.[21] Some of these recommendations were eventually put into practice but not until several years later (see "Ambassadors and the Gender Action Plan" and "Breaking the 'Macho Culture'?").

Target numbers continued to play a strong role during the 1990s, but as the Ministry of Defense admitted in retrospect, "There were no success stories."[22] The share of women in the armed forces increased rather steadily but slowly; over fifteen years (1983–1996), a 3 percent increase, from 3.5 percent to 6.7 percent, was achieved.

Connecting a Better Gender Balance to UNSCR 1325 Objectives

Following the Beijing Platform for Action and subsequent gender-mainstreaming recommendations by the UN Economic and Social Council (ECOSOC) and the UN General Assembly, the Ministry of Social Affairs and Employment published a letter outlining the government's approach to gender mainstreaming in June 2001.[23] This official position paper outlined the positive effects of gender mainstreaming as a tool for taking the "male/female perspective" into account in policy development and implementation. Conditions necessary for improved gender mainstreaming were identified as commitment at the senior level, explicit gender policy with clear objectives and responsibilities, availability of gender expertise, and availability of resources and tools.

The gender-mainstreaming research that led to the official policy paper had already been commissioned when in October 2000 UNSCR 1325 was unanimously adopted. UNSCR 1325 addressed not only the inordinate impact of war on women but also the pivotal role women should and do play in conflict prevention, conflict resolution, and peace building. The resolution, adopted five years after the Fourth World Conference on Women in Beijing, was the result of intense lobbying by women's civil society groups and collaboration between a range of member states.[24]

In 2002 a working group formed by the Ministries of Foreign Affairs and Defense started to assess whether new policy was needed to properly implement the resolution. Regarding the defense organization, the working group concluded that (1) gender needs to be embedded in training and instructions, (2) the gender perspective needs to be integrated into peace operations, (3) gender needs to be mainstreamed in policies and briefings, and (4) a well-balanced composition of male and female defense employees needs to be achieved, including in deployments.[25]

The latter recommendation established a clear link between the need to recruit and retain female personnel and the implementation of UNSCR 1325. Later, in 2007, the Ministry of Defense assessed that the working group's conclusions had led to a change of direction by shifting the focus "from the equal opportunities process in personnel policy to gender in the core business of the defense organization, namely crisis management operations."[26] The second part of this chapter focuses more in depth on the gender perspective in operations, but it is important to note that UNSCR 1325 implementation for the Netherlands meant investing both in better gender balancing and in gender mainstreaming in operations.

Ambassadors and the Gender Action Plan

In 2002 State Secretary of Defense Cees van der Knaap assumed office and took on a visibly strong position regarding the benefits that a more diverse workforce could reap for the armed forces. In autumn 2002 deputy commanders of the four services (army, navy, air force, and military constabulary) were appointed gender ambassadors. These ambassadors were expected to invest in gender (mainly in the form of better gender balancing) within their branches and act as points of contact for gender-related matters. During the kickoff meeting of the gender ambassadors network in October 2002, the gender ambassadors were also asked to identify three specific areas in which they would personally commit to follow up. As an example, the deputy commander of the military constabulary committed to ensuring that every commanders' meeting he attended would have gender on the official agenda.[27]

Also under Van der Knaap, an ambitious gender action plan (2004–10) was presented. The plan integrated both gender-mainstreaming objectives and the UNSCR 1325 working group recommendations.[28] The main aim of the plan was described as "the improvement of the balance in workforce composition within the defense organization." The action plan offered an approach focused on attracting and retaining more women to the defense organization. The following concrete deliverables were identified:

- a 30 percent share of women in the inflow to initial military training;
- an increase in the share of military women in the organization to 12 percent and in the share of civilian women to 30 percent by 2010 (up from 9 and 22 percent, respectively);
- an increase in the number of high-profile and influential female role models; and
- the creation of a climate in which both men and women feel a sense of belonging within the organization and are able to develop to their maximum capabilities.[29]

The action plan included detailed subplans for the different branches of the defense organization, and the gender ambassadors were given the lead responsibility for the plan's implementation in the respective branches. Reporting criteria were introduced, and a communication plan with both internal and external activities to raise the profile of the gender agenda was put into effect. Besides pushing an increase in numbers, the plan also focused on making certain role models more visible and gaining stronger leadership buy-in for implementing the agenda.

The tone of the action plan was progressive and seemed to capture the momentum around a desire for real change. At the same time, it was clear that a pushback was to be expected. As Van der Knaap noted, "With the implementation of this action plan a state of affairs, customary until now, is being broken through. This is eroding certain positions and is leading to pushback. The groups that already have a place within the organization are experiencing competition from other groups. This is understandably leading to discussions. The action plan gives me the confidence that within the defense organization the courage is there to enter the conversation and translate words into actions."[30]

By 2005 all branches had implemented a considerable number of action points. Recruitment campaigns focusing specifically on increasing the inflow of women were highlighted as a positive example of action taken. In the first year of the action plan, there was, however, no major progress in terms of numbers of women joining the organization. At the time Van der Knaap claimed that for a real breakthrough moment "more time, more action and even a cultural change" would be necessary.[31] In 2009 Van der Knaap's successor found that efforts under the Gender Action Plan had led to mixed results. In spite of increased attention on the topic of gender within the organization and a 2 percent increase in the percentage of female civil servants, the percentage of female military personnel remained at the same level as it had been in 2006 (9 percent).

Although more women joined the military and made their way through the ranks, retention was identified as a key obstacle. The state secretary noted that women leaving the defense organization quoted career opportunities, work level, and external career possibilities as main reasons for departure. The challenge of balancing work and caregiving responsibilities was cited less so. Nonetheless, several initiatives aimed at bettering work-life balance were launched. High deployment pressure, especially since the NATO-led operation in Afghanistan, was also mentioned as a possible reason for departure, although no supportive data for this claim was presented.[32] In general, solid publicly available retention and attrition data, including reasons quoted by women leaving the service, still remain hard to come by.

Breaking the "Macho Culture"?

During a period of positive efforts under the Gender Action Plan, claims of sexual intimidation and abuse aboard the navy ship HNLMS *Tjerk Hiddes* hit the news. Van der Knaap created an independent commission, known as the Staal Commission, to investigate the *Tjerk Hiddes* claims and to provide broader insight on issues relating to misconduct in the armed forces. In September 2006 the commission presented its report and concluded that bullying, discrimination, and sexual intimidation were occurring "too often" in the armed forces, including in comparison with other governmental organizations.

The navy scored worst with respect to the prevalence of sexual intimidation and harassment. Young women who had been serving in the armed forces for only a short while were identified as most prone to being the target of harassment and misconduct. The Staal Commission, furthermore, concluded that superiors generally did not react appropriately when confronted with or notified about cases of misconduct. The commission also established that the support to victims was not well organized. Among its recommendations, the commission called for a better gender-balanced workforce, including more women in high-level positions.[33]

The Staal Commission's findings were followed by a report from an independent commission (Visitatiecommissie Emancipatiebeleid) tasked by the Ministry of Social Affairs and Employment with reporting on gender-mainstreaming and empowerment policies within the different ministries. The commission specifically pointed out that the changes the state secretary was actively promoting were facing too much resistance linked to the organizational culture. The commission added that the existing culture, described as "macho culture," made the defense organization not a safe place for everybody to work.[34]

In response to the Staal Commission's findings, the chief of defense staff released a five-point Code of Conduct in January 2007 covering all personnel within the Ministry of Defense and armed forces. The Code of Conduct also covered out-of-duty time, individual responsibilities to tackle misconduct, and "social management" (investing in the social aspects of management) to mitigate and prevent misconduct. Stricter rules regarding alcohol and drug use were set, and for instance, the viewing of pornography in public spaces on board ships or military bases was explicitly forbidden.

Extensive data from periodic surveys on bullying, undesirable sexual behavior, aggression, and discrimination were published in the four years following the Staal Commission investigation. The available data show some notable but overall limited progress. The periodic surveys showed improvement in 2006–10, with the rates of women experiencing undesirable sexual behavior dropping from 67 percent to 43.8 percent, but improvements mainly occurred in 2006–8 and little progress was made in 2008–10. The data regarding women experiencing "structural bullying" on the job remained the same for 2006–10. Young women were again identified as a high-risk group suffering from sexual intimidation and bullying.[35]

Since 2011 no such detailed data as presented in the periodic surveys have been released publicly, which makes it difficult to assess the current situation and the lasting impact of the Staal Commission's recommendations. Research from 2010 and 2014 that focused on the culture and behavioral norms of military academies and institutes concludes, though, that a culture leading to high risk of unwelcome behavior, including bullying and sexual harassment, prevails.[36] The 2014 report called for "driving out the everyday sexism" within the officers' academy and noted with concern an apparent reluctance to formally report incidents.

It is beyond the scope of this chapter to analyze in depth any cultural change within the defense organization, including trends in attitudes and behavior toward women, but it is relevant to note that over the years certain incidents and trends have clearly pointed at the continuous need to pay critical attention to the organizational culture in order to ensure a safe working environment for all.

From Gender to Diversity Policy

In December 2007 the state secretary of defense presented a letter to Parliament on gender and diversity.[37] He explained that until the end of 2007, the ministry had upheld "target group policies" that specifically focused on women, homosexuals, and ethnic minorities, with the position of women receiving particular attention. He concluded that the target group policies lacked an overarching vision. The decision was therefore made to move from target group policies, including the gender policy, to a diversity policy in order to create more synergy between the efforts to empower, prevent discrimination against, and strengthen acceptance of minority groups.

The motto of the new diversity approach was summarized as follows: general action where possible, specific action where needed.[38] The gender ambassadors transformed overnight into diversity ambassadors and became responsible not only for gender but also for policies aimed at the inclusion and acceptance of ethnic and cultural minorities as well as lesbians, gays, bisexuals, and transgender persons (LGBT) within the armed forces. In January 2009 State Secretary Jack de Vries introduced the Action Plan Diversity 2009–12 to Parliament. At that time women made up 24 percent of civilian staff and 9 percent of the armed forces.

The diversity action plan was based on the following assumptions: diversity policy supports operations (with mixed teams performing better than single-gender teams and women in missions and operations offering operational advantages, such as facilitating easier access to local female populations), diversity policy contributes to finding more suitable candidates to fill a substantial number of vacancies, and diversity has a positive influence on the culture within the defense organization. When presenting the new action plan, the state secretary highlighted the progress in the appointment of women to high-visibility positions; there were now two female generals, a female commander of a frigate, and a female commander of a battalion. The number of women in management positions had also increased. Mentor projects were identified as contributing to this development. Looking back, the secretary concluded that gender awareness had increased within the defense organization but that cultural change is nonetheless a "long-term process."[39]

The Quality Debate

In 2010, when new diversity target numbers were to be presented, the political climate had changed the trajectory of progress on gender and diversity issues. The new government's coalition accord, based on a minority cabinet with support on key issues from the right-wing populist party Partij voor de Vrijheid (PVV), included the following commitment: "The Cabinet ends the diversity/preferential treatment policy on the basis of gender and ethnic background. Selection has to occur on the basis of quality."[40] This meant not only abandoning the diversity action plan but also taking a leap backward on the promotion of diversity's benefits for the defense organization. In concrete terms, the coalition accord meant letting go of target numbers for the inflow and retention of women and other minority groups. Specific mentoring and internship programs were also discontinued.⁴¹ Commitments by the Ministry of Defense on UNSCR 1325 were upheld, though.

The minority government with PVV support fell in early 2012. When a new cabinet took office later that year, investing in diversity in the armed forces appeared poised to make a comeback. The cabinet committed itself to appointing more women in senior government positions. In the same period, representatives from nine (out of eleven) political parties committed to the Gender Multiparty Initiative, a joint approach, transcending party lines, to increasing focus on gender and women's rights, particularly in foreign policy. In addition, Jeanine Hennis-Plasschaert joined the new cabinet as the first-ever female minister of defense.

Less than two months after she had taken office, while she was defending the defense budget in Parliament, Minister Hennis-Plasschaert was asked about her plans regarding gender in operations and gender balancing. She stated that sexual orientation and gender "did not matter"; recruitment and retention were, ultimately, all about the merit or quality of each individual.⁴² When in July 2013 Minister Hennis-Plasschaert presented her plans on diversity, she emphasized the relevance of diversity policies linked to operational effectiveness.⁴³ Interestingly, though, no significant new plans were launched. Already existing activities were to continue, but the defense minister did not make very clear what these initiatives entailed or what impact was expected. In any case, the gender or diversity ambassadors were not reinstated, and no target numbers were presented. In November 2014 Hennis-Plasschaert reiterated the quality argument in relation to recruitment efforts, stating, "Sex does not play a role in this process."⁴⁴

And yet Dutch women were still being excluded from serving in the marine corps and on submarines. Members of Parliament, especially from the Dutch Labor Party and the Democrats '66, continued to raise this discrepancy and ask questions about why quotas for women and an increase in women at high ranks were not being realized. Moreover, representatives from the two parties pushed for a more or less symbolic change in the law that would subject women to the draft, should it be recalled in the future.

Although it is hard to say whether pressure from Parliament or perhaps more internal considerations formed a tipping point, Minister Hennis-Plasschaert in 2016, less than a year before upcoming elections, committed to implementing several gender-balancing initiatives. She committed to opening the marine corps to women by January 2017 and requested that the navy aim for the "accommodation" of women when acquiring new submarines. Moreover, in 2016 Parliament adopted a law saying women would be included in the draft should it ever be reinstated.

Integrating a Gender Perspective in Operations

In retrospect the Ministry of Defense noted that the adoption of UNSCR 1325 had led the Netherlands to shift focus from the equal opportunities process in personnel policy to gender mainstreaming in operations. Noteworthy, though, is that in the years immediately following the adoption of UNSCR 1325, reference to the actual resolution was rather minimal in policy documents. Nonetheless, the realization that inclusion of women in operations would lead to increased operational effectiveness became a more prominent narrative in the early years of the twenty-first century.

Genderforce

In 2005 Genderforce was initiated by the Netherlands Ministry of Defense and in part funded by the European Social Fund (ESF). The initiative entailed a project-based approach and the intention to share knowledge and experience gained with other nations or regions that also received ESF subsidies (Sweden, Austria, and Scotland). Genderforce was meant to bring together existing initiatives aimed at strengthening the role of women within the defense organization and to give these initiatives extra impetus. The objective was to bring about cultural and structural change in the defense organization, all linked to the understanding that Genderforce would improve performance levels in operations by

- incorporating gender in training courses;
- integrating the gender perspective into crisis-response operations;
- mainstreaming gender by including gender aspects as an integral part of both the operational management process within the defense organization and in the various documents and briefings surrounding crisis-response operations; and
- realizing a more balanced male-female ratio in the composition of the defense organization workforce in general and with special regard to crisis-response operations.[45]

These four themes were split up into subprojects with specific deliverables. The Netherlands served as the lead nation on gender mainstreaming in operations. Despite the focus on operations, the initiators and the coordinators of the Genderforce project were mainly based in the Personnel Directorate of the Ministry of Defense.

Genderforce brought in additional resources and expertise to incorporate both gender balancing and gender mainstreaming in the operations agenda.

Several initiatives described later in this chapter—such as the inclusion of gender perspective in pre-deployment training and the development of a gender checklist and a gender expert job description—found their basis in the Genderforce project. Several experts interviewed for this research deemed Genderforce a particularly important vehicle for improving the visibility and knowledge of "the power of gender." However, judging from the project documents, the operational angle of Genderforce focused largely on the importance of deploying women to operations and less on the importance of including a gender perspective in conflict analyses and operational planning, in part by involving local women.

Operations in Afghanistan: The Bottom-Up Experience

In 2002 the Netherlands deployed its first troops to Afghanistan. Initially, troop presence was mainly centered in the capital, Kabul. The extreme stratification between men and women in Afghan society was obvious to those deployed, and the status of women in Afghanistan figured highly in the political debates regarding the mission.[46] In early 2006, after the NATO-led International Security Assistance Force (ISAF) extended its area of responsibility, the Netherlands committed to deploying troops to the southern province of Uruzgan. In addition to Task Force Uruzgan (TFU), consisting of approximately 1,200–1,400 troops, the Netherlands became the lead nation of the provincial reconstruction team (PRT) in Uruzgan, with the 3D (integrated development, diplomacy, and defense) concept as the basis of its efforts.

In the four years that Dutch forces, diplomats, and development experts were active in Uruzgan, many practical lessons were learned on the importance of integrating a gender perspective in operations. These lessons ranged from backlash against male troops' entering women's quarters in Afghan houses to the need to search women in burqas for explosive devices in a culturally sensitive way. Reaching out to women to get information and to allow them to share their concerns and security needs (as the TFU did specifically regarding improvised explosive devices) was not an easy task. Having women in military units proved beneficial to the operation, and at the same time, it became increasingly clear that there was more to integrating a gender perspective than having women on board.

In total about 16,000 Dutch troops deployed to Uruzgan. As one interviewee from civil society involved in pre-deployment initiatives noted: "I think in Uruzgan the military were for the first time really confronted with gender as an operational obstacle which made them think about how to deal with that." During the Uruzgan years especially, the gender perspective agenda was increasingly seen as a useful tool benefiting operational effectiveness, or as one former commander put it, a gender perspective was "helpful to prevent body bags." In this context the Netherlands contributed the first gender advisor to ISAF. The navy lieutenant commander took up her position in Kabul in October 2009 and focused both on training fellow international military members on gender perspectives and on engaging local women's organizations and mentoring Afghan national security forces on gender perspectives. Over the years sixteen military women have been deployed as gender advisor to Afghanistan by the defense organization.

Dutch involvement in Afghanistan shifted from southern Uruzgan to the northern province of Kunduz between 2010 and 2011. In Kunduz several hundred troops formed the Police Training Group (PTG). The aim of the PTG was to train, advise, and mentor Afghan police forces, and due attention was given to gender and human rights training as well as the training and mentoring of female recruits. On paper a gender perspective was very well integrated in the PTG efforts, with a clear push coming from the political level, but the realities on the ground in Kunduz were different from the experiences in Uruzgan. There was much less contact between the PTG and the local population in Kunduz, and several interviewees described the political and media attention toward the few female police officers as disproportional. Whereas the Uruzgan "bottom-up" experiences had proved the relevance of integrating a gender perspective in operations, the mission in Kunduz focused on gender perspective more because of "top-down" pressure.

First National Action Plan UNSCR 1325

In December 2007 the Netherlands became the seventh UN member-state to launch a national action plan (NAP) for implementing UNSCR 1325.[47] All those interviewed for this chapter, ranging from civil society representatives to representatives from the Ministries of Defense and Foreign Affairs, identified the first Dutch NAP as an important driver for enhanced focus on gender perspective in military operations and for strengthened cooperation among the Ministry of Foreign Affairs, Ministry of Defense, and civil society. The NAP was unique as the only plan in the world that was signed jointly by the government and civil society.[48] The NAP development process allowed for unprecedented discussion and synergy of efforts, leading, for example, to nongovernmental organizations' providing gender and civil society expertise during military exercises.

The most important goal of the 2008–11 National Action Plan was to achieve systematic attention, recognition, and support for women's roles in conflict and post-conflict situations. The plan was to serve as a launchpad for renewed cooperation among different agencies and organizations concerned with the position of women during and after conflict. The NAP set out seventy-two actions to be performed by state and civil society actors. Due attention was given to the gender perspective in operations, including the commitment to provide civilian and military peacekeepers with context-specific training on the roles and capabilities of women. The NAP also paid attention to the need for peacekeepers to adhere to codes of conduct and to tackle misconduct within the ranks. It, furthermore, included a specific focus on the number of women in the Netherlands armed forces and the need to improve the existing figures with a clear link to advancing operational objectives.[49]

In early 2008 both a new gender advisor in the Ministry of Defense (Personnel Directorate) and the first NAP coordinator at the Ministry of Foreign Affairs took office. A period of close cooperation resulting in the development of new initiatives commenced, linked to, as one interviewee described, "driven individuals benefiting from the political attention attributed to UNSCR 1325 and the increasing awareness that this agenda would benefit operations." Besides a range of well-attended high-level events, in which the minister of defense continued to highlight the link between gender perspective and operational effectiveness, a publication was launched on lessons learned in integrating gender into operational activities in Afghanistan, Burundi, and the Democratic Republic of the Congo, and a bilateral training initiative saw light.[50]

The first training course, A Comprehensive Approach to Gender in Operations, took place in June 2011 and was a collaboration between the Spanish and Dutch Ministries of Foreign Affairs and Defense. The one-week course continues to run twice a year, and according to one of the course board members, over five hundred military and civilian participants from more than twenty-five countries have by now participated.[51] Most of the participants have subsequently been deployed to missions and operations. A former gender advisor who was heavily involved both in Genderforce and later in the bilateral training initiative highlighted the importance of bilateral commitments: "The fact that there is a commitment made to the other nation (e.g., Sweden and Spain) in reaching certain joint gender goals made the Dutch defense organization feel much more obliged to work hard on realizing the agreed objectives."

Institutionalizing Gender Perspective in Operations

The Genderforce project, experiences in Afghanistan, and the development of the first NAP 1325 all led to valuable insights on how to implement UNSCR 1325, including the gender perspective in peace and security operations. Many of these lessons were also being institutionalized and made available to the wider defense organization. In early 2006 a Chief of Defense Staff Directive (CDS A-104) made gender perspective a permanent part of central operational management. CDS A-104 states that attention should be paid to the differential positions of men and women in an operational theater and to the different impact operations could have on men and women, taking into account the fact that women are more than victims but also actors in conflict, conflict prevention, and peace negotiations. CDS A-104 stipulates that applying the gender lens is a shared responsibility: "The presence of female military personnel is no guarantee that gender aspects will be emphasized during the deployment. The male and female military personnel present should focus attention on the various gender aspects."[52]

A year later a gender checklist of stakeholders was introduced to the Operations Directorate, making gender a permanent point of attention during the planning, execution, and evaluation of operations. The checklist contains an overview of analyses and actions needed to properly use the so-called gender lens. Furthermore, progress was made in institutionalizing gender perspective in operations in relevant trainings. In 2007 the Civil Military Cooperation (CIMIC) Centre of Excellence in the Netherlands, for instance, developed a special gender module for CIMIC courses, and the School of Peace Missions, the institute responsible for pre-deployment trainings, developed a module on gender in crisis-response operations.[53] Moreover, in 2009 the Ministry of Defense launched its first-ever internal Defense Action Plan 1325. The plan was inspired by the first NAP but with an eye to relevant actions for the defense organization.

Dutch Parliament also played a noteworthy role in ensuring efforts and lessons learned were being institutionalized. In late 2008 Parliament adopted a motion to gain more insight into concrete action undertaken to implement UNSCR 1325 objectives.[54] Parliament requested that the government include a paragraph on the situation of women in all relevant state-of-affairs letters, which outline for Parliament the political, security, and developmental progress in focus countries and indicate the Dutch contribution to this progress. In the following year, the cabinet and Parliament reviewed the "Testing Framework" (Toetsingskader), which is the standard instrument to structure the debate between government and Parliament on the deployment of armed forces in operations.[55] The review was dominated by the Netherlands' experience in Afghanistan. This led to gender ("the participation of women, impact on women and other aspects of gender policy") also being added to the standard list of considerations of the Toetsingskader. Although critics could claim this approach was more an add-on versus true gender mainstreaming, gender was structurally injected into the debate on military deployments. As the former NAP coordinator summarized: "1325 moved from the personnel and humanitarian sphere to the heart of the security agenda."

The period 2005–11 was very important to integrating gender perspective objectives in the cycle of missions and operational planning and execution. This change came both from within the Ministry of Defense, which benefited from good cooperation with the NAP coordinator at the Ministry of Foreign Affairs and other NAP partners, and from Parliament. However, some of the instruments established in that period could be reinvigorated since interviews with current personnel at the Ministry of Defense indicate the gender checklist, for instance, has fallen out of use. Moreover, the internal action plan has never been made available to the public, making it hard to assess progress, and it seems no set reporting on implementation is currently taking place. The Ministry of Defense has, however, engaged in the development of a third edition of the NAP and committed to updating the internal action plan. This could create momentum and will likely lead to more clarity regarding reporting and coordination responsibilities.

Positioning of the Gender Advisor

The positioning of gender expertise within the ministry illustrates developments in the so-called gender and the armed forces agenda—which includes both the integration of women in the armed forces and the integration of a gender perspective in operations—over the last decade. Gender expertise was initially placed in the Personnel Directorate and was boosted to 4.5 full-time equivalents (fte) during the Genderforce years. Gender advisors active in Genderforce, however, soon identified the need to also have gender expertise in the Operations Directorate. This push for change further translated to mission areas; the first ISAF gender advisor made available by the Netherlands came from the Genderforce team, and one of her first achievements was to move the position of the gender advisor in ISAF from CJ1 (Personnel) to Stability Operations in early 2010. Within the ministry this change was harder to establish, but eventually the gender advisor moved from the Personnel Department to the Operations Directorate in 2011. She was placed in the Planning Branch (J5) and thereby allowed to influence the planning cycle to make sure gender perspective was well integrated in missions and operations.

This move in itself was an important signal of the more general shift of priorities from improved gender balancing to gender perspective in operations. When in early 2011 the Ministry of Defense, in line with the coalition accord, informed Parliament about the discontinuation of the 2009–12 Diversity

Action Plan, commitments by the Ministry of Defense to UNSCR 1325, including NAP 1325, were explicitly upheld.[56] The factors most likely driving this decision were a strong internal lobby coming from the ministry's gender advisor, supported by the Ministry of Foreign Affairs, and the momentum that had been created in previous years regarding the link between gender perspective and operational effectiveness.

Although the position of the gender advisor within the Operations Directorate was not negatively affected by the discontinuation of diversity policies, the severe budget cuts of 2012 and 2013 did have an impact. The gender advisor position went from 1 fte to 0.5 fte and moved from Planning to CIMIC (J9); the head of the CIMIC Branch now also became the gender advisor. The Personnel Directorate currently also has a full-time officer working on diversity, including gender. The number of positions focused on gender expertise in the organization have dropped since the Genderforce years. At the same time, thanks to deployments in Afghanistan and the Dutch-Spanish training course, a larger network of personnel with gender expertise exists. This network and a network of gender focal points in the different directorates are, according to several interviewees, currently being formalized and strengthened.

In the meantime, Parliament is keeping the pressure on with a May 2016 motion requesting that the Ministry of Defense include full-time gender expertise within several directorates and units, referring to NATO operational standards.[57] It will be interesting to follow how and to what extent this request will be implemented.

Contributions beyond Afghanistan: MINUSMA

Dutch contributions to the NATO-led operations in Afghanistan affected the way gender was perceived and integrated in operational planning and execution. Yet with the NATO-led operation scaling down in Afghanistan, it is important to consider, even if only briefly, other missions and operations in which the Netherlands is involved in order to see to what extent lessons learned in Afghanistan are being integrated in other operational theaters.

In November 2013 the Netherlands confirmed its military contribution to the UN Multidimensional Integrated Stabilization Mission in Mali (MINUSMA). Currently nearly four hundred troops are deployed to Mali with a key focus on conducting reconnaissance and intelligence gathering. Gender perspective was included in the "Testing Framework," and the Ministry of Foreign Affairs was particularly vocal on the importance of integrating UNSCR 1325 objectives into the Dutch integrated approach—which is essentially the successor to the 3D approach rolled out in Afghanistan—in Mali.

The topic of gender perspective in operations and an introduction to UNSCR 1325 have been integrated in pre-deployment trainings for MINUSMA troops. However, much of the initial training material on gender perspective in operations that the defense organization used was based on the Afghanistan context and therefore was less useful for the Mali context, according to two interviewees familiar with gender and MINUSMA.

Dutch contributions to MINUSMA remain by and large focused on strengthening the intelligence picture to enhance UN situational awareness and thereby also protect of civilians and the force. At least during the initial troop rotations into MINUSMA, no engagement strategy appeared to be in place to ensure women could contribute to establishing a full picture of security needs and concerns. Moreover, the male-only Special Forces, at least initially, was making the most contact with the local population to gather intelligence. No gender advisor has so far been deployed to Mali as part of the Dutch military contingent.

Conclusion

Women have come a long way in the Netherlands armed forces since the establishment of the first female corps in 1943. Important milestones were achieved in the 1970s and 1980s: most formal barriers to women's participation in the military were removed, and globally ambitious empowerment policies were adopted. In the last decade, however, the percentage of women in the armed forces has stagnated at 9 percent, just below the current average of the twenty-eight NATO allies. At the same time, there has been a significant shift in the gender and armed forces agenda, with the Netherlands looking beyond the integration of women toward also paying due attention to the integration of gender perspectives in operations. Regarding the latter, the Netherlands has been an active player—a front-runner even—on the international level, but currently investments in safeguarding and expanding on gender-mainstreaming approaches do not seem to mirror the efforts or enthusiasm of experiences several years ago. Tools that were developed to facilitate the integration of a gender perspective in operations, such as the gender checklist, seem to be disregarded or underutilized.

The Genderforce project, the large-scale military deployments to Afghanistan, and the development of the first NAP 1325 served as important change catalysts that deepened the understanding of gender mainstreaming in operations within the defense organization. Of key importance here was the message that integrating a gender perspective was not about being politically correct but about enhancing operational effectiveness. Moreover, driven individuals at the working level were instrumental in moving the agenda forward, including through cross pollination between the Ministries of Defense and Foreign Affairs and in cooperation with civil society. High-level political support for UNSCR 1325 and the momentum of increased international attention to gender dimensions in peace and security also proved consequential. Furthermore, bilateral and multilateral commitments provided key opportunities for innovation, deepening of experience, and sharing of lessons.

Regarding change catalysts having pushed forward better gender balancing, societal change in the late 1960s and 1970s and the subsequent ratification of EEC and UN gender equality standards led to the opening of the defense organization to women. However, at the time women were merely "to be accommodated." Later, in the post-conscription era, they were simply much needed to reach recruitment targets. In the early 2000s, the understanding that a more diverse workforce could lead to a better organizational culture and skill set began to gain ground. The operational effectiveness argument, mentioned in the context of gender mainstreaming, influenced views on mixed units and the need to further integrate women in the armed forces. Again, individuals left an important mark on the gender-balancing agenda. The leadership of State Secretary Van der Knaap, from 2002 to 2007, proved to be a change catalyst for a greater understanding within the defense organization of the benefits of gender mainstreaming and balancing.

There has been an overlap in change catalysts pushing the related gender-balancing and gender-mainstreaming agendas forward. Both agendas benefited from the development of and messaging around concrete and ambitious goals and targets. Members of Parliament played an important and consistent role in keeping the pressure on the Ministry of Defense. Whereas the development of NAP 1325 was essential in supporting gender mainstreaming in operations, the gender action plans under Van der Knaap were of great importance in boosting the visibility and understanding of the gender-balancing agenda. Change processes diverged at points as well. The politically motivated 2011 debate on merit and quality of individuals had a negative impact on the gender-balancing agenda but less so on broader UNSCR 1325 priorities.

Looking ahead, there appears to be consensus among those interviewed and in the existing literature on the subject that political attention and external pressure will remain necessary to advance, and prevent a backslide in, gender balancing and gender mainstreaming in operations. Better and more consistent data collection on reasons women and men join and leave the defense organization would be useful for achieving a better understanding of gender-balancing challenges and opportunities. Currently, the message from the armed forces leadership is that individuals are hired and promoted according to their quality and competence (regardless of sex), but this assumes a level playing field has been achieved when in fact the reality is not so definitive. When it comes to the armed forces' ability to establish an organizational culture that truly fosters a diverse workforce, the views of interviewees are still somewhat pessimistic. As one former gender advisor notes, "Every move forward has been met with internal resistance.... External pressure will remain necessary for progress, although an internal drive would ... lead to quicker and more sustainable results."

While this case study of the Dutch experience does not provide a clear-cut or easily transferable solution to expanding the participation of women and integrating gender perspectives in operations of the armed forces, it has offered an insight into the range of operational, policy, and leadership factors that, especially when taken jointly and consistently, can have incremental and aggregate impact.

Notes

This chapter is based on both historic and current data and a literature review. The chapter has also greatly benefited from interviews the author held with several key actors who are or have been involved in efforts aimed at gender balancing or gender mainstreaming in operations. The views of several counterparts at the Ministry of Foreign Affairs and civil society organizations have also been incorporated in this analysis. A special word of thanks for their inputs and support goes to Lt. Col. Björn de Heer, former head of CIMIC and gender advisor in the Operations Directorate, and Capt. (Navy) Mary Riemens, former diversity advisor in the Personnel Directorate, from the Netherlands Ministry of Defense. Overview of interviews: Interview through email correspondence with former military Genderforce staff member and former gender advisor in Afghanistan, June 8, 2015; interview through email correspondence with former military gender advisor in Afghanistan, October 20, 2015; email correspondence and interviews from May 2015 to August 2016 with former military diversity advisor, Personnel Department; interview with current diversity advisor, Personnel Department, August 25, 2016; email correspondence and interviews from June 2015 to November 2016 with former head of CIMIC and gender advisor, Operations Directorate; interview through email correspondence with former military gender advisor, J5 Operations Directorate, September 19, 2016; interview with officer deployed to MINUSMA, September 15, 2015; interview through email correspondence with UNSCR 1325 civil society expert, May 27, 2015, with follow-on correspondence on June 18, 2015; interview with former coordinator NAP 1325, Netherlands Ministry of Foreign Affairs, September 10, 2015.

1. Ministry of Foreign Affairs and Ministry of Defense, "Beantwoording vragen van de leden Hachchi en Sjoerdsma over achterblijvende resultaten om meer vrouwen te betrekken bij militaire vredesmissies" [Answers to questions posed by Members of Parliament Hachchi and Sjoerdsma about results to involve more women in military peace and security missions lagging behind], Ref. No. 2014Z19554, November 25, 2014.

2. "Integration of gender perspective is a way of assessing gender-based differences of women and men reflected in their social roles and interactions, in the distribution of power and the access to resources.... It is used synonymously with implementing the requests of UNSCR 1325, related resolutions ... the aim of which is to take into consideration the particular situation and needs for men and women, as well as how activities ... have different effects on them. More fundamentally, implementing a gender perspective is done by adapting action following a 'gender analysis.'" NATO, Bi-strategic Command Directive (BI-SCD) 40-1, August 8, 2012.
3. H. P. Staal, "De persoonlijke dienstplicht der vrouw" [The personal duty of service of a woman], *De Gids* 72 (1908), accessed September 10, 2016, http://www.dbnl.org/tekst /_gid001190801_01/_gid001190801_01_0050.php.
4. M. P. F. G. Thissen, "Integratie van de vrouw in de Nederlandse Landmacht van 1895 tot 1984" [Integration of women in the Netherlands army from 1895 to 1984], *Aspecten van de Afrikaanse historiografie* 122 (1993); Sophia Kruyswijk-van Thiel, *Het Vrouwenkorps-KNIL* [The women's corps–KNIL] (Amsterdam: Dutch University Press, 2004).
5. Ministry of Defense, *The Netherlands National Report to the NATO Committee on Gender Perspectives* (2012), http://www.nato.int/cps/en/natohq/topics_132097.htm.
6. De Legerkoerier, "15 jaar MILVA Herinnering aan jaren die men nimmer vergeet" [15 years MILVA memories of years one will never forget], July 1959, accessed September 10, 2016, http://www.prinsesirenebrigade.nl/15_jaar_milva.htm.
7. Ministry of Defense, "Eerste vrouwelijke militair Francien de Zeeuw overleden" [First female soldier Francien de Zeeuw has passed away], September 11, 2015, https://www .defensie.nl/actueel/nieuws/2015/09/11/eerste-vrouwelijke-militair-francien-de-zeeuw -overleden.
8. The Dutch Women's Committee was a national umbrella organization of women's organizations. Its first president was Marie Anne Tellegen, an important figure in the Dutch resistance movement during World War II. Andere Tijden, "Vrouwen ten strijde!" [Women into battle!], *Nederlandse Publieke Omroep* video, 30:05, November 11, 2012, http://www.npogeschiedenis.nl/andere-tijden/afleveringen/2012-2013/Vrouwen-ten -strijde.html.
9. House of Representatives, "Nota: Vrouw in de Krijgsmacht" [Policy note: Women in the armed forces], 1985–1986, Ref. No. 16565, no. 3-4.
10. Ibid.
11. Ibid.; "Discussie dienstplicht Vrouwen beëindigd" [Discussion on conscription for women has come to an end], *Reformatorisch Dagblad*, January 27, 1987.
12. Jaime Karremann, "Zuiderkruis bevoorradingsschip" [Zuiderkruis supplyship], *Marineschepen.nl*, February 2, 2015, http://marineschepen.nl/schepen/zuiderkruis.html.
13. "Raad voor de Krijgsmacht: 'Alle legerbanen open voor vrouw'" [Council for the Armed Forces: All military positions open to women], *Leidsch Dagblad*, April 27, 1984, accessed September 10, 2016, http://leiden.courant.nu/issue/LD/1984-04-27/edition /0/page/5; "Vrouwen in leger ook in gevechtsfuncties" [Women in armed forces also in combat positions], April 27, 1984, http://www.digibron.nl/search/detail/012e9905 aaf3e53973a5989d/vrouwen-in-leger-ook-in-geyechtsfuncties.
14. Ministry of Defense, "Plan voor positieve actie voor de integratie van de vrouw in de krijgsmacht" [Plan for positive action for the integration of women in the armed forces], House of Representatives, 1988–1989, no. 34, February 15, 1989.

15. Ministry of Social Affairs and Employment, "Beleidsprogramma Emancipatie, Met het oog op 1995" [Policy programme Emancipation, with a view on 1995], November 19, 1992, http://www.emancipatie.nl/_documenten/emb/dce/algemeen/beleid/bpeoog95/def.htm.
16. Ibid.
17. Ibid.
18. Helena Carreiras, *Gender and the Military: Women in the Armed Forces of Western Democracies* (London: Routledge, 2006), 145.
19. Letter from the State Secretary of Defense, "Emancipatiebeleid Defensie" [Empowerment policy defense organization], House of Representatives, 1996–1997, Ref. No. 25 436, no. 1, June 25, 1997.
20. Jolande Bosch, *DVN-Denktank 'Emancipatiebeleid in actie' oplossingen voor de knelpunten in het emancipatiebeleid van Defensie* ["Empowerment policy in action" solutions to the barriers in the empowerment policy of the defense organization], November 22, 2000, http://docplayer.nl/14120227-Dvn-denktank-emancipatiebeleid-in-actie-met-oplossingen-voor-de-knelpunten-in-het-emancipatiebeleid-van-defensie.html.
21. Ibid.
22. Ministry of Defense, *Netherlands National Report*.
23. Letter from the State Secretary of Social Affairs, "Meerjarennota emancipatiebeleid" [Multiple year policy document on empowerment policy], Ref. No. 27 061, no. 15, June 26, 2001.
24. Nicola Pratt and Sophie Richter-Devroe, "Critically Examining UNSCR 1325 on Women, Peace and Security," *International Feminist Journal of Politics* 13, no. 4 (December 2011): 489.
25. Ministry of Foreign Affairs and Ministry of Defense, "Notitie 'Stand van zaken m.b.t. de uitvoering van de aanbevelingen Veiligheidsraad Resolutie 1325 Vrouwen Vrede en Veiligheid'" [Policy note 'Status of the implementation of UNSCR 1325 recommendations on women, peace and security'], March 27, 2003.
26. Ministry of Defense, *Netherlands National Report*.
27. Defensie Vrouwen Netwerk (DVN), "Nieuwsbrief" [Newsletter] no. 2, December 2002.
28. Letter from the State Secretary of Defense, "Gender Actie Plan" [Gender Action Plan], House of Representatives, Ref. No. 29 800, no. 27, November 17, 2004.
29. Ibid.
30. Ibid.
31. Letter from the State Secretary of Defense, "Vaststelling van de begrotingsstaten van het Ministerie van Defensie voor het jaar 2006" [Adopting the budget of the Ministry of Defense for the year 2006], House of Representatives, Ref. No. 30 300, no. 64, December 22, 2005.
32. State Secretary of Defense, "Antwoorden op vragen van de vaste commissie voor Defensie over het Actieplan Diversiteit Defensie 2009–2012" [Answers to questions by the Defense Committee regarding the defense organization's Action Plan for Diversity 2009–2012], Ref. No. P/2009004024, March 13, 2009; State Secretary of Defense, "Rapportage genderbeleid 2006–2008 aan Tweede Kamer" [Report gender policy 2006–2008 to the House of Representatives], Ref. No. P/2009017326, November 12, 2009; Ministry of Defense, "Doorstroom Defensievrouwen door Actieplan Gender" [Career development women in the defense organization based on Gender Action Plan], November 12, 2009,

https://www.defensie.nl/actueel/nieuws/2009/11/12/doorstroom-defensievrouwen-door-actieplan-gender.
33. Commissie Onderzoek Ongewenst Gedrag [Commission Investigating Undesirable Conduct], "Rapportage over onderzoek naar vorm en incidentie van en verklarende factoren voor ongewenst gedrag binnen de Nederlandse Krijgsmacht" [Report on the investigation into form and occurance of, and explanatory factors for, undesirable conduct within the Netherlands armed forces], September 29, 2006, https://zoek.officielebekendmakingen.nl/kst-30800-X-6-b3.pdf.
34. Visitatiecommissie Emancipatie [Review Committee Empowerment], "Emancipatiebeleid en gender mainstreaming bij het Ministerie van Defensie" [Empowerment policy and gender mainstreaming within the Ministry of Defense], VCE-07-03, January 2007.
35. Bedrijfsgroep Defensie Personele Diensten Gedragswetenschappen [Defense Organization Personnel Services Behavorial Science], "Ongewenst gedrag, Defensie onderzoek 3" [Undesirable conduct, Defense research 3], no. GW~1O-167, 2010.
36. Governance & Integrity B.V. en Centrale Organisatie Integriteit Defensie [Governance and Integrity and Central Organization Integrity of the Defense Organization], "Rapportage Risicoanalyse Integriteit" [Report Risk Analysis Integrity], based on research at Netherlands Defense Academy during academic year 2012–13; Letter from the Minister of Defense, "Risicoanalyse integriteit NLDA" [Risk Analysis Integrity Netherlands Defence Academy], Ref. No. BS201400447, February 17, 2014; "Rapportage omgangsvormen: een onderzoek naar omgangsvormen binnen 6 opleidingsinstituten van Defensie" [Research into social behavior within 6 educational institutes of the defense organization], Blauw Research, Ref. No. 32 123-X, no. 152, August 2010.
37. Letter from the State Secretary of Defense, "Vaststelling van de begrotingsstaten van het Ministerie van Defensie voor het jaar 2008" [Adopting the budget of the Ministry of Defense for the year 2008], House of Representatives, Ref. No. 31 200 X, 2007–8, no. 78, December 14, 2007.
38. Ibid.
39. Letter from the State Secretary of Defense, "Rapportage genderbeleid 2006–2008" [Report gender policy 2006–8], Ref. No. P/2009017326, November 12, 2009.
40. Coalition Agreement between the parties VVD and CDA, "Vrijheid en verantwoordelijkheid" [Freedom and responsibility], September 30, 2010, https://www.rijksoverheid.nl/documenten/rapporten/2010/09/30/regeerakkoord-vvd-cda.
41. Letter from the Minister of Defense, "Vaststelling van de begrotingsstaten van het Ministerie van Defensie voor het jaar 2011" [Adopting the budget of the Ministry of Defense for the year 2011], House of Representatives, Ref. No. 32 500 X, no. 84, February 9, 2011.
42. Verslag wetgevingsoverleg [Report on legislative deliberation], "Vaststelling van de begrotingsstaten van het Ministerie van Defensie voor het jaar 2013" [Adopting the budget of the Ministry of Defense for the year 2013], House of Representatives, Ref. No. 33 400 X, no. 23, December 5, 2012.
43. Letter from the Minister of Defense, "Vaststelling van de begrotingsstaten van het Ministerie van Defensie voor het jaar 2013" [Adopting the budget of the Ministry of Defense for the year 2013], House of Representatives, Ref. No. 33 400 X, no. 90, July 5, 2013.
44. Ministry of Foreign Affairs and Ministry of Defense, "Beantwoording vragen van de leden Hachchi en Sjoerdsma over achterblijvende resultaten om meer vrouwen te betrekken bij militaire vredesmissies" [Answers to questions posed by Members of

Parliament Hachchi and Sjoerdsma about results to involve more women in military peace and security missions lagging behind], Ref. No. 2014Z19554, November 25, 2014.
45. Genderteam hoofddirectie Personeel [Genderteam Personnel Department], "Genderforce: vrouwen en mannen presteren beter samen" [Genderforce: Women and men perform better together], 2005; Christianne Vermue, *Genderforce 2005–2007: The Power of Gender; A Report on Gender Policy at the Netherlands Ministry of Defence* (2008), http://www.nato.int/ims/2008/win/briefing/Lt%20Col%20Vermue%20-%20Speaking%20Notes%20%20Briefing%20Gender%20Force%2002%20June%2008.pdf.
46. This also translated to initiatives such as the policy discussions (*Verkenning*) held in 2005 by the Ministry of Defense in cooperation with the Ministry of Foreign Affairs and the Visitation Commission Empowerment under the header "Peace, Security, Development, Women's Rights and Equality: The Afghanistan Case."
47. Ministry of Foreign Affairs, *Dutch National Action Plan on Resolution 1325: Taking a Stand for Women, Peace and Security* (The Hague: 2007).
48. A cooperation that had already been strengthened by the June 2007 Schokland Pact, in which representatives of the private sector, civil organizations, knowledge institutes, and governmental bodies (including the Ministry of Defense) pledged to work together toward reaching the Millennium Development Goals.
49. Ministry of Foreign Affairs, *Dutch National Action Plan on Resolution 1325: Taking a Stand for Women, Peace and Security* (The Hague: 2007).
50. Booklet titled *The Dutch Do's on Women, Peace and Security Diplomacy, Defence and Development in Partnership*.
51. Email from Annemieke Verrijp, board member of the ESDC course "Gender in Operations," September 26, 2016.
52. Ministry of Defense, "CDS Aanwijzing A-104, ONDERWERP: Genderbeleid" [Instruction A-104 by the Chief of Defense Staff, Subject: Gender policy], December 15, 2005.
53. Vermue, *Genderforce 2005–2007*.
54. Motie van het lid Diks c.s. [Motion initiated by Member of Parliament Diks c.s.], "Vaststelling van de begrotingsstaten van het Ministerie van Buitenlandse Zaken voor het jaar 2009" [Adopting the budget of the Ministry of Foreign Affairs for the year 2009], Ref. No. 31 700 V, no. 53, November 13, 2008.
55. It includes a list of political and military points of interest such as suitability and availability of Dutch units, duration of the participation, and an overview of other nations' participation.
56. Letter from the Minister of Defense, "Vaststelling van de begrotingsstaten van het Ministerie van Defensie voor het jaar 2011" [Adopting the budget of the Ministry of Defense for the year 2011], Ref. No. 32 500 X, no. 84, February 9, 2011.
57. *Motie van het lid Belhaj* [Motion initiated by Member of Parliament Belhaj], "Vaststelling van de begrotingsstaten van het Ministerie van Defensie voor het jaar 2016" [Adopting the budget of the Ministry of Defense for the year 2016], Ref. No. 34 300 X, no. 105, May 24, 2016.

Women and Gender in the US Military

A Slow Process of Integration

Brenda Oppermann

Women have contributed to national defense since the Revolutionary War; yet fully integrating them into the military—much less the notion of a gender perspective—has been a perennial struggle. However, despite many obstacles, progress has indeed been made. The purpose of this chapter is to provide a historical overview of American women's participation in military affairs, activities undertaken to more formally integrate them into the armed forces as well as efforts to incorporate a gender perspective in military operations conducted by the United States. By doing so, it underscores the importance of women and gender perspectives as integral components of war fighting and peace building. Improving understanding in this regard should, in turn, help to accelerate and streamline integration efforts, thereby more rapidly improving military effectiveness at strategic, operational, and tactical levels.

The chapter highlights five key historical events that served as tipping points for integrating women and a gender perspective in military operations and discusses the political and social contexts surrounding them. The five events are (1) passing the Women's Armed Services Integration Act; (2) passing Public Law 94-106, authorizing women to be admitted into the service academies; (3) rescinding the Direct Ground Combat Definition and Assignment Rule (also known as the Combat Exclusion Rule); (4) conducting combat operations in Iraq and Afghanistan; and (5) implementing the US National Action Plan (NAP) on Women, Peace, and Security (WPS). The first three events facilitated the integration of women into the armed forces. The last two served to incorporate a gender perspective that, in turn, also more fully integrated female soldiers in military operations.

In 1948 Congress passed the Women's Armed Services Integration Act, granting women permanent status in the military subject to military authority and regulations and entitling them to veterans' benefits. Essentially, this law formally recognized women's heretofore "temporary" contributions to the country's defense by laying the legal groundwork for their permanent participation. Public Law 94-106, passed in 1975, authorized women to be admitted into the service academies. Since US service academies are considered the ultimate training ground for future military leaders, women's admission paved the way for women not only to receive this esteemed education and training but, more important, to assume leadership positions. While these laws greatly facilitated women's entry into the armed forces, the existence of the 1994 Direct Ground Combat Definition and Assignment Rule, which prevented women from serving in combat arms positions, remained a considerable obstacle to integrating women throughout the services. The rescission of this rule in 2013 removed one of the final barriers to women's complete integration into the armed forces.

While efforts to integrate women in military operations have continued for generations, efforts to adopt a gender perspective are relatively new. Tactical operations in Iraq and Afghanistan (starting in 2001) first compelled the military to consider the role of gender in conflict since culturally mandated gender segregation precluded soldiers from operating as usual. Because local cultural norms precluded American male soldiers from interacting with Iraqi and Afghan women, military units had to modify their tactics, techniques, and procedures (TTPs) to adequately deal with this situation. The US NAP on WPS, instituted in 2011, represented the first "official" government action requiring gender perspectives to be included in military operations. The Department of Defense (DOD) has been slow to implement the NAP in comparison to other government entities, like the Department of State and the US Agency for International Development, but awareness about the importance of integrating a gender perspective in military operations is increasing and leading to concrete actions.

In addition to examining five key events that facilitated American women's inclusion in military operations, this chapter also features a case study of how the US Army 10th Mountain Division (10th MTN) integrated a gender perspective in military operations during its combat mission in Kandahar, Afghanistan (September 2010 to September 2011). Serving as a regional command headquarters in an area of operations (AO) that was a Taliban stronghold, the 10th MTN launched efforts in this regard that were remarkable for their scope—gender integration occurred at operational and tactical levels for both hostile actions and peacebuilding operations—and for their success in an area of operations (AO) that was in a near constant state of violent conflict. By covering real-life experiences, this case study concretely illustrates what worked, what did not, and what challenges are associated with incorporating a gender perspective in military operations. In doing so, it provides not only valuable insights but also guidance concerning future gender-integration efforts.

The case of the US is noteworthy since it reveals the power of cultural norms, specifically American cultural norms surrounding gender roles. History has repeatedly shown that including women in military operations directly contributes to successful outcomes. Similarly, incorporating a gender perspective improves situational understanding leading to the design and execution of appropriate and effective strategies, operations, and tactics. Despite this evidence, the DOD continues to resist calls to fully integrate women and gender perspectives in military operations, largely because many of its members continue to believe that women and gender dynamics play little to no role in military affairs.

Since change in cultural norms occurs very slowly, it is recommended that DOD provide continued—and more robust—education about the importance of women and gender in military operations, especially to senior leaders. Over time education will help make these concepts the rule rather than the exception. This will ensure that military members have a solid understanding of how women, men, and gender norms contribute to both peace and conflict, enabling the US military to more effectively prevent and mitigate violent conflict and, if necessary, fight.

Background

American women have a long history of involvement in US military operations. Beginning with the Revolutionary War (1775–83), they served in military camps as laundresses, cooks, and nurses. During the American Civil War (1861–65), they served in both Union and Confederate battlefield hospitals as hospital administrators, nurses, and cooks. It is estimated that around 6,000 women performed nursing duties for the Union forces alone. Women also served as spies, and some, disguised as men, served as soldiers. During the onset of the Spanish-American War, the surgeon general requested and promptly received congressional authority to appoint women nurses under contract. Approximately 1,500 civilian women served as nurses assigned to army hospitals in the US. Hundreds more served as support staff and spies, and once again, disguised as men, some served as combatants. Although women's labor and support were critical to the success of American forces during these wars, the military establishment did not officially accommodate women who wished to serve, nor were women generally recognized for their service by the military.[1]

The establishment of the Army Nurse Corps on February 2, 1901, opened the door for women to serve officially in the military. Nurses were appointed to the Regular Army for a three-year period but were not actually commissioned as officers in the Regular Army during their tenure. When the US government got involved in World War I on April 6, 1917, some parts of the military became serious about using women in the armed forces, as evidenced by the navy and marine corps allowing women to enlist for the first time. The army, however, never allowed women to officially join but instead continued to rely on women's labor as contract employees and civilian volunteers.[2]

The Navy Nurse Corps was formed in 1908. Unlike the army, the navy and marine corps actively recruited women to serve in World War I. The Naval Act of 1916 facilitated this recruitment by including broad language that essentially provided a loophole for women to enlist. While the act called for recruiting those with prior naval experience (i.e., men), it also called for "all persons who may be capable of performing special useful service for coastal defense." Clarifying the meaning of "all persons," the secretary of the navy concluded that the language did not prohibit women from enlisting in the reserves. As a result, in 1917 commanders of naval districts began to recruit women to the Naval Coast Defense Reserve to be "utilized as radio operators, stenographers, nurses, messengers, chauffeurs, etc. and in many other capacities in the industrial line."[3]

Women's successful performance of their duties in World War I set an important precedent for their involvement in World War II and subsequent wars. During World War II, more than 400,000 women served at home and abroad as mechanics, ambulance drivers, pilots, administrators, nurses, and other noncombat roles. Eighty-eight women were captured and held as prisoners of war. During the Korean War, over 50,000 women served at home and abroad, including in combat zones. During the Vietnam War, over 7,000 women served, mostly as nurses, in all departments of the military.

While women's historical participation in wars has been significant, their integration into the American armed forces has followed a series of advances and setbacks, with advances closely tied to shortages of qualified males, usually during wartime.[4] Viewed as auxiliary support for the most part, women's permanent and full integration into the armed forces has proved largely elusive for most of the country's history. Despite significant resistance from many corners over time, today more than 200,000 women serve on active duty, making up approximately 15 percent of the armed forces.[5] The reasons for this are discussed in the following sections.

American Armed Forces' Integration of Women

Women have served in the military for generations but were not considered permanent, regular members of the US Armed Forces until 1948. This shift in status was a major step to further incorporate women into the armed forces. However, full integration of women requires more. Women must have the opportunity to participate in all aspects of military service and be given the support necessary to do so. The following actions have contributed significantly to facilitating this ongoing process.

Integration Tipping Point #1: Women's Armed Services Integration Act

Women's indispensable and admirable service during wartime contributed to expanding their roles in the military overall and also greatly assisted in fostering the military establishment's acceptance of their service in the US armed forces. As a result, in 1948 Congress passed the Women's Armed Services Integration Act, granting women permanent status in the military subject to military authority and regulations and entitling them to veterans' benefits. The act also provided women with pay and rank equal to men. While affording women permanent status, the law limited the number of women who could serve in the military to 2 percent of the total forces in each branch.[6]

Although the significant contribution of women to the World War II war effort created a political and social environment that made the Women's Armed Services Integration Act possible, this progressive view of women's roles was soon reversed. Social trends of the late 1940s and early 1950s promoted a feminine ideal of domesticity and maternalism, and thus, the drive to recruit women into the armed forces was at odds with these shifting gender norms. The result was telling. When the Korean War began in 1950, the army, navy, and air force combined had only 60 percent of the projected need for nurses.[7]

In 1967 the limit on the percentage of women in the military was repealed, and the number of women serving continued to grow through the next three decades.[8] Despite continued resistance to women's full participation in the military, the Women's Armed Services Integration Act laid the groundwork for their inclusion. In addition to increasing the percentage of women serving in the military, the act also facilitated women's promotion into senior leadership positions, some in traditionally male units. The first woman to serve as a deputy commanding general in an army combat division was selected in 2012, and the first woman to serve as a deputy commanding general in one of the army's light infantry divisions was selected in July 2015.

Integration Tipping Point #2: Women's Admission into Service Academies

The second tipping point concerning the integration of women was Public Law 94-106, signed on October 7, 1975, authorizing women to be admitted into the service academies.[9] In 1976 the first females were admitted to the US Military Academy at West Point, US Naval Academy at Annapolis, and the Air Force Academy.[10] Much debate surrounded this decision. During the 1970s women were perceived as a potential threat to the productivity and cohesion of the service academies. Their admission into the academies also challenged the cultural values and gender roles of a male-dominated niche in the armed forces.[11] However, in counterpoint, the women's rights movement was also gaining influence during this period and began to affect policies concerning women in military service, as evidenced, in part, by the passage of Public Law 94-106.

As of January 2015, there were 2,600 female military academy cadets and midshipmen as a direct consequence of Public Law 94-106.[12] The impact of this law on the number of women officers over time is significant. Females constituted 3 percent of officers in the 1960s and 1970s. This number steadily increased, reaching 8.5 percent in 1980 and 16.4 percent in 2013.[13]

Integration Tipping Point #3: Rescission of the Direct Ground Combat Definition and Assignment Rule

On January 24, 2013, DOD rescinded the 1994 Direct Ground Combat Definition and Assignment Rule for women as part of a plan to remove gender-based barriers to service. This policy change opened two categories of positions to women: combat arms occupational specialties and noncombat specialties assigned to combat units (e.g., a medic serving in an infantry company).[14] While DOD's goal in canceling the rule was to ensure that military missions used the best-qualified and most-capable people regardless of gender, women continue to face significant obstacles. The Women's Armed Services Integration Act and Public Law 94-106 established a legal foundation for women's integration but could not sway public opinion opposed to it, and repealing the direct combat exclusion rule had a similar effect. The repeal was an important step in eliminating gender barriers by providing women an equal opportunity to serve in all military occupations, but it did not remove stiff resistance from various fronts. The marine corps, for example, resisted the change, going so far as requesting exemptions from the secretary of defense (who refused).[15] Other military members, and civilians, continued to oppose having women serve in combat roles.

This policy change occurred because of two primary issues: (1) female soldiers had been (unofficially) serving in combat roles in Iraq and Afghanistan for many years, and (2) various commissions and other groups had been conducting extensive reviews of women in the military and policies concerning their assignment and career progression. For example, the Military Leadership Diversity Commission conducted a study and issued a report in 2011 on the "establishment and maintenance of fair promotion and command opportunities for ethnic- and gender-specific members of the Armed Forces." Among its recommendations, the commission said that DOD should take deliberate steps to open additional career fields and units involved in direct ground combat to women. This prompted Congress to direct DOD to conduct a review to "ensure that female members have equitable opportunities to compete and excel in the Armed Forces."[16]

To comply with Congress's directive, all military departments and the US Special Operations Command (USSOCOM) advanced studies and efforts to validate operationally relevant, occupationally specific, and adopted gender-neutral performance standards. All military departments and USSOCOM also continued to study the effects of integration from the standpoint of doctrine, training material, leadership and education, personnel, facilities, and policy. DOD also notified Congress of its intent to integrate approximately 28,000 more positions and maintained its goal to integrate women into newly opened positions and units as expeditiously as possible, but no later than January 1, 2016.[17]

Although all exclusions on women serving in combat arms positions were removed in 2016, the military has had mixed results integrating women into these occupations. The army has made slow but steady progress with more than six hundred women recruited for or transferred to combat positions as of early 2018. More than seventy female officers have completed the infantry or armor basic leader courses, and twelve women graduated from Ranger school.[18] In response to DOD's requirement to integrate women, the Marine Corps initially requested a waiver. The waiver was denied, and female integration efforts were undertaken. The Corps is made up of 8 percent women with ninety-two female marines serving in combat arms billets, eleven of whom are in infantry positions. Special Operations Forces (SOF) constitute an area in which women have largely been unsuccessful in meeting the bar for entry because of extremely high physical standards required by these units.[19]

Integration Tipping Point #4: Combat Operations in Iraq and Afghanistan

The conflicts in Iraq and Afghanistan required a change in how the US fights wars. Since conventional warfare methods were ineffective in the irregular wars being waged, the US military engaged in counterinsurgency (COIN) operations. These consisted of lethal and nonlethal activities, that is, engaging in combat and also "winning the hearts and minds" of local populations through stabilization activities. COIN operations, in turn, facilitated the integration of both a gender perspective and women in military operations.

Two principal situations drove this change: the nature of irregular warfare and local customs governing gender relations. In irregular warfare frontline combat is not delineated; the front line can be anywhere at any time. As a consequence, female soldiers found themselves in situations requiring them to engage in direct combat. In addition, because local customs in Iraq and Afghanistan precluded male soldiers from engaging local women, female soldiers were often the only ones qualified for certain missions, such as searching women and offering assistance to women as part of stability operations. As a result, in 2003 the marine corps created the Lioness Program in Iraq, the first military program to incorporate gender considerations to achieve mission objectives.

The Lioness Program attached female volunteer marines to combat units and was the forerunner of female engagement teams (FETs). Facing similar gender-based constraints to achieving mission success in Afghanistan, marine corps and army units were required, once again, to call on female military members for assistance. Female soldiers and marines charged with dealing with Afghan women were called FETs. (For a more detailed look at the use of FETs, see the 10th MTN case study later in this chapter.) Seeing the need for FETs, Special Operations Forces eventually trained and deployed their own teams, called cultural support teams (CSTs). In addition to FETs and CSTs, military units also worked with human terrain teams, provincial reconstruction teams, and district support teams as means to engage with Afghan women to increase situational awareness, improve security, and promote peace and stability.

Integration Tipping Point #5: US National Action Plan on Women, Peace, and Security

The US NAP on WPS was released in December 2011 to empower women "as equal partners in preventing conflict and building peace in countries threatened and affected by war, violence and insecurity." Although all US government agencies are accountable for implementing the policies and initiatives endorsed in the NAP, the plan contains explicit commitments by DOD, the Department of State, and the US Agency for International Development to assist in achieving the plan's goals "to advance women's inclusion in peace negotiations, peace building activities, and conflict prevention; to protect women from sexual and gender-based violence; and to ensure equal access to relief and recovery assistance, in areas of conflict and insecurity."

The US NAP can be considered a culminating event of sorts. Activists have long highlighted the need to consider and leverage women's perspectives and actions domestically and internationally. In 1995 these issues came into unprecedented focus during the Fourth World Conference on Women in Beijing. In preparation for the conference, the US government had pledged to implement a list of commitments on behalf of women that would take advantage of existing foreign and domestic policy instruments.[20] Despite these commitments, however, little progress was made, particularly regarding the military establishment. It took Executive Order 13595, legally mandating the implementation of the NAP, for DOD to get serious about integrating women and gender throughout the organization.

DOD has made some progress in this regard, especially concerning education and training, since the release of the NAP. WPS has been included in the Joint Professional Military Education (JPME) system as a special area of emphasis (SAE). While this is a positive development, JPME colleges are only encouraged—not required—to incorporate SAEs in their curricula.[21] To fill the training and education gap on WPS within DOD, the Gender Awareness 101 course module was developed in April 2014. In addition, numerous studies and many conferences and seminars focusing on WPS have been conducted.[22] Several DOD components, including US Africa Command, US Southern Command, US Northern Command, and US Pacific Command, have also included WPS in their orientation courses to familiarize new personnel. Others have begun to integrate WPS issues into their planning documents.[23]

While educating military members about gender and WPS is a foundational step in achieving the NAP's goals, genuine and sustainable integration of gender and WPS in DOD also requires incorporating these issues into activities that serve to operationalize them, such as training exercises (field, command post, simulation, etc.) and pre-deployment training. In this regard, DOD's progress has been somewhat lacking. For instance, while DOD developed an NAP implementation guide that serves as a tool for applying US NAP objectives into the strategic, operational, and tactical environments, there is no requirement to address these objectives in DOD pre-deployment training.[24] Although the North Atlantic Treaty Organization (NATO) could assist in filling this gap through accredited gender training materials and courses, which have been available to all NATO member nations for several years, DOD has sent only sixteen of its members to participate in gender training sessions.[25] None of the NATO-accredited materials have been formally adopted into the DOD pre-deployment training curriculum.

When it comes to training exercises, there is also room for improvement. According to annual DOD reports detailing "progress in advancing the objectives outlined in the Executive Order 13595, 'Instituting a National Action Plan on Women, Peace, and Security,'" the department essentially includes WPS issues solely in peacekeeping training exercises designed to prepare *non-US armed forces* for deployment to UN peacekeeping missions. WPS is not generally integrated into exercises conducted to prepare for war.

One notable exception is the US-Australia biannual exercise, Talisman Sabre. More than 30,000 service members representing all military branches participate in Talisman Sabre, an exercise that fully simulates a high-intensity war-fighting environment. Implementing UN Security Council Resolution (UNSCR) 1325 on WPS was one of the top three training objectives of Talisman Sabre 2015 (TS15). While the Australian Defence Force was responsible for including WPS in the exercise for the first time, Pacific Command, its partner command, actively met the challenge. US Army I Corps, playing the role of Coalition Forces Land Component Command (CFLCC), was notable for establishing a WPS cell to successfully address the topic.[26] All other units at every level—strategic, operational, and tactical—also had WPS representatives, that is, gender advisors. Conflict-related sexual violence, child soldiers, protection of women and children, and the engagement of female key leaders were some of the issues woven throughout the exercise. Although most TS15 participants were unfamiliar with UNSCR 1325, the exercise greatly improved the knowledge and understanding of both senior leadership and subordinate commands since they could experience the impact of WPS issues in the context of a (simulated) battle. Considering it key to mission success, senior leadership ensured that WPS was substantively dealt with from beginning to end.

Integrating Women and Gender Perspectives: A Case Study of the US Army 10th Mountain Division in Kandahar, Afghanistan

Historically, wartime needs—and the laws they generate—have been the chief drivers for integrating women and gender perspectives into military operations. The same holds true today. The US NAP on WPS represents the newest way forward in this regard; it addresses not only the role of American women in conflict but also the role of indigenous women living in conflict zones and gender relations in those places. However, before the NAP was developed, wartime necessities in Iraq and Afghanistan had spurred this integration as well.

The US Marine Corps and Army, the services principally responsible for the human domain, recognized the importance of dealing with local women, acknowledging them as key participants in those conflicts. Iraqi and Afghan women actively contributed to violent conflict in assorted ways, including smuggling arms, serving as suicide bombers, and sustaining combatants through the provision of food, shelter, and medical care. On the other hand, local women were also some of the strongest advocates for peace and stability, bridging political divides between conservatives and progressives, resolving disputes peaceably, and strengthening communities by providing health care, education, and social assistance. Representing a diversity of views, knowledge, and activities, marines and army personnel engaged local women to improve intelligence collection, enhance situational awareness, mitigate conflict, and promote stability.

To glean lessons from and thereby improve future attempts at integrating a gender perspective into military operations, this section examines the efforts of the 10th MTN in Afghanistan. This case study provides some brief background information about the 10th MTN's role during its tour of duty in Kandahar, Afghanistan (2010–11), and about the defense policy regarding gender considerations. It also discusses why the 10th MTN decided to integrate a gender perspective into operations halfway through its tour and presents the many activities undertaken to achieve this end. Equally important, the case study examines the obstacles and challenges—for example, the lack of adequate policy and guidance and a dearth of soldiers sufficiently trained about gender and female outreach—impeding the integration process. Factors that facilitated the integration process—such as the development of a gender annex as part of the command's operations order (OPORD), support by senior military leaders, and a FET training program—are also discussed.

Background

The 10th MTN was in command of Regional Command–South (RC-South) in Kandahar, Afghanistan, from September 2010 to September 2011. Its AO included some of the most unstable, highly kinetic territory in the country and is considered the spiritual birthplace of the Taliban. Kandahar, along with the other provinces in RC-South's AO, produced a steady supply of insurgents who kept military units working overtime to maintain a modicum of stability. In addition to regular attacks, firefights, and other forms of violence, the

RC-South territory is also one of the most repressive parts of Afghanistan for women. Primarily rural and tribal, this area is inhabited predominantly by Pashtuns, who are renowned for their oppressive treatment of women. Females living in this area have little freedom of movement, fewer than 10 percent are literate, and girls are subjected to *baad*, a traditional practice in which young girls are given away as payment to settle disputes. In this trying environment, the 10th MTN attempted to integrate women and gender into RC-South's military operations.

Lack of Policy and Guidance

The 10th MTN's efforts to integrate gender considerations and women in its operations can essentially be summed up by the proverb "Necessity is the mother of invention." Whereas other military operations are guided predominantly by doctrine, DOD had no doctrine to offer when it came to addressing the role of gender and women in the continuum of conflict. Moreover, the doctrines most frequently applied in Afghanistan—COIN and stability operations—failed to adequately address gender and women. While NATO had in 2009 issued Bi-Strategic Command (Bi-SC) Directive 40-1, requiring NATO units—including the International Security Assistance Force–Afghanistan (ISAF)—to implement UNSCR 1325 on WPS, this directive seemed to be largely ignored, as evidenced by the "poor awareness of the provisions and content of UNSCR 1325 and Bi-SC Directive 40-1, as well as in the limited understanding of basic gender concepts" by ISAF.[27] Further, on May 31, 2010, Gen. Stanley A. McChrystal, then commander of ISAF (COMISAF), issued a directive titled "Engagement with Afghan Females," which provided guidance for standardizing engagements. However, like Bi-SC Directive 40-1, few commands were aware of it.[28] Since 10th MTN's predecessor at RC-South, the United Kingdom's 6th Infantry Division, did not act on this COMISAF directive during its command of the AO, no information about gender or female engagements was available for sharing with the 10th MTN during the command handover process. In addition, the 10th MTN was not aware of this COMISAF directive. Plus, at the time the 10th MTN commanded RC-South, the US had not yet developed an NAP on WPS. The NAP was not issued until December 2011, three months after the end of the 10th MTN's deployment to Kandahar.[29]

Some tactical units operating in places like Iraq and Afghanistan acknowledged the important role that gender plays in those countries and, consequently, implemented a gender perspective and integrated female soldiers into military operations. However, DOD overall lagged in this regard. Despite years of boots-on-the-ground evidence that engaging local women in areas of conflict was critical to mission success, both in terms of improving security and fostering stability, no guidance in this regard emanated from the Defense Department.

Deficient Military Doctrine

In addition to the overall dearth of policy and plans concerning gender and women and conflict available before December 2011, DOD's revised doctrine—specifically, the Department of the Army's Field Manual (FM) 3-07, *Stability Operations*, and FM 3-24, *Counterinsurgency*—failed to adequately address these topics. This is striking since both FMs were updated (FM 3-24 in 2006 and FM 3-07 in 2008) years after several tactical units and their operational commands began to engage with local women to improve operational effectiveness. Remarkably, FM 3-07 claims to serve as "a roadmap from conflict to peace," yet it only mentions women six times in its 208 pages.[30] Moreover, the only discussion dealing with the "role of women" occurs in appendix E, "Humanitarian Response Principle," concerning disaster relief efforts. This appendix is also the only part of the FM that mentions a gender perspective.[31] Besides this section, FM 3-07 mentions the term "gender" in only five other instances, none of which explains gender roles and the way they influence stability operations.

Like the stability operations FM, FM 3-24 on COIN does not provide much, if any, guidance for addressing women and gender. This 282-page manual mentions women just two times. The first instance is found under "Social Norms," a section that calls for the "appropriate treatment of women and children" and notes that husbands and wives have different statuses.[32] Appendix A, "A Guide for Action," includes a paragraph concerning the need to engage women because "in traditional societies, women are hugely influential in forming the social networks that insurgents use for support. . . . [But if they] support COIN efforts, families support COIN efforts."[33] Considering the multiple roles of women in a COIN environment and the need for explicit knowledge and appropriate resources to fully engage women, this manual falls far short of providing adequate guidance.

Why Integrate Women and Gender Perspectives?

When the 10th MTN assumed command of RC-South, no US directive or policy required the division to integrate women and gender into its operations. So why did they do it? Several months after taking command of RC-South, Maj. Gen. James Terry attended a commanders' conference during which US Marines discussed the benefit of using FETs in their operations in Helmand

Province.³⁴ The logic of the argument convinced the commanding general (CG) to establish FETs in RC-South and integrate women and gender into the command's overall operations. While the intention of improving units' operational effectiveness by integrating women and gender was spot-on, the outcome was less than ideal.

Operational Structure

The 10th MTN integrated a gender perspective into military operations in a variety of ways, including developing official guidance, educating military members, and expanding military roles.

Operations Order Gender Annex

To meet the significant challenge of operationalizing gender, the command incorporated this capability through the military plans process. The command created a gender annex as part of the division's OPORD. This annex was eventually issued as a fragmentary order (FRAGO) so that subordinate commands could be tasked to execute the guidance.³⁵ A small group of military members and civilians working for the 10th MTN and its civilian counterpart organizations, such as the US Agency for International Development, was brought together to draft the gender annex. The gender annex answered what, why, and how by providing basic information, like definitions of key terms and explanations of concepts, and guidance concerning the command's goals for integrating gender. Importantly, as the command's primary operations plan, the OPORD (including the gender annex) also established much-needed legitimacy.

Although the annex provided basic, foundational information and an overarching framework, there was no doctrinal basis and insufficient follow-on guidance or direction from the US Army. This situation created additional organizational resistance since units were already extremely busy fighting the Taliban and other insurgent elements while trying to set conditions for conducting stability operations. Commanders had little impetus to take on what was viewed as a "new" issue amid other pressing concerns, and with insufficient guidance to effectively address it. As a result, they generally failed to exploit one of the primary enablers for executing the gender annex FRAGO: FETs.

Female Engagement Teams

Establishing FETs was a key component of the command's efforts to integrate gender into operations. Subordinate commanders were directed to establish FETs using female soldiers who were already in their units. The civilian contractor appointed by the command to serve as the gender coordinator initiated this effort with the support of the Training Section of the Operations Cell at RC-South Headquarters (HQ). The Training Section was extremely supportive of this initiative, providing critical logistical support. It also accessed FET educational resources and was instrumental in drafting the FRAGOS that were central to enabling female soldiers to participate in FET training.

Three FET training sessions were conducted in 2011. Each five- to seven-day session was held at RC-South HQ and included female soldiers from RC-South as well as other locations in Afghanistan. Approximately fifty to seventy women (soldiers and interpreters) participated in each session. Women soldiers who participated in FET training had no particular background, making them more or less suitable to serve in this capacity since the command relied on the personnel available in the command's AO at the time. Essentially, they were women who either volunteered to serve on a FET or were ordered to accept the extra duty of serving on a FET. Consequently, some FET members were highly motivated to succeed in this role and contribute to mission effectiveness. Others had little enthusiasm and performed accordingly.

Perhaps the greatest misstep of the FET training program was its focus on FET members rather than on commanders, who needed to learn how to use this battlefield asset. Only much later in the program did a couple of commanders attend a FET training session.[36] The dearth of military leaders who understood the role of gender relations and Afghan women in relation to the conflict weakened the overall FET initiative. In sum, unless a commander is educated about how to use an asset and is willing to do so, that asset will remain largely unexploited. This was the case for the 10th MTN.

Key Leader Engagements

The command's push to include women and gender in its operations also affected its efforts to work with "key leaders." For the US Army, key leaders are local residents who have the potential to influence others—ideally in terms of possibly reducing or minimizing armed conflict. Before the CG's initiative to integrate women and gender into operations, all Afghans in RC-South who were designated key leaders were men. This was the direct result of the command's—and the US Army's—limited and flawed understanding of Afghan society and of its inherent organizational bias favoring men in leadership roles. The move to integrate women into operations provided the space to expand the notion of key leaders. One instance in particular is revealing. The command had been trying to meet with a specific tribal leader, but he rebuffed all attempts from the army to engage him. The 10th MTN's cultural advisor suggested that RC-South representatives meet with women parliamentarians as a way to influence tribal elders to engage in peace building and reconciliation.

She knew that some Afghan women were very influential in parts of Kandahar, and equally important, they were nonthreatening compared to men. Upon following this advice, the command was finally able to communicate with the tribal leader who had eluded them. Although the tribal leader had long refused to speak to members of the US military, he agreed to speak with a female parliamentarian who convinced him to meet with Major General Terry.[37] Despite some (female) key leader engagement successes, the command's integration of women and gender remained ad hoc with regard to its key leader efforts. One officer summed up RC-South's overall gender integration effort by stating, "Gender was at the bottom of the list for everyone, even the civilians."

Assessments

The command's assessment team used a combination of scientific and social techniques to gauge the organization's progress toward (or away from) command goals, objectives, or milestones. The assessment team initially relied on data that were collected almost exclusively from Afghan men since team members did not consider that women's perceptions and concerns might be different from men's and, therefore, present a different picture about an area's security. With the 10th MTN's move toward integrating women and gender into operations, the assessment team soon realized that its initial efforts suffered from a less robust engagement and data-collection capacity than other similar engagement efforts. When it came to female engagements, this initiative had no separate dedicated team.

Although they didn't account for women initially, over time assessment team members came to believe that the most telling information concerning the level of security in a particular area might indeed come from the area's women and children. For example, an Afghan District Center that is vibrant with the business of men likely sends a different message about security than one busy with women and children. Knowing whether the women seen in public were longtime local residents or had relocated from a dangerous place to an area they considered safe could also be helpful. This type of data assisted the team in developing a more comprehensive and nuanced understanding of the security situation.

In attempting to integrate women and gender, the assessment team faced three primary obstacles. The first was the nature of coalition survey infrastructure. Large, unwieldy, and consisting of many different types of longitudinal surveys, the survey infrastructure was not agile enough to modify the type of data collected and the manner in which data were collected in the middle of a deployment. Despite this situation, the assessment team came up with a plan to retool one of the surveys to include information from and about Afghan women.[38]

Challenges

The 10th MTN faced numerous and varied challenges to integrating gender into RC-South military operations. Command and control, always critical to conducting effective operations, was one of the greatest obstacles, followed by ISAF members' insufficient understanding of gender and women's roles in peace and conflict, inadequate staffing, and a tactical-operational divide, among others.

Unity of Effort

Integrating women and gender effectively in a multinational and multiorganizational context would benefit from adequate command and control in order to facilitate coordination and ensure that engagement activities were designed to consider gender and to suit the local context. This proved to be impossible for the 10th MTN since each organization in RC-South working on gender—the US Marine Corps and SOF, civilian government organizations, Canadian Armed Forces, British Armed Forces, and so forth—had its own approach. The marines, for instance, would often have FETs go to many villages only once to provide health care and social assistance in order to cover large and multiple AOs. In contrast, army SOF (ARSOF) teams that had CSTs would generally include them on all missions in one AO over time. This enabled CSTs to become an integral part of the ARSOF team and to establish trust with local communities through ongoing engagements, both of which were key to mission success. In addition to conducting female engagement differently, the lack of doctrine and guidance made it impossible to identify which approach should be used with certain communities or which organization should be in the lead in an AO. As one senior military officer noted, instead of focusing on designing and conducting appropriate engagement activities, "there was more energy spent arguing between organizations about who had the better model."

Lack of Key Personnel

Although NATO required the establishment of gender advisor positions to provide expertise on UNSCR 1325, women and gender perspectives, and cultural awareness, RC-South, like most ISAF commands, did not have a gender advisor.[39] (It had created the position of gender coordinator, which should not be confused with the official NATO gender advisor position.) A scope of work for gender advisors was drafted and submitted to the 10th MTN chief of staff for staffing and approval. The request seemed to languish despite repeated inquiries about its status. By the time the 10th MTN departed in the fall of 2011, a gender advisor had not yet been hired.

Insufficient Resources

In addition to a lack of DOD doctrine and insufficient guidance, the 10th MTN had to achieve its objective of integrating women and gender solely with the resources deployed to Afghanistan with it. Critically important was the fact that no extra personnel would be made available. As a consequence the command had to staff FETs with female soldiers who were already engaged in their regular, full-time jobs. In addition, the command needed to find females among its pool of interpreters since few female soldiers spoke Pashto, the local language.

Inexperience and Lack of Understanding

The FET initiative suffered primarily from a lack of experienced personnel at all levels. The gender coordinator, brigade and subordinate commanders, and the female soldiers recruited to serve as members of FETs were all novices when it came to understanding the role of gender and women in the continuum of conflict. While the US Army provided limited cultural awareness training for both military members and civilians deploying to Afghanistan, scant attention was paid to the role of gender in Afghan society. Those working in Afghanistan learned that strict gender segregation defined Afghan society to a large degree. As a consequence male soldiers were not allowed to speak with or otherwise engage with Afghan women, especially in rural areas.[40] The practice of *purdah*, secluding women from public view, resulted in the belief by US military members that Afghan women had no role in the insurgency or the mission objective of fostering peace and stability. This limited knowledge proved to be a massive obstacle in terms of operationalizing FETs. Commanders tended to believe that because Afghan women were restricted in their actions and movements and hidden from the view of non-family members, they were not at all involved in the conflict. This impression made FETs unnecessary in their view.

Into this uninformed, misinformed, and "gender-integration resistant" environment, the command's gender coordinator was placed. While the decision to appoint a gender coordinator made sense, the command's lack of understanding about the role of women and gender in conflict resulted in the selection of a person who lacked the requisite knowledge or experience to lead the effort. Although the gender coordinator had studied gender in an academic setting and was very enthusiastic, she had no field experience working on this issue, much less in a conflict environment. In addition, her lack of experience working with the military proved to be another obstacle to achieving the command's desire to fully integrate women and gender into operations. Her inexperience served to stiffen resistance rather than facilitate the integration process. The gender coordinator's inability to effectively convey the integration message to a military audience left many convinced that the initiative was a waste of valuable time. In sum, facilitating this process in such an inconducive environment would have been extremely challenging even for someone with subject matter experience and expertise—both in terms of gender and the army—much less a person without it.

FET training was a critical component of the command's integration efforts. Ensuring that FET members were sufficiently prepared was important for operational reasons and for reasons of perception, specifically, of male commanders and soldiers. There were three primary reasons to provide solid FET training: (1) it allowed female soldiers to successfully carry out FET missions, thereby contributing to units' comprehensive understanding of the operational environment; (2) on combat missions, well-trained FETs decreased the risk of violent reactions to units by reducing Afghan men's concerns about the proper treatment of Afghan women; and (3) competent FETs encouraged male commanders to see the value of accounting for the role of women and gender in counterinsurgency and stability operations.

Initial FET trainings provided valuable information to female soldiers but were also insufficient in many respects.[41] A key component of the training, for example, was helping FET members to gain a deeper understanding of Afghan life in the AO so that they could understand the gender roles of both Afghan women and men within their families and society. Gender roles are determined and enforced in Afghan society primarily through customary law. Based on Islamic law and traditional practices and beliefs, customary law (*Pashtunwali* in southern Afghanistan) guides the everyday behavior of Afghans. A US Army lawyer—a prosecutor who had never dealt with customary law—was selected to teach the rule of law session during the first FET training. Needless to say, while FET members were educated about women's rights according to Afghanistan's Constitution, they were ill prepared to confront the realities of Afghan women's lives under customary law.

FET Composition

The female soldiers who volunteered or were ordered to serve on FETs were also novices at engaging with Afghan women (and men) as part of stabilization and COIN efforts. Trained to serve in a variety of military occupational specialties—as intelligence analysts, medics, administrative clerks, logisticians, and so forth—these women generally had little to no understanding of what they were being asked to do. Further, lacking adequate combat training, many were poorly prepared to accompany combat units on tactical missions. In addition, like their commanders, they too tended to believe that Afghan women had no agency or power in society.

From a purely military standpoint, one of the greatest detriments to the FET concept was a dearth of credible senior noncommissioned officers (NCOs) and officers on the teams. Most of the FET members were young enlisted soldiers since senior higher-ranking females were considered too valuable in their current roles to participate in an activity that was not a priority. According to a human terrain team member, "What was needed were female soldiers who could contribute to the security posture of a unit, carry their weight, have situational understanding, and be seen by their peers as a soldier." The lack of NCOs and officers was problematic for several reasons. First, the young soldiers were unable to communicate requirements effectively. The ability to communicate requirements was important because the FETs were in direct competition with other unit members for funds to support assorted activities. The young soldiers' inexperience with articulating requirements meant FETs lost out on funding for projects designed to assist Afghan women. This in turn made the teams less effective. The young team members were also inexperienced at briefing senior officers, and their ineffective briefings were often not considered credible.

Commanders' Situational Awareness

In discussing why the US military waited so many years to engage Afghan women, one general officer said, "We let the cultural barriers get in the way." Cultural barriers to engaging Afghan women, combined with a very lethal operating environment, are key to understanding the 10th MTN's somewhat limited success in integrating gender and women. By focusing primarily on combat operations and, moreover, incorrectly equating Afghanistan's strict gender segregation practices with a complete lack of agency and influence among Afghan women, military forces ignored Afghan women for the most part.

Another obstacle to integrating women and gender in military operations was commanders' lack of understanding about women's roles in Afghan society and in military operations. Commanders received virtually no education or training about these issues. US military culture has a blind spot when it comes to considering women as part of operations or conflict. To complicate matters, the gender coordinator's effort to educate subordinate commanders about the gender annex—to include the role of gender and women in operations—served to reinforce commanders' doubts about the need to address these issues rather than dispel them. As one senior member of the command noted, "Sending a representative who lacked legitimacy in the eyes of military commanders to prepare them to incorporate FETs into their missions essentially guaranteed the failure of this initiative."

Army Organizational Culture

Despite both formal and informal efforts to use FETs and thereby integrate a gender perspective into military operations, the organizational culture of the military proved to be a persistent and substantial impediment. Commanders and their—primarily male—soldiers did not believe that FETs had the requisite skills and training to carry their weight on missions. Since most male soldiers were trained in combat arms and women were not legally allowed to train for those positions, the men were concerned that having female soldiers on missions would be a burden and create undue risk.

The role of organizational culture as an obstacle to fully integrating women and gender into military operations was also apparent in the few units that were receptive to the FET concept. Even units that saw the need for FETs and successfully worked with them did not fully integrate them into the military planning process. For example, every step in a patrol needs to be planned, so to ensure success, it is vital to consider all aspects and potentialities of a mission. Nevertheless, unit commanders did not consider FET leaders to be decision makers and, consequently, did not include them in the planning process for patrols. This situation precluded FET members from contributing insights and knowledge that could have improved patrols and thereby contributed to mission success.

The Tactical-Operational Divide

While RC-South senior leadership supported integrating women and gender into operations, the response of subordinate commanders was less than enthusiastic. Consequently, despite setting up this initiative for success by creating a gender annex—requiring commanders to establish FETs, providing FET training, and appointing a gender coordinator—implementation of the program was another matter.

Many brigade- and battalion-level commanders were unwilling to address the role of gender and women. They would pay a lot of lip service to integrating women and gender, but as evidenced by the lack of reporting and discussions during FET monthly meetings, they generally did the bare minimum. Many gender focal points in the field were ambitious and had very good ideas about how to improve mission success by leveraging local women, but these ideas were often quashed by commanders. For many commanders, gender was the last item on their list of things to do. It was considered an add-on, time and resources permitting.

The unwillingness to address women and gender was also manifested by commanders' failing to discuss these issues with their soldiers. While senior leaders at the HQ believed that their message was reaching all the way to tactical units, this did not generally happen. A stability operations advisor working for the 10th MTN who accompanied assorted units on patrols regularly asked soldiers whether they included Afghan women as part of their stabilization activities. The response was almost always no. Most soldiers and officers had simply never considered reaching out to women or discussing this topic with male community members with whom they worked, even though they had conducted a wide range of stability operations projects designed to strengthen communities.

Resistance to the integration process also occurred with respect to peacebuilding efforts, such as the Afghan Peace and Reintegration Programme (APRP). The APRP commenced in June 2010 and addressed reintegration when low-level fighters put down their arms and needed to transition to civilian life. ISAF played a significant part in facilitating APRP processes. In Kandahar, for example, a US military officer was assigned to work closely with the APRP provincial-level committee to design, fund, and manage activities. Although the process to include women and gender in all operations had been underway in the command for several months by the time the APRP Kandahar provincial committee was established, no Afghan women served on the committee, nor did any of the committee's activities include women. The RC-South stability operations advisor spoke to the officer about this situation and offered guidance about how to reach out to Afghan women and include them. The officer highlighted how women were already promoting peace in their communities and noted that they had an important stake in the success of the process since they were directly affected by returning ex-fighters who often continued to perpetuate violence and threaten communities. Despite these discussions, no action was taken, and the APRP process in Kandahar continued to be a male-only initiative.

Convincing Commanders

Although the 10th MTN's attempt to integrate women and gender into operations by having the gender coordinator educate and inform commanders was not optimal, the senior leadership and staff of the 10th MTN stressed its importance. For example, Major General Terry took the time to speak with subordinate commanders about the importance of and philosophy behind engaging Afghan women to improve operational effectiveness. He introduced these concepts during regularly scheduled commanders' conferences, battle rhythm briefings, and informal discussions during visits to subordinates' AOs. RC-South also issued formal orders concerning the application of the female engagement philosophy in operations. The officer in charge of the Civil Affairs Section made a point of visiting the heads of FETs to learn about and support their efforts and to emphasize the importance of FETs to their commanders. While senior leadership supported integrating women and gender perspectives, tactical units' limited efforts in this regard revealed that full integration would require more than verbal support and formal orders.

Tactical commanders' personal experience dealing with these issues in an operational context proved to be more effective at convincing their peers and soldiers to integrate women into military operations. A few company commanders who had served on previous deployments, for instance, saw how including female soldiers on missions increased their security and made life for their units more predictable. They realized that without female soldiers to search and manage Afghan females during missions, they were contributing to local hostility and increasing the risk of violence to their soldiers. However, there were too few of these commanders to significantly facilitate the integration process. Moreover, while integrating female soldiers into missions made sense, the idea of including a gender perspective was entirely absent.

Lessons Learned

Too often the term "gender" becomes conflated with "women," resulting in activities designed to include women without ever truly incorporating a gender perspective. This was the case for the 10th MTN. While its efforts to integrate women and gender into RC-South operations were commendable, they were more focused on recruiting female soldiers to engage with Afghan women for information-gathering purposes rather than on considering the gendered aspects of conflict. The Afghan Local Police (ALP) program is a prime example of how a failure to consider gender perspectives increased conflict rather than reduced it. ISAF established the ALP—a loose network of local defense forces designed to mobilize and arm local civilians to defend their communities from the Taliban—in 2010. Although it improved security in some areas, the ALP was also responsible for repeatedly violating Afghan civilians, including harassing women and committing acts of violence against them. Had a gender analysis of the ALP program been conducted to reveal the different protection needs of men and women, potential abuses would have been anticipated and, in turn, possibly prevented or mitigated. Instead, the primary effort was to train more and more female soldiers to engage with Afghan women rather than analyze initiatives through a gender lens.

Perhaps more important, the 10th MTN's attempt to integrate women and gender goes beyond the operational imperative to improve effectiveness by underscoring the importance of culture and beliefs when trying to effect change. Despite taking the steps necessary to ensure that the existing command administrative infrastructure and processes accounted for gender and women, the 10th MTN was unable to do the same for the organizational culture of the army. Predominantly male and valuing physical prowess and fighting ability above all else, the army culture was not amenable to a change that required a shift in this worldview. Integrating gender and women effectively called for commanders and soldiers not only to acknowledge the importance of these issues in conflict but to redefine their understanding of conflict and, more important, their role in it. While some were able to do this, many more could not.

The lessons learned from the 10th MTN's forward-leaning attempt to enhance RC-South military operations by integrating a gender perspective provided many valuable insights that could have been used to facilitate future integration efforts. The withdrawal of US troops from Afghanistan, however, proved to be a major stumbling block in this regard. In June 2011 President Obama announced plans to withdraw troops from Afghanistan "at a steady pace" until the United States handed over security to the Afghan authorities in 2014.[42] In response to the decision to rapidly decrease the size of the US military footprint, Gen. John Allen, then commander of ISAF, decided to forgo COIN operations in favor of accelerating the handover of security responsibilities to Afghan security forces. This decision significantly diminished subordinate commands' interest in focusing on local populations and, on a related note, gender considerations. The overall result has been a sort of amnesia in the military. The lessons concerning the military's experience with integrating a gender perspective into military operations have been all but forgotten. This situation has made implementing the NAP even more challenging.

For the most part, efforts to integrate gender perspectives in military operations are not shaped and designed using the prior knowledge gained in Afghanistan and Iraq but, instead, treated as something new and novel.

Conclusion

The integration of women, much less a gender perspective, in US military operations has been a slow process marked at times by considerable advocacy promoting its benefits, as well as stiff resistance. As a result, the number of women serving in the military and their level of participation has fluctuated greatly over time. Because women's early service was voluntary and tied to war-related needs like freeing up men to fight, caring for them when they were wounded, and filling billets when no men were available, the end of fighting correlated with a rapid and considerable decrease in the number of female service members. This cycle was repeated with each war the US engaged in. Even legislation like the Women's Armed Services Integration Act of 1948, which altered the temporary status of women by enabling them to permanently serve, was insufficient to stop this perpetual and cyclical vacillation. Instead, post–World War II social norms promoting female maternalism and domesticity proved more persuasive, with many women opting to stay home rather than pursue the long-term military careers the act facilitated.

The 1975 passing of Public Law 94-106, authorizing women to be admitted to the service academies, helped to change this situation. Based on a "gender equality" argument for integrating women rather than wartime needs (i.e., operational effectiveness), this law essentially acknowledged women as permanent members of the armed forces and, as such, entitled to the same opportunities as their male counterparts. Progress toward integrating women into military operations got another boost from the wars in Iraq and Afghanistan. The nature of irregular warfare, in which the tactical definition of "front line" is irrelevant, meant that female soldiers were often engaged in direct combat. Women's combat experience led to the eventual rescission of the Direct Ground Combat Definition and Assignment Rule since battlefield exigencies revealed that the rule could not be consistently enforced and, furthermore, there was no logic in doing so.

US military experience in Iraq and Afghanistan was also instrumental in drawing attention to the vital role that gender plays in combat and stability operations. Culturally mandated gender segregation in Islamic cultures, which precluded male soldiers from interacting with local women, meant that in many instances female soldiers were the only ones able to conduct certain missions. This situation led US officers and soldiers to acknowledge the importance of gender dynamics and, in turn, incorporate a gender perspective into military operations. However, while advances were made in this regard as evidenced by the Lioness Program and FETs, for example, they were tied to tactical needs and were consequently ad hoc rather than officially and doctrinally part of how the military operates.

The US NAP on WPS played a consequential role in moving beyond ad hoc efforts to integrate a gender perspective in military operations by legally requiring DOD to do so. It also obliged DOD to more fully integrate women. By explicitly addressing the need to integrate women and gender, the NAP helped the US move beyond its heretofore limited understanding of and actions concerning strengthening national defense, improving security, and effectively addressing global instability. This is important because ensuring full integration requires political will more than formal requirements, and political will can be fostered through a "top-down" forcing function, such as the NAP, that enhances understanding and compliance.

In sum, while laws, practical experience, cultural evolution, and increased understanding have done much to more fully integrate women and gender perspectives into US military operations, work in this regard is far from finished. Current efforts, such as opening combat arms positions to female soldiers and moving toward incorporating WPS considerations into training exercises, signal a significant and promising shift in attitudes. And a change in attitude is crucial to ensuring that women and gender perspectives are no longer considered as an add-on but as integral to creating an effective military.

Notes

Telling the story of the US military's experience with integrating women and gender from the Revolutionary War until today could easily fill several volumes. Trying to do so in several pages has called for omitting, truncating, and condensing to an extreme degree. Consequently, I apologize up front for any perceived and real inadequacies in relating this history.

Since the writing of this chapter, the US government has enacted the Women, Peace, and Security Act of 2017, which was signed into law on October 6. Perhaps this new law will reinvigorate gender integration efforts. According to the Office of the Assistant Secretary of Defense for Special Operations and Low Intensity Conflict, following the signing of the act, the "Defense Department is advancing its efforts to include more women in peacebuilding and conflict resolution processes following the signing of the 2017 Women, Peace and Security Act." Chuck Broadway, "DOD Works to Incorporate More Gender Perspective in Operations," DOD News, March 8, 2018, https://www.defense.gov/News/Article/Article/1461815/dod-works-to-incorporate-more-gender-perspective-in-operations/.

1. Two notable exceptions are Deborah Sampson and Dr. Mary Walker. Sampson served for over a year during the Revolutionary War in General Washington's army disguised as a man. After she had been wounded, her gender was discovered, and she was honorably discharged. Later, she received a military pension from the Continental Congress. During the Civil War, Dr. Mary Walker served as a field surgeon and became the only woman to receive the Medal of Honor, the nation's highest military honor.
2. "The Army Nurse Corps," WW2 US Medical Research Centre, accessed July 24, 2015, http://med-dept.com/articles/the-army-nurse-corps/.
3. Nathaniel Patch, "The Story of the Female Yeomen during the First World War," *Prologue Magazine* 38, no. 3 (Fall 2006), http://www.archives.gov/publications/prologue/2006/fall/yeoman-f.html.
4. Maureen Murdoch et al., "Women and War," *Journal of General Internal Medicine* 21, no. S3 (2006).
5. "National Women's History Month," US Department of Defense, accessed July 30, 2015, http://www.defense.gov/home/features/2015/0315_womens-history/.
6. *Encyclopaedia Britannica Online*, s.v. "Women's Armed Services Integration Act," accessed July 24, 2015, http://www.britannica.com/event/Womens-Armed-Services-Integration-Act.
7. "1950s: Recruitment," Office of History and Collections of the Women in Military Service for America Memorial Foundation, accessed July 28, 2015, http://chnm.gmu.edu

/courses/rr/s01/cw/students/leeann/historyandcollections/history/lrnmre1950rec.html.
8. Kristy N. Kamarck, *Women in Combat: Issues for Congress*, Rep. No. R42075 (Washington, DC: Congressional Research Service, 2015), 4, https://fas.org/sgp/crs/natsec/R42075.pdf.
9. Department of Defense Appropriation Authorization Act, Pub. L. No. 94-106, 89 Stat. 537 (1975).
10. It is interesting to note that the first legislation regarding the admission of women into the service academies was introduced into Congress in November 1944. Congressman Eugene E. Cox of Georgia introduced a bill proposing a plan to create a service academy for women, a step toward giving them permanent military status (H.R. Res. 314, 1944). The bill never went anywhere. In 1945 Congressman James G. Fulton of Massachusetts introduced a bill to establish an academy for aviators and another for women (H.R. Res. 3403, 1945). This bill also failed miserably. In February 1955 Senator Dennis Chavez of New Mexico introduced a joint resolution to establish a Women's Armed Services Academy. This too failed. See A. C. Showers, "Rocking the Boat: Women Enter Military Academies" (unpublished paper, University of Colorado at Boulder, April 22, 2008), 3.
11. Showers, "Rocking the Boat," 7.
12. "National Women's History Month."
13. Mary K. Trigg and Eunsung Lee, "Women in the U.S. Military Services," Rutgers Institute for Women's Leadership, September 30, 2009, http://iwl.rutgers.edu/documents/njwomencount/Women%20in%20Military%202009%20Final.pdf.
14. Kamarck, *Women in Combat*, 13.
15. Matthew Cox, "Female Soldiers Cleared to Serve in Infantry, Ranger, Special Forces," *Military.com*, December 3, 2015.
16. Kamarck, *Women in Combat*, 12.
17. Department of Defense, *Annual Report on Implementation of Executive Order 13595 and the U.S. National Action Plan on Women, Peace, and Security* (Washington, DC: Department of Defense, 2015).
18. Andrew Swick and Emma Moore, "The (Mostly) Good News on Women in Combat," Center for a New American Security, April 19, 2018, https://www.cnas.org/publications/reports/an-update-on-the-status-of-women-in-combat.
19. Ibid.
20. Valerie M. Hudson and Patricia Leidl, *The Hillary Doctrine: Sex and American Foreign Policy* (New York: Columbia University Press, 2015), 19.
21. Department of Defense, *Annual Report*, 4.
22. Ibid., 9.
23. Anne A. Witkowsky, "Integrating Gender Perspective within the Department of Defense," *Prism* 6, no. 1 (2016): 37–38.
24. Department of Defense, *Annual Report*, 8.
25. Data received from US DOD Joint Staff J7, Individual Training and Learning (June 4, 2018). The sixteen DOD members participated in gender training at the Nordic Centre for Gender in Military Operations (NCGM), the primary organization providing NATO-accredited gender training, seminars, and materials.
26. The WPS Cell consisted of one civilian subject matter expert, one army colonel, and one army sergeant major.

27. Helené Lackenbauer and Richard Langlais, eds., *Review of the Practical Implications of UNSCR 1325 for the Conduct of NATO-Led Operations and Missions* (Stockholm: Swedish Defence Research Agency, 2013), http://www.nato.int/nato_static/assets/pdf/pdf_2013_10/20131021_131023-UNSCR1325-review-final.pdf.
28. Because ISAF did not track its own efforts to implement UNSCR 1325, accurate data concerning the degree and extent of WPS implementation is not available. However, interviews conducted to write this chapter, in-depth literature reviews, and many discussions concerning this topic that the author engaged in while posted in Afghanistan during this time frame revealed that few military units were even aware of WPS considerations or understood the concept of gender.
29. Executive Order 13595 legally mandated the implementation of the NAP and directed DOD, the Department of State, and the US Agency for International Development to submit agency-specific implementation plans to the assistant to the president and national security advisor within 150 days.
30. Department of the Army, *Stability Operations*, FM 3-07 (Washington, DC: University of Michigan Press, 2008), E-6.
31. Ibid., E-7.
32. Department of the Army, *Counterinsurgency*, FM 3-24/MCWP 3-33.5 (Washington, DC: Marine Corps Warfighting Publication, 2006), 3-8.
33. Ibid., A-6.
34. Terry retired in 2016 as a lieutenant general.
35. The OPORD serves as the base order; subsequent orders are published as FRAGOs.
36. Data concerning commanders' participation in FET training was not collected. This estimate comes from an interview with an army officer who was familiar with RC-South FET training efforts.
37. Interview with a Canadian army officer who served in RC-South, April 2015.
38. For a variety of reasons, this survey had not yet been conducted by the time the 10th MTN left Kandahar.
39. NATO, "Integrating UNSCR 1325 and General Perspective into the NATO Command Structure," Bi-Strategic Command Directive 40-1 (Brussels: NATO, 2009).
40. In urban areas of Afghanistan, gender segregation was generally not as strict, allowing non-Afghan men to interact with Afghan women in certain circumstances.
41. FET trainings improved significantly with each iteration.
42. Mark Landler and Helene Cooper, "Obama Will Speed Pullout from War in Afghanistan," *New York Times*, June 22, 2011, http://www.nytimes.com/2011/06/23/world/asia/23prexy.html?hp&_r=1.

7

Women, Gender, and Close Combat Roles in the UK

"Sluts," "Bitches," and "Honorary Blokes"

Anthony King

In July 2016 the United Kingdom—the very last major Western power in NATO to do so—decided to lift its ban on female personnel serving in ground combat units. It was an important moment in British defense policy and concluded a debate that had been going on a number of years. Following operations in Iraq and Afghanistan and in light of Secretary Leon Panetta's decision to rescind all gender restrictions in the American military, the United Kingdom reconsidered its combat exclusion between 2013 and 2016. In the spring of 2014, both Philip Hammond, the defense secretary, and Gen. Peter Wall, the chief of the General Staff, publicly stated their support for a rule change. Their position was affirmed by Prime Minister David Cameron on December 20, 2015. In anticipation of the 2016 Ministry of Defence ruling, Cameron declared, "The Defence Secretary [Michael Fallon] and I are united in wanting to see all roles in our Armed Forces opened up to women in 2016. We've already lifted a number of barriers in our Armed Forces with the introduction of female submariners and women reaching the highest ranks in all Services. We should finish the job next year and open up ground combat roles to women."[1] The prime minister noted that current British policy was out of line with public feeling and with the UK's closest allies in NATO. The new policy will be implemented by the end of 2018. At that point, women will be allowed to serve in the ground combat units in the British Army.

In fact, women had already been effectively serving in these roles for some years. Since 2001 Western forces have been involved in military campaigns of unexpected duration and intensity in Iraq and Afghanistan. One of the most remarkable aspects of these campaigns has been the formal access of women to ground combat roles or, in the British and American armed forces, where women were officially excluded, to service alongside combat troops in military operations.[2] In the latter cases, although formally defined as attached to combat units rather than assigned to them, women have endured the same risks as their male counterparts, and in numerous cases they have engaged enemy fighters at close quarters. Indeed, since British forces have been heavily involved in combat in both Iraq and Afghanistan, the UK ironically has more female soldiers who are genuine combat veterans than any other NATO nation except for the United States. By any objective standard, these women have served in combat with combat units, and females will serve in close combat in the future. The de facto and future de jure accession of women to the combat arms in Britain's armed forces demands some explanation. This chapter provides a brief overview of this important transformation and seeks to describe the conditions for and limits of contemporary female accession to the combat arms in the United Kingdom.

Discrimination against Female Soldiers in the UK

Feminist scholars have shown that female accession to the armed forces has been consistently resisted by men. According to Enloe, the armed forces are a key pillar of patriarchy and one of the state's most potent agents of female suppression. The state and the military seek to "militarize" women's lives, thereby subjecting women to intense masculine control through the most diverse and indirect means. According to Enloe, to preserve patriarchy, women have been excluded from the military as a pillar of masculine power, and they "cannot qualify for the entrance to the inner sanctum, combat."[3] Indeed, Enloe argues, "To *allow* women entrance into the essential core of the military world would throw into confusion *all* men's certainty about their male identity."[4] Megan MacKenzie has also shown how the myth of the Band of Brothers has been used to block the accession of women to the combat arms.[5]

There is clear evidence of such resistance in the British armed forces today. Although many female soldiers have served on the front line and have been accepted, British military culture remains masculinized. The armed forces, and the combat arms in particular, remain overwhelmingly male, after all.[6] Specifically, for many—perhaps even most—male soldiers, even within a highly professionalized force, femininity is still equated almost exclusively with heterosexuality and sex itself; women are essentially seen as being for sex. Male soldiers often do not know how to interact with females, defined only in sexual terms, in any other way than by solicitation; moreover, they expect females to comport themselves in sexualized ways toward them.

As a result of these entrenched attitudes, it is possible to identify the emergence of a now well-established, even hegemonic, gender construct in the British military—namely, a "slut-bitch" binary. This construct appears almost ubiquitously in discussions with female service personnel as they describe their experiences. It is extremely prevalent in the American literature. For instance, Kayla Williams, who served as an interpreter in a US intelligence battalion in Iraq, insightfully concluded on the basis of her service that "sex is key to any woman soldier's experience in the American military."[7] However competent a woman might be, her relations with male soldiers are finally determined by their sexuality; women were either "sluts" or "bitches."[8] This classification is corroborated widely by scholars.[9] Kronsell records the use of the category "bimbo," which is equivalent to the slut.[10]

The phenomenon is pronounced in the British forces. One female British soldier described how "women got called a lot of degrading names by some, but not by all men, usually from peers." British female soldiers have routinely acknowledged the existence of this gender binary, around which they are compelled to negotiate their service. Indeed, one female British soldier described the discrimination and outright harassment she had faced during her career:

> I, and all other women, are expected to put up with men, using the feminine as insults. For example, men considered weak being called "you're a girl's blouse," "you're a fanny," "you're a vagina," "you're a girl." If a woman complains, then she immediately becomes a non-team player, the trouble-maker. We get told to "get a life," to develop a "sense of humour" or that it was "only banter." We get the same reaction if we object to male sexual attention, whether that is another touching or speaking with you in a way that you consider inappropriate, or by a male in the chain of command asking you to "fuck him."[11]

As this evidence reveals, the slut-bitch binary has become so institutionalized in the British forces that women are often denied any agency in this process of classification; whatever they do, they will be defined by it.[12] They are defined either as sluts (sexually available) or bitches (sexually unavailable); lesbians or "dykes" (self-evidently unavailable) are a subcategory of bitches. This symbolic coding materially obstructs female participation in the armed forces not because they are deemed instrumentally incapable of performing their roles but purely and solely because they are women.

The thorough, even hegemonic, institutionalization of the slut-bitch binary in British military culture self-evidently represents a major obstacle to integration.

If femininity is exclusively associated with sex for most male soldiers, women have to repress their sexuality if they are to be accepted by men.[13] If a woman wants to be treated equally in the British Army, she has typically to avoid all sexual contact with male soldiers. Indeed, British female soldiers have recorded that sexual abstinence has to be extended even to the point of rejecting friendships with male soldiers, lest they be misinterpreted by the colleague or by others.[14] For example, a highly competent female British officer formed a close professional bond with her senior noncommissioned officer (NCO), only to find that this relationship had been interpreted as sexual and had reportedly invoked a notable response from her commanding officer: "My wife would not behave like that."[15] According to this man, the female officer was behaving like a slut; close professional relations were imputed to be something else. She was accused of flirting or consorting with a male colleague. Of course, male soldiers who fraternized with women and who were, therefore, minimally equally responsible for any breakdown of discipline that ensued, normally avoided any sanction from their peers: "Somehow everyone got it that getting laid was okay for the guys."[16] Any sexual activity automatically re-invokes the slut-bitch binary because it once again affirms that a female soldier is to be defined in purely sexual terms as a woman. Despite their increasing integration even into the combat arms, female soldiers in the British forces, and the British Army in particular, have faced severe discrimination.

The Integration of Women

Women have certainly faced resistance as they served with British combat units in Iraq and Afghanistan, then. However, it is important to recognize that some successful integration has taken place, even without a change in policy. Some women have been accepted and included in the combat arms on the front line in the last ten years; they have been respected, valued, and indeed, in several cases, decorated for their services.

The preceding section showed how entrenched gender definitions have played a critical role in excluding women from service. Significantly, as women have been integrated into combat units in the United Kingdom, new gender definitions that have facilitated women's acceptance by male colleagues have become apparent. In her work on the women in the US Marine Corps, Connie Brownson has advocated a concept of equivalence to explain changing gender relations in the armed forces.[17] Because of the typical disparity in physical capacity and the fact that they were assigned to different, noncombat roles, women could not be accepted as absolute equals by male combat marines.

However, they were accepted as "equivalents"; they were accepted as "sisters," valued female comrades, who offered the unit an important new capability. Their difference was recognized but celebrated.

The concept of equivalence is not invalid, and Brownson provides evidence of its usage, but in fact, recent research shows that some women have been accepted as more than equivalents; they have been accepted as professional equals in combat units, though in potentially problematic ways in gender terms (discussed later in the chapter).[18] A small but potentially highly significant transformation has begun to take place in the last decade. In the course of the Iraq and Afghanistan campaigns, a new gender category has begun to emerge among British—and other Anglophone—forces. Accordingly, it has become increasingly common for female soldiers to describe how on recent operations they have been accepted as "one of the boys," "one of the lads," "one of the guys," or "one of us."[19] "I can remember being pleased when I'd been classed as 'an honorary bloke.'" The term "bloke" is used even by women to refer to other female soldiers.[20] Competent female soldiers have been accepted on the ground that they are conceived no longer in sexual terms as women but, in professional military terms, as equals. Since the armed forces are understood to be a masculine organization by male soldiers, respected female soldiers have been coded as men too. Women have been integrated into the British Army and its combat units as "honorary men," therefore. A third gender category has emerged beside the slut-bitch binary: the honorary man.

Of course, not all female soldiers have consented to the concept of the honorary man. For instance, one female informant who had once aspired to being an "honorary man" considered herself old and senior enough to survive without this ascription: "By this stage in my life I had grown into the age of being a mature woman and so had the attitude of 'I'm not a bloke, I am a woman, accept me for who I am or not at all.'"[21] However, this female soldier fully recognized the pertinence of the honorary man category. Consequently, some female soldiers have been accepted as equals to their male counterparts and assigned a masculine status. They have been thoroughly incorporated into the male combat group; they have become "honorary men." This is an important gender transformation in the British forces that deserves considerable academic attention.

Several factors might be invoked to explain the acceptance of some proven women into combat units under the ascription of an honorary male status. The advance of feminism and changes in occupational structures are clearly significant here; more women now serve in the armed forces, and traditional concepts of gender have been substantially displaced. However, the professionalization of Western armed forces is also of immediate relevance to the emergence of "the honorary man." Indeed, since the 1990s and especially in the last decade, scholars have highlighted the importance of professionalization to the armed forces; professionalization has increased the combat effectiveness of the military, but it has also changed the very culture and cohesiveness of the armed forces. This is particularly apparent in small combat units, where cohesive bonds need to be very close. The research by Elizabeth Kier and Robert MacCoun played an important role here.[22] Against traditional accounts of masculine bonding, they have argued that social cohesion or "likeness" was not so important in the primary groups of the contemporary professional force. Here, teamwork, not interpersonal bonds, becomes crucial. Kier, for instance, writes: "The sense of group cohesion based on 'teamwork' has little to do with whether members enjoy one another's company, share an emotional bond or feel part of some 'brotherhood of soldiers.'"[23] In the mass citizen armies of the twentieth century, racial, ethnic, sexual, and gender homogeneity was normally crucial to cohesiveness. Today, cohesion depends rather on the group's level of professionalism, its training, and members' effectiveness at their job. In a professional force, soldiers can be trained to perform together, irrespective of their social backgrounds and interpersonal relations.

There is now a well-developed literature that argues training and, specifically, professionalism—not male social homogeneity—are the crucial determinants of cohesion at the small group level.[24] Social scientists have increasingly observed that professional soldiers unite around quite impersonal procedures and drills, which they have learned in training, whatever their background. This has produced the possibility of a novel form of cohesion, described as "swift trust" by Ben-Shalom and colleagues.[25] Professional soldiers do not necessarily need to share a common social background or personal relations to cooperate; they can perform with each other by reference to common drills and adherence to shared doctrine. In this context, the personal bonds between males in dense primary groups, once regarded as essential to cohesion, becomes less relevant or even supererogatory.[26] Under the intensified professionalism of the twenty-first century, performance, not social background, has become primary. Soldiers have developed solidarities with each other through the competent performance of their mutually allotted tasks, out of which they build up dense networks of trust.

In the twenty-first-century all-volunteer professional army, social cohesion based on the homogenous male primary group, so typical of twentieth-century armies, has been increasingly replaced by a more impersonal form of solidarity based on competence. Individuals are accepted on the basis of whether they can perform their assigned role efficiently, whatever their social, ethnic, or racial background, to form, in many cases, very dense solidarities on a professional basis. For Western soldiers, comradeship has become a function of performance.[27] The performative dimension of soldiering is critical to understanding the process of female integration.

Crucially, professional cohesion has allowed for the integration of once excluded population groups, such as ethnic and racial minorities or homosexuals.[28] By extension, professionalism may be critical in facilitating the accession of women to the combat role. In the case of women, like homosexuals and racial and ethnic minorities before them, gender might become simply another arbitrary social category—of no more significance than skin color—in determining military participation. On this account, in a highly professionalized military culture, as long as a woman can perform, she might be accepted by male colleagues. The professionalizing ethos of armed forces has provided a cultural context for the accession of women into the combat arms. Professionalization is the cultural precondition that has allowed women to be incorporated into combat units and be judged by their combat performance, not by their sex.

There is substantial evidence to corroborate the thesis that professionalization has been the critical factor in the emergence of the honorary man category. Decisively, male soldiers have collectively changed their view of women and their capabilities. They have been willing to incorporate them into their primary groups on a specifically professional basis. For instance, one NCO from the British Parachute Regiment maintained that because of recent operations and increased training, "the British army is in a better state than it has ever been." Specifically, he noted how this professionalism had manifestly improved the quality and maturity of junior soldiers; while the older generation were "more concerned with image," "the younger cadre are much more professional."[29] The implication was that the advance of professionalism had involved a revision of traditional concepts of military masculinity. Soldiering was no longer understood purely in gendered terms as an expression of manhood, still less in sexualized terms. Rather, soldiering was a professional activity that relied on the acquisition of expertise. Indeed, connecting professionalism to a revision of gender norms, he explicitly concluded, "We had a female medic. She was awesome. She carried the same weight as the blokes. She was doing her job, performing as well or better than the men. Why should sexuality affect cohesion?"[30]

Among elite British forces, for instance, which are typically considered to be the most masculine, there is evidence, provided by women, that male soldiers have begun to accept females, interpreting them as professional colleagues. For instance, female British soldiers attached to the Royal Marines and Parachute Regiment recorded similar experiences. Chantelle Taylor, a medic attached to 16 Air Assault Brigade in Helmand in 2008, confirmed the statement from the male Parachute Regiment NCO cited previously. In a striking episode, she helped to fire a mortar during a firefight: "There was a time that this would have been unheard of—a female helping out. Blokes down here weren't bothered anymore. It didn't matter what cap badge you were so long as you could do the job."[31]

The experience of another British female medic, who spent four months in frontline patrol bases with the Royal Marines, corroborated the point. Throughout the period she carried her own equipment, including body armor, weapon, medical kit, and water. She recorded that she was completely accepted by the young Marines. Once she had been attached and demonstrated her ability to cope with the environment physically and to perform her role professionally, her status as a woman became irrelevant, especially when she was under fire and treating wounded marines:

> In the patrol bases the relations were so close. We were a nine man team, there wasn't twenty minutes when you weren't thinking about the team. In Tombstone [a major base in Helmand away from the front line], there was no guy in my room but in the patrol base, we did everything together. When I first arrived, they felt protective of me and they worried that I was ok but it was more that than girls and boys getting romantic. They were like family, like brothers. In Bastion, the officers were different but in the PBs [patrol base] it was all together. It was very professional. The lads were aware of that. I was under as much pressure as them: I was literally one of the lads.[32]

This statement affirms the thesis about professionalization and female accession. By working, sleeping, and eating so closely together, this female medic and the Marines were united. This process of feminine effacement is particularly obvious in the statement of the British medic cited previously. Precisely because there was no possibility of "getting romantic," she could be treated as a fellow Marine.[33] In effect, the marines found it impossible to equate her femininity (i.e., their perception of female sexuality) with her role, and consequently, to be able to work with her at all and accord her full membership of their group, they simply erased her gender from their relations. She became "one of the lads" because she was no longer an object of sexual interest. Close codependence changed her status from a potential object of sexual interest into an equal professional partner. In this way, she usefully summarized in detail the precise means by which professionalization has facilitated gender integration and the incorporation of women as honorary men into combat units. Selected women who have demonstrated their competence have been accorded an honorary male status in combat units. They have been incorporated into the male primary group as equal professionals. As a result of professionalization, gender relations and gender definitions have been renegotiated even in once fiercely masculine combat units.

Conclusion

Of course, it is important to avoid any idealization about the reformation of gender relations in the British forces. The concept of the honorary man does not represent a major transformation of gender norms or concepts. On the contrary, it affirms traditional norms, including the slut-bitch binary, because only a few selected individual women are accorded this status. They are included in a substantially unrevised masculine grouping; gendered concepts, language, and practices remain broadly unchanged. The concept involved further problems because it put women in a contradictory position. Discussing the issue of the honorary man was difficult for informants because they were, in effect, being asked to consider reflexively whether they had played into gender stereotypes, which might be damaging to women in general. Indeed, some informants were explicitly aware that their status as honorary males meant that they complied with definitions of women as sluts and bitches. Officers have recorded that they have been able to sustain themselves as honorary men only by allowing male soldiers to disparage other less competent women in sexist ways.[34] Honorary man status is problematic because it often reaffirms rather than invalidates the slut-bitch binary. Ultimately, the concept of the honorary man relies on and reinforces a rather conventional concept of gender—but that is the only one available to women. The fact that some individual women can be "men" is taken to prove that most are rightly dismissed as "sluts" and "bitches."

Nevertheless, the acceptance of some female British soldiers by British Army and Royal Marines combat units is a novel departure that is likely to be of great significance in the future, especially once the current gender restrictions on women serving in combat units are lifted at the end of 2018. In fact, the rule change is unlikely to have a radical effect on gender relations in the combat arms in the United Kingdom. Very few women will want to or be capable of serving in combat units. Denigrating gender categories are likely to persist. Yet the accession of women into the combat arms will not be insignificant. Not least, it will legally recognize that the only proper basis for selection for the combat arms and the forces more widely is competence—whatever the sex, sexuality, ethnicity, or race of an individual. This ruling will establish professionalism as the sole criteria of inclusion and acceptance. It is likely, in this context, that the concept of the honorary man will be deepened and extended in ways that might actually generate a reformed gender settlement in the military in which not sex but mere performance and competence becomes primary.

Notes

1. Tim Ross, "British Army's Women Soldiers to Go into Combat," *Telegraph*, December 20, 2015, http://www.telegraph.co.uk/news/uknews/defence/12060225/British-Armys-women-soldiers-to-go-into-combat.html.
2. Katia Sorin, "Women in the French Forces: Integration versus Conflict," in *Challenge and Change in the Military: Gender and Diversity Issues*, ed. Franklin C. Pinch, Allister T. MacIntyre, Phyllis Browne, and Alan C. Okros (Kingston, ON: National Defence Academy Press, 2006); G. Harries-Jenkins, "Institution to Occupation to Diversity: Gender in the Military Today," in Pinch et al., *Challenge and Change in the Military*; Gerhard Kümmel, "Complete Access: Women in the Bundeswehr and Male Ambivalence," *Armed Forces and Society* 28, no. 2 (2002): 555–73.
3. Cynthia Enloe, *Does Khaki Become You?* (London: Pluto, 1983), 15.
4. Ibid.
5. Megan MacKenzie, *Beyond the Band of Brothers: The US Military and the Myth That Women Can't Fight* (Cambridge: Cambridge University Press, 2015).
6. Rosabeth Moss Kanter, *Men and Women of the Corporation* (New York: Basic Books, 1997); Carol Cohn, "'How Can She Claim Equal Rights When She Doesn't Have to Do as Many Push-ups as I Do?' The Framing of Men's Opposition to Women's Equality in the Military," *Men and Masculinities* 3 (2000): 131–51.
7. Kayla Williams and Michael E. Schaub, *Love My Rifle More Than You: Young and Female in the US Army* (London: Weidenfeld and Nicolson, 2006), 22, 72, 199, 207.
8. Ibid.
9. Helen Benedict, *The Lonely Soldier: The Private War of Women Serving in Iraq* (Boston: Beacon Press, 2010), 6; Connie Brownson, "The Battle for Equivalency: Female US Marines Discuss Sexuality, Physical Fitness and Military Leadership," *Armed Forces and Society* 40, no. 4 (March 2014): 770; Melissa S. Herbert, *Camouflage Isn't Only for Combat: Gender, Sexuality and Women* (New York: New York University Press, 2000), 67.
10. Annica Kronsell, "Gendered Practices in Institutions of Hegemonic Masculinity: Reflections from Feminist Standpoint Theory," *International Feminist Journal of Politics* 7, no. 2 (2010): 51.
11. Interview with anonymous source, January 19, 2015.
12. Victoria M. Basham, "Everyday Gendered Experiences and the Discursive Construction of Civilian and Military Identities in Britain," *Nordic Journal of Masculinity Studies* 3, no. 2 (2008): 156–57; interview with OF-4a female, British Army, May 13, 2010.
13. Williams and Schaub, *Love My Rifle More Than You*.
14. Anthony King, "The Female Combat Soldier," *European Review of International Relations* 22, no. 1 (2016): 122–45.
15. Interview with OF-4a, British Army, May 13, 2010.
16. Williams and Schaub, *Love My Rifle More Than You*, 21.
17. Brownson, "Battle for Equivalency," 770.
18. Anthony King, *The Combat Soldier*, 401; King, "Female Combat Soldier," 122–45.

19. Ibid.
20. Email communication with OF-4a female, British Army, March 20, 2014.
21. Ibid.
22. Elizabeth Kier, "Homosexuality in the US Military: Open Integration and Combat Effectiveness," *International Security* 23, no. 2 (1998); Robert J. MacCoun, "What Is Known about Unit Cohesion and Military Performance," in *Sexual Orientation and US Military Personnel Policy: Options and Assessment*, National Defence Research Institute (Washington, DC: RAND, 1983); Robert J. MacCoun and William M. Hix, "Unit Cohesion and Military Performance," in *Sexual Orientation and US Military*; Robert J. MacCoun, Elizabeth Kier, and Aaron Belkin, "Does Social Cohesion Determine Motivation in Combat? An Old Question with an Old Answer," *Armed Forces and Society* 32, no. 4 (July 2006): 646–54.
23. Elizabeth Kier, "Homosexuality in the US Military," 19.
24. Hew Strachan, "Training, Morale and Modern War," *Journal of Contemporary History* 41, no. 2 (April 2006): 211–27; Uzi Ben-Shalom, Zeev Lehrer, and Eyal Ben-Ari, "Cohesion during Military Operations: A Field Study on Combat Units in the Al-Aqsa Intifada," *Armed Forces and Society* 32, no. 1 (2005): 63–79; Eyal Ben-Ari, Zeev Lehrer, Uzi Ben-Shalom, and Ariel Vainer, *Rethinking Contemporary Warfare: A Sociological View of the Second Al-Aqsa Intifada* (New York: State University of New York Press, 2010); Edward J. Coss, *All for the King's Shilling: The British Soldier under Wellington, 1808–1814* (Norman: University of Oklahoma Press, 2010).
25. Ben-Shalom, Lehrer and Ben-Ari, "Cohesion during Military Operations," 63–79.
26. King, *Combat Soldier*, 374.
27. Ibid.
28. Kier, "Homosexuality in the US Military," 5–39; MacCoun, "What Is Known"; MacCoun and Hix, "Unit Cohesion and Military Performance."
29. Cited in King, *Combat Soldier*.
30. Ibid.
31. Chantelle Taylor, *Bad Company: Face to Face with the Taliban* (London: DRA, 2011), 223.
32. King, *Combat Soldier*.
33. Interview with OR-2 female, Royal Navy, 2013.
34. King, "Female Combat Soldier," 122–45.

Are Women Really Equal in the People's Army?
A Gender Perspective on the Israel Defense Forces

Hanna Herzog

Israel is the only country that, since its establishment in 1948, has had compulsory military service for women and men.[1] In this sense it is an interesting test case for examining the changes that have taken place over the years in the way women have been integrated into the army, and for investigating whether, and in what way, the inclusion of women was accompanied by gender sensitivity that influenced the structure of the army, its rules, and its gender equality. These questions have particular importance because in Israel, an immigrant society, the military is perceived as the melting pot of the Jewish community. Military service is a means for acquiring human capital that can be converted in the labor market and in politics.[2] Furthermore, the young people enlisting in the army at age eighteen serve for at least two years, during the period of their lives when they are most impressionable in regard to the formation of their social identity, in general, and their gender identity, in particular. Thus, the policies and practices of inclusion and exclusion of women, the meaning attached to them, and the methods of coping used by women and policymakers go far beyond the period of military service, and as such, these policies and practices play a central role in shaping Israeli society.[3]

In Israel, as in other countries, the army is associated with fighting and hence with the masculine body and masculinity. Being a state institution, the military has a close relationship with masculinity.[4] The gender regime that distinguishes between men and women is deeply intertwined in the organizational structure of the army, its methods of operation, and its organizational identity. Thus, if military service is compulsory, the major question to be addressed is how Israeli women have been included in such a gendered institution.

As many studies have indicated, women's inclusion in the military is associated with two major processes: the first follows and reproduces the "gender regime" in Connell's terms, and the second is the de-gendering that Lorber defines as a process of blurring the binary gender regime by recognizing that the two genders are not homogeneous groups and that women can serve in so-called men's roles and conversely men can serve in so-called women's roles.[5]

However, these two opposing trends are not merely intra-military processes; rather, they intersect with wider sociocultural and political arenas. My claim is that the Israeli case highlights these complex relations. There is no way to talk about the "military" as a universal category or as confined within itself. It is a dynamic changing hybrid organization that is continuously reshaped at the intersection of various sociocultural and political forces. Such too is the case regarding the issue of women's inclusion within military systems.

This chapter addresses the major intra- and inter-logics that act simultaneously as formal and informal mechanisms of gendering and de-gendering the structure, organizational norms, and practices of the Israeli army. In the first part, I briefly discuss four major logics, the intersections between which mold women's inclusion in or exclusion from the Israel Defense Forces (IDF). I then follow the changes in the encounters among these logics over the years. I examine the processes of change against sociocultural obstacles, the strategies that were developed for de-gendering, and the social carriers of the gendering and de-gendering processes.

I argue that since 1948 and up to the end of the 1980s, the encounter between these logics reinforced the gendering of the IDF. From the 1990s onward, various active strategies were developed for de-gendering. The intersections among these forces in the field stimulate processes of de-gendering. However, they do not form one clear, linear trend of development but rather disrupt the deep, gendered structure of the IDF. A multitude of facets of gendering and de-gendering can be found; these often exist simultaneously.

Women's Integration in the Israel Defense Forces

The issue of women's integration within militaries is not unique to Israel. In the following I track the complex relations between sociocultural and military inclusion and exclusion of women in the IDF. Analytically, there are four intra- and inter-military cultural logics whose changing forms of intersection affect the ways women are integrated into the IDF. The four are Western-state logic, security logic, military organizational logic, and the Jewish national religious logic.

Western-State Logic

From time immemorial, armies all over the world have been considered the world of men; the incursion of women has been perceived as partial or as temporary. The incorporation of women as combatants or in supporting roles, such as for medical care or administrative purposes, is characteristic of societies undergoing a national struggle for independence or war.[6] The need for legitimization of the struggle and for maximum mobilization of the population has opened the military's doors to women. In many instances, when the war ends or national independence is achieved, the gendered order returns to its former state, and women are once again relegated to their traditional roles.[7] It was only in the 1970s that most of the armies went over to voluntary induction of women as part of the demands of feminist movements. The Israeli case suggests a different path. From the founding of the IDF in 1948, the Israeli army based itself on the principle of universal conscription whose aim was to include women in the army by means of a law. The State of Israel was founded during a military struggle with its neighbors, and the enlistment of women was thought of as part of the nation building; but this women's enlistment also responded to the army's enormous need for personnel. As part of the nation-building process, the army was perceived, by both the political leadership and society at large, as the site for the melting pot of the Jewish waves of immigration arriving in Israel—men and women alike.[8]

The Security Service Act of 1949 viewed compulsory drafting as the means for redefining the new Israeli-Jewish collective and as an integral part of defining republican citizenship.[9] As such, it was embedded in the civic discourse of Western culture that spoke in terms of the nation-state. The Western liberal meritocratic ethos was adopted, with the army being a site for personal social mobility and for contributing to the nation-state.[10]

The decision about compulsory military service was much disputed and eventually resulted in the Security Service Act, which only appeared to call for universal conscription.[11] The law addressed compulsory induction into the army for all, but it defined rules for gendered service conditions, among which were shorter mandatory service periods for women, different reserve duties (men were to serve longer than women), and exemption for women from compulsory service because of marriage, pregnancy, parenting, and declaration of religious lifestyle.[12] The law adopted the traditional gendered role divisions between men and women. Motherhood, either in practice or in potential, was, and continues to be, the main reason for releasing women from army service, with motherhood seen as women's civic contribution to the collective. This gendered inclusion enabled the military-organizational logic to institutionalize gendered frameworks and roles to the extent that it was possible to refer to the army as having two separate tracks for men and for women.

Security Logic

The concept of security in the Israeli discourse has a mythical aspect. It relates to basic perceptions about law and order, safeguarding the individual from all harm, including concrete threats of violence and war. In the deepest sense, security is also thought of as the ability to maintain a sovereign Jewish state. In short, the term has implications for broad swaths of existence and survival—of the individual and of the national community.[13]

This perception persists despite Israel's military and economic resilience. Israelis' belief in their ability to withstand threats against their security does not prevent the Jewish citizens of Israel from continuing to adhere to thought frames that view the security threat as a fundamental problem.[14] Military service, reserve service, and repeated wars have placed the army at the center of the Israeli experience and of the formation of Israeli identity. The security threat constitutes the central platform on which relations between individuals and the state are given expression and are implemented.[15] Life in the shadow of security matters sharpens the gendered division of labor in Israeli society, with army and soldiering being the center of Jewish male identity, leaving family as the province of women.[16]

Military Organizational Logic

The masculine principle is the basic logic guiding the army as an organization, and in this the IDF does not differ in any essential way from other armies around the world. But it was precisely the 1949 Security Service Act, which both included women in compulsory service and also excluded them in granting them an exemption on the basis of their socially prescribed gender roles as wives and mothers, that is a testament to the degree to which the military's perception is masculine.[17] The gendered distinctions drawn in the act and in the regulations of the Ministry of Defense, as asserted by Amram-Katz, were honed by means of the bureaucratic mechanism of the military system: the Women's Corps was formed, and in every corps in which women served, they were legally subordinate to the officers of the Women's Corps.[18] Personnel selection, training, and placement were based on gendered distinctions and gendered segregation. However, as various studies have demonstrated, it is precisely in the military organizational logic that the seeds were sown for the de-gendering of the organization; this allowed women, under the auspices of the army and its needs, to break out of the gendered institutional roles.

Over the years the guiding organizational principle in the military bureaucratic system was of exploiting manpower. When women began to take on "masculine roles," this was undertaken in accordance with a model of "women substituting for men." At times when the need for combat manpower became widespread, new roles were opened up for women. Such was the case in the post–Six Day War period (1967), when the boundaries of the state were expanded and there was a need to police the occupied territories. Similarly, after the Yom Kippur War (1973) when the army established many additional combat battalions and was in need of men, women took on instructors' roles in field units. During the First Lebanese War (1982) and the First Intifada (1987), women replaced men in instructors' roles, inspection, and essential operations.[19] Reduction of the military budget in the 1980s also increased the need to use women's service more effectively, and this was accompanied by a policy change that permitted the stationing of women in the occupied territories where women are likely to confront Palestinians directly. The researchers who investigated these changes claim that despite the blurring of the gendered boundaries, the entrance of women into these roles did not change the gendered hierarchical perception that is the core of the military-organizational logic. Women took up positions that were usually low status, and this was often associated with a structural change that diminished the status of the roles that they filled.[20] Moreover, as soon as these positions were identified as roles for women, men avoided taking on these roles. Amram-Katz points out that the army profited from this because it got highly qualified women and at the same time made these positions less attractive to men.

Jewish National Religious Logic

Israel is defined as the national state of the Jewish people. The definition of the Jewishness of the state is embedded in the religious tradition carried forward over many generations. However, the meaning of Jewishness was expanded and endowed with new aspects as secularism developed, on the one hand, and modern nationalism, on the other hand. Prompted by the desire to bridge the gaps between the perception of a modern state and that of Jewish tradition, compromises were made that accorded privileged status to religion in legislation and in various social arrangements, including those related to the military.[21]

Thus, the Security Service Act (1949) granted an exemption from military service to religiously observant women based on the reasons given by religious members of the Knesset, who expressed their concern for moral family values and female modesty that might be infringed in shared spaces. Additional reasoning was based on religious commandments forbidding women to carry instruments of war or to participate in war.

Other arrangements included the exemption of Ultraorthodox men who were studying in Yeshivas and incorporation of religious precepts, such as keeping kosher food regulations, observing the Sabbath—which prohibits carrying out any work or operation of any machinery—and the founding of the military Rabbinate. Until the early 1980s, most of the military Rabbinate's activity focused on shaping the Jewish character of the army, laying emphasis on observing the Sabbath and laws of kashrut, instilling knowledge about Jewish heritage, and creating conditions that enabled religious soldiers to play their part in the army, which was largely secular.

Over the years religious practices expanded by means of halakhic religious rulings on the subject of the army and war issued by the first military Chief Rabbi Goren.[22] In the initial decades after the establishment of the state, this did not find expression in the way the army was run, but the practices gradually expanded after the Six Day War, when proponents of religious Zionism who had been on the political and social sidelines in the army began to enter into the core political discourse and saw influence over the military as an avenue through which to reinforce their position. They looked on the occupation and its military command positions as a way of ensuring the dominance of their political and religious perception of the world.[23]

The inclusion of secular women in the first decades of the state had not constituted a problem from the religious point of view, both because the number of women soldiers was relatively small and because their army trajectories were separate, and this prevented intense interaction between men and women.[24]

To recap, up to the 1980s, the four logics, by and large, supported one another in shaping a gendered military structure. The mandatory enlisting of men and women did not challenge gendered perceptions. Women's entry into the military meant entering into a male domain. It was supported by the Western binary perception of private-public spheres that overlap the gender division of roles. Similarly, life under a protracted conflict has given priority to the security logic whereby men's role is protecting the family and women's roles are caregiving and nurturing. Masculinity is also at the basis of the organizational logic of the army structure. Women's inclusion depends on the military needs for the replacement of men. Thus, until the 1980s this entailed mainly service roles that supported the gendered structure. These perceptions fit perfectly with the national religious logic that supports gender separation according to halakhic norms. Processes of de-gendering of roles in the army expanded gradually after the 1967 Six Day War and the 1973 Yom Kippur War—first and foremost, owing to the army's own needs and largely owing to the need to respond to the political or economic priorities of the country's leaders. However, the basic gendered logics have not been challenged; disruption in the gendered order mostly followed the military bureaucratic logic that perceives women as substitutes for men. The turning point came in the encounter between processes that disrupted these gendered logics.

The Breakthrough: Reframing of the De-Gendering of the Army

Starting in the 1980s and through the turn of the century, the gendered division of roles as immovable was challenged. From a bureaucratic category based on an essentialist perception of men and women, there began a long-lasting process of disrupting the gender distinctions. The requirements of the organizational military logic to use personnel correlated with the broader social trends that were pressing for de-gendering the army.

I examine the processes of de-gendering the military as part of what is referred to in the literature of political sociology as state feminism. State feminism denotes the emergence of feminist or pro-feminist practices within the institutions of the state.[25] Analytically, feminist engagement with the state developed in three main consecutive perspectives.[26] The first is a demand for "adding women in"— advancing the presence of women in institutional bodies. Most of the demands come from below. The second is "extending the boundaries"—giving women a voice by promoting them into the ranks of policymakers in order to incorporate women's concerns and interests into policymaking. This is a mostly top-down approach. The third is a "re-conceptualizing of core concepts" by employing a strategy of gender mainstreaming. The three perspectives very often coexist, and moreover, the outcomes of these processes are not necessarily linear.

While most studies use this analytical scheme to analyze political changes, I suggest using these stages to analyze changes within the army as one of the major state institutions.

Descriptive Representation—Adding Women

During the 1990s military service ceased to be perceived only as a contribution to the collective and was increasingly considered an avenue through which to gain social mobility with symbolic and practical advantages. At the same time, the perception that the army was the only avenue through which to contribute to the collective identity eroded—particularly among the middle class.[27] Moreover, with the strengthening of civil and political discourse on rights and equality of opportunity, Israel underwent a constitutional revolution.[28] The political-legal arena became the site in which the struggle for de-gendering of the army was carried out.[29]

The military-organizational logic was challenged in 1995 by Alice Miller, a woman soldier who made an application to the High Court of Justice with the demand to allow her to apply for the prestigious pilot's course that was considered a combat course closed to women. She won her court case, and this led to an amendment to the Security Act (2000). The High Court of Justice's decision in Alice Miller's case forced the army to open all its ranks to women. Alice Miller's struggle was supported by the Women's Lobby, the Association for Civil Rights, and then–member of Knesset Naomi Chazan. In the wake of this court ruling, the Security Service Act was amended in 2000 to say that women had the same rights as men to serve in any position.[30]

All of this led the army to take some important steps to de-gender basic organizational practices that challenged the boundaries between women and men. Various mechanisms, which distinguished between men and women, were dismantled. The first step was the abolition of the Women's Corps (2001). Then joint training programs for men and women officers replaced the previously segregated courses, basic training exercises, and vocational courses, which became mostly gender-integrated. In many domains the training was determined by the soldier's intended job and not by gender. Women entered new technical combat support roles, such as freight truck drivers and auto mechanics. At the same time, there was a reduction in the proportion of women in clerical jobs that had been identified as, and in many cases still are considered to be, the main role of women in the army.[31] Combat roles previously closed to women, such as positions in the naval officer's course and security units in the border guard—including on the boundaries between Israel and the Palestinian Authority—opened up. A low-intensity combat regiment composed of men and women was established, and it was stationed on the peaceful borders with Egypt and Jordan. These changes made the army more dependent on women in crucial operational roles. Studies indicate that the map of gendered occupations changed: the proportion of mixed jobs rose from 16 percent to 66 percent. Nevertheless, even after the gradual changes, more than 20 percent of jobs remained dominated by either men or women.[32]

Institutionalization of gender equality and the aspiration to remove all impediments to equal integration were formalized in a 2004 amendment to the General Staff Order that included the following statement: "Every man and woman soldier has an equal right to fill any position in the army service, or to carry out any activity during that service, unless the essential character of the job or activity does not make this possible."[33] Research on women in combat roles reveals that their integration is based on "exclusionary inclusion," meaning they are channeled to different jobs and tasks within the combat units.[34] The model of the soldier remained mostly masculine. Women took up positions that had previously been closed to them, but to a great extent, the expectation was that they would behave like men and view masculine practices as the fulfillment of military service. The strategy of "adding women" failed to question the basic gendered perception of the IDF.

Extending the Boundaries—Bringing in Women's Voices

The second phase of state feminism is based on the idea of "extending the boundaries" by giving a voice to women within institutions and incorporating women's concerns into policymaking and policy-implementing processes. Hernes, who coined the term "state feminism," emphasizes the dynamic relationships between governmental policies and agents (feminism from above) and the mobilization of women in political and cultural activities (feminism from below).[35] In the military case, the processes of de-gendering were accompanied by the creation of the role of advisor on women's issues to the chief of staff in 2001. A research department was also established to investigate gender equality and to expose mechanisms that created inequality. Sasson-Levy notes that the position of advisor is, by its very nature, a conflicted one.[36] It is part and parcel of the military system, and at the same time, its role is to challenge the system and to promote the status of women in the army. To overcome the role's internal and inherent limitations, women scholars from outside the army were invited to take part in the research setup and the planning teams. The various research studies conducted in this framework have become an important tool for critique and for creative thinking about the methods of change and ways to cope with gender inequality.

A major step in incorporating women's concerns into the army policy began with a systematic enforcement of a policy against sexual harassment. It is worth mentioning that the army's commitment to prevent sexual harassment already existed in a general staff order of 1978, well before the general law in the country was passed in 1998. However, it was rarely enforced. The broad systemic enforcement of the order and the various amendments introduced in general staff orders took place following the state legislation. The major amendments related to the utilizing of power relations. The division of the army women's advisor began to conduct surveys of sexual harassment reporting. These surveys show that the law and ordinances prohibiting social harassment are well-known in the system and were followed by a decrease in reports of practices of sexual harassment, but they did not disappear.[37] Researchers claim that the drop in the number of those reporting sexual harassment is more an indication of women soldiers' lack of trust in the military system and its treatment of the matter rather than an actual decrease in the prevalence of sexual harassment.[38] Moreover, a study of male soldiers in all ranks found that familiarity with the law is not translated into internalization of a gender egalitarian worldview of power. Law and the ordinance are imposed through means rather than cultural assimilation.[39]

Challenges of Gender Mainstreaming

The third stage of state feminism relates to gender mainstreaming and signifies paradigmatic changes in the way policies were formulated. Accordingly, it is not enough to follow flows of information from above and below. It is also crucial to analyze the feminist perspective framing interpretations and actions of all agents involved in policymaking, implementation, and especially the public.

The idea of gender mainstreaming, the integration of gender perspective across programs and policies, is based on the theoretical shift in feminist thought that claims that the gendered structure is rooted in deep thought patterns and social arrangements that translate these patterns into everyday practices. Thus, gender mainstreaming is a process of revision of key concepts and practices.[40] It requires a radical redefinition of policy values and practice in order to change the gendered world.[41]

It is precisely because gendered practices filter down into every social site that integration of gender perspective into the army could not arise voluntarily from the goodwill of that organization or the public or from its commitment to an equitable social order. It requires multilevel transformative strategies.[42]

Moreover, the commitment to responsiveness and sensitivity to women's experiences requires a move from the binary approach of men versus women to the intersectionality perspective that takes into consideration various systems of inequality.[43] Thus, the challenge for gender-mainstreaming policy is to incorporate gender perspectives into mainstream policies.[44]

In the Israeli case, from the middle of the first decade of the twenty-first century, army researchers claimed that the army could not be treated as a unified organization and that, in practice, there are various "armies," each operating according to different logics.[45] There are strong correlations among ethnic origin, class, and gender in enlistment in these units, and there are clear hierarchies among them: the prestigious combat units, the technical units that are mostly blue-collar vocational units, and the home guard units.[46] Women who serve in different "armies" don't have the same experiences or the same opportunities. Thus, for example, women who volunteer for combat units that are more prestigious have a strong tendency toward de-gendering the service. However, at the same time, they have to adopt the masculine model of the fighter. Studies show that officers' training courses serve simultaneously as a mechanism for de-gendering and re-gendering.[47]

In low-prestige technical support jobs, the army is interested in de-gendering—recruiting women who are often of higher quality than the men—but many of these women, like their male colleagues, do not want to serve in these units that lack prestige. They are put in undesirable jobs and encounter demeaning and discriminatory attitudes from the male soldiers and commanders who re-gender their experience. Hence, they pay the price of de-gendering enjoyed by women who volunteer for prestigious combat units. On the other hand, in the support units and roles, women find themselves in positions that reproduce traditional perceptions.[48] Gendered occupational assignments direct many women into clerical jobs and replicate the perception that a woman's place is in the private-domestic sphere and that she carries these skills with her when she enters the public sphere. As the "office wife," the woman is expected to take on traditional feminine roles, like cleaning the office, taking care of food and drink, and at times serving as a hostess for those invited to discussions with the commanding officer. This replicates the traditional division of labor, emphasizes power relations, and marks the work of the female clerk as nonprofessional.[49] A study conducted by Sasson-Levy, commissioned by the advisor on women's issues, found that making coffee was felt by many women soldiers to be demeaning and over time became the essence and characteristic of the whole job.[50] An attempt to abolish this demand to carry out personal services for commanders by means of clear, official rules was never issued.[51]

In 2007, at the recommendation of the advisor on women's issues and with the support of the head of the Division of Human Resources, the Segev Committee was established to examine women's service in the IDF.[52] Though not formally declared, the background to this move was UN Security Council Resolution 1325 of October 2000.[53] The resolution, which calls for gender mainstreaming in peacemaking and conflict resolution, especially in armed conflict zones, prompted changes to policies for women's integration in armed forces in many countries.[54]

The Segev Committee was assigned three tasks: to examine the situation at the time of the committee's establishment; to make note of existing gaps as compared with values, social aspects, and the utilization of personnel; and to formulate operational proposals for the integration of women and their utilization in military service. Committee members included representatives from various corps; experts in physiology; researchers from diverse relevant fields such as organizational sociology, gender scholars, military experts; and representatives of various civil society organizations who were invited to participate at the pleasure of the committee head and with the approval of the army.[55] A comprehensive survey of models for integrating women used in various armies in the North Atlantic Treaty Organization (NATO) was presented to the committee. The Segev Committee drafted a formative document that outlined the principles for integrating gender mainstreaming. Emphasis was placed on "the need for a fundamental change and an organized, systematic and well-budgeted arrangement starting with the planning stage, equipment, acquisitions, training programs and personnel programs."[56] During the discussions in the committee, disputes arose among committee members who supported gender mainstreaming and those who opposed an equitable integration of women. Some members expected the committee to recommend a return to the gendered patterns of women's service, calling for the need to exclude women from combat roles and command roles in the field. This position was characteristic of some of the officers' attitudes even if it was not openly expressed. Moreover, representatives of the national religious lobby who appeared before the committee clearly stated their opposition to equitable military service for women. Their reasoning was based on various studies conducted in other countries that told of the difficulties faced by women in combat positions, but also largely on internationally renowned Israeli military historian Martin van Creveld. Using the security logic, Van Creveld claimed that the inclusion of women in armies caused those armies to weaken.

Sasson-Levy uses this case to illustrate the reciprocal influence and the tendency for isomorphism among militaries. She claims that all members of the Segev Committee studied the gender arrangements in foreign militaries and used their knowledge to justify their pro or con stance regarding women's integration in the army.[57]

Despite the objections the Segev Committee unanimously recommended the adoption of strategies for the integration of gender mainstreaming. The dominant principle decided on by the committee was the replacement of military service based on gender by the principle of "the right person in the right job." The committee also recommended the implementation of gender mainstreaming in the entire military system so that it would become an integral part of decision-making processes, planning, and oversight. In its recommendations, the committee addressed the issues of recruitment, classification, duration of service, training, building, equipment, combat, and budgeting and also endorsed the creation of a clear-cut gender code that would ensure equitable treatment, respectful and efficacious for men and women in everyday life in the army.

Owing to political pressures, the committee report was not published and was not adopted in its entirety. Tzipi Hotovely, a female member of Knesset for the right-wing Likud Party, a religiously observant woman who headed the Knesset Committee on the Status of Women, agreed to discuss the Segev report in her committee after many attempts to persuade her on the part of women's organizations. But the debate took place without the participants' receiving the report, so the discussion did not allow for an explanation of the serious meaning of integrating gender mainstreaming into the reorganization of the army. Lerer argues that it would not have been possible to reject the committee's recommendations on professional, rational, or legal grounds.[58] In other words the Segev report appropriated the military organizational logic, claiming that the military in general would benefit from gender mainstreaming. In practice the status of the recommendations remained vague even though the overall vision was adopted. The methods for implementing them remained dependent on negotiation and changing organizational practices. Some sections of the report have filtered down into practices, interpretations, and inconsistent decisions adopted in negotiations between the various military entities, including the advisor on women's issues.

From the 1990s onward, as the analysis shows, strategies were developed for de-gendering the army and integrating women into various units, including diverse field units. This process stood in stark contrast to the strengthening of the religious contents in military arrangements. In those years there was a turning point in the composition of military service for national-religious soldiers. Preparatory programs for military service were established, and these looked on military service as having a special value in and of itself. The men received a one-year postponement of their military service and, upon completion of their pre-military program, enlisted in the army in the regular way.[59] The rabbis at the preparatory programs encouraged participants to enlist in mixed units of men and women, although this was opposed to their previous inclination to have them congregate in homogeneous religious units. Within a few years, the proportion of those enlisting in combat service in command roles increased, and they began to constitute a critical mass in combat units alongside secular soldiers; they demanded recognition of their special needs. Among other things this included demands for gender separation on the grounds of religious and halakhic norms mandating modesty and gender separation.[60]

From the organizational point of view, the military service of both groups—women and the national religious—became essential for the army together with the integration of these groups into combat lineups, combat support professions, and training roles. However, pressure from rabbis outside the army as well as from religious soldiers and commanders within the army resulted in the 2002 formulation of rules governing "appropriate service." The aim of these rules was to facilitate the joint service of women and religious soldiers without excluding women but with due consideration given to the needs of religious soldiers. These rules referred to modest clothing, separation of men's and women's living quarters, and separate training of men and women wherever there was a concern about physical contact or being at close quarters. These rules stated that religiously observant soldiers could not be compelled to serve in a mixed combat unit. Initially, this move was supposed to facilitate women's military service, but religious entities outside the army as well as within it took steps to use this as a means for excluding women from mixed units. Pressure from the religious leaders to adopt a narrow interpretation of the appropriate integration grew. In 2004 an administrative body on appropriate integration was established; in effect this became a kind of modesty police force and a mechanism for excluding women. The army conducts continuous negotiation about the interpretation of the order in relation to field operations as well as military and nonmilitary rabbis.[61] This activity is part of the resurgence of religiosity that the army is undergoing. It involves the strengthening of the power of the Military Chief Rabbinate and increasing involvement of the political forces of the national religious bodies both inside and outside the army. The undeclared aim is to subjugate the army not only to religious values but also to the political agenda.

The order on appropriate integration became a mechanism for re-gendering: some of the officers' training courses were made separate, the physical strength testing requirements were increased, and the character of the gendered tasks was changed.[62] These trends corresponded with the masculine logic that attempts to preserve the perception of the combatant as the archetype of masculinity.[63]

The efforts to re-gender the military took place at the same time the Segev Committee recommended an equitable model of service and gender-mainstreaming policy to de-gender army service. Even though there were many attempts to delegitimize the members of the Segev Committee, particularly the female members, the committee's recommendations that equal opportunity for a meaningful and respectful service should be granted in accordance with skills and abilities was formally accepted.[64] In practice 8 percent of all the professions in the army, mostly those connected with attacking and conducting maneuvers, are still closed to women. The proportion of women combatants is 4 percent of all combatants.[65] Women's jobs are still on the periphery of combat roles.

Beginning in the late 1990s, new actors entered the de/re-gendering pendulum: religious women who enlist in the army despite the rabbis' opposition. Owing to the army's desperate need for personnel, it is promoting this recruitment, making accommodations for religious women, and ensuring that they are satisfied with the jobs they are given. In the army's Division of Personnel, a section was created to deal with religious women. The jobs suited for them were expanded, and they are assigned to them in groups so as to make it easier for them to function in a secular milieu. In 2009 a female officer was appointed in the military Rabbinate to support the integration of women, and for the first time, a religious woman was appointed as the advisor on women's issues. This integration of religious women raises the question of whether the appropriate integration will be suppressed and the separation between men and women reinforced. Since the numbers of these women are still low, it is too early to answer this question. It is possible that since these women are mostly members of the national-religious camp, they are likely to support the men's position that segregation between men and women should be reinforced in military service.

Conclusion

The Israeli case demonstrates that internal military gender regimes intersect with cultural and political forces within and outside the military itself. A sociohistorical overview of women's military service in the IDF shows that. Four intra- and inter-logics act simultaneously as formal and informal mechanisms of gendering and de-gendering the structure, organizational norms, and practices of the Israeli army. The Western political logic brought about the legislation of universal conscription but simultaneously exempted married women owing to the binary perception of the private/domestic that is taken for granted and the public spheres that espoused a gendered division of roles. The dominance of the security logic that says the state is under a protracted security threat bolsters this gendered perception. So too do the logics of Jewish religious tradition. These combined into a military logic that views the army, especially the combat forces, as belonging to the world of men and as an expression of masculinity. Up to the end of the 1980s, there was a clear distinction between the military service of men and of women. But beginning in the 1990s, various notions disrupted the gendered structure. The increasing needs of the army led to the opening of various positions to women, but filling these positions was still subject to the logic of "women replacing men." Beginning with the end of the 1990s, it is possible to identify changing attitudes that pressed for the reframing of women's service.

The military is undeniably an arm of the state, and for that reason I have proposed viewing the changes in the light of varying perceptions of the feminist discourse. In the initial phase, there were claims, based on the resurgence of the discourse on rights and equality of opportunity, accompanied by demands for representation. The Alice Miller case in the High Court of Justice resulted in the abolition of organizational mechanisms that distinguish between men and women and even brought about a change in the Security Service Act. In the second phase, the army was expected to exhibit gender sensitivity toward women's needs and concerns, and in the third phase, with the establishment of the Segev Committee, the concept of gender mainstreaming began to filter down. Together these phases acted to disrupt the gendered structure of the army. Nonetheless, the gendering logics still view—particularly in combat roles—men and masculinity as the essence of military service and, therefore, continue to be the major forces that reproduce gendered structures.

From the 1990s, dramatic reframing of gender inclusion in the military was supported by feminist civilian advocacy and the political climate of the time, but at the beginning of the new millennium, new religious actors have actively engaged in re-gendering the army. This is related to the increasing commitment of national-religious groups to enlist in the army and to take on senior command roles. From individual claims connected with religious ideology on behalf of religiously observant soldiers and up to the appropriate integration order that enables them to serve in a mixed army, their actions moved over to the army's internal politics even as the senior officers convert this into the army's special interest. These processes act to segregate men and women and to re-gender or to call a halt to the process of de-gendering of various jobs, particularly in field missions and in combat units. The army's dependence both on women and on religious soldiers leaves in effect the dual processes of gendering and de-gendering alongside each other.

The Israeli case suggests that the army is a dynamic changing hybrid organization that is continuously shaped at the intersections of inter- and intra-sociocultural forces. Thus, while there are commonalities among armies, policies for social integration of women should take into consideration the local forces operating in a given society. Any policy for social change should be aware of those forces.

The second important lesson is that the complex intersections among forces operating within and outside the military organization create a pendulum of gendering and de-gendering processes. Thus, there is no one clear, linear trend of development but rather a multitude of facets of gendering and de-gendering processes that often exist simultaneously.

Women have already disrupted the gendered regime of militaries. The de-gendering processes that enabled women to enter a variety of roles previously considered "male" increase the dependence of the military on women power. This is a springboard for negotiation about their rights, needs, and roles.

Last but not least is the fact that in situations of protracted armed conflict when the tendency is to recruit more men, women's interests must be given greater consideration so as to pave the way for peaceful solutions.

Notes

1. It is important to note that compulsory military service applies to the Jewish population only; Palestinian Arab citizens of Israel— except for the Druze population, which is included in the law, and the Bedouins, who are entitled to volunteer—are exempt from military service. Military service is a powerful mechanism for marking out the boundaries between Jewish and Palestinian citizens of Israel. It forms the distinction between the liberal principle of citizenship and the republican principle that mainly refers to Jews. See Gershon Shafir and Yoav Peled, *Being Israeli: The Dynamics of Multiple Citizenship* (Cambridge: Cambridge University Press, 2002).
2. Dafna N. Izraeli, "Gendering Military Service in Israeli Defence Forces," *Israel Social Science Research* 12, no. 1 (1997): 129–66; Iris Jerby, *Double Price: Women Status and Military Service in Israel* [in Hebrew] (Tel Aviv: Ramot Publication, 1996).
3. Izraeli, "Gendering Military Service"; Orna Sasson-Levy, "Constructing Identities at the Margins: Masculinities and Citizenship in the Israeli Army," *Sociological Quarterly* 43, no. 3 (2002): 357–83. Owing to the central importance of the army in Israel, military research is multifaceted. For a survey of studies on the army and gender and trends in their development from a theoretical and empirical perspective, see Orna Sasson-Levy, "The Military in a Globalized Environment: Perpetuating an 'Extremely Gendered' Organization," in *Handbook of Gender, Work and Organization*, ed. Emma Jeanes, David Knights, and Patricia Yancey Martin, 391–410 (Oxford: Wiley-Blackwell, 2011).
4. Cynthia Enloe, *Does Khaki Become You? The Militarization of Women's Lives* (London: Pandora / HarperCollins, 1988); Carole Pateman, *The Disorder of Women: Democracy, Feminism and Political Theory* (Cambridge: Polity Press, 1989); and Sasson-Levy, "Military in a Globalized Environment."
5. Raewyn W. Connell, *Gender and Power: Society, the Person and Sexual Politics* (Stanford, CA: Stanford University Press, 1987); Judith Lorber, *Breaking the Bowls—Degendering and Feminist Change* (New York: W.W. Norton, 2005). See also Orna Sasson-Levy and Sarit Amram-Katz, "Gender Integration in Israeli Officer Training: Degendering and Regendering the Military," *Signs* 33, no. 1 (2007): 105–35.
6. Mady Wechsler Segal, "Women's Military Roles Cross-Nationally: Past, Present, and Future," *Gender and Society* 9, no. 6 (1995): 757–75. In the Israeli case, during the Second World War, women took part in fighting organizations that preceded the establishment of the state. They joined Jewish units and British ones in which they made up some 20 percent of the personnel. Women were perceived not only as participating in the support units but also as serving as equals in field positions and as combatants; to put it another way, they proved themselves to be able and worthy. However, various studies have shattered the myth that there was gender equality in these organizations; see Orna Sasson-Levy, "Research on Gender and the Military in Israel: From a Gendered Organization to Inequality Regimes," *Israel Studies Review* 26, no. 2 (2011): 73–98.

7. Nira Yuval Davis and Floya Anthias, *Women-Nation-Gender* (London: Macmillan, 1989).
8. Sarit Amram-Katz, "From Coffee to Rifle: Gendering and Disruption in the People's Army," [in Hebrew] in *Sociology of the People's Army*, ed. Hadass Ben Eliyahu and Ze'ev Lerer (Tel Aviv: Association of Military Sociology, 2009). In practice the idea of modernity and Westernization marked the immigrants from the Arab countries as lacking in suitable resources, and the army through its sorting and selection methods for the various military corps became the mechanism that paved the way for these immigrants to be diverted to lower-valued jobs; it reproduced the ethnic-class inequality and thereby contributed to the formation of the Mizrahi identity in Israel. Maurice Roumani, "The Military, Ethnicity, and Integration in Israel Revisited," *Armed Forces and Society* 3 (1991): 51–80; Sasson-Levy, "Constructing Identities."
9. Nitza Berkovitch, "Motherhood as a National Mission: The Construction of Womanhood in the Legal Discourse in Israel," *Women Studies International Forum* 20, no. 5 (1997): 605–19; Shafir and Peled, *Being Israeli*.
10. Ze'ev Lerer and Hadass Ben-Eliyahu, "The People's Armies: Structure, Identities and Supervison," in Ben-Eliyahu and Lerer, *Sociology of the People's Army*, 396.
11. There is selective conscription of different groups by means of the army's selection strategies as well as exemption for military service on the grounds of religion, particularly for Ultraorthodox men. It is worth noting that gender identity was not a reason for discrimination in the early years of the army, largely because many remained in the closet until the late 1970s, but also because the army never treated gender identity as a criterion in selection processes.
12. Berkovitch, "Motherhood"; Joyce Robbins and Uri Ben Eliezer, "New Roles or 'New Times'? Gender Inequality and Militarism in Israel's Nation-in-Arms," *Social Politics* 7, no. 4 (2000): 309–42.
13. Hanna Herzog and Ronen Shamir, "Media Discourse on Jewish/Arab Relations," *Israel Social Science Research* 9, nos. 1–2 (1994): 82.
14. Asher Arian, *Security Threatened: Surveying Israeli Opinion on Peace and War* (Cambridge: Jaffee Center for Strategic Studies, Tel Aviv University, and Cambridge University Press, 1995), 24–53; Hanna Herzog, "Gendering the Discourse on Occupation: A Sociological Perspective," in *The Impacts of Lasting Occupation Lessons from Israeli Society*, ed. Daniel Bar-Tal and Izhak Schnell, 359–79 (Oxford: Oxford University Press, 2013).
15. Sara Helman, "Militarism and the Construction of Community," *Journal of Political and Military Sociology* 25 (Winter 1997): 305–32.
16. Hanna Herzog, "Homefront and Battlefront and the Status of Jewish and Palestinian Women in Israel," *Israeli Studies* 3, no. 1 (1998): 61–84; Herzog, "Gendering the Discourse."
17. Nira Yuval Davis, "Front and Rear: The Sexual Division of Labor in the Israeli Army," *Feminist Studies* 11, no. 3 (1985): 649–75; Berkovitch, "Motherhood."
18. Amram-Katz, "From Coffee to Rifle."
19. Izraeli, "Gendering Military Service"; Robbins and Ben Eliezer, "New Roles."
20. Amram-Katz, "From Coffee to Rifle."
21. Yagil Levy, *The Divine Commander: The Theocratization of the Israeli Military* (Tel Aviv: Am Oved, 2015).
22. Halakhic religious rulings are the collective body of Jewish religious laws and regulations derived from the written and oral Torah that dictates people's behavior in everyday life.
23. For an expanded discussion of this issue, see Levy, *Divine Commander*.

24. Levy, *Divine Commander*, 250–52.
25. Jonathan Dean, *Rethinking Contemporary Feminist Politics* (Basingstoke: Palgrave Macmillan, 2010); Dorothy E. McBride and Amy Mazur, *Comparative State Feminism* (Thousand Oaks, CA: Sage, 1995).
26. Judith Squires, *The New Politics of Gender Equality* (Basingstoke: Palgrave Macmillan, 2007).
27. Yagil Levy, Edna Lomsky-Feder, and Noa Harel, "From 'Obligatory Militarism' to 'Contractual Militarism': Competing Models of Citizenship," *Israel Studies* 12, no. 1 (2007).
28. Noya Rimalt, *Legal Feminism from Theory to Practice: The Struggle for Gender Equality in Israel and the United States* [in Hebrew] (Haifa: Pardes Publishers, 2010).
29. Guy I. Seidman and Eyal A. Nun, "Women, the Military and the Court: Israel at 2001," *Review of Law and Women's Studies* 11 (2001): 91–154.
30. Noya Rimalt, "From Law to Politics: The Path to Gender Equality," *Israel Studies* 18, no. 3 (2013): 5–28.
31. Orna Sasson-Levy, "Contradictory Consequences of Mandatory Conscription: The Case of Women Secretaries in the Israeli Military," *Gender and Society* 21, no. 4 (2007).
32. Amram-Katz, "From Coffee to Rifle," 97–99.
33. Levy, *Divine Commander*, 250.
34. Amram-Katz, "From Coffee to Rifle."
35. Helga Marina Hernes, *Welfare State and Woman Power: Essays in State Feminism* (Oslo: Norwegian University Press, 1987), 153.
36. Sasson-Levy, "Military in a Globalized Environment."
37. Shelly Shtarker and Yael Topel, *Sexual Harassment in the IDF: Study among Women Soldiers and Officers in Conscript Service* [in Hebrew] (Tel Aviv: Advisor on Women's Issues to the Chief of Staff, IDF, 2007).
38. Ibid.; Sasson-Levy, "Military in a Globalized Environment," 82.
39. Yael Topel, "Gender, Discourse, and Sexuality in Organizations: Social Construction of Sexual Harassment among Men in the Israeli Defense Force" (PhD diss., Tel Aviv University, 2017).
40. Emanuela Lombardo, "Integrating or Setting the Agenda? Gender Mainstreaming in the European Constitution-Making Process," *Social Politics* 12, no. 3 (2005): 296–311; Sylvia Walby, "Gender Mainstreaming: Productive Tensions in Theory and Practice," *Social Politics: International Studies in Gender, State and Society* 12, no. 3 (2005): 321–43.
41. Alison Woodward, "European Gender Mainstreaming: Promises and Pitfalls of Transformative Policy," *Review of Policy Research* 20, no. 1 (2003): 65–88.
42. Carol Bacchi and Joan Eveline, *Mainstreaming Politics: Gendering Practices and Feminist Theory* (Adelaide: University of Adelaide Press, 2010); Teresa Rees, "Reflections on the Uneven Development of Gender Mainstreaming in Europe," *International Feminist Journal of Politics* 7, no. 4 (2005): 555–74.
43. Joan Acker, "Inequality Regimes: Gender, Class, and Race in Organizations," *Gender and Society* 20, no. 4 (2006): 441–64.
44. Emanuela Lombardo and Lut Mergaert, "Gender Mainstreaming and Resistance to Gender Training: A Framework for Studying Implementation," *NORA—Nordic Journal of Feminist and Gender Research* 21, no. 4 (2013): 296–311; Mieke Verloo, "Multiple Inequalities, Intersectionality and the European Union," *European Journal of Women's Studies* 3 (2006): 211–29.
45. Ibid.

46. Ibid.; Orna Sasson-Levy, "Military, Masculinity and Citizenship: Tensions and Contradictions in the Experience of Blue-Collar Soldiers," *Identities: Global Studies in Culture and Power* 10, no. 3 (2003): 319–45.
47. Sasson-Levy and Amram-Katz, "Gender Integration."
48. Amram-Katz, "From Coffee to Rifle"; Lerer and Ben-Eliyahu, "People's Armies."
49. Sasson-Levy and Amram-Katz, "Gender Integration."
50. Sasson-Levy, "Military, Masculinity and Citizenship."
51. Ze'ev Lerer, *Equality for Women in the IDF? The Tenth Anniversary of the Amendment to the Security Law* [in Hebrew] (Jerusalem: Center for the Advancement of Women in the Public Sphere, Van Leer Jerusalem Institute, 2010), 8n15.
52. The committee was named after Gen. (Res.) Yehuda Segev, who headed it. Segev served as the head of the Personnel Division in 1998–2001.
53. Lerer, *Equality for Women*.
54. Sasson-Levy, "Military in a Globalized Environment."
55. For the purposes of full disclosure, I was a member of the committee. However, since the report of the committee was not approved for publication, the discussion of what transpired in the committee will be confined to information that reached the public in various contexts, such as the debate in the Knesset Committee on the Status of Women and conferences and articles that referred to the subject.
56. Lerer, *Equality for Women*, 8.
57. Sasson-Levy, "Military in a Globalized Environment."
58. Lerer, *Equality for Women*, 17.
59. As mentioned previously, religiously observant women are exempt from conscription. Those wishing to contribute to the state can volunteer for civilian national service.
60. Yagil Levy, "The Clash between Feminism and Religion in the Israeli Military: A Multilayered Analysis," *Social Politics: International Studies in Gender, State and Society* 17, no. 2 (2010): 127–48.
61. Levy, *Divine Commander*, 266–72.
62. Sasson-Levy and Amram-Katz, "Gender Integration."
63. Lerer, *Equality for Women*, 15–17.
64. Sasson-Levy, "Military in a Globalized Environment," 90; Levy, *Divine Commander*, 277.
65. Levy, *Divine Commander*, 278.

The Case of Australia
From "Culture" Reforms to a Culture of Rights

Susan Harris Rimmer

For many Australian women, the story of Lt. Cdr. Robyn Fahy, aired on Australian television in 2006, remains hard to forget. Fahy was the first female graduate of the Australian Defence Force Academy (ADFA) in 1987 and graduated top of her class. When she made her way to the front to collect the award, her uniform was soaking in spit from her angry colleagues. She told the national broadcaster about her time in the academy, "I can't remember a day where I wasn't punched or hit, or slapped or spat upon."[1]

Flashing forward to late 2015, Australia appointed its first female defense minister with the unexpected promotion of Senator Marise Payne.[2] This appointment capped a decade of significant reform and interest in the integration of women in the Australian armed forces—albeit a decade filled with scandals, world famous responses to said scandals, strategies, and setbacks. The Australian example is noteworthy because the gender equality agenda remains cogent and urgent despite a range of policy responses, including "culture" reviews (examined in depth later in the chapter) and the lifting of restrictions on frontline combat roles. Can strategic reform really be achieved through responding to scandalous incidents rather than through a proactive commitment to reform?

More modest reforms have taken place in relation to the application of gender perspectives in military operations through the adoption of the Australian National Action Plan on Women, Peace, and Security, new gender advisor positions, doctrinal reforms, and Australia's ongoing work as a nonmember contributor to the North Atlantic Treaty Organization (NATO). The Australian

Defence Force (ADF) is not alone in these reforms, as the Australian Federal Police and Australia's diplomatic corps are also seeking to strengthen gender integration and policy at the strategic level.

The two pillars of gender equity and gender perspectives reform have been pursued separately in the ADF and have proceeded in fits and starts. The February 2016 defense white paper should be seen as a modest breakthrough in that it did mention links between internal and external reform.[3] It stops short of making clear that the best warrior for a mission may be a woman.

The key finding of this analysis is that the reforms in the ADF have been highly dependent on certain personnel and external drivers rather than on a systemic approach to creating a modern armed force fit for purpose. This dependence is disappointing in an institution that aims for excellence in strategic thinking and planning. The internal and external goals are clearly linked as a high order imperative to have the best "capability" in terms of "enabling workforce" and the best chance of operational success in population-centric operations. However, the modernization impulse is often limited to equipment and technology rather than to habits of gender analysis. There is still too little accountability placed on the ADF for gender equality outcomes either at home or abroad. The objective for this chapter is to demonstrate that the last decade has set shaky foundations for more sustained reforms, if political will could be focused to that end. The Australian Parliament should be more focused on the quest to modernize the armed forces and change the "warrior" culture to suit modern society and contemporary military operations, should insist that the ADF be more receptive to the feedback of external actors, and should insist on the ADF's accountability to Parliament.

Background: About the ADF

The Australian Defence Force began at the birth of the commonwealth in 1901. It consists of the Royal Australian Navy (RAN), the Australian Army, the Royal Australian Air Force (RAAF), and several "tri-service" units, all volunteers. The 2016 defense white paper sets out plans for the permanent ADF workforce to increase to around 62,400 over the next decade to return it to its largest size since 1993. The white paper also provides for a future Australian Public Service (APS) workforce of around 18,200 full-time equivalent (FTE) employees, down from 22,300 FTE employees in June 2012. Around 2,500 ADF personnel are currently deployed on operations overseas and on border protection duties.

The ADF has been active in thirteen major conflicts since 1901, usually through alliances with the United Kingdom and the United States ("forward defense"). The Australian mainland came under attack by Japan in World War II during 1942–43.[4] Australia's most famous military engagement was defeat at Gallipoli at the hands of the Turks in World War I (1915). The battle is celebrated every April 25 as Australian and New Zealand Army Corps (ANZAC) Day, a national holiday with services and veteran marches.[5] The Australia, New Zealand, and United States Security Treaty (ANZUS Treaty), signed in 1951, remains key to Australian security. Australia and the US have run the Joint Defence Facility Pine Gap, an intelligence center in Central Australia, since 1966. Since April 2012, 2,500 US Marines rotate through Marine Air-Ground Task Force in Darwin.

Owing to Australia's geography and climate, the ADF plays an important "aid to the civil power" role. The ADF supports state and territory emergency response personnel to help communities respond to natural disasters such as floods and bushfires and is often deployed to assist in disaster response through the near region.

The 2016 defense white paper sets out Australia's strategic defense interest as "a secure, resilient Australia."[6] The three strategic defense objectives underpinning that aim are as follows:

1. to deter, deny, and defeat any attempt by a hostile country or non-state actor to attack, threaten, or coerce Australia;
2. to secure the nearer region, encompassing maritime Southeast Asia and the South Pacific (the ADF will support the governments of Papua New Guinea, Timor-Leste, and the Pacific island countries to build and strengthen their security); and
3. to ensure stability of the Indo-Pacific region and rules-based global order that supports Australian interests.

The government plans to fund the white paper goals by increasing the defense budget to 2 percent of Australia's gross domestic product by 2020–21, providing approximately $195 billion over ten years.

Methodology

This research is informed by a feminist methodology focused on gender equality and gender-based violence against women and men. Gender refers to "the economic, social, political and cultural attributes and opportunities associated with being male and female."[7] Gender-based violence is also defined by the United Nations in the 1993 UN Declaration on the Elimination of Violence against Women. Sex is not gender. As Hilary Charlesworth explains,

First, it [sex] links gender with biology, implying that gender is a fixed, objective fact about a person. It does not capture the ways in which gender is constructed in a particular society so as to make some actions seem natural and others controversial. It reaffirms the "naturalness" of female/male identities and bypasses the performative aspects of gender.... Most significantly, the association of the term "gender" primarily with women leaves both the roles of men and male gender identities unexamined, as though they were somehow natural and immutable.[8]

I seek to examine the following question through the lens of the lived experience of women held against human rights standards; as Enloe might say, What if the ADF were designed to fulfill the rights of women?[9] During the research phase of this chapter, activist colleagues outside the defense community often told me that feminist academic engagement with the gender reforms at the ADF was misplaced—at best naive, at worst a waste of energy and time. There is considerable academic debate on the subject of gender reform in the military between those opposed to women's military participation in any form and those who support gender reform.[10] Australia is not alone. In Canada, Ireland, and the US, we see scandal-motivated reforms, ongoing struggles with implementation, and the legacy of gender restrictions in deployment.

Encouraging reforms in the ADF could itself be seen as anti-feminist. As Cynthia Enloe writes, "The newest maneuver has been to camouflage women's service to the military as women's liberation."[11] To put the argument in essence, militaries and militarism are hardwired to oppress women; this oppression is inherent in an organization that defines itself by positing women as "the other."[12] There is serious doubt about whether re-gendering the military is possible if its primary function remains organizing the use of violence to achieve national objectives devised by groups that include few women. Therefore, women and men who do not embrace a hypermasculine culture should not be encouraged to follow military careers.

At the same time, most feminist strains encourage choice for women in every sphere of life, respect for sexual diversity, and wider acceptance of diversity in masculinity. Empirically, considerable progress has been made in policy frameworks, strategy, and training, reinforced by developments in regional security institutions such as NATO.[13]

Indeed, the current reform process includes a degree of ritualism, but I do believe that research and engagement is timely, if only to refresh and inform complex discussions within the ADF and Department of Defence. Former lieutenant general David Morrison AO, chief of army, said at a UN Commission for the Status of Women side event in New York: "We do need to bond our soldiers to one another and instil toughness and resilience into them. But when this goal is invoked to degrade and demonise women and other minorities it is undermining rather than enhancing capability. We need to define the true meaning of teamwork to embrace a band of brothers and sisters."[14] This kind of sentiment, even if still instrumentalist, might be encouraged by feminist scholars.[15] The ADF is a site of resources (195 billion AUD) and constitutional power in Australian society. The women within the ADF and Defence Department are citizens with agency who deserve support and accountability for violations of their human rights. In my view the reforms deserve scrutiny, and if the reforms are to succeed, then a measure of engagement unencumbered (but perhaps tempered) by cynicism is necessary.

As a theoretical framework for this analysis, I consider what the sociological literature calls "total institutions" that might be seen as similar to the ADF and explain its resistance to certain norms. Total institutions are defined by sociologist Erving Goffman as those institutions in which the "subjects' every movements, choices, and behaviour are governed by institutional objectives and influence, wherein the rituals of daily life occur in the company of others."[16] Goffman included the asylum, the monastery, the prison, the orphanage, and the army barracks. In this sense Steven Talbot, using Goffman's theory, writes, "The army barracks is a total institution: new recruits are interned, stripped of their identities (mortification of the self), and volunteer their agency (and lives) to the state and defence force."[17] Goffman argues that life within institutions like the military is an all-consuming, routinized, intensely scrutinized, and regulated existence.[18]

Within this "bounded" notion of the ADF, Talbot writes, historical notions of the "warrior" and particular constructions of "operational necessity" are likely very resistant to structural reform and even the reality of successful modern militaries and their missions.[19] Maj. Craig Orme in his personal conduct review draws on Talbot's paper but with a much rosier reflection on military cohesion.[20] I find the total institutions theory has potent explanatory power in answering the question, Why has the ADF struggled to make the strategic changes necessary to fulfill its mandate according to its own goals?

Warfare has changed, even if ADF doctrine states that war itself has not.[21] Modern armed conflict is fought among the population and within communities and is increasingly based on technological advantage.[22] War is not predominantly fought between male soldiers in discrete geographic areas on the basis of physical strength (if indeed it ever was). Certain biological differences between the sexes should not be considered as essential to including or excluding individuals from modern soldiering as they once were.[23] Modern militaries also undertake a range of activities that are not war fighting, such as peacekeeping and responding to natural disasters at home and abroad.

Therefore, the high levels of abuse in the military also target and affect many men, particularly young men and homosexual men, as found by the Defence Abuse Allegations Review. While women may be targeted because of their minority status, clear evidence also indicates that there is substantial stigma and other barriers to reporting abuse against men, especially abuse linked to the victim's homosexuality or perceptions thereof.[24] Nowhere in the ADF response to the culture reviews has this issue been adequately dealt with, except perhaps in the concept of training in sexual ethics.

Integration of Women in the Australian Armed Forces

The current defense workforce is made up of around 58,000 permanent members of the ADF, around 19,500 paid and active reservists, and around 17,900 FTE APS employees. As of April 1, 2015, the defense website states that 5.4 percent (8,823) of the ADF permanent workforce is female. Women make up less than 5 percent of the five-star ranks and less than 8 percent of warrant officers.[25] The breakdown is 2,637 (19.0 percent) in the navy, 3,517 (12.0 percent) in the army, and 2,669 (18.7 percent) in the air force. Of the total deployed force, 14.9 percent, or 266, are women serving on current overseas ADF operations.

The proportion of women in ADF rose from 14.4 percent on June 30, 2013, to 15.0 percent on June 30, 2014. This reflects a net increase of 482 women. The 2016 white paper acknowledges this issue:

> 6.24 Women are under-represented in Defence. Presently, 15 per cent of the ADF workforce and 41 per cent of the APS workforce are women. Increased female participation in the Defence workforce, and in senior leadership, will continue to be a focus in order to broaden Defence's access to the considerable skills and capabilities within the Australian community. To grow and advance the female workforce in Defence, the organisation is focusing on attraction, recruitment and retention of women, the removal of barriers to progression, and facilitating development through mentoring and development opportunities. Defence APS graduate recruitment will continue to include a focus on increasing the representation of women at this important entry point to the APS.
>
> 6.25 Defence will increase the attractiveness of a military career for women, including through targeted recruitment initiatives, retention

measures and career support. Defence will improve the representation of women across Defence, including in leadership and technical areas, and has already removed the gender-based barriers preventing women from serving in ADF combat roles. This commenced with the opening up of combat roles that have previously been restricted to women already serving in the ADF. From 2016, all ADF combat roles will be open to new female recruits and Defence Force Recruiting will market all Defence roles to all prospective ADF members.[26]

The ADF has other problems with diversity. Men who speak English at home make up 80 percent of the ADF, yet men who speak English at home represent less than 40 percent of the general Australian population. Australia is frozen at its 1990 demographic. Also, numbers in the eighteen to twenty-four age group—the ADF's traditional recruiting pool—have flatlined.

The ADF has achieved only a 1 percent increase in the recruitment of women over the last ten years and 2 percent over the last twenty. Attrition rates are 18.9 percent of enlistment. There is considerable occupational segregation by gender. In each service health and logistics, administration, and support have the highest proportion of women, while the groups with the lowest proportion of women are combat and security; engineering, technical, and construction; and aviation.

These are worrying figures for an organization that prides itself on attracting and retaining talent. Some more promising trends are outlined in the following section.

The Breakthroughs

In the UN Women *Global Study on Women, Peace, and Security*, the ADF merits a feature page on positive changes wrought through human resources policy.[27] How did the ADF get from the Fahy case to this point within a decade? It was in large part because of a series of scandals that forced reforms. I argue the accountability for these reforms is still weak and not based on structural, sustainable change, partly owing to the incident-driven nature of forced reforms versus the more strategic approach that may drive voluntary reform.

A professional military occupies a special position in the polity. The Australian military carries a special constitutional role and receives many exemptions from the legal responsibilities of ordinary citizens. These exemptions are necessary for the ADF to perform its constitutional function to protect the state; the state allows the military to bear arms on the state's behalf and rewards the soldier for being willing, if necessary, to die in defense of the national interest.[28]

The Australian military thus exists in a state of exceptionalism in relation to "ordinary" law but is still bound through the constitution by the rule of law and civilian control.[29] These exemptions do not encompass individuals outside the reach of the law when it comes to the unequal treatment of men and women serving in the ADF and impunity for criminal behavior perpetrated by ADF members against each other.

International law includes Australia's obligations under the Convention for the Elimination of All Forms of Discrimination against Women (CEDAW)—incorporated into the Sex Discrimination Act of 1984 (Cth) and the Criminal Code Act of 1995 (Cth)—as well as other international human rights obligations, such as the right to privacy, personal integrity, and family life.[30] Implementation of these obligations is also set out in the policy framework titled *National Plan to Reduce Violence against Women and Their Children 2010–2022*.[31]

Relevant domestic law includes administrative law, criminal law, military justice, and defense instructions and regulations.[32] The implementation of these norms within ADF structures has proved difficult, as the most recent reviews have demonstrated.

Culture Reviews

The gender challenges for Australia's military institutions were made clear in the 2011–12 culture reviews of the ADF (outlined later). Defence Minister Stephen Smith ordered these reviews to examine systemic issues arising out of the so-called Skype scandal (also described later). I examine the outcomes of these culture reviews, explain the progress to remove restrictions for women on frontline combat, and chart the implementation of the reforms until December 2017.

Since 1995 there have been thirteen substantial inquiries into sexual abuse in the Defence Department, of which the Defence Abuse Allegations Review is the most comprehensive. Minister Smith ordered thirty-three major reviews of the department from September 2010, when he took office, to 2013, at a substantial cost.[33] This chapter focuses on the Defence Abuse Allegations Review and a subsequent task force and on the Broderick review (phase 2) as it relates to discrimination and sexual abuse. I note the range of reviews undertaken in 2011.

2011–12 Defense Reviews

On April 11, 2011, Minister Smith announced a series of wide-ranging reviews into aspects of ADF "culture." He also announced the Review of Allegations of Sexual and Other Forms of Abuse in Defence, which would consider complaints and assess whether credible complaints of abuse had not been dealt with.[34] All reports were final. The post-review task force, called the Defence Abuse Response Taskforce (DART) and led by Len Roberts-Smith QC, completed its work in September 2016.[35] The reports included the following:

- Report of the Review of Allegations of Sexual and Other Forms of Abuse in Defence;[36]
- Review of Personal Conduct of ADF Personnel;[37]
- Review of the Use of Alcohol in the ADF;[38]
- Review of Social Media and Defence;[39]
- Review of the Management of Incidents and Complaints;[40]
- Review of Employment Pathways for APS Women in the Department of Defence;[41] and
- Review into the Treatment of Women in the Australian Defence Force Academy (phase 1 and phase 2).[42]

Minister Smith called for these reviews in response to two incidents in 2011, one at the ADFA and one on an RAN vessel, HMAS *Success*. There have been subsequent incidents at the academy and on board *Success*. Also, in 2010 a gay hate Facebook page, which included disturbing posts about gay members of the ADF, was discovered, and gay soldiers have received death threats.[43]

Skype Incident

In March 2011 a female cadet (known to the public only as "Kate") was filmed having sex with a fellow cadet, Daniel McDonald, allegedly without her knowledge.[44] The act was broadcast on Skype, an Internet-based telephone/video-conferencing application, to a group of cadets in a nearby room. In her statement in the Australian Capital Territory (ACT) Magistrates Court, which was leaked to the media and reported, the female cadet said that after she had returned to her room, she discovered a message on her Facebook site. "The content of the message stated, 'I'm about to root a girl n[sic] and have a webcam set up to the boys in a nother [sic] roomwin?'" When she asked him about the message, McDonald told the woman, "Someone else must have posted it as a joke."

On April 1 the Australian Defence Force Investigative Service (ADFIS) allegedly told the cadet she had been filmed and broadcast. The cadet took her story to the media—namely, Channel 10—allegedly after she had been told the men would face minor disciplinary conduct. The public record is unclear, but the incident appears to have been referred to the Australian Federal Police (AFP), which initially did not find an offence given the facts. How ADFA's disciplinary response proceeded was not public, but it is certain the female cadet also faced disciplinary offences unrelated to the incident.

The then vice chief of the Defence Force tasked Andrew Kirkham QC to undertake an independent inquiry into the ADFA's management of the Skype incident and its aftermath (called the Kirkham inquiry). The minister responded to the inquiry report on March 7, 2012, clarifying several allegations, but the report was not released.[45]

McDonald was subsequently arrested by the AFP and faced the ACT Magistrates Court on charges of using a carriage service to cause offense and an act of indecency. Fellow cadet Dylan De Blaquiere faced one count of using a carriage service to cause offense. Both were granted bail. As of August 2013, McDonald had returned to ADFA, Kate had not but stayed with the Defence Department at a Queensland base, and De Blaquiere had returned home to South Australia. De Blaquiere and McDonald, both charged with using a carriage service in an offensive manner, faced a jury trial in the ACT Supreme Court in August 2013. McDonald was also accused of committing an act of indecency on the young woman, who was eighteen at the time.[46] McDonald and De Blaquiere were found guilty in late August 2013 but not jailed.

Other parts of the culture reviews dealt with some aspects of the Skype case, including the incident itself and the effects of binge drinking and social media on unacceptable conduct in the defense environment.

Then–chief of the Defence Force (CDF) Angus Houston made several public comments about the incident, as did previous CDFs. There was significant debate in the public arena about the incident and the minister's response to ADFA officials, especially head of ADFA Commodore Bruce Kafer, who was stood down for a period.[47] The minister launched the suite of reviews shortly after the Skype incident was made public in April 2011. The public discussion of the incident can be summarized very broadly as follows:

- The cadets were ten weeks into their training and, therefore, "brought behaviour with them," or alternatively, the ADFA induction process had failed.
- Was the cadet's decision to approach the media with her situation correct?
- Did the AFP and the ADFIS perform adequately in determining whether an offence had been committed? What were the legal implications of the new phenomenon of real-time broadcasting using social media of otherwise consensual sexual behavior?
- Were training institutions like ADFA appropriate mechanisms for preparing soldiers? Perhaps the ADP should allow postgraduate entrance in the same manner as other professions, such as medicine or law.

- Were there differences between the social mores of the wider community and of the ADF? Would the cadets have been expelled or fired from a civilian institution, or would nothing have happened to them?[48]
- Was the public losing patience? What were the outcomes of the various reviews into previous issues at ADFA and the Defence Department more broadly? Did we expect a higher standard of behavior from defense personnel than from the wider community? Should we, owing to defense personnel's special role?

The Skype incident raised sexual assault issues particular to more closed facilities within the department, especially those with higher proportions of younger people, such as training institutions like ADFA and ships. It also raised the issue of interaction between civilian authorities and defense processes, which could lead to amplification of difficulties or confusion over the pathway to redress for victims of sexual assault or other violations. Questions raised included the following:

- What is the outcome for ADF members who seek to complain outside the internal defense system?
- What are the incentives and disincentives of the current system viewed from the victim/survivor's perspective?
- What are the physical and mental issues for victims, and how effectively are their needs addressed?
- What are the duties or responsibilities of bystanders or whistleblowers in these situations?

The incident also raised the issue of how ADF members understand and implement defense standards and values, both those expressed clearly or exemplified by their leaders—for example, "unacceptable conduct," the ADF Code of Conduct, or "keeping mates safe"—and what the civilian community might understand these values and standards to mean in practice.

HMAS Success

The HMAS *Success* inquiry reviewed a series of incidents while the vessel was on deployment in Asia, some involving inappropriate sexual behavior and verbal and physical confrontations between serving men and women in public. The HMAS *Success* Commission of Inquiry was conducted by the Hon. Roger Gyles AO QC. It primarily focused on proper process and the adequacy of disciplinary proceedings, but it also considered the role of alcohol abuse in prompting inappropriate behavior. During the inquiry crew members' behavior on shore in ports of deployment was described as "out of control," and it was further reported that "discipline had broken down."[49] The inquiry did not focus in any depth on gender or inequality issues. More rape allegations against crew members on board *Success* have been made since the commission was concluded, and these cases are currently in the court system.

Report of the Review of Allegations of Sexual and Other Forms of Abuse in Defence

As noted, on April 11, 2011, Minister Smith announced an external review of allegations of sexual and other forms of abuse that were raised following the ADFA Skype incident.

The minister engaged three lawyers: Gary Rumble, Melanie McKean, and Dennis Pearce AO, then with the law firm DLA Piper. The remit was to review each allegation methodically and at arm's length from the Defence Department in order to make recommendations to the minister and secretary for further action. Key events were as follows:

- October 11, 2011—Volume 1 of the report, *General Findings and Recommendations*, was submitted, along with the first tranche of volume 2 about individual allegations.
- March 7, 2012—The minister announced the release of redacted extracts of volume 1, *Facing Problems of the Past—General Findings and Recommendations*.
- April 17, 2012—The minister announced he had received the final tranche of volume 2.
- June 14, 2012—The unredacted executive summary to volume 1 became public under Freedom of Information provisions.
- July 10, 2012—The *Final Report* of phase 1 of the Review of Allegations of Sexual and Other Abuse in Defence was released.
- November 26, 2012—The minister announced the government's response to the review.

Volume 1 and the supplement to volume 1 identified some findings, broad recommendations, and systemic issues for phase 2 consideration. Volume 2 included initial assessments of all the specific 1,100 or so allegations and made thousands of recommendations (as laid out in the "Explanatory Material" for volume 2, which is appended to the supplement to volume 1). Minister Smith's March 2013 letter to the Senate committee,[50] and later the evidence of Roberts-Smith, indicated that the government did not accept or reject *any* of the review's volume 1 or volume 2 findings and did not accept or reject *any* of the recommendations. All findings, systemic issues, and recommendations from the DLA Piper review were transferred to the DART.

The DLA Piper review received allegations from over a thousand people. Thousands more were received by the DART, which in April 2013 imposed a final deadline for complaints, which was then extended to August 2016. The review identified a range of allegations from 775 sources that fell within ITS terms of reference and found the overwhelming majority of the allegations to be plausible. These plausible allegations dated from 1951 to 2012 and involved minors and both women and men. The review also found that ADF environments typically have factors that indicate a "high risk of abuse occurring" (finding 1). The review found present risks to the ADF's operational capability: "The apparent failure of Defence to call to account perpetrators of abuse and/or mismanagement of allegations of abuse in the past carries risks for Defence now because some of those persons may be in positions of senior and middle management within the ADF (Finding 5)."

The minister did not pass the report on to the secretary of the Department of Defence, contrary to the review's terms of reference, but otherwise broadly accepted most the review's findings.[51] The government response included the establishment of the DART, as noted, as well as a parliamentary apology to victims of abuse, delivered by the defense minister; access to a capped compensation scheme for individual claims made to DLA Piper and then DART ($50,000 maximum); and a free telephone hotline for complaints and referral to services.[52]

The DART was responsible for liaising with those who made allegations of abuse in order to determine appropriate responses, which included the following:

- restorative justice / conciliation processes in which a victim and alleged perpetrator were brought together in a facilitated process;
- referral to counseling (the DART was funded to provide counseling services beyond those generally available to defense personnel or veterans), health, and other existing services;
- compensation, to a maximum of $50,000;
- referral of appropriate matters to police for formal criminal investigation and assessment for prosecution; and
- referral of appropriate matters for disposition by the military justice system or other Defence Department process (for example, consideration under the Public Service Act).

The DART recommended further investigation by a new royal commission into matters identified in the review team's report, particularly those related to ADFA and to alleged events at the naval base HMAS Leeuwin in the 1960s and 1970s.

The DART operated with several extensions until September 2016 and reported to Parliament through the minister for defense. The task force found at least 1,100 abusers still in the ADF with impunity.[53] The DART report accounts for 2,224 cases of abuse relating to more than 1,650 male and female victims over about six decades. Reparation payments, totaling 46.705 million AUD, have been made in 1,159 cases.

Broderick Review into the Treatment of Women in the ADF

Much more positive in governance and accountability terms were the outcomes of the review by Sex Discrimination Commissioner Elizabeth Broderick, which may be the brightest legacy of the entire culture review exercise. Minister Smith announced on November 26, 2012, that Defence had accepted all twenty-one recommendations from the phase 2 report of the Broderick Review into the Treatment of Women in the ADF, six in principle and fifteen in full. Key measures included the following:

- establishing a dedicated Sexual Misconduct Prevention and Response Office to coordinate timely responses, victim support, education, policy, practice, and reporting for any misconduct of a sexual nature, including sexual harassment and abuse;
- implementing restricted reporting so that personnel can make confidential reports of sexual harassment, sex discrimination, and sexual abuse (a recommendation also offered by the Defence Abuse Allegations Review);
- introducing waivers for initial minimum provision of service and return of service obligations for victims of sexual assault and harassment so they can discharge from the ADF expeditiously and without financial penalty;
- increasing diversity on promotion boards and in selections for most senior positions;
- introducing growth targets for recruiting women; and
- producing an annual "Women in the ADF" report on implementation of the review's recommendations and related initiatives.[54]

If the intent and the recommendations of both the Defence Abuse Allegations Review and the Broderick review were fully implemented, gender equality outcomes would clearly have a much stronger governance footing in the ADF. It remains to be seen how the government will implement the comprehensive recommendations from this suite of reviews over time. The ADF's response, set out in the document *Pathway to Change*, is examined later in the chapter and was referenced in the 2016 defense white paper.[55]

The Apology

The major symbolic outcome of the reviews was a parliamentary apology, delivered by Minister Smith on November 26, 2012, and given bipartisan support by opposition Defence Department spokesman Stuart Robert. Both spoke of the "great betrayal" suffered by victims of abuse and said that such violations of trust erode public confidence in the ADF.[56] CDF David Hurley also issued an apology on the same day. He said that the number of allegations in the review indicated that there must have been abuse but did not acknowledge any of the evidence provided by the desktop survey of previous reports. He did not acknowledge that the review indicated the scale of the problem was much larger than the numbers who registered complaints. The apologies were well received by some victims according to the limited press coverage, although no victims of abuse were alerted, and so they were not present in the chamber.

The *Pathway to Change* document, in contrast, was released with much fanfare but was underwhelming in content. Its language is that of grudging acceptance of partial failure. It is not a frank admission of the victims' perspective and suffering, nor an avowal of serious failures of governance and current operational risk, nor an acknowledgment that public confidence has been eroded.

> Despite our great strengths as an organisation, it is all too apparent that *we are not uniformly good*. We and Australia rightly expect that Defence will deliver to consistently high standards, whether in theatres of operations, capability development, support to our operations, our everyday personal behaviour or in how we treat our colleagues. We have learnt, to our cost, that we do not consistently meet these high standards and, more worryingly, that our culture has tolerated shortfalls in performance. Most of these failures are personal, but our inability to consistently address them quickly points to flaws and gaps in Defence's processes and the need to reshape aspects of our single Service and whole of Defence culture. Put simply, *we cannot be entirely satisfied* with all aspects of our current culture; there are parts that serve us poorly, which limit our performance, hurt our people and damage our reputation.[57]

This follows the tone of the March 2012 parliamentary hearing during which sympathetic parliamentarians asked whether Defence felt singled out by the media over what were societal trends: "These incidents do not define Defence, but that is what people are using them to do. A lot of external commentary defines Defence by these incidents. I utterly reject that. . . . We are about growing people, not damaging them. We are about taking young kids off the street and giving them a great opportunity to develop life skills and career skills and be part of a great institution."[58]

Pathway to Change can be read as a wide range of inputs and activities, but it can also be read as the ADF's doing precisely what it had intended to do before the reviews. It can also be read as a statement of good intentions, and there have been previous statements of this kind.[59] Some sections of the document raise concerns. For example, according to the section on recruitment and promotion of women, "Women in our organisation have been recruited, deployed and promoted on merit. They tell us explicitly that they do not want special treatment."[60] This statement represents a willful misunderstanding of the situation of women outlined with painstaking care in the Broderick report.

However, the messages about female talent being crucial to the ADF's future seem to have been accepted as a business case and governance model. Maj. Gen. Gerard Fogarty said, "With more women in the ADF, and more women in combat roles, we will have a far more capable military force. For example, women serving in combat will make a positive contribution to the modern battlefield, accessing and interacting with local communities and cultures that may otherwise be closed to us if we only employ men. More generally, diversity improves decision making in teams."[61] This may be a breakthrough. A more promising section from a governance perspective dealt with establishing a reporting culture, although there is still the language of grudging qualification:

> We will also take actions to shift attitudes and willingness to speak up when we become aware of inappropriate behaviour by a colleague in Defence. Several of the Reviews indicate that we do not do this sufficiently. The Pathway to Change stipulates that our people must put each other's safety and dignity before loyalty to a peer group.
>
> We particularly need to remove the stigma of communicating distress to those who have a responsibility for our welfare; whether it relates to injury or other ailment, perceived threat, intimidation or harassment. There is no pride to be found in watching others suffer or for remaining in denial about a serious problem. As one Review termed it, we need to adopt a 'Reporting' culture.[62]

Pathway to Change appears to be very resistant to influence from international or comparative law—or any type of law at all as a regulatory or governance framework. The ADF appears to float in a realm where international law that pertains to its internal operations is absent, but such standards might be beneficial. Nevertheless, most of the recommendations of the suite of reviews were adopted; the exception was the Defence Abuse Allegations Review, which was handed over to the DART. The question is whether the ADF accepted responsibility for past mistakes or whether it still feels that its exceptional status does not extend to being the same or better than the "ordinary" community at promoting gender equality in its ranks.

For most Australians, a more convincing statement of the ADF's commitment to changing its culture was video footage of Chief of Army David Morrison in July 2013 telling members of the so-called Jedi Council—that is, senior officers who had shared footage of sexual encounters online without the women's knowledge—"Those who think that it is OK to behave in a way that demeans or exploits their colleagues have no place in this army. . . . If that doesn't suit you, get out."[63] Many members of the Jedi Council were jailed in due course.

Defence made complicated arguments throughout these cases that the department was part of society and therefore reflected wider norms. The most thorough and recent examination of gender-based harms in Australia and policy responses is in the ten-year National Action Plan to End Violence against Women, based on the *Time for Action* report and launched in 2010 with bipartisan support. This report from the National Council to Reduce Violence against Women and Their Children, chaired by Libby Lloyd, paints a bleak picture of Australian society.

Around one in three Australian women will experience sexual violence in her lifetime, and many will experience abuse early in life that can affect their material well-being in almost every aspect of life.[64] The most rigorous study by an international team involved a sample of 4,000 Australian women and confirmed this prevalence of sexual offences, with thirteen years the average age for rape victims. The study also maps the causal link to mental harm experienced by victims/survivors. The national action plan lays out a series of steps to prevent and respond to violations and considers the role alcohol abuse plays in such incidents. In the report, violations are understood as the result of the dynamics of dominance, power, and control rather than of sex or biology; this perspective holds true for group interactions, male-on-male violations, and female-on-male violations. It is regrettable that the Defence Department did not see this national action plan as relevant to the men and women who make up the ADF. However, the Broderick report was informed by the plan.

Can Australia's military institutions respond to the interplay between public and international law on questions of gender equality? Or will the role of the ADF as an institution dwindle in social importance as women and men who do not conform to a limited notion of a warrior withdraw their talent? The ADF has consistently been resistant to the idea of external accountability and independent inquiry and also to the concept that the problem might be structural and not just the result of a few rotten apples.

Is the ADF as an institution ready to effectively address the gendered nature of conflict and to apply gender analysis to itself, and does it accept that challenge?[65] The Australian National Action Plan on Women, Peace, and Security includes compulsory government reporting to improve the gendered response to peace and security challenges regionally and internationally. Between the national action plan and *Pathway to Change*, the ADF has both internal and external criteria for measuring improved gender outcomes.

Rotten Apple Delusion

Gary Rumble, one of the authors of the Defence Abuse Allegations Review report, stated in March 2013 that he held deep concerns that victims might give up on the process and that perpetrators might wait out the public attention.[66] The report is frank about resistance to the review process itself:

> During the course of this Review, the Review members have heard a lot about the ADF's need to maintain operational capability and about "moving forward." Central aspects of the ADF's operational capability are the loyalty of serving men and women to the ADF and broad community confidence in the ADF.
>
> It was, therefore, not a surprise to the Review members when we encountered resistance in our discussions with current and former leaders of the ADF when we tried to take them back to discuss past problems of abuse and what might be done now to respond to the ongoing effects of that past abuse.
>
> At one level there has been hostility simply because we outsiders—civilian lawyers—have been questioning "their" ADF on the particularly sensitive issue of abuse by members of the ADF inflicted on other members of the ADF.
>
> At another level there is a concern that a report by the Review drawing attention to past abuse in the ADF could damage the ADF's current reputation and, thus, damage the ADF's operational capability.[67]

Minister Smith also made statements about the need for more robust cycles of parliamentary reporting and oversight by parliamentary committee. This is a promising initiative, although committees have often been far too deferential to ADF evidence in the past. A specific reporting focus on complaints now that there is baseline data may prove useful over time, as would a focus on CEDAW compliance in particular and human rights in general.

Many Defence Department leaders since the 1970s have talked about bad or rotten apples, peripheral to the organization's overall success and unfairly focused on by external critics. The 1996 Grey report took on the rotten apples talk and responded that the barrel was rotten—in other words, that normal young Australians arrived at ADFA and the academy culture affected them. Chalking up problems to a few bad apples ignores the consistent finding of many reports—listed in chapter 6, volume 1 of the Defence Abuse Allegations Review—that problems are underreported. With underreporting, ADF leaders cannot be confident they know the full picture.

The Defence Department has resisted acknowledging or admitting structural or systematic gender exclusion, violations of rights, and the prevalence of "factors which indicate a high risk of abuse occurring" within the ADF as a modern example of a total institution in which the participation of women is low.[68] Admittedly, many of these violations and exclusion are found in society outside the Defence Department, as shown by the January 2013 establishment of the Royal Commission to Investigate Institutional Responses to Child Sexual Abuse. But Defence cannot aspire to excellence in all other forms of endeavor and reputation, and not in this area of crucial reputational risk, especially when it has itself accepted that diversity leads to better team decision making and therefore more effective operational capability.

The pressure for the current suite of ADF reviews came from politics, the media, and external social factors. Defence would not have undertaken the culture reviews itself. Many of the key actors, like Minister Stephen Smith (who stepped down in the September 2013 election) and Commissioner Elizabeth Broderick (who stepped down in 2015), have moved on to new posts. Few of the mainstream defense or foreign policy think tanks have engaged with the culture reviews as crucial to operational outcomes. The current ADF leadership team is likely to wait out the executive interest in gender reforms for the ADF or make small but highly visible concessions to particular senior women who accept the parameters of ad hoc reform.

But maybe all of Australia's total institutions are receiving the message that it is much easier in a digital age to evade the boundaries of total institutions. Why not harness reform efforts to globally agreed standards of gender equality and suffer less the vagaries of the politics of the day? Why not accept the truth that Defence has not been uniformly good at putting the rights of women at the center of operational effectiveness or gender equality at the heart of the values of a modern warrior? Rectifying gender issues is a true test of leadership because, as Clare Burton writes, "Discrimination issues are leadership issues first and foremost."[69]

Gender equality measures that focus on human resources may at least increase the relative number of women in the ADF and thus may start to remove one of the most significant abuse risk factors—being in a minority group. Integrating women could become a self-reinforcing positive spiral:

gender equality increases the proportion of women in the ADF, which reduces the risk of women's experiencing abuse in the ADF. The reduced incidence of abuse should encourage more women to enter or stay in the ADF and thus further raise the proportion of women to men—and so on in a virtuous spiral.

But addressing the structural gender issues that relate to both women and men in the ADF—this is the start of a long road. ADF leaders need to accept that external accountability and independent advocacy are necessary to achieve gender equality. The 2016 defense white paper both embraces these reforms and is defensive about the department's perceived complacency:

> 6.36 Defence has made substantial progress in addressing a range of cultural issues, but the organisation cannot become complacent. Gender equality and increasing female participation in the Defence workforce and in senior leadership roles is fundamental to achieving Defence capability now and into the future.[70]

Lifting of Combat Restrictions

In the media the culture reviews' headline outcome was the removal of sex barriers to direct combat roles announced on September 27, 2011.[71] Allowing women to undertake combat roles that they had previously been barred from might be considered an important step for equal opportunity in a constitutional and citizenship sense, even if feminist and other opinion was divided over the issue.[72] But the lifting of combat restrictions is not the focus of this chapter; here the focus is on attitudes to governance, particularly accountability for violations of women's rights, and on the incorporation of sources of law that encourage gender equality.

The debate over frontline combat roles had been ongoing for at least a decade since the passing of the Sex Discrimination Act in 1985. Indeed, it could be argued that agreeing in 2011 to the phased reforms over five years was a red herring to distract from more widespread reforms to enshrine equality in the ADF. The most wide-ranging of the international human rights treaties devoted to women is CEDAW, adopted by the UN General Assembly in 1979 and now having 186 state parties (but with many states making serious reservations to certain provisions). Australia signed CEDAW at a special ceremony in Copenhagen at the UN World Conference for the Decade of Women on July 17, 1980, sending a strong delegation of experts led by Robert Ellicott (minister for home affairs in the Fraser government). The treaty then entered into force in September 1981. After a long consultation period with the states and territories, Australia ratified the treaty on July 28, 1983, but made some reservations to the treaty; these reservations were revised in 2000.[73] "The Government of Australia advises that it does not accept the application of the Convention in so far as it would require alteration of Defence Force policy which excludes women from combat duties."[74] Even with these reservations, Australia's ratification of CEDAW became part of the intense domestic and partisan debates that affected the passage of the Sex Discrimination Act of 1985 (Cth).

In 2000 Australia removed a previous exemption in the legislation with respect to women in ADF combat-related employment areas through an amendment to the Sex Discrimination Amendment Act of 1995 (Cth). Almost 90 percent of all employment areas in the ADF were made open to women, the exemptions being areas of "combat duties" in which the duties required a person to commit, or to participate directly in the commission of, an act of violence against an adversary in time of war. As the new combat positions phase in, Australia can withdraw this reservation altogether.

The Application of Gender Perspectives in Military Operations

The 2016 defense white paper acknowledges the importance of gender expertise as part of the Defence Department's ongoing engagement in efforts to maintain peace and security:

> 5.79 Defence will continue to support United Nations training and education activities and will provide expertise to support the Australian National Action Plan on Women, Peace and Security 2012–2018 that implements United Nations Security Council Resolution (UNSCR) 1325. UNSCR 1325 recognises that security, stability and peace can only be achieved through a gender inclusive approach to conflict resolution and peace building. Defence is responsible for implementation of 17 of the 24 actions in the National Action Plan. The National Action Plan sets out what Australia will do, at home and overseas, to integrate a gender perspective into its peace and security efforts, protect women and girls' human rights and promote their participation in conflict prevention, management and resolution. Under the National Action Plan, ADF women are playing a more prominent and influential role on operations in which the ADF is involved.

> 5.80 Australia is promoting the active participation and integration of Afghan women in Afghanistan's national security institutions. In recent

years, ADF personnel have performed the role of Gender Advisor to the NATO-led Resolute Support Mission in Afghanistan, providing guidance on the provision of safe and appropriate facilities and equipment for women serving in Afghan security forces, and training for men and women in the prevention of gender-based violence and harassment.[75]

Harassment of personnel based on actual or perceived diversity can combine with trauma experienced on deployment to bring great harm to individuals. A special investigation in August 2016 has found that forty-one military personnel and veterans have taken their own lives in one year, the same as the number of Australians who were killed in Afghanistan during thirteen years of war.[76]

Australian National Action Plan on Women, Peace, and Security

In this section I outline UN Security Council resolutions implemented in national policy (but not legislation) through the Australian National Action Plan on Women, Peace, and Security.[77] The plan applies to any overseas operations the ADF undertakes, especially peacekeeping and emergency or disaster response. When ADF members are deployed on a peacekeeping mission to restore international peace and security under Security Council authorization, they are required to understand the security threats to the female population and incorporate the perspectives of women into peace processes to ensure sustainable security responses. The focus of the UN's women, peace, and security (WPS) agenda is the full participation of women as important security actors.

A cluster of UN Security Council resolutions makes up the WPS agenda: UNSCR 1325 (2000), UNSCR 1820 (2008), UNSCR 1888 (2009), UNSCR 1889 (2009), UNSCR 1960 (2010), UNSCR 2106 (2013), UNSCR 2122 (2013), and UNSCR 2242 (2015).[78] In July 2013 Resolution 2106, the fourth to focus on conflict-related sexual violence, was passed during the United Kingdom's presidency. This resolution adds greater operational detail and a focus on women protection advisors. It reiterates that all actors, including not only the Security Council and parties to armed conflict but also all member states and UN entities, must do more to implement previous mandates and combat impunity for these crimes.[79] In October 2013, after an open debate on women, rule of law, and transitional justice in conflict-affected situations, Resolution 2122 was adopted to request more regular briefings from relevant UN agencies, more attention to WPS issues when issuing or renewing mandates of UN missions, and commitment to a high-level review of implementation of WPS in 2015. In October 2015 the UN Security Council adopted Resolution 2242, which recognizes the importance of including gender expertise and considering the role of women in relation to global responses to terrorism and violent extremism.

In essence the UNSCR 1325 agenda states that women and girls experience conflict differently from men and boys.[80] Women have an essential role in conflict prevention, peace building, and post-conflict reconstruction, and states are required to ensure women are represented in all decision making.[81] WPS resolutions after 1325 focus on ending impunity for sexual violence in conflict and increasing the participation of women in the UN's own "good offices" roles in mediating conflict and negotiating peace. Resolution 1325 was groundbreaking, and the WPS agenda led to the appointment of a new special rapporteur on sexual violence in conflict, Margot Wallström, in 2010, as well as annual reporting by the secretary general.[82] One of the key actions of the agenda is for states to design and implement national action plans. Thus far, only around forty countries have implemented national action plans, few are funded, and there are few or no baseline data for many of the actions.[83] This has led to claims that the institutional commitment is more rhetorical than real.

Even the rhetoric has proved controversial. In the last three years, debates on the thematic agendas (such as the focus on sexual violence during election violence) have been criticized as extending beyond the Security Council's mandate.[84] But some evidence indicates that WPS issues are being considered more routinely in debates, affecting mandate design and adding weight to the zero-tolerance policy for UN peacekeeping forces. Some commentators argue that the resolutions and resulting actions have focused too much on the protection of civilians agenda, and then only on sexual violence and not enough on participation and conflict prevention—in other words, women's agency.[85] There are critiques that WPS has struggled with gender mainstreaming, the gendered nature of peace and security institutions, and the lack of sex-disaggregated data required to underpin policy.[86]

As a piece of polylateral diplomacy linked to both regional and global social movements, the WPS agenda is strong despite wide acknowledgment of its flaws.[87] Advocates argue that the core premise of the WPS agenda remains being attentive to the security needs of half the world's population and thereby builds the legitimacy of the Security Council as a normative actor.

The Australian National Action Plan on Women, Peace, and Security was developed in 2010, driven by Australia's successful campaign for the UN Security Council. The Defence Department is responsible for seventeen out of twenty-four actions. Progress on the plan is tabled in Parliament annually.

The ADF developed the Defence National Action Plan Implementation Plan and created the position of director of the National Action Plan for Women, Peace, and Security, in August 2013. The director reports directly to the CDF. Another appointment was a new post of gender advisor to Australia's CDF, who provides advice on women's access to leadership opportunities and factors affecting the recruitment and retention of women in the ADF.

Defence has made progress on updating key strategic guidance documents, including the 2014 refresh of the Defence Corporate Plan, the 2014 Defence Annual Plan, the Defence International Engagement Strategy, and the Defence Regional Engagement Strategy. Operational guidance on WPS will be included in the CDF planning directives, which inform strategic direction and planning for operations.

Former defense officer and civil-military advisor Susan Hutchinson has identified several areas in which the WPS doctrine could affect the deliberate planning and conduct of joint military operations. These areas include the "legal framework for operations; intelligence process for conflict analysis; deliberate planning processes and products; security sector reform; disarmament, demobilisation and reintegration; transition assistance; and disaster response."[88]

Thus far Australia's strengths have been in doctrine, training, and advisor positions, and the nation has been active in NATO on this issue (again led by former Commissioner Broderick). In comparison Australia's allies have gone further with operational matters. Canada now has new WPS doctrine.[89] The Irish Defence Forces have mainstreamed a gender perspective into all unit and subunit patrols. They have updated standard operating procedures and reporting pro formas for tactical maneuver units, subunit patrols, and Civil Military Cooperation village assessments. Information from these reports is collated in the regular gender advisor report that is collated by the deputy commander. Reports now include sex-disaggregated population data; female leaders and influencers; women's groups; roles of men and women in security forces, armed groups intelligence, and law enforcement; access to social services; a sex-disaggregated list of protection threats; and differences between men and women, boys and girls.

Despite Australia's being involved in a range of operations in which the WPS doctrine was relevant, such as the Solomon Islands, Timor-Leste, and Afghanistan, the work in this area has been limited, and the 2016 white paper makes little reference to gender in bilateral relationships.[90] Other gaps in the white paper include the new countering violent extremism agenda and disaster response. The white paper makes no specific reference to gender expertise or the need to address the disproportionate impact of emerging security threats on women and girls. The Australian Strategic Policy Institute argues that consideration should be given to the appointment of military gender advisors or focal points throughout different levels of the ADF and on deployment to assist in gender-related efforts, especially for peace operations (an approach that has been adopted by several NATO countries and suggested by UN military guidelines).

Australia has not resolved issues around quick-impact projects used in Afghanistan to target women. Robert Egnell and colleagues argue that gender advisors should focus their energy on internal organizational matters, such as deliberate planning, and that external aid projects for women should be abandoned:

> Such "external projects," performed by military units, have seldom improved women's conditions in the area of operations, or won the "hearts and minds" of the local population. Even if external projects may at times produce small measurable improvements in women's rights or local support, the limited nature of such results must be measured against the potential to increase military effectiveness by helping the rest of the unit conduct operations, win local legitimacy, and increase its cultural understanding of a gender perspective.[91]

Talisman Sabre 15

The strongest example of gender integration in the ADF was the way the WPS doctrine formed a key part of Australia's engagement with the US in Exercise Talisman Sabre 2015. Talisman Sabre is a biannual bilateral military exercise involving up to 30,000 personnel. The ADF worked closely with US counterparts to ensure that gender advice was considered in the lead-up to the exercise (through education and training) and throughout the planning and conduct of operations. The culmination of the exercises was the 2014 Australia-US Ministerial Consultations (AUSMIN) communiqué, referencing WPS objectives as crucial to the exercise.

Conclusions

In this final section, I question whether the Australian military will continue to undertake law and policy reform to progress a gender equality agenda and what the obstacles to lasting reform might be. In governance terms, my hypothesis is that the ADF wants to deal with gender issues on a policy basis that treats the ADF as an exceptional institution, with as much discretion as possible. The ADF may enact a raft of administrative and policy reforms in response to past scenarios, but conceptually and structurally there has yet to be engagement with deeper normative challenges to future practice posed by a commitment to women's rights as fundamental to the ADF mandate. I call this the rotten apple delusion (explored further later), although some progress has been made in attitudes expressed by ADF leadership since 2013. The impulse for reform was forced on the ADF by scandals reported to the media, political leadership, and long-term advocacy. I analyze what internal motivations might strengthen reform efforts for the future but conclude that it is up to the federal Parliament to force long-term accountability for gender diversity and for gender abuse on the ADF.

A possible reform for the future is to establish a permanent service complaints commissioner, as the UK did in 2006, discussed in the Defence Abuse Allegations Report at section 8.22.[92] This would elevate the functions given to the defense force ombudsman in 2016. The UK commissioner has a special remit to deal with unacceptable behavior, including bullying, harassment, discrimination, victimization, and dishonest or improper behavior. In these cases the commissioner has to be kept informed by law about the handling of a complaint and the outcome. The commissioner presents an annual public report to Parliament on how efficient, effective, and fair the complaints process has been during the year. The defense force ombudsman is undertaking this role at present, informed by the experience of DART—the task force was designed to wind up in 2013 but was extended until August 2016. Given how many complaints both the Defence Abuse Allegations Review and the task force have received, plus the ongoing rate of complaints, the demand for a stand-alone complaints commissioner with direct access to the Parliament is clear.[93]

The one aspect of comparative practice that the Defence Department implemented was the recommendation of the Broderick review that a new entity be set up to take reporting sexual misconduct out of the chain of command. The Sexual Misconduct and Prevention Office (SeMPRO) was launched in July 2013 and is explicitly informed by international practice on creating victim-centered complaint processes in military settings.[94]

Senior leadership of the ADF has been historically, and remains in some aspects, a hyper-masculinist institution, as the outgoing chief of army informed the United Nations in 2013. The ADF has been under significant pressure to reform since 2011 in response to a series of high-profile scandals, some involving new technology. Several previous reviews in the decade prior documented violations of human rights, serious discrimination, and incidents of gender-based violence against women and men within the ADF and have met with an institutional response that has failed to meet community expectations.

Since 2011 the ADF has undertaken a series of culture reviews to reform this aspect of its governance as both a capability issue and an equity issue to ensure respect and promotion of women's rights. Of course, Australia is not the only Western military organization facing this kind of pressure. In some respects the ADF has followed the workplace reforms undertaken by the militaries and assessed lessons learned in its comparator framework (the US, the UK, Canada, and New Zealand). But in other respects, the Australian reforms are unique, owing to the lack of a human rights act of any kind at a federal level, the long history of abuse claims in a series of Australian institutions, and the relative weakness of parliamentary scrutiny of the portfolio. The ADF has shown a deep unwillingness to accept the norms and standards of international law and due process and to incorporate them into their own governance framework in relation to ending discrimination and sexual and other forms of gender-based violence. This is because of its well-established culture of extralegal exceptionalism as a total institution.

I have argued that the current culture reforms have been driven by specific reactions to incidents and given impetus by personalities and events, such as Defence Minister Smith, Sex Discrimination Commissioner Broderick, and Chief of Army Morrison. These actors, rather than a committed acceptance of gender reform's utility for improved operational effectiveness at a structural level by the institution itself, have wrought change. Nevertheless, these actors have successfully introduced several reforms that could provide sustainable change to the ADF institutional framework toward gender equality outcomes.

These include the DART, which has completed expedited compensation proceedings for those who suffered abuse in the ADF before April 1, 2011. The reviews and DART have created a much clearer record of structural injustice in the history of the ADF. The creation of a permanent complaints function and fund in the ombudsman is a positive move. Another important measure is the establishment of an improved process for the reporting of sexual violence outside the chain of command. The CDF has created more gender advisor positions within the ADF and made several important appointments of women at senior levels. The ADF has key tasks to acquit for Australia's National Action Plan on Women, Peace, and Security by 2018.

There are, however, also signs that point to an ADF culture that weathers storms but then reverts to previous structures when active leadership and public pressure lessens. The more integrated gender equality outcomes and gender analysis are in operations, the better the outcomes for women inside the ADF are likely to be. But that kind of integration is progressing very slowly. After six years the *Pathway to Change* reforms have ended in a cul-de-sac.

Parliament should appoint independent gender advocates who can monitor progress in the ADF, both in integration and operations. Parliament should further mandate that gender equality is fundamental to achieving the mission of the ADF as a foundational Australian public institution and set standards that reflect international human rights standards. If this parliamentary oversight does not occur, the ADF will continue to respond to gender abuse in an ad hoc manner, laboring under what I term the rotten apple delusion—that the fault lies with individuals who can be expunged from the organization, not with the organization itself—and waiting out reformist impulses. The ADF should embrace parliamentary scrutiny and accept external monitoring from independent gender equality advocates. In the long term, the ADF will be forced to strive for excellence and leadership in this key area to improve operational capability and social acceptance of the ADF's role.

Notes

1. Mark Bannerman, "Naval Officer Breaks Silence on Harassment," *News*, Australian Broadcasting Corporation, May 15, 2006, television program transcript.
2. Madonna King, "Meet Marise Payne, Australia's First Female Defence Minister," *Sydney Morning Herald*, December 19, 2015, http://www.smh.com.au/good-weekend/meet-marise-payne-australias-first-female-defence-minister-20151215-globcd.html.
3. Department of Defence, *Defence White Paper* (Canberra: Defence Publishing Service, 2016).
4. On February 19, 1942, Japan launched an air raid on Darwin in the Northern Territory and then Broome in Western Australia two weeks later. By the end of September 1943, Japanese pilots had flown ninety-seven air raids against towns and bases in northern Australia. On May 31, 1942, three Japanese midget submarines entered Sydney Harbour. In June 1942 a submarine lightly shelled the eastern suburbs in Sydney and then Newcastle. Japanese submarines also attacked coastal shipping, causing the loss of some sixty lives and 29,000 tons of shipping during May and June 1942.
5. Joan Beaumont, *Broken Nation: Australians in the Great War* (Sydney: Allen & Unwin, 2013).
6. Department of Defence, *White Paper*.
7. OECD Development Assistance Committee, *Guidelines for Gender Equality and Women's Empowerment in Development Co-operation* (Paris: OECD, 1998).
8. Hilary Charlesworth, "Not Waving but Drowning: Gender Mainstreaming and Human Rights in the United Nations," *Harvard Human Rights Journal* 18 (2005): 1.
9. Hilary Charlesworth, "Feminist Methods in International Law," *American Journal of International Law* 93, no. 2 (1999): 379–94; Cynthia Enloe, *Bananas, Beaches and Bases: Making Sense of Feminist Politics* (Berkeley: University of California Press, 1989), 3; Lucinda M. Finley, "Breaking Women's Silence in Law: The Dilemma of the Gendered Nature of Legal Reasoning," *Notre Dame Law Review* 64 (1989): 886.

10. Claire Duncanson and Rachel Woodward, "Regendering the Military: Theorizing Women's Military Participation," *Security Dialogue* 47, no. 1 (2016): 3–21.
11. Cynthia Enloe, *Maneuvers: The International Politics of Militarizing Women's Lives* (Berkeley: University of California Press, 2000), 45.
12. Elizabeth Broderick et al., *ADFA Gender Audit* (Canberra: Defence Publishing Service, 2013), 78.
13. Helena Carreiras, *Gender and the Military: Women in the Armed Forces of Western Democracies* (London: Routledge Cass Military Studies, 2006).
14. David Morrison, "Implicit Stereotypes, Explicit Solutions: Overcoming Gender-Based Discrimination in the Workplace" (remarks delivered at Commission for the Status of Women Session 57, New York, March 8, 2013); Craig Orme, *Beyond Compliance: Professionalism, Trust and Capability in the Australian Profession of Arms—Report of the Australian Defence Force Personal Conduct Review* (Canberra: Defence Publishing Service, 2011), 29.
15. Angela Ballard, *Sexual Assault Prevention and Intervention in a Military Environment* (Canberra: Winston Churchill Memorial Trust of Australia, 2009); Major Kathryn Quinn, *Sexual Harassment in the Australian Defence Force* (Canberra: Australian Army Psychology Corps, 1996), http://www.defence.gov.au/fr/reports/SHinADF.pdf; Bronwen Grey, *The Grey Report—Report of the Review into Policies and Practices to Deal with Sexual Harassment and Sexual Offences at the Australian Defence Force Academy* (Canberra: Defence Publishing Service, 1998); S. J. Brubaker, "Sexual Assault Prevalence, Reporting and Policies: Comparing College and University Campuses and Military Service Academies," *Security Journal* 22 (2009): 56–72; Saskia Stachowitsch, "Military Gender Integration and Foreign Policy in the United States: A Feminist International Relations Perspective," *Security Dialogue* 43 (2012): 305–21.
16. Erving Goffman, *Asylums: Essays on the Social Situation of Mental Patients and Other Inmates* (London: Anchor Books, 1991), 6.
17. Steven Talbot, "Warriors, Warfighting and the Construction of Masculine Identities," DSTO Discussion Paper 1811 (Canberra: Defence Publishing Service, 2011), 19.
18. Goffman, *Asylums*, 5.
19. Talbot, "Warriors," 20.
20. Orme, *Beyond Compliance*.
21. See Department of Defence, *Capstone Series ADDP-D 2012* (Canberra: Defence Publishing Service, 2012), para. 2.27, pp. 2–7: "Change is ever-present in warfare. Some of the factors that may influence change in the characteristics of warfare include technology, asymmetry, globalisation, political and legal constructs, changing demographics, and social and cultural factors." Also paras. 2.16–2.17, pp. 2–5: "The nature of war—imposing your will on the adversary and making them comply—is immutable. Additionally, war will always involve terror, violence, chaos, suffering, social and economic dislocation, and destruction of life and property."
22. Department of Defence, "Defending Australia in the Asia Pacific Century: Force 2030," White Paper (Canberra: Defence Publishing Service, 2009).
23. C. H. Gray, "Posthuman Soldiers in Postmodern War," *Body and Society* 9, no. 4 (2002): 215–16.
24. ABC TV, "Chamber of Horrors," *Four Corners Report*, aired June 9, 2014, http://www.abc.net.au/4corners/chamber-of-horrors/5512000.

25. Senate Joint Standing Committee on Foreign Affairs Defence and Trade, *The Report of the Review of Allegations of Sexual and Other Abuse in Defence, Conducted by DLA Piper, and the Response of the Government to the Report* (Canberra: Commonwealth of Australia, 2013), https://www.aph.gov.au/Parliamentary_Business/Committees/Senate/Foreign_Affairs_Defence_and_Trade/Completed_inquiries/2010-13/dlapiper/index.
26. Department of Defence, *White Paper*.
27. UN Women, *Global Study on the Implementation of Security Council Resolution 1325 (2000)* (New York: United Nations, 2015), 138.
28. Section 51(vi), *Constitution of Australia*, plus Sections 61 and 68. See also Department of Defence, *The Strategic Framework 2010* (Canberra: Defence Publishing Service, 2010), 8–9.
29. See Department of Defence, *Capstone Series ADDP-D 2012*, 5-1. See also Sir Ninian Stephen opinion in *Defence Abuse Allegations Review*, vol. 1 (Canberra: Defence Publishing Service, 2012), appendix 39.
30. UN General Assembly, Resolution 34/180, Convention on the Elimination of All Forms of Discrimination against Women, A/34/46 (Dec. 18, 1979), at 193 (hereafter cited as CEDAW).
31. Commonwealth of Australia, *National Plan to Reduce Violence against Women and Their Children, 2010–2022* (Canberra: Commonwealth of Australia, 2012).
32. *Criminal Code Act*, 1995 (Cth); *Defence Force Discipline Act*, 1982 (Cth). See especially Defence Instruction (General) PERS 35-4, Management and Reporting of Sexual Offences, February 2004; Defence Instruction (General) PERS 35-3, Management and Reporting of Unacceptable Behaviour, June 2009.
33. Ian McPhedran, "Defence Reviews Tally $20m and Rising," *Adelaide Advertiser*, January 16, 2012, http://www.adelaidenow.com.au/news/national/defence-reviews-tally-20m-and-rising/news-story/2eb7f3e2c200f3d3f37a1ab669321882.
34. Michelle Smith, "Women in Australia's Military: On the Frontline of the Gender War," *Conversation*, November 11, 2011.
35. The government announced an expanded complaint mechanism within the Defence Force Ombudsman's Office. This new function commenced on December 1, 2016.
36. Gary A. Rumble, Melanie McKean, and Dennis Pearce, *Report of the Review of Allegations of Sexual and Other Abuse in Defence: Facing the Problems of the Past*, vol. 1, *General Findings and Recommendations* (Canberra: DLA Piper, 2011).
37. Orme, *Beyond Compliance*.
38. Margaret Hamilton, *The Use of Alcohol in the Australian Defence Force—Report of the Independent Advisory Panel on Alcohol* (Canberra: Defence Publishing Service, 2011). Valerie M. Hudson et al., "The Heart of the Matter: The Security of Women and the Security of States," *International Security* 33, no. 3 (2009): 7–45.
39. Ibid.
40. G. Earley, *Review of the Management of Incidents and Complaints in Defence, including Civil and Military Jurisdiction—A Report by the Inspector General Australian Defence Force* (Canberra: Defence Publishing Service, 2011).
41. Catherine McGregor, *The Review of Employment Pathways for APS Women in the Department of Defence* (Canberra: Department of Defence, 2011).
42. Broderick et al., *ADFA Gender Audit*.
43. ABC TV, "Chamber of Horrors."

44. Deborah Snow, "Women in Uniform 'Have Advantage,'" *The Age*, August 2, 2011, http://www.theage.com.au/national/women-in-uniform-have-advantage-20110801-1i8iz.html#ixzz1U4Uc3aSV; "ADF Cadet's 'Friend with Benefits' Claim," *Sydney Morning Herald*, April 29, 2011, http://www.smh.com.au/national/adf-cadets-friend-with-benefits-claim-20110429-1e07z.html#ixzz1U4VZjQtd.
45. Stephen Smith, "Minister for Defence—Outcomes of the Kirkham Inquiry," media statement, March 7, 2012.
46. Louis Andrews, "ADFA Skype Scandal Trial Set," *Canberra Times*, February 28, 2012, http://www.canberratimes.com.au/act-news/adfa-skype-scandal-trial-set-20120227-1tztm.html.
47. Commodore Kafer was reinstated at ADFA in 2012. Minister Smith announced the promotion of Brig. Simone Wilkie to major general in charge of the Australian Defence College beginning in August 2013.
48. Australian Human Rights Commission, *Change the Course: National Report on Sexual Assault and Sexual Harassment at Australian Universities* (Sydney: Australian Human Rights Commission, 2017).
49. Department of Defence, *HMAS Success Commission of Inquiry: Allegations of Unacceptable Behaviour and the Management Thereof* (Canberra: Defence Publishing Service, 2011), 1.
50. Senate Joint Standing Committee, *Report of the Review of Allegations*.
51. Gary Rumble, "Evidence of Gary Rumble to the 'Parliamentary Inquiry into the DLA Piper Review,'" March 14, 2013, in ibid.
52. Smith, "Minister for Defence."
53. "Welcome to the Defence Abuse Response Taskforce," Defence Abuse Response Taskforce, last updated September 13, 2017, http://www.defenceabusetaskforce.gov.au/Pages/default.aspx.
54. Stephen Smith, "Government Response to the Review into Allegations of Sexual or Other Forms of Abuse in Defence," November 26, 2012, http://www.minister.defence.gov.au/2012/11/26/minister-for-defence-government-response-to-the-review-into-allegations-of-sexual-or-other-forms-of-abuse-in-defence/.
55. Ibid.
56. House of Representatives, *Debates*, November 26, 2012, http://parlinfo.aph.gov.au/parlInfo/search/display/display.w3p;query=Id%3A%22chamber/hansardr/c94905e2-4370-462f-b408-d06e0d0a5c8e/0000%22
57. Department of Defence, *Pathway to Change: Evolving Defence Culture: A Strategy for Cultural Change and Reinforcement* (Canberra: Defence Publishing Service, 2012), 1 (emphasis added).
58. Department of Defence, "Evidence of General David Hurley (Transcript)," *Joint Foreign Affairs Defence and Trade Committee Chapter 7 Review of "The Defence Annual Report 2010–2011"* (Canberra: Parliament House, March 16, 2012).
59. For a graphic representation of implementation of the reviews, see "Figure 1: Key Inputs to Pathway to Change," in Department of Defence, *Pathway to Change*, 4, http://www.defence.gov.au/PathwayToChange/Docs/120410%20Pathway%20to%20Change%20-%20Evolving%20Defence%20Culture%20-%20web%20version.pdf.
60. Ibid., 11.

61. Alisha Welch, "Heading in the Right Direction," *Defence Magazine* 6, no. 7 (2012): 1, http://www.defence.gov.au/defencemagazine/issue/6/index.html.
62. Department of Defence, *Pathway to Change*, 23.
63. ABC News, "Chief of Army David Morrison Tells Troops to Respect Women or 'Get Out,'" June 14, 2013, http://www.abc.net.au/news/2013-06-14/chief-of-army-fires-broadside-at-army-over-email-allegations/4753208.
64. KPMG, *The Cost of Violence against Women and Their Children*, Safety Taskforce, Department of Families, Housing, Community Services and Indigenous Affairs (Canberra: Commonwealth of Australia, 2009).
65. There is almost no reference to women except for the need for more diversity in recruitment in the key strategic document *Force 2030*. In the white paper released in mid-2013, women are referred to in the context of personnel retention (102), but there is also reference to the National Action Plan on Women, Peace, and Security.
66. ABC News, "Chief of Army."
67. Rumble, McKean, and Pearce, *Report*, 4.
68. Ibid., xxiii.
69. Clare Burton, *Women in the Australian Defence Force: Two Studies* (Canberra: Defence Publishing Service, 1996), [2.1].
70. Commonwealth of Australia, *National Plan*, 23.
71. Geoffrey Barker, "Defending Defence Equity," *Inside Story*, September 28, 2011, http://insidestory.org.au/defending-defence-equity; Mark Dodd, "Combat Roles Offered to Women," *The Australian*, April 12, 2011; Smith, "Women in Australia's Military"; Jeremy Thompson, "Combat 'Too Dangerous' for Female Soldiers," ABC News, April 12, 2011.
72. Anne Summers, "The Lady Killers: Women in the Military," *The Monthly*, December 2011–January 2012: 24–27; Natalie Sambhi, "Why I Want to Serve on the Front Line, Despite Challenges for Women at War," *The Conversation*, October 3, 2011, https://theconversation.com/why-i-want-to-serve-on-the-front-line-despite-challenges-for-women-at-war-3622.
73. Including the "federalism" declaration Australia makes regarding most international treaties. Australian practice is to make a short "federal declaration" on ratification of treaties if states will play a role in implementing the treaty. The CEDAW reservation follows the sample declaration attached to the Principles and Procedures for Commonwealth—State Consultation on Treaties: "Australia has a Federal Constitutional System in which Legislative, Executive and Judicial Powers are shared or distributed between the Commonwealth and the Constituent States. The implementation of the Treaty throughout Australia will be effected by the Commonwealth State and Territory Authorities having regard to their respective constitutional powers and arrangements concerning their exercise."
74. This is the current text. Effective August 30, 2000, Australia withdrew the part of the reservation that read: "The Government of Australia advises that it does not accept the application of the Convention in so far as it would require alteration of Defence Force policy which excludes women from combat and combat-related duties. The Government of Australia is reviewing this policy so as to more closely define 'combat' and 'combat-related' duties."
75. Department of Defence, *White Paper*, 137.
76. "Defence Gets Helping Hand under Federal Government Plan," *The Australian*, August 11, 2016, http://www.theaustralian.com.au/national-affairs/defence/defence-force-gets

-helping-hand-under-federal-government-plan/news-story/db9fdb9ce06add29b8ad597fc8096b18.

77. Chapter 7 of "Charter of the United Nations," June 25, 1945, accessed December 1, 2016, http://www.un.org/en/charter-united-nations/.
78. The full texts of the WPS core resolutions are available under the year of adoption from http://www.un.org/documents/scres.htm.
79. UN Security Council, S/RES/2106 (June 24, 2013).
80. Laura J. Shepherd and Jacqui True, "The Women, Peace and Security Agenda and Australian Leadership in the World: From Rhetoric to Commitment?," *Australian Journal of International Affairs* 68, no. 3 (2014): 257–84.
81. Louise Olsson and Theodora-Ismene Gizelis, "An Introduction to UNSCR 1325," *International Interactions: Empirical and Theoretical Research in International Relations* 39, no. 4 (2013): 425–34.
82. The current special rapporteur on sexual violence is Pramila Patten. Christine Bell, *Women and Peace Processes, Negotiations, and Agreements: Operational Opportunities and Challenges* (Oslo: Norwegian Peacebuilding Resource Centre, 2013).
83. Aisling Swaine, *National Implementation of the UN Security Council's Women, Peace and Security Resolutions* (Oslo: Norwegian Peacebuilding Resource Centre, 2013).
84. Security Council Report, *Third Cross-Cutting Report on Women Peace and Security, April 2013* (New York: Security Council Report, 2013), http://www.securitycouncilreport.org/cross-cutting-report/women-peace-and-security-sexual-violence-in-conflict-and-sanctions.php.
85. Inger Skjelsbaek, "Responsibility to Protect or Prevent? Victims and Perpetrators of Sexual Violence Crimes in Armed Conflicts," *Global Responsibility to Protect* 4, no. 2 (2012): 163.
86. Christine Bell and Catherine O'Rourke, "Peace Agreements or Pieces of Paper? The Impact of UNSC Resolution 1325 on Peace Processes and Their Agreements," *International and Comparative Law Quarterly* 59, no. 4 (2010): 941–80; Chantal de Jonge Oudraat, "UNSCR 1325—Conundrums and Opportunities," *International Interactions* 39, no. 4 (2013): 612.
87. On polylateral diplomacy, see Geoffrey Wiseman, "'Polylateralism' and New Modes of Global Dialogue," Discussion Papers No. 59 (Leicester: Leicester Diplomatic Studies Programme, 1999), 41: "My working definition of this concept is: 'the conduct of relations between official entities (such as a state, several states acting together, or a state-based international organisation) and at least one unofficial, non-state entity in which there is a reasonable expectation of systematic relationships, involving some form of reporting, communication, negotiation, and representation, but not involving mutual recognition as sovereign, equivalent entities.'" For regional and global social movements, see NGO Working Group on Women, Peace, and Security, http://www.womenpeacesecurity.org/about/; Women's International League of Peace and Freedom (WILPF), http://www.peacewomen.org/; and a wide array of academic and activist groups. For similar responsibility-to-protect groups, see the International Coalition for the Responsibility to Protect (ICRtoP), http://icrtopblog.org/; the Global Center for R2P, http://www.globalr2p.org/.
88. Susan Hutchinson, *Operationalising United Nations Security Council Resolution 1325 within the Australian Defence Force*, Report for Joint and Operations Analysis Division

Defence Science and Technology Group DST-Group-GD-0909 (Canberra: Defence Publishing Service, 2016), 12.
89. Canada Defence Services, CDS Directive for Integrating UNSCR 1325 and Related Resolutions into CAF Planning and Operation, January 2016, last modified July 21, 2017, http://www.forces.gc.ca/en/operations-how/cds-directive.page.
90. Lisa Sharland, "DWP 2016: Women, Gender Advice and Future Defence Capabilities," *The Strategist*, March 8, 2016, http://www.aspistrategist.org.au/dwp-2016-women-gender-advice-and-future-defence-capabilities.
91. Robert Egnell, Petter Hojem, and Hannes Berts, *Gender, Military Effectiveness, and Organisational Change—The Swedish Model* (Basingstoke: Palgrave Macmillan, 2014), 9–10.
92. "Service Complaints Ombudsman," Service Complaints Ombudsman for the Armed Forces, accessed December 1, 2016, http://armedforcescomplaints.independent.gov.uk.
93. The total number of reports received between December 1, 2016, and April 30, 2018, is 517. See further Commonwealth Ombudsman, "Reporting Abuse in Defence," accessed May 31, 2018, http://www.ombudsman.gov.au/making-a-complaint/australian-defence-force/reporting-abuse-in-defence.
94. Ballard, *Sexual Assault*.

10

Three Waves of Gender Integration

The Causes, Consequences, and Implications for the South African Armed Forces

Lindy Heinecken

South Africa has a long history of women's involvement in war. During the battles against the indigenous black tribes, white Afrikaner women assisted with the loading of rifles and other support functions.[1] Afrikaner history contains many examples of women's involvement in legendary battles, with some reaching near mythical status. However, as with many other Western nations, it was only during the world's major wars that women became part of the nation's armed forces on a part-time basis. During World War I, women served as nurses in support of South African troops in Europe and East Africa. Their roles expanded during World War II, when they served in a number of female auxiliary corps in the medical services, army, navy, air forces, and military police. Here they performed various support roles, such as drivers, signalers, radiographers, and even coastal artillery. However, this was short-lived as after the war the women's auxiliary corps was disbanded and women came to play a very minimal role in the military.[2]

It was not until the seventies that women reentered the military on a permanent basis, owing to an acute shortage of white males during the height of the South African Border Wars. In 1971 the first group of women was recruited into the military on a voluntary basis, essentially to relieve men for combat and operational duties. This marked the first wave of gender integration, in which women were permitted to serve but limited to noncombat support roles. As the security threat grew, so their roles and deployments expanded. While white women were fighting against a perceived communist threat and defending white supremacy under the apartheid regime, black women were fighting against the repressive apartheid regime. Many joined the liberation forces in the 1970s and 1980s as part of the African National Congress's anti-apartheid struggle. But even here, their roles were limited, and issues of gender equality remained subservient to the political goal of eradicating racial suppression and white supremacy.[3]

The plight of women changed significantly after the end of the Cold War and demise of apartheid. The adoption of a new Constitution for the Republic of South Africa (RSA) and emphasis placed on the eradication of all forms of racial and gender discrimination paved the way for gender reforms. This marked the beginning of the second wave of gender integration. Following a liberal equal rights agenda, the newly formed South African National Defence Force (SANDF) was obliged to open up all positions, including combat, to women. A Gender Sub-Directorate was established within the Equal Opportunities Chief Directorate to oversee the implementation of new SANDF policies to ensure equal treatment and monitor the advancement of women.[4] During this second wave of gender reforms, including women in combat roles and increasing the number of women in leadership positions dominated the gender agenda. This was a period of adaptation to existing norms and practices and amendment of policies, rather than gender reform.

Around 2008 a major shift in gender integration occurred, prompted by international treaties and protocols, associated with gender mainstreaming. A concerted effort was made to shift gender binaries and address the factors that influenced women's full participation and utilization in the SANDF. Linked to this was the commitment to increase the number of women in the military and in leadership positions, as well as the deployment of more women on peacekeeping missions. The focus shifted from issues of equality to the importance of having more women in the military for instrumental reasons and purposes of security sector reform. In this regard, South Africa is a particularly interesting case study for several reasons. Although many of the South African debates resonate with those of other countries in terms of gender integration, few countries have adopted such an assertive process of gender reform. Not only do women now serve in combat roles, but they represent more than a quarter of the full-time forces. Added to this is the intersectionality of race, culture, and politics that plays out alongside and influences attitudes toward gender integration.

Accordingly, the aim of this chapter is to discuss the systemic conditions that have facilitated women's exclusion and inclusion during the three waves of gender integration and the tensions this has created over the past fifty years. To place the discussion in context, a brief outline of the unique security, political, and social contexts is provided for each wave of gender reforms. Hereafter, how gender-equality and gender-mainstreaming initiatives have been implemented is described and reflected on. The last section evaluates what tensions gender integration has evoked and whether women's increased numbers have shifted gender binaries.

First Wave: Admission of Women to the Military

To grasp what led to women's integration into the military in South Africa, it is important to understand the wider political and security context that influenced their admission into the military during the Apartheid era.

Political and Security Context

During the sixties the country was caught in the midst of two main conflicts, the first being the perceived communist threat north of South Africa's borders and particularly from Angola, and the second the increasing violent uprisings within the country against the apartheid state. Combined, these threats were referred to as the "total onslaught" on the country—a "communist invasion" that was engulfing the country.[5] Externally, the South African military became increasingly embroiled in several border wars during the period 1966–83 to stem this threat, and internally, it worked to suppress popular black resistance against the apartheid state. With the state facing acute manpower shortages, compulsory military conscription of white men was introduced in 1967 and systematically increased to meet manpower requirements. At the time blacks were not conscripted; they were later invited to volunteer but were initially permitted to serve only in support roles. This changed for blacks in the seventies as the security situation worsened, giving rise to a number of combat units organized along ethnic lines.[6]

During this time the decision was made to permit women to join the military to augment the South African Defence Force's (SADF) manpower capacity. Although the conscription of women was considered at one stage, this never materialized. Instead, women were permitted to volunteer for military service for a two-year period and could then join the permanent force, should they so desire.[7] What is important to realize at this point is that only white women were permitted to join the SADF as permanent force members.

Women's Roles and Functions

While initially women only enrolled and trained to provide civil relief, from the seventies their roles were expanded but restricted to noncombat support branches, such as finance, personnel, logistics, intelligence, medical service, and welfare. They received their basic training separately from men at the South African Women's Army College, but other than adaptions in physical training, they had to meet the same standards as men upon completion of their basic training. Hereafter, all other military courses were integrated, and women were remunerated and promoted on the same basis as men but did not enjoy all the same service benefits. For example, women were not entitled to medical benefits for their dependents, there was a differentiation between the pension benefits of men and women, and women did not have equal access to military accommodation if married.[8] Added to this, women were not permitted to serve in combat roles, and weapons training was limited to self-defense. Thus, women were never deployed to the front line but did serve as instructors on weapons systems in the armor, artillery antiaircraft corps and even in the infantry (especially the equestrian branch).[9]

Numerous reasons were cited for women's exclusion from combat roles. According to Meyer, this had more to do with the conservative attitudes of broader society toward women than with the military itself.[10] She writes that during the seventies (white) South Africans were not ready to see women in a fighting role, given that men are expected to perform the role of protector. What this meant was that women were not appointed to any position that could result in close combat, direct enemy fire, or positions with substantial risk of capture.[11] This, and concerns about the effect that wounded women could have on men's effectiveness, were cited as reasons for women's exclusion from combat roles. Other reasons included the usual claims related to women's suitability for combat roles, physical and physiological impediments, and the effect women's presence would have on male bonding.[12]

This gendered division of labor served to maintain patriarchal values and notions of masculinity, which were reinforced by the emphasis placed on women to maintain their "feminine" qualities and image as women.[13] They were reminded that they were "women in uniform," were encouraged to uphold this image and maintain high standards of dress, and were even taught how to use makeup and how "to retain their fine femininity."[14] In so doing, gender roles remained intact, and the masculine image of the soldier as the "defender and protector" was maintained.[15] Although many admired the tenacity of these young women, their presence within both the military and broader society was met with some ambiguity. Within the military, their exclusion from combat roles, coupled with the emphasis placed on the maintenance of their femininity, meant that they were not seen as "real soldiers." The public in turn was divided on whether the inclusion of women in the military was proper; some questioned why women would consider serving in the military, while others admired their sense of patriotism.[16]

What is important to point out at this stage is that South Africa had become a highly militarized society, in which white women in general played an important role in upholding the ideology of apartheid and white supremacy. Women contributed to this militarization in several ways. Through various civil society organizations, such as the Southern Cross Fund, they provided material support by raising funds to provide aid and comfort for soldiers, recreational facilities, and organizing lifts for national servicemen. They became involved in civil defense organizations and in mobilizing the support of the civilian population for the total onslaught. White women also became increasingly active in commando units in rural areas in counterinsurgency activities and equipped in the use of weapons. Added to this, many were employed in the formidable armaments industry.[17]

On the other side of the political spectrum, black women came out on numerous occasions to protest against the apartheid regime and the repression they experienced. Some left the country to join the African National Congress (ANC) armed wing, Umkhonto we Sizwe (MK), and the Pan African Congress (PAC) armed wing, the Azanian People's Liberation Army (APLA), in the liberation struggle. By 1991 women made up 20 percent of MK membership. As members of the revolutionary forces, these women trained alongside male soldiers. Unlike their female counterparts in the SADF, they received infantry-type training and were accustomed to a military culture that emphasized equal rights for women.[18] However, in practice they too were often relegated to support functions, did not serve on the front line, and were underrepresented in positions of leadership and authority.[19] In this regard the inclusion and utilization of black women in the liberation forces was strikingly similar to that of white women in the SADF. Between 1976 and 1990, the inclusion of women in both armed forces was fueled by levels of threat perception and manpower shortages. In both they remained excluded from combat and underrepresented in leadership and authority.[20]

Second Wave: Equal Rights and Opening the Combat Arms to Women

By the end of the Cold War and the subsequent unbanning of the ANC and PAC, both black and white women had become a permanent feature of their respective armed forces. These women came out strongly in support of gender equality as the political and security situation in the country changed in the nineties.

Political and Security Context

The end of the Cold War in 1989 and the subsequent demise of apartheid ushered in a new era in the history of South Africa. Within a few years, from 1990 to 1994, the mission of the SADF changed from countering a communist threat and weakening the ability of neighboring countries to support the ANC's low-level insurgency campaign to literally searching for a new mission. In 1994 the new SANDF was formed out of seven different armed forces, and in 1996 its tasks were defined in the new constitution, Article 200 (2), as "to defend and protect the Republic, its territorial integrity and its people in accordance with the Constitution and the principles of international law regulating the use of force."[21]

The first and primary role of the SANDF was defined as defense against external aggression, but it was for its secondary functions—to defend and protect its people and regional security—that the SANDF would be most operational. The new defense doctrine showed a definite shift away from an offensive posture to one of conflict prevention, common security, and cooperation with other states in southern Africa. While initially the SANDF was employed in support of the police, it was systematically withdrawn from this internal role. Regionally, its role was limited to humanitarian aid assistance to countries affected by floods or other disasters. At the time, South Africa had very little experience in peacekeeping operations, and it was not until 1999, with the promulgation of the *White Paper on South African Participation in Peace Missions*, that the country became more involved in such missions.

The end of hostilities and advent of democracy with an emphasis on equal rights profoundly affected the gendered division of labor of the SANDF. In post-apartheid South Africa, the achievement of gender equality became part of the country's political agenda. These ideals were built into the 1996 white paper on national defense, which stated that the SANDF would develop a nonracial, nonsexist, and nondiscriminatory institutional culture; that the composition of the SANDF would broadly reflect the composition of South Africa; and that women had the right to serve in all ranks and positions, including combat roles.[22] Since the establishment of the SANDF, there has been a strong commitment to gender integration and equity. Consequently, instructions were issued that all arms of service employ, train, and promote women on the same bases as their male counterparts.[23] This led to the closure of the South African Women's Army College in 1998, ending an era of separate basic training of men and women.

Roles and Functions

With the establishment of the SANDF in 1994, both the gender and the racial composition of the military changed significantly. At the time, women constituted 11 percent of the full-time forces. However, the vast majority were white women from the SADF (5,714) compared to only 712 black women (mainly from the former MK). While numerically in the minority, the women from MK were ideologically and politically more predisposed to enforce a more radical equal rights agenda. They had served alongside men in infantry-type roles during the liberation struggle and insisted that all positions in the SANDF be open to women. To ensure their fair and equal integration, a female former MK brigadier general was appointed as head of the Chief Directorate Equal Opportunities (CDEO), established in 1997.

The task of CDEO was to oversee the process of achieving gender equality, and specific funds and human resources were allocated to this. An affirmative action plan was put in place to promote women to senior positions and to increase their representation across all branches and ranks. This legal and politically driven process led to a rapid increase in the number of women in uniform serving in the SANDF, from 11 percent in 1994 to 19.5 percent in 2007. In addition, by 2007 women made up almost 11 percent of the senior leadership positions above the rank of brigadier general.[24] Similarly, women's numbers in the combat branches grew steadily during this second wave of gender integration. By 2007 an estimated 14 percent of women now came to serve in the armor corps, 18 percent in artillery, 8 percent as infantry, 21 percent in combat navy, and 6 percent as aircrew (including pilots).[25]

This did not mean that prejudice against women's serving in combat roles did not persist. A survey conducted by the Defence Inspectorate in 2006, for example, found that only half (53 percent) of respondents felt that the strict application of gender equality would have no effect on the striking power of the SANDF. Roughly the same number (48 percent) believed it was possible to have more women in combat posts without compromising the effectiveness of the military.[26] Men were particularly guarded in their views of whether women should serve in the Special Forces, which require exceptional endurance, courage, mental strength, and the ability to operate alone and far behind enemy lines for lengthy periods. Men still considered women more suited to support positions because they are physically weaker and unsuited to serve on the front line.[27]

Important to realize at this stage is that for many women the issue was no longer whether they were permitted or able to serve in traditional male roles but whether they could do so in a gender-friendly environment. It took quite a number of years before discriminatory policies related to the employment benefits of women in terms of health care, pension, and housing were brought in line with men. True equality cannot be achieved when the support structures are lacking and when attitudes that render women inferior remain. Women continue to be disadvantaged by maternity leave and the way leave affects their ability to attend and complete military courses. Even though women receive the same training, many claim that they do not receive the same recognition and experience feelings of social isolation and discrimination.[28] Isolation and discrimination are experienced differently by white and black women.

Menon and Kotze, for example, found that white women feel less empowered and integrated because they are not regarded as professional "career" soldiers, given that they serve mainly in support roles and face role ambiguity in terms of homemaker versus career woman.[29] Black women experience subordination more in terms of African culture, which is steeped in patriarchy and the subservience of women to men. Compared to white women, they carry a heavier burden in terms of child-care responsibility, with more African women being single parents. What this has meant is that women are under greater stress in trying to balance their roles as wives and mothers than men are, which affects their ability to attend military courses, availability for deployment on peacekeeping missions, and ultimately their career progression. At this point in time, women were included in the military, but with little due recognition of the different gendered needs to enable equal participation and promotion.

An independent assessment found that the policy frameworks of the Department of Defence (DOD) were not adequately aligned with international compliance frameworks such as the Convention on the Elimination of All Discrimination against Women (CEDAW) and UN Security Council Resolution (UNSCR) 1325. The audit also found that women were still inadequately represented in senior decision-making forums; that insufficient attention was being given to gender issues such as facilitating work-family balance; that support to women in leadership was lacking; and that sexism and sexual harassment were rife. Furthermore, gender issues related to peacekeeping were not adequately addressed.[30]

Third Wave: Gender Mainstreaming and Valuing Difference?

A third wave of gender reforms followed, as South Africa became more involved in peacekeeping operations on the African continent and came to implement gender mainstreaming policy to address the gendered nature of security.

Political and Security Context

In response to the independent assessment in June 2008, the DOD's gender mainstreaming policy was promulgated to ensure that a gender perspective would be infused in all policies, planning, and reforms related to defense management. This effort included the need to align the SANDF's policies and practices with international, continental, and regional obligations. Besides CEDAW and UNSCR 1325, the DOD's gender mainstreaming policy reiterated the need to commit to continental-level agreements, such as the Namibian Plan of Action on Mainstreaming a Gender Perspective in Multidimensional Peace Support Operations (2000) and the African Union (AU) Solemn Declaration on Gender Equality in Africa (2004). The policy also included commitments to the Southern African Development Community Declaration on Gender and Development (1997) and the Addendum on the Prevention and Eradication of Violence against Women and Children. A commitment was made to strive to meet a 30 percent target for women's involvement at all levels of decision making and in peacekeeping operations. A premium was placed on the role of women in post-conflict reconstruction and development and on their participation in security sector reforms, "not as a matter of political correctness" but as key to "operational effectiveness."[31]

Associated with this was the implementation of an assertive affirmative action campaign to increase the number of women serving in the military and in higher ranks. Recruitment targets were increased to 40 percent in order to create a significant pool of women in the military. In addition, the target was set to attain 30 percent representation of women in all decision-making levels in the DOD. Measures were also put in place to monitor the progress with respect to gender equality and the ways policies, plans, and actions were being implemented. In addition, steps were taken to ensure that when military equipment was acquired, it would be gender friendly. Closer attention was paid to the need to accelerate women's role in peacekeeping and peace building and to address some of the challenges facing women on deployment.[32]

By this time South Africa had become extensively involved in peacekeeping and post-conflict reconstruction and development on the continent. Serving mainly in Burundi, the Democratic Republic of Congo, and Darfur/Sudan, it was now one of the largest troop-contributing countries on the continent.[33] Given this, and the growing importance assigned to women in peacekeeping and security sector reform, the SANDF came under pressure to deploy more women on peacekeeping operations. Of the total number of 3,057 members deployed on peacekeeping missions in May 2015, 429 (14 percent) were women.[34] Besides increasing the number of women, the commitment was made to enhance women's participation in the development of the Africa Standby Force and early warning systems and to deploy more women as contingent commanders on UN/AU missions. Added to this, a gender perspective was now incorporated in all military development courses and in mission readiness training.[35]

Roles and Functions

This commitment meant that more women had to be trained to serve in peacekeeping operations abroad. As peacekeeping troops are typically drawn from the infantry battalions in South Africa, the majority of women recruited were now destined to serve there. The recruitment targets for women were raised to 40 percent, which could be met given the high number of applications received. The problem, however, was that the selection criteria for both men and women was based on health specifications, academic qualifications, and aptitude, with little due consideration to physical capabilities. In South Africa as elsewhere, training in the infantry remains steeped in the warrior ethos, which is constructed around ideals of physical strength, bravery, and aggression. Many women indicated that they were unaware of the physical demands of their mustering at recruitment and did not have a choice about how they would be utilized. This placed a strain on gender relations, especially in the teeth arms musterings.[36]

As gender mainstreaming started to take effect and the number of women pushed into the infantry increased, so the attitudes toward women in combat roles hardened. On the one hand, there was acceptance of women's right to serve in combat musterings, but on the other, resentment grew over the effect their "inferior" physical capabilities were having on standards, competency, and military effectiveness. As their visible presence increased, so support among army members for women in combat roles plunged from a high of 57 percent in 2004 to just 39 percent in 2009.[37] Poor selection of capable women for combat musterings meant that the old stereotypical debates about whether women are suited to serve in frontline combat positions continued.[38]

Despite this, there has been growing recognition that women are in a position to make a unique contribution to peacekeeping on the basis of attributes commonly associated with women, namely, that they are less aggressive and more compassionate and conciliatory.[39] As elsewhere, these essentialist claims have led to the belief in the SANDF that female peacekeepers are able to enhance the access of local women to services, improve community relations, reduce the incidence of sexual and gender-based violence (SGBV), and break down traditional views that discriminate against and marginalize women.[40] While this is certainly possible, often these ideals are not met or are context specific. Far more important is the ability to communicate with the local community and cultural considerations. For example, a lack of understanding of the cultural context can lead to hostility, as was the case in Sudan, where local women were often hostile toward the female peacekeepers for failing to respect their culture.[41]

Similarly, many dispute claims that female peacekeepers are able to break down traditional values against women, given their small numbers and the fact that their identity is often concealed behind their helmets. In terms of improving the security of local women and children, female peacekeepers thought the locals placed more trust in male soldiers because "they [did] not know how to judge female soldiers." Also questioned was their supposedly greater ability to ensure access to assistance for women who had been victims of SGBV. The female peacekeepers indicated they were not trained to assist in this role and knew very little about the gender dynamics in the communities. What this shows is that women peacekeepers are not making the contribution that many claim based on their gender, primarily because they serve in the same capacities as men and are not trained, deployed, or used in capacities in which they can make a difference "as women." This has meant that their value, while recognized, has remained contested.[42] It also contributes to a kind of reversal of women to roles that are considered more suited to women based on socialization and cultural ascriptions attached to gender.

What one should not forget is that even where women are fully integrated, their utilization is often influenced by the hypermasculine peacekeeping environment associated with high levels of violence and abuse against women. This environment is hostile to women at various levels. When gender harassment and sexism are rife, this denigrates women and is used to undermine their authority. Added to this, when the threat of sexual assault or violence exists, this is used as a means of exclusion or suppression of women. The implication is that a hostile environment reinforces patriarchy and a militarized masculinity in which women are seen as vulnerable and in need of protection. Added to this are concerns that women pose a "gendered" security threat when women's presence makes the peacekeeping force more vulnerable to attack. The hostile environment brings forth another level of resistance and exclusion from roles that entail engagement with rebel forces or combat, which ultimately maintains the ideological structure of patriarchy.

Discussion: Reflecting on the Process

Reflecting on gender integration in the South African armed forces, one sees three distinct shifts in women's representation over time from the motivation for the inclusion of women in the military to their utilization in different roles and functions to their numeric representation and attitudes toward women serving in combat musterings. During the first wave, women were admitted into the military primarily because of a shortage of white men. The patriarchal nature of society and the SADF's involvement in offensive missions barred them from combat and service on the front line. Women's utilization was restricted to noncombat support roles, in support of men. In the SADF they were ladies first and soldiers second. Given their "place" in society and the emphasis on the need to maintain their femininity, they never posed a threat to the hegemonic masculinity of male soldiers or the warrior ethos of the military. The gendered division of labor remained largely accepted and reinforced by society.

The changed political dispensation in the country marked the second wave of gender integration. The motivation to include women and open all positions, including combat, to women was driven by a political liberal equal rights agenda and *not* by internal dynamics in the SANDF. Nor was there any active feminist movement pressing for changes in the military.[43] Hence, legal reforms and political pressure compelled the SANDF to allow equal opportunities for women. Women were to be recognized as "soldiers first" and then "women." However, they were still referred to as "ladies." Nonetheless, by the end of the second wave, women's numbers had increased steadily to just below 19 percent. The increase in numbers was not the only change. By 2007 white women represented a mere 22 percent of women in the SANDF, with African women 65 percent, colored (i.e., of mixed descent) 12 percent, and Asians 1 percent.[44]

The third wave, associated with an assertive affirmative action campaign to advance women and to mainstream gender, pushed gender integration along a different trajectory. Now the motivation was not merely the inclusion of women but the consideration of women's needs in development, planning, and resource allocation. This marked a shift away from an essentially liberal equal rights agenda to a more radical feminist approach based on differential arguments that served to recognize, value, and acknowledge gender differences. Backed by international, continental, and regional political agreements, pressures were placed on the SANDF to increase the recruitment of women to 40 percent and to increase the number of women involved in decision making to 30 percent. In addition, women's participation in peacekeeping became a focus. As of May 2015, women represented 25 percent of the total strength of the SANDF, of which 17 percent served in the senior ranks (brigadier general to general). Women's representation in the combat services increased to 19 percent and in combat support to 31 percent.[45]

This rapid promotion of women based on quotas has resulted in somewhat of a gender backlash. There are many reasons for this. First, the drive to recruit

40 percent women has tended to overlook the selection criteria related to certain posts, which has meant that the person-post fit is often not met. Added to this, the rapid promotion of women to meet gender quotas has meant that the most qualified or competent are not always promoted or appointed to certain posts. This has a negative effect on gender equality. Many have become critical of the "window dressing" and "numbers game" driven by political rather than operational or organizational concerns. Women themselves acknowledge that the appointment of incompetent women in senior positions compromised the status of all women in the DOD.[46] Men are more critical of women's ability, and it is clear that women continue to be judged by their gender rather than their competence.

Although gender mainstreaming is driven by the need to infuse alternative views and perspectives into decision making, it is a slow process largely because women are expected to assimilate masculine values, norms, and standards. The SANDF's military culture is still rooted in the warrior ethos, which is embedded in each and every layer of the military: in the training, the culture, the uniform, and the technology. This is aptly reflected in a comment made by a female peacekeeper:

> The flak jackets don't fit us, the trousers don't fit us, nothing in this organisation is designed for women. The boots I wear are two sizes too big. I wear size 3 and there are no army boots that are size 3, so I have to wear extra socks and it is so difficult to walk in these big boots. You just don't have a choice, you must just cope. Because your boots don't fit your feet, they become swollen and your toenails become blue. They say it is a man's world. We challenge this but . . . eish [*expression of exasperation*] . . . but nothing happens.[47]

Patriarchy persists, and many women report that if they serve in positions of authority, they are often not respected or their instructions are ignored. In addition, one finds that gender and sexual harassment are used to denigrate women, and this creates mixed reactions. On the one hand, women indicate that they continue to experience high levels of sexism, and on the other, men claim that women use their femininity in inappropriate ways to gain favors. "That women 'expect' special treatment—that they are ladies first and soldiers second—and some say that women have double standards—citing equality when it benefits them or claiming to be the fairer sex when they have to work hard."[48] In general, femininity is not valued and is seen as a threat and liability to the organization. Although some recognize that women are able to make a "different" contribution to peacekeeping, in reality this view tends to be limited and more highly regarded by women than men.[49]

Thus, the feminist agenda based on valuing gender difference and infusing alternative values is subsumed and seen as incompatible with military culture. Even when women are represented in significant numbers, they have little choice but to "contribute to the war system, which reinforces gender roles."[50] This is no different in the SANDF, as reflected in the comment of one female peacekeeper: "If those rebels see you ... you must walk like a man, you talk like a man ... behave like a soldier, not a woman and must always be aggressive."[51] However, most tend to agree that it is essential to have gender-mixed sections and platoons during peacekeeping operations. At the decision-making level, women's voices are being heard, but whether they are in fact infusing a gender perspective is uncertain. A senior white female colonel recently remarked to me that she has never been a feminist (few military women are) but that recently she feels as if "she is choking in testosterone." Despite being the most senior, experienced, and educated, she said, her inputs are ignored or not taken seriously.

Concluding Remark

To conclude, there is no doubt that women in the South African military have come a long way. The debates are no longer whether women are permitted or able to serve in combat. Men accept that women have equal rights, but whether those rights are supported remains a contentious issue. The issue is not that women are not seen as able. Rather, the processes of affirmative action and gender mainstreaming have been numbers driven and not focused on ensuring that the right women (and men) are in the right post according to the person-post fit. This is a leadership failure, not a gender issue, but still it has affected attempts to achieve gender equality and to change organizational culture.

Because masculine traits continue to be privileged and valued more than feminine traits, women, despite the significant increase in their numbers, have been unable to bring about a more gender-balanced or androgynous military culture. Gender integration and the ideals of UNSCR 1325 are not just about gender equality, the numbers, or women serving in combat but about a shift in perspective on war and peace. Where hegemonic masculinities remain at the heart of military culture and the "value" of the female voice and contributions remain unappreciated, it is difficult (but not impossible) to infuse alternative values. Nonetheless, there is evidence of some re-gendering of the soldier profile in which traditional masculine qualities, such as bravery, ambition, and steadfastness, are valued alongside feminine qualities, such as caring, patience, and empathy.[52] One hears this from both male and female soldiers, but the change is slow—yet evident as women's numbers and influence in decision-making processes increase. In terms of international comparison, South Africa is such an interesting case study because of the progression of gender integration, the various tensions that have arisen, and the enduring influence of military culture on gender relations.

Notes

1. E. M. Meyers, "Die Suid-Afrikaanse vrou in landsverdediging: Agtergrond en perspektief" [The South African women in national defence: Background and perspective], *Scientia Militaria* 16, no. 1 (1986): 33.
2. Ibid., 4.
3. Lindy Heinecken, "Affirming Gender Equality: The Challenges Facing the South African Armed Forces," *Current Sociology* 50, no. 5 (2002): 715–28.
4. Ntsiki Motumi, "Gender Equality: A Challenge for the Department of Defence," *African Security Review* 8, no. 3 (1999): 26–29.
5. Republic of South Africa, *White Paper on Defence* (Pretoria: Government Printers, 1973), 3.
6. Jakkie Cilliers and Lindy Heinecken, "South Africa: Emerging from a Time Warp," in *The Postmodern Military*, ed. Charles Moskos, John Allen Williams, and David Segal (London: Oxford University Press, 1999), 242–64.
7. Jacklyn Cock, "Manpower and Militarisation: The Role of Women in the SANDF," in *War and Society: The Militarisation of South Africa*, ed. Jacklyn Cock and Laurie Nathan (Cape Town: David Phillips, 1989), 65.
8. Motumi, "Gender Equality," 28.
9. Meyer, "Die Suid-Afrikaanse," 41.
10. Ibid., 44.
11. Laurie Nathan, *The Changing of the Guard* (Pretoria: HSRC Publishers, 1994), 164.
12. Cock, "Manpower and Militarisation," 60–61.
13. Ibid., 60.
14. Este Kotze, "Historical Perspectives on Masculinity, Femininity and the South African Military: Gender Relations with Specific Focus on the Impact of the South African Army Women's College and the SADF (1971–1998)" (Master thesis, Stellenbosch University, 2015), 90.
15. Cock, "Manpower and Militarisation," 62.
16. Kotze, "Historical Perspectives," 92.
17. Cock, "Manpower and Militarisation," 53–55.
18. Jacklyn Cock, "Forging a New Army out of Old Enemies: Women in the South African Military," *Women's Studies Quarterly* 23, nos. 3–4 (1995): 105.
19. Shirleen Hassim, *The ANC Women's League* (Scottsville: University of KwaZulu-Natal Press, 2006), 57.
20. Cock, "Forging a New Army."
21. Republic of South Africa, *Constitution of the Republic of South Africa* (Pretoria: Government Printers, 1996), 1–3.
22. Department of Defence, *South African White Paper on Defence* (Pretoria: Department of Defence, 1996).

23. Department of Defence, "Employment of Women in Uniform," *CNDF Internal Communications Bulletin* (Pretoria: Department of Defence, 1994).
24. Lindy Heinecken, "A Diverse Society, a Representative Military? The Complexity of Managing Diversity in the South African Armed Forces," *Scientia Militaria* 27, no. 1 (2009): 37.
25. Lindy Heinecken and Noelle van der Waag-Cowling, "The Politics of Race and Gender in the South African Armed Forces: Issues, Challenges and Lessons," *Commonwealth and Comparative Politics* 47, no. 4 (2009): 527.
26. Adriaan Van Breda, *Status of Women in the DOD: A Review of Women in the South African Department of Defence* (Pretoria: Department of Defence, 2010), 12.
27. Heinecken, "Diverse Society," 38.
28. Motumi, "Gender Equality," 29.
29. Sanjay T. Menon and Elize Kotze, "Human Resource Integration in the South African Military: A View from the Trenches," *Human Resource Management* 46, no. 1 (2007): 73.
30. Van Breda, *Status of Women*, 8–9.
31. Department of Defence, *Gender Mainstreaming Strategy, No 1 of 2008* (Pretoria: Department of Defence, 2008).
32. Van Breda, *Status of Women*, 9.
33. Lindy Heinecken and Rialize Ferreira, "Fighting for Peace: South Africa's Role in Peace Operations in Africa (Part I)," *African Security Review* 21, no. 2 (2012): 20–35.
34. Department of Defence, "South African National Defence Force Transformation Status," Briefing to the Joint Standing Committee on Defence (Cape Town: Parliament, May 21, 2015).
35. Van Breda, *Status of Women*, 10.
36. Ibid., 13.
37. Lindy Heinecken, "South African Officers' Views on Aspects of Military Culture: Grappling with Change and Realising What Needs to Be Done," in *On Military Culture: Theory, Practice and African Armed Forces*, ed. Francios Vrey, Abel Esterhuyse, and Thomas Mandrup (Cape Town: University of Cape Town Press, 2013), 249–65.
38. Lindy Heinecken, "Are Women 'Really' Making a Unique Contribution to Peacekeeping? The Rhetoric and the Reality," *Journal of International Peacekeeping* 19, no. 4 (2015): 227–48.
39. Siniša Malešević, *The Sociology of War and Violence* (Cambridge: Cambridge University, 2010).
40. Henry Carey, "Women and Peace and Security: The Politics of Implementing Gender Sensitivity Norms in Peacekeeping," *International Peacekeeping* 8, no. 2 (2001): 49–68; Nadine Puechguirbal, "Gender Training for Peacekeepers: Lessons from the DRC," *International Peacekeeping* 10, no. 4 (2003): 113–28.
41. Heinecken, "Are Women 'Really' Making," 240.
42. Ibid., 231–40.
43. Cock, "Forging a New Army," 107.
44. Heinecken, "Diverse Society," 37.
45. DOD, "South African."
46. Van Breda, *Status of Women*, xiii.
47. Heinecken, "Are Women 'Really' Making," 243.
48. Van Breda, *Status of Women*, xiii.
49. Heinecken, "Are Women 'Really' Making," 247.

50. Joshua Goldstein, *War and Gender: How Gender Shapes the War System and Vice Versa* (Cambridge: Cambridge University Press, 2001), 412.
51. Heinecken, "Are Women 'Really' Making," 232.
52. Heinecken, "Conceptualising the Tensions That Gender Integration Evokes," *Armed Forces and Society*, November 18, 2016, 1–19.

11

Integrating Gender Perspectives at NATO

Two Steps Forward, One Step Back

Charlotte Isaksson

The North Atlantic Treaty Organization (NATO) is not the first international organization that comes to mind when one is studying the implementation of gender perspectives. Most readers will therefore be surprised to learn of NATO's substantial work in this area. NATO, as an international organization and a military alliance with tremendous reach and impact, is of great relevance as it has the potential not only to influence the behavior of its member states but also to influence the host nations in the areas where its forces operate.

This chapter will describe some of the key achievements and challenges regarding the implementation of United Nations Security Council Resolution (UNSCR) 1325, related resolutions, and a gender perspective within NATO. The organizational focus is the military strategic commands: NATO Allied Command Operations (ACO), encompassing all NATO operations and missions, and Allied Command Transformation (ACT), which is responsible for education, training, and transformation. The chapter highlights the importance of managing the change process to achieve substantial and sustainable effect in the organization. Furthermore, this chapter argues that the progress until now has been both top-down and bottom-up; a handful of committed individuals have operated as entrepreneurs using their agencies within the organizations, thus contributing to the first steps toward transformation.

The chapter follows the themes of women's integration into the armed forces and the integration of gender perspectives into operations. Finally, it lists some of the remaining challenges for full implementation of the women, peace, and security (WPS) agenda, within NATO and possibly in other similar organizations as well.

Background

The WPS agenda, which grew out of UNSCR 1325, was, and is, a novelty that questioned the traditional perspectives on security policy. The WPS agenda both embodies and catalyzed an important paradigm shift in how security and peace are achieved and sustained. Given NATO's purpose to guarantee the freedom and security of its members through political and military means, it was likely that this agenda would be brought forward by the alliance.

NATO and UN Security Council Resolution 1325

NATO comprises the twenty-nine nations of the alliance and its twenty-six partners; translated, this means broad national diversity regarding policies and procedures on gender balance and gender mainstreaming. Thus, issues involving women's integration, recruitment and retention, human resource policies, and women's roles and equal place within the military, as well as military operations conducted with an integrated gender perspective, are approached within NATO with a broad variety of interpretations and priorities.

NATO is fully committed to implementing UNSCR 1325 as well as the subsequent and related UNSCRs on WPS, including conflict-related sexual violence.[1] The ambition is that this implementation should be an integral part of the everyday business in both the civilian and military structures. The work on WPS is fundamental to the realization of NATO's common values of individual liberty, democracy, human rights, and the rule of law; the obligations under the Charter of the United Nations; and other sources of international law.[2] NATO recognizes that such common values and legal obligations cannot be fulfilled if women cannot participate fully and freely or if their rights are not respected. This reasoning is in line with Cynthia Enloe's ideas that the everyday experiences of women are important to ensure that we do not end up "with a political analysis that is incomplete, even naïve."[3]

Since the 2007 adoption of the NATO Euro-Atlantic Partnership Council (EAPC) Policy on the Implementation of UNSCR 1325, considerable progress has been made in integrating a gender perspective within NATO and in encouraging nations and partners to improve their gender balance and national policies. NATO has adopted policy frameworks including issues that recognize the disproportionate impact conflict and post-conflict situations have on women and girls and the importance of ensuring women's active and meaningful participation in decision making in security institutions. NATO and its partners state that they will continue to work toward the participation of women in prevention, management, and resolution of conflicts and in peace building as well as in post-conflict efforts and cooperation.

NATO's fundamental and enduring purpose is to safeguard the freedom and security of all its members by political and military means. In accordance with the strategic concept, the three core tasks of the alliance are crisis management, cooperative security, and collective defense.[4] In April 2014 a third revised NATO/EAPC policy was released, providing the organization with the necessary direction and tools to further enhance the integration of a gender perspective into these three core tasks of the alliance at the strategic, operational, and tactical levels.[5]

Furthermore, during the four previous NATO summits in Lisbon (2010), Chicago (2012), Wales (2014), and Warsaw (2016), gender and WPS considerations were given increasing attention in the resulting declarations. The declarations provide a clear commitment to the protection of women's and girls' rights, taking due consideration of their security and protection needs and the prevention of conflict-related sexual and gender-based violence (SGBV). NATO and its partners aim to change the mind-sets and behaviors in their institutions and promote awareness and positive changes. Due regard is given to the social roles of both men and women and the way these may lead to different risks and security needs. Attention is also given to how these roles may translate into different contributions to conflict prevention and resolution. One of the ways to ensure accountability is through the involvement of civil society. NATO and its partners also recognize the key role civil society continues to play in promoting women's and girls' empowerment and in protecting their rights. Moving from policy to practice, NATO established the civil society advisory panel through which representatives from women's organizations have formally been given a role in NATO's development and implementation of its policy on WPS.[6] The first meeting was convened in October 2016 and focused on NATO's policy and action plan for the implementation of UNSCR 1325 and related resolutions on WPS across the three core tasks of the alliance.

An additional significant and symbolic step was taken at the Chicago Summit when the Norwegian diplomat Ms. Mari Skåre was appointed special representative to the NATO secretary general on WPS. This moved the WPS presence high up on the political agenda, which in turn facilitated a swifter and effective implementation. The second incumbent of the position was the Dutch ambassador Marriët Schuurman. Since its initial establishment, the position has gone from being "a first" to being institutionalized. In October

2014 another significant step was taken when the position was then changed from being linked solely to the secretary general to becoming a NATO special representative, a permanent position that indicates WPS should not be linked to a specific individual but rather must be an organizational responsibility.

Owing to an internal realignment of staff in October 2015, the portfolio of the special representative expanded to include protection of civilians, together with children and armed conflict. Merging all perceived "soft security" topics under the same leadership has been cause for some concern and mixed reactions as the objectives and expertise to address these topics are vastly different. What is clear is that nine months after the merger, the special representative's office retained staff support with the required expertise, but these individuals have subsequently been reallocated internally. At the time of this chapter submission, a third special representative, Ms. Clare Hutchinson, has been appointed after a recruitment selection process. This appointment marks a shift as the coming incumbent does not originate from the diplomatic corps but instead brings substantial experience and expertise on the topic, both on the policy and operational levels.

Moving down one level in the organization from the political to the strategic command level, the implementation of UNSCR 1325 and related resolutions in all planning, preparation, execution, and evaluation of NATO operations and missions is now well underway and significantly improved in comparison to before the 2013 review was conducted, upon request of the NATO nations.[7] Both ACO and ACT have, since 2011 and 2012, respectively, been staffing gender advisor positions. Many of the advancements are attributed to the initial appointment of an ACO gender advisor by the former Supreme Allied Commander Europe (SACEUR) Adm. (ret.) James Stavridis.[8] Initially, these gender advisor positions were placed lower in the organizational hierarchy. However, it was decided that the gender advisors should be organizationally elevated, and they now report directly to the commander. This rationale and process will be described later in this chapter.

The gender advisors are, and have been, the key tool for NATO's implementation work, especially in terms of working resources and knowledge. It has been recognized that upon appointment or through the course of their work, not all gender advisors have been perfectly equipped or fully supported. This remains a weakness that both ACO and ACT emphasize and need to rectify. While this has not yet been accomplished, the evolution following the first deployed gender advisors presents an undisputable positive trend. However, limited resources remain one of the key challenges. This challenge is exacerbated when NATO members and partners issue ambitious political guidance that comes with high expectations but do not provide sufficient resources to ensure effective implementation of their directives. As many military colleagues in the alliance frame it, "Nations must put their money where their mouth is." This has not been the case so far. Thus, the formal structures and positions created through great effort are left vacant, not only hampering work efficiency but also sending a signal, internally and externally, that the issue at hand is something spoken about but not necessarily addressed with real action.

NATO Policies on the UN Women, Peace, and Security Agenda—Definitions

Coherence in terminology is critical to effective change processes. Thus, the partial adoption of formalized NATO key terminology and definitions is in place and was initially disseminated through a document known as Bi-Strategic Command (Bi-SC) Directive 40-1, released in 2009 and updated in 2012 and 2017.[9] The (partial) introduction of an agreed terminology on gender has been instrumental to the results achieved so far. While the terminology is not fully established and continues to be misunderstood by external audiences, I have chosen to include crucial definitions from Bi-SC Directive 40-1 Revision 2 (2017) that have served as a common language when speaking about these topics within NATO.[10]

Gender Perspective

Integration of gender perspective is a way of assessing gender-based differences between women and men as reflected in their social roles and interactions and in the distribution of power and access to resources. In the strategic commands' activities, a gender perspective has been used to enable implementing the requests of UNSCR 1325 and related resolutions, as well as additional directives and policies from NATO. The aim is to consider how a situation affects the needs of men, women, boys, and girls and if and how NATO's activities affect them differently. More fundamentally, integrating a gender perspective is done by adapting action following a gender analysis.

Gender Mainstreaming

Gender mainstreaming is defined as a strategy used to achieve gender equality by assessing the implications for women and men of any planned action, in all areas, and at all levels in order to ensure that the concerns and experiences of both sexes are taken into account. This includes legislation, policies, and programs in all areas and at all levels to ensure that the concerns and experiences of women and men are taken into account in the design, implementation, monitoring, and evaluation of policies and programs in all political, economic, and societal spheres. These considerations should lead to ensuring equal opportunity to women and men. Gender mainstreaming in this context is the process whereby the role gender plays in relation to NATO's activities, including operations, missions, and exercises, is recognized. Gender mainstreaming does not focus solely on women but recognizes women's disadvantaged position in various communities.

Gender Equality

Gender equality refers to the equal rights, responsibilities, opportunities, and access for men, women, boys, and girls. Equality does not mean that women and men will become the same but that women's and men's rights, responsibilities, and opportunities will not depend on whether they are born female or male. Gender equality implies that the interests, needs, and priorities of both women and men are taken into consideration, recognizing the diversity of different groups of women and men. Gender equality is not just a women's issue; it concerns men and men's roles as well as women and women's roles.

Women's Integration into the Military and Security Domain

While there is no disagreement that the achievement of gender equality requires both gender balance and gender mainstreaming, NATO has admittedly had more success with gender mainstreaming than gender balance. This is in part owing to the reality that gender balance is solely a national responsibility; nations decide who to appoint and deploy to different positions. What this means for NATO is that the organization can only ask and encourage nations to appoint women, but the decisions remain national and, consequently, progress has been slow.[11]

In 2016 the number of female personnel and staff in the armed forces of NATO was 10.9 percent, compared to the yet lower 7.14 percent in 1999, signifying that NATO is not yet an equal opportunity workplace.[12] Most women in the national militaries that constitute NATO hold lower ranks, in supportive roles and as noncommissioned officers.[13] It could be argued that these are positions of less influence and fewer opportunities. A common justification for the current situation is that women's integration takes time; growing through the ranks requires a minimum number of years to yield results. However, substantial research and anecdotes demonstrate that the explanation is not that simple.[14] More recent numbers from March 2017, based on data from the fourteen

ACO headquarters, show that 7 percent of the working staff (both seconded from allies and partners as well as NATO staff) are women, which is lower than the numbers presented in the 2016 report from the NATO Committee on Gender Perspectives (NCGP).[15]

Military institutions are the visible incarnations of intertwined security relations within and between states. As a result, they are among the most gendered of all governmental and related activities.[16] The military and police have for a long time been dominated by men together with masculine norms in the thinking, processes, and activities that make them "institutions of hegemonic masculinity."[17] Women entering the military must conform to the dominating norm, which by virtue of history has been masculine. Anthony King describes how women entering combat roles become subjected to an institutionalized cultural code that denies them equality and recognition, no matter their behavior.[18] Simultaneously, some women become accepted "and a new cultural classification has been developed—'honorary men'"—whereby women make the transition from what sociologist Norbert Elias called an outsider to more of an insider position.[19] King argues that this constitutes an opportunity for armed forces to integrate women and perhaps re-gender gendered structures, but at the same time, he points out that this classification is so narrow that it is difficult for women to maintain it.[20]

One of the main barriers to retaining women in the military is the presence of SGBV, the existence of which is not exclusive to conflict or post-conflict settings. SGBV occurs in all NATO member states, including partner nations, within organizations, and within the military ranks of member countries. A study done in 2014 by the European Union (EU) Agency for Fundamental Rights shows that one in three women has experienced physical or sexual violence since the age of fifteen, one in five women has experienced stalking, and every second woman has been confronted with one or more forms of sexual harassment.[21] This phenomenon has been further visualized globally through a campaign centered on the social media hashtag #metoo that gained momentum in the autumn of 2017 and generated a previously unheard number of women stepping up and publicly admitting that they too had been victims of various forms of sexual harassment and violence.

The 2015 theme of the NCGP Conference was the recruitment and retention of women in the armed forces of NATO. In July 2015 NATO released its "Military Guidelines on the Prevention of, and Response to, Conflict-Related Sexual and Gender-Based Violence."[22] While these guidelines build on the foundation of the UN Security Council resolutions on conflict-related sexual violence and form NATO policy, the full continuum of SGBV spreading from the internal to the external requires a holistic, not a fragmented, approach.

Thus, sexual harassment, discrimination, sexual abuse, and sexual assault within NATO's own institutions must not be left out of the picture when the alliance addresses the threat of SGBV to peace and security.

The tendency to oversimplify and overlook the entirety of the continuum of gender-based violence is a continuous challenge. The political narrative and will to focus on sexual violence in conflict have come at the cost of the marginalization of other areas of equal importance within the WPS mandate. For example, the fragmentation of this continuum of violence can be seen through the disassociation of prevention and protection aspects of WPS in women's participation in peace building and conflict resolution. Thus, the internal situation of women's roles within the organization cannot, and must not, be left out of the discussion. Ignoring such internal aspects negatively affects the execution of operations and missions. If there is no respect and protection within a unit, the ability to deliver respect and protection for the local population can, and will, be questioned. Bi-SC Directive 40-1 gives direction and guidance in this regard: "Linkage between external and internal integration of gender perspective must be emphasized and recognized as a matter of credibility. Internal aspects including measures to remove barriers for the active participation of women in relation to the execution of operations and missions must be emphasized."

During the finalization of this chapter, the second revision of the Bi-SC Directive 40-1 was released. It is worth elaborating and drawing attention to one part of the continuum of SGBV: sexual exploitation and abuse (SEA). In the newest revision, the broad definition of SEA reflects a lack of coherence with the broader international community. This is potentially detrimental; clarity is a must when it comes to SEA. The reason is clear: trust is fundamental for unit cohesion. Thus, perpetrators of any form of SEA (i.e., fellow soldiers, officers, or other officials within an organization) must be identified and held accountable.

As we have seen, slight variations among entities (UN, EU, NATO) on the definition of SEA may exist, owing to their different styles and priorities on reporting and management of information, but this should not affect the common understanding of the terminology. By broadening the NATO definition of SEA to possibly include other areas relevant in other contexts (e.g., prostitution or forced labor), the latest Bi-SC Directive 40-1 becomes vague, lacking first and foremost a clear definition of what SEA means and what it represents. Instead, the new version highlights some categories that are considered within the realm of SEA without pointing precisely to the differences between, for example, sexual abuse and sexual exploitation. Since the topic is complex, spans different areas, and varies from context to context (e.g., SEA in conflict regions), it is critical to work from coherent and clear definitions. The previous version of the directive presented the concept straight to the point. It indicated the main differences between exploitation and abuse. By expanding the definition, the 2017 revision of Bi-SC Directive 40-1 marks a shift in both ambition and substance that could be seen in the light of a new reality.

In stark contrast to NATO, the UN has increased its ambition by appointing Ms. Jane Holl Lute as a special rapporteur on SEA. Out of several achievements, this appointment demonstrated not least the strong commitment of UN Secretary General António Guterres on this topic. Guterres established the circle of leadership, the high-level advisory board, and the launch at a high-level event during the UN General Assembly of the voluntary compact on preventing and addressing SEA. The far-reaching, progressive compact was signed, or indicated that it would be signed, by twenty-six of the NATO allies.[23] It is founded on the zero-tolerance agreed definition for SEA. In detrimental contrast the NATO deviation in the latest revision of the Bi-SC Directive 40-1 raises significant questions. This also makes the NATO approach to SEA weaker and vaguer than the approaches of the UN, EU, and African Union (AU).

However, one positive sign is that the pervasive "boys will be boys" attitude within military institutions, including peacekeeping operations, is slowly changing. In Australia, Canada, and the US, among other countries, military culture is under increasing scrutiny, and the armed forces are trying to better understand, prevent, and respond to cases of sexual harassment, assault, abuse, discrimination, and sexualized treatment of female, as well as male, personnel. These nations, among others, are also trying to eradicate the widespread culture that blames and encourages silence and hostility toward victims.

According to the website Protect Our Defenders, the US military had 20,300 (10,600 men and 9,600 women) reported sexual crimes cases in 2014, a rate unchanged from 2010.[24] Most victims were sexually assaulted more than once, resulting in over 47,000 assaults in 2014 alone. Even if these are troubling statistics, we must also remember that underreporting is a norm in cases of SGBV. It has been debated whether this is a US-specific problem or whether the situation reflects most NATO members and partners, in which the majority of the domestic defense organizations have not yet investigated the presence or frequency of these problems or have not made the results public. This problem is yet to be fully understood. Even still, it hampers the achievement of gender equality and negatively affects both the recruitment and retention of women and some men (as shown in the statistics, many of the sexual assaults in the US military are perpetrated against men).[25]

Clearly, SGBV is not prevalent only in the Global South and in traditional conflict settings. NATO and its partners cannot demand that host nations address gender equality, including eradicating a culture of permissive sexual harassment, assault, and abuse, without also turning inward. But as we have seen, it is always easier to criticize and advise externally rather than address the problems "at home." An example of how serious accusations of SEA were handled by a NATO partner is the case of sexual assault allegations against French peacekeeping troops in the Central African Republic (CAR) in 2014.[26] The aftermath of the French CAR case—which was closed in the French legal system without charges—highlights the challenge of addressing accusations of SEA internally and demonstrates the different yardsticks used to measure and interpret misdeeds done by foreign forces within a host nation. As we have repeatedly seen, the international community expects that all standards of behavior are respected by the host nation, yet these same standards do not seem to apply, or can fall to the wayside, in respect to those carrying out the mission. On a multiplicity of levels, not least including a resurrection of the specter of neocolonialism and moral obligation, this is problematic. NATO's credibility risks being questioned when it is cooperating with other nations or host nation forces. What is more, the essential relationship of trust between NATO forces and the population where NATO operates could deteriorate.

Work within ACO so far indicates that it is more acceptable to focus on gender-related issues "somewhere else," be it Afghanistan or Kosovo, or on the fact that the US military ("and not us") is under scrutiny for sexual assault in its own forces. It is rather convenient to focus on what might not work very well somewhere else. Paying more attention to internal gender-related aspects has been met with massive reluctance, both within and outside the gender community of practice. The perceived balance to be struck between what NATO's structure could and should do to become a gender-equal organization and the notion of national sovereignty and control over aspects related to internal matters have proved difficult to overcome and have stalled NATO's ability to act and lead by example in these matters. This actively leaves NATO behind other regional and global actors that have been forced to grapple with these issues and find a way forward as an organization. By avoiding these issues today, NATO is just delaying future problems and possible scandals.

From Policy to Practice through Organizational Change

But what does it mean for a military organization to mainstream gender and include gender balance? How should a military organization address this "new" form of security threat, that is, conflict-related SGBV, in support of the global WPS agenda? And what aspects need to be considered as NATO seeks to achieve lasting organizational change?

While NATO has successfully established many of the necessary internal structures to address the problem of SGBV in its operational mandates, effective implementation throughout the chain of command remains to be fully realized. The work must start internally. It should be mentioned that NATO has an external focus, and this focus has reinforced the internal processes so that both the internal and external gender dimensions are imprinted in the organizational DNA.[27]

Prior experience with organizational change indicates one common reason for failure—neglecting the organization's culture. In a military organization, it is imperative to understand military culture and its potential impact on a change process. In this context, terminology is important. For example, the language that ACO and ACT continue to use is the integration of gender perspectives as the primary, individually performed and comprehended method of the strategy gender mainstreaming.

It is also vital to accept that there may be resistance to change at the organizational and individual levels. Such resistance occurs for several reasons since a change process can be perceived as a threat to one's position and the proposed change can challenge existing values and culture. Most important, if the reasons behind a change process are not fully understood, resistance is much more likely to occur. As the primary internal agents for change, the gender advisors must face and ultimately deal with a lot of this resistance. Adding to this, since the gender advisors have been few and under-resourced since their establishment, the correlation between the perceived lack of results is evident and self-explaining.

Military organizations have long dealt with the challenge of having a deeply rooted culture and values that make resistance to top-down changes common. Yet as in most organizational environments, successful change is achieved when the commander or senior leaders support new ideas and empower gender advisors to make changes by giving them access and opportunities. Thus, from the start the gender advisors (at all levels from political and policy to operational and tactical) have focused, and are still focusing, much of their efforts on securing this senior leadership support. One could argue that it was mainly driven from the bottom up in the first phases, but later the process was driven from the top down. To enable success, ACO spent a lot of effort on anchoring the change processes and focused on bringing on board key leaders, both formal and informal, throughout the organization. As the personnel turnover is relatively high (even at the senior leadership level), work on educating colleagues needs to be continuously restarted since a "system" is not yet in place in which nations deploy candidates that are already knowledgeable about gender equality and the WPS dimensions related to their leadership and tasks.

But changing the mind-set of the whole organization takes time. Creating and fostering change is not only about building competence on gender and women's rights; it requires skills in social interactions and change management and not least comprehensive knowledge about the organizations' modus operandi. It must be understood that the sustainable integration of a gender perspective will be made mainly on the organization's own terms, and thus organizational ownership of these issues is a must.

Dealing with Change

The approach to internal ACO implementation has been to transform the thinking, planning, and conduct from within. By altering the normative organizational behavior through the integration of UNSCR 1325 and gender perspectives into existing structures, systems, and processes, the success rate in achieving gender-related objectives in ACO has been significant.

In complex military structures, one of the biggest challenges for the gender advisors has been to gain access to the core business. Identifying existing structures, systems, and processes and integrating UNSCR 1325 into the organization has been key. From the beginning ACO recognized that the creation of something new and unknown would likely generate a great deal of resistance. Nevertheless, a delicate balance had to be struck. On the one hand, the change process must be continuously and firmly grounded within the transformative WPS mandate: the demand of primarily preventing conflict and ensuring women's participation together with the objective of achieving gender equality. On the other hand, for this change process to be successful and effective, it must also be on the organization's own terms. Managing these two sides has been a craft and is akin to the work that a gender advisor is expected to undertake. For example, gender advisors are expected to support and advise "upon request" but also "when he/she considers appropriate."[28] This specific example highlights that the balance must constantly be fine-tuned and surveyed, with interventions provided as necessary.

Dealing with a theory of change has been instrumental for ACO's transformation and implementation. In the study *Implementing a Gender Perspective in Military Organizations and Operations: The Swedish Armed Forces Model*, there is a description of a process that served as a model for the ACO transformation.[29] In short, it deals with the concepts of leadership commitment, active involvement, local ownership, and responsibility—first and foremost, the commander's responsibility but also the responsibilities of everyone else. If one's aim is to achieve sustainable change, one must involve local actors and stakeholders. For ACO this resulted in identifying and defining the internal stakeholders and actors who would assume responsibility for the change process and for reaching the desired end state.

Individuals with an established strong platform and status were given primacy to participate in the first echelon. The agents for change have been, by purpose, individuals with substantial understanding and knowledge of the organization they should try to affect. This meant that they could easily communicate and relate to both the people and the tasks conducted. The ownership and active involvement from the organization was crucial. Having a very good understanding of the military and organizational culture and structure was key. In this culture all external actors (civilian, political, etc.) are often viewed with suspicion. Thus, gender advisors and gender focal points were identified and tasked. These individuals have been invaluable agents for change in the work so far. But as messengers for change, these individuals have faced many challenges. Some of them continue to be un/under-supported in an unwelcoming environment, facing significant resistance. The accomplishments achieved to date are attributed to a small, dedicated group of individuals who have persevered in the face of many difficulties and even hostility. However, while this is still true, there is light at the end of the tunnel, meaning progress has been achieved and the gender advisors and gender focal points today face fewer obstacles (although obstacles still exist). At least structures are in place now, as was not the case when the first gender advisory functions were deployed. Furthermore, today political, strategic, and operational direction and guidance and job descriptions exist, although, according to some, they are overwhelming in scope. Progress is being made, and safeguarding achievements is important.

One identified challenge area has been monitoring and evaluation, including the frequency and content of reports. The question is, Should there be stand-alone gender- and WPS-related reports, or should everything be mainstreamed into already existing reports? Guidance on reporting has been issued, though it is currently too early to draw any conclusions. At the time of writing, the perception is that this area still needs improving. However, the latest direction and guidance are that reporting should normally be comprehensive.

Impact of the Change Process

When NATO first began to address UNSCR 1325 and related resolutions, gender was marginalized to a few documents and policies. Today, gender is fully present at the core of the organization.

One of the main achievements of NATO's military component is the state-of-the-art blueprint containing practical proposals and guidelines for implementing UNSCR 1325 through the revised Bi-SC Directive 40-1. The directive, first approved in 2009, has been revised twice, in August 2012 and in October 2017.[30] It is the only document of its kind to have been endorsed both by NATO's highest governing body (the North Atlantic Council [NAC]) and by the Defense Ministers of the Alliance through their approval of the Bi-Strategic Implementation Plan in October 2013. Bi-SC Directive 40-1 is a comprehensive directive providing relevant guidance regarding the who, what, why, and how of ensuring the implementation of UNSCR 1325 and the related resolutions and the integration of a gender perspective into military organizations and forces within the NATO Command Structure and NATO-led operations. If properly disseminated, reinforced, and implemented, the directive responds to several challenges regarding the implementation of UNSCR 1325 and related resolutions.[31]

The directive is clear and understandable. It is presented in a form that is familiar and easily recognized by individuals within the organization. The message was straightforward: "doing gender" is just like doing any other task. This understanding has been a key to success. However, an overzealous focus on awareness raising at all levels of the organization has hampered continued implementation. No one would suggest constantly and quantitatively demonstrating the operational benefits of intelligence, strategic communications, or special operations, so one might question using "awareness" and "proofs and evidence" to motivate gender training. Gender should not be sidelined or perceived as needing special treatment that no other topic in the organization requires. Thus, the ACO and ACT approach has been to use strong and active verbs when speaking and writing about gender so it becomes clearer that action and commitment are expected from everyone.

In addition to Bi-SC Directive 40-1, NATO has created a working structure to ensure the implementation of UNSCR 1325 and gender mainstreaming. The analysis was made early: if NATO wanted results, it had to invest. The integration of a gender perspective in NATO activities requires resources, just as any other area or topic does. The math is simple: limited resources equals limited results.

NATO's investments are reflected through the establishment of gender advisor positions throughout the organization, which includes the joint force commands (operational level). Gender advisor positions were also established at the tactical (theater) level. The gender advisor job descriptions used to list the prerequisite of undertaking the biannual NATO-accredited gender advisor course; however, this course is now listed as a "desirable requirement," thus signaling a devaluation of sufficient professional training before deployment. One of the reasons for this change may be the difficulty of having nations fill these posts. The job description may have been amended to open the positions to a larger group of eligible candidates and to enable recruitment to be done first and training thereafter. At the same time, given similar circumstances, would NATO have revised the job descriptions for any other position, for example, legal advisors, political or human rights advisors, or cyber experts?

All gender advisors are to report directly to the commander with the rationale being that direct access provides better effectiveness. This requirement has been a challenge to enforce for various reasons, including commanders' and advisors' different personality types and the desire to break certain social codes in order to prove one's place in an established group.[32] In addition to gender advisors, gender focal points (dual-hatted positions) are also being appointed, ensuring a working network throughout the entire structure and organization. The appointment of gender focal points supports the work toward full integration of a gender perspective as the primary, individually performed method of strategy of gender mainstreaming. The main objective is that every part of the structure (individuals included) works with an integrated gender perspective on their own tasks and responsibilities, in complement to the subject matter experts. This work is conducted by women and men, and within ACO most individuals holding these positions are men.

In support of the education and training of the gender advisory structure, a system was established in 2012 under the NATO global programming approach. A strategic training plan for gender was developed and endorsed at the Military Committee, which officially appointed the Nordic Centre for Gender in Military Operations as the first gender department head in a partner nation. The ACO gender advisor was designated as the requirements authority, responsible for identifying and developing all training requirements for NATO at the strategic level and below. The professional approach to gender education and training has allowed for gender to be integrated into the current structure and has served as an example for other subject areas to follow.

In addition to the previously mentioned achievements, several operational and military force–led efforts are being more effectively accomplished with an integrated gender perspective. Such efforts involve security tasks, including guarding, patrolling, and escorting individuals or groups in vulnerable situations, as well as targeting insurgents and illegal combatants. Both in monitoring and in reporting the security situation (including SGBV) of men, women, girls, and boys, the presence of security forces has a deterring effect and creates safety where those forces are deployed. Maj. Gen. Karl Engelbrektson, a former battalion commander in NATO's Kosovo Force (KFOR) during the Balkan Wars, describes certain parts of Kosovo where women felt so insecure that they and their families could not function.[33] These women were too afraid to go out to buy food, take their children to school, or perform other daily tasks.

Because of this, some of the deployed NATO forces planned publicly known and random patrols in certain areas to increase freedom of movement for the women. This is a classic military task of creating a safe and secure environment through the conduct of military operations.

NATO has also integrated a gender perspective into its regular tasks of training, advising, and assisting local forces. The importance of military personnel as role models and positive agents for change in this regard should not be underestimated, especially in mentoring and training. This is particularly true in the context of security sector reform and security force assistance, as well as in other capacity-building exercises for the local security forces. These activities aim to increase the local ability to address and deal with issues of SGBV and to provide equal security for men, women, girls, and boys. The most significant and relevant example is the political decision surrounding the transition to the current Resolute Support Mission in Afghanistan. In the lead-up to the mission, the NAC issued the NAC Initiating Directive (NID).[34] For the first time, UNSCR 1325 and gender equality were presented as part of the military strategic objectives. This facilitated the integration of a gender perspective throughout the planning cycle. Whereas in previous operations military planning had been solely based on policy, the NID for Afghanistan provided an impetus for a wholly different process in analysis and military planning. Including gender equality and UNSCR 1325 in the NID demonstrated that gender could not be marginalized; it must be integrated everywhere at all levels to facilitate effective implementation. This has spurred continued institutionalization, although the misconceptions of what "gender really means" and how it should be translated have led to the attempted inclusion of other seemingly related subjects (e.g., children and armed conflict, protection of civilians, LGBTQI rights) without them being anchored in the same WPS mandate.

Identifying and targeting specific key documents to include gender within the ACO structure have been critical for establishing and sustaining implementation. It was imperative to revise relevant intelligence, planning, reporting, and assessment tools so that they included a gender perspective, with the objective of facilitating gender mainstreaming through all phases of NATO operations. The integration of a gender perspective into the NATO Comprehensive Operational Planning Directive (COPD) was one of the first and significant steps. This meant that direction and guidance were sent to all planners within the alliance and it militaries seeking inspiration from NATO about how a gender perspective could be integrated. The deliberate use of the doctrine, directives, and handbooks as tools for integration and institutionalization was prioritized. In 2018 the COPD was revised, and the achievements made since the first version (e.g., within the area of conflict-related SGBV) were integrated.

Already in July 2015, a crucial step was taken with the release of the Gender Functional Planning Guide (FPG).[35] The Gender FPG is a practical tool on how to integrate, in concrete terms, gender analysis and perspective into planning at all levels from the military strategic to the operational and tactical levels. It also presents a gender analysis tool, something that had been previously lacking and thus hampering the conduct of gender analysis. Equally important for a systematic and effective approach is making sure that the implementers understand "how" this should be done. The Gender FPG not only supports planners at the headquarters but also influences exercises, training, and education for personnel taking part in NATO operations and missions. This is an example of how to work with an integrated approach building on existing structures and systems rather than creating something new and potentially in parallel. The Gender FPG has also been a way of providing the planners in NATO with a concrete hands-on tool that facilitates and supports them in integrating gender without necessarily requiring a gender advisor. This approach has served to support the overarching strategy of gender mainstreaming.

Embedding a gender perspective into all planning phases related to a crisis is crucial in promoting the change process. ACO has integrated a gender perspective into its existing analytical processes and has introduced gender analysis as the primary tool to improve the result of any analysis, though this is still a work in progress.[36] Gender has also been integrated into the ACO *Comprehensive Crisis Operations Management Handbook*, ensuring that gender is institutionalized into crisis identification, horizon scanning, early warnings, and all other similar assessments.[37]

Another important cornerstone in the integration of gender in ACO has been the revisions to SACEUR's Annual Guidance on Education, Training, Exercises and Evaluation (SAGE). For several years gender has been an identified priority in this publication.[38] For example, the evaluation of headquarters and forces has integrated gender criteria. The inclusion of a gender perspective into the evaluation criteria for all headquarters—initially an area that posed a potential challenge—has been remarkable. A headquarters cannot be considered fully operationally capable if these criteria are not sufficiently met. This has meant that implementing the mandate of WPS has become a requirement and is no longer voluntary, thus demonstrating that the change process has been given substantial force within the existing system. The inclusion of gender-related criteria in the evaluation and certification process sent a clear message to the subordinate headquarters; to be certified within NATO, a headquarters has to demonstrate that it has sufficient gender capability and capacity. This requirement led several national headquarters with the ambition to be certified to appoint their own gender advisors, even if they did not necessarily understand the importance of the issues or undergo training.[39] In the 2016 evaluation cycle, the NATO Rapid Deployable Corps (Turkey) Headquarters demonstrated the professionalization of this work by fully engaging the gender advisor and all staff and by reviewing all procedures and processes to ensure the integration of a gender perspective throughout the planning cycle. This work is now being extended to the forces level through the review of the Combat Readiness Evaluation (CREVAL).[40]

Harnessing the Power of the Community: The Military Wives of SHAPE WoMen

Most people within NATO and ACO working in gender-related positions over the years have had to come up with some atypical solutions and innovative methods, sometimes in an unwelcoming environment, in order to promote awareness and change. In 2012 at the Supreme Headquarters Allied Powers Europe (SHAPE) in Belgium, an independent initiative called SHAPE WoMen was established with the aim to unite the SHAPE community (NATO workers and their families) and deepen the understanding of gender-related issues. One of SHAPE WoMen's goals is to bridge the gap between the people working for SHAPE headquarters and their female spouses who are also working either in the military or as civilians, as these relations often create unique challenges for the professional women.[41] In 2016 a women's professional network, albeit only for the military women, was established in ACT. Both of these networks are examples that demonstrate some of the creative and unique initiatives that were needed to push the envelope.

Challenges to Full Implementation

Gender mainstreaming as a strategy has been questioned because as long as the fundamental associations among security threats, military capacity, and the masculine soldier ideal persist, any efforts aimed at gender mainstreaming will only continue to take the form of integrating women into already defined masculine structures.[42] NATO has made some clear headway and could be described as state of the art, with the creation of a solid policy framework, education and training, the integration of gender perspectives into operational planning, and consultation with civil society organizations. Nonetheless, the organization admittedly continues to struggle with how to incorporate the ideas and changes needed to fully integrate a gender perspective. The ability to address and deal with gender inequalities, SGBV (including SEA), and women's limited influence and participation requires a comprehensive approach. "Review of the Practical

Implications of UNSCR 1325 for the Conduct of NATO-Led Operations and Missions" concludes for ACO that the structure, policies, and directives are in place to support UNSCR 1325, but implementation remains a challenge.[43]

This extensive review, headed by internal and external experts, academics, and practitioners, also found that there is a lack of knowledge and understanding about both the principles behind UNSCR 1325 and the way it should be implemented. This is particularly negative news for the commanders and senior leadership who are responsible for the implementation. Another challenge is a lack of cooperation and collaboration among security forces, civil organizations/society, and women's organizations. There are also unclear mandates on how to address gender perspectives and SGBV. An example of the politicization of the WPS mandate is the monitoring, analysis, reporting, and assessment tool developed by the UN and adopted through the NATO Military Guidelines. Unfortunately, the tool overlooks the needs of survivors, who are treated more as numbers than humans since forces are not trained on how to address SGBV.

While there are good practices in place (such as training initiatives, protective measures, cooperation between military and civilian actors, leadership, and reporting), they are not systematically disseminated or made readily available. Security forces and other security actors are, for the most part, not sufficiently directed, trained, or skilled in working with gender as an integrated part of their military or security-enhancing capability.

Gender equality must encompass and consider both men's and women's parts in the problem and in the solution. The ability to deal with all these aspects is affected by several challenges to full implementation. Overcoming such challenges requires extensive reflection, cooperation, coordination, and understanding of the WPS agenda. This agenda is and remains transformative and practical, but all stakeholders must avoid contributing to the mandates' becoming political tools and bargaining chips. The politicization of UNSCR 1325 within NATO is evident. One indicator of this is the seeming lack of resources for staffing or support to develop specific programs to implement the WPS agenda, both at the strategic and operational levels. One impediment to the overall staffing cycle of gender advisors is the lack of recognition of the professionalization of the gender advisory capacity in many national militaries, although it must be noted that this should not be viewed as a satisfactory reason to justify the lack of gender advisors within NATO.

One of the challenges of the gender advisory structure has been the dilemma posed by vacant positions. Equally disconcerting has been the number of cases in which nations post gender advisors who are not fully qualified or motivated to generate the momentum needed for change. Following political direction and guidance, ACO established the current gender advisory structure. When these positions, at various levels, are left vacant, directives and orders related to UNSCR 1325 and Bi-SC Directive 40-1 cannot be effectively implemented. This situation also constitutes a gap between the "talk" and the "walk" by the nations that highlight the importance of gender equality and the need to staff gender advisors yet do not post gender advisors into the organization. This is illustrated in both of NATO's current major theaters of operations: the KFOR and the International Security Assistance Force (ISAF). The KFOR deputy gender advisor position has not been filled since its creation in 2012. Similarly, thirteen nations actively promoted establishing a brigadier general position as the gender advisor to ISAF in an attempt to strengthen the work with gender by NATO in Afghanistan in 2012; however, no nation offered to fill the position for almost two years. The position was finally filled through an atypical approach involving not only influential actors at SHAPE who lent their direct support but also clever maneuvering of the staff work process to ensure that supportive decision makers were presiding at the time. At the time of writing, the ACO gender advisor position is unfilled and is likely to remain so until summer 2018. Taken together, the lack of will for action can be perceived as a reflection of the true commitment.

Another remaining challenge has been bridging the gap between the internal aspects of sexual harassment, exploitation, and abuse and the external delivery of security and operational effectiveness. This discrepancy is evident in the development of the revisions to Bi-SC Directive 40-1. Great differences of opinion on the clear link between internal and external aspects of sexual harassment, exploitation, and abuse and between both strategic headquarters delayed the release of this critical policy document, with a possible retrograde on the horizon. While the arguments that gender is a force multiplier and provides operational effectiveness have been essential in gaining traction within nations and in getting the appropriate buy-in from the organization, the overt de-extrapolation of the internal vice external aspects of gender reflects a lack of understanding of the WPS mandate. We have seen an overemphasis on the external applications focusing on "operational effectiveness" in education and training, resulting in many gender advisors being ill-equipped to respond to all aspects of gender dimensions within a headquarters. Achievements and investments that were once well entrenched in the structure have been challenged. Some nations have taken a stance against the Bi-SC Directive, both actively and passively, demonstrating that this difference of opinion is based on a national political will's attempting to influence NATO structures. Just as solely pursuing gender balance initiatives will not lead to gender equality, the continued oversimplification and emphasis on operational effectiveness will not live up to the fulfillment of UNSCR 1325.

Working with the integration of a gender perspective, UNSCR 1325, and related resolutions and being a woman in a highly gendered and male-dominated context still constitute challenges. The similarities between applying the external mandates and being a woman within the organization are many and are primarily based on gender norms, gender relations, gendered power structures, and figuration theory. Taken together, the challenges impede implementation and create an atmosphere that prevents new individuals from joining the cause because it is perceived as too difficult.

Conclusion and Recommendations on How to Move Forward

NATO is a large, international political-military organization with the ability to demonstrate best practices in, for example, capacity building and local security forces training. This ability makes NATO a key element in establishing upstream security in what will be a future paradigm for any military organization. NATO could help national security forces take the lead in integrating a gender perspective and improving the gender balance simply by setting, and living up to, the standards stipulated in UNSCR 1325 and the related resolutions on WPS, as well as by promoting public diplomacy, liaising, and mentoring. These efforts could be enhanced by developing training activities, establishing train-the-trainer programs, strengthening structures and systems (e.g., for the recruitment and retention of women), and supporting leadership programs for local security institutions. Additionally, in the countries where NATO currently operates, it must work comprehensively with the other organizations operating in the security field to ensure an integrated gender perspective based on the principles supporting women's meaningful participation, the protection of women's bodies and rights, and the prevention of conflict as well as SGBV.

One key to accelerating the implementation of the WPS agenda is closer collaboration on all levels between international, regional, and local organizations and other relevant stakeholders. Identifying and singling out common prioritized areas would support unified and focused efforts and would most likely lead to even more effective implementation.

Even if NATO faces improvements regarding the creation of a working structure of trained individuals, there is still room for improvement regarding the actual implementation of UNSCR 1325. The 2013 NATO review found that the structure to support and facilitate the implementation of UNSCR 1325 is in place and the policies and directives are mainly in place, but that the implementation is still hampered. One challenge is the lack of knowledge and understanding about the principles behind UNSCR 1325 and the way these principles should be carried out. Since the commanders and the senior leadership are formally responsible for this implementation, they play a special, and powerful, role in promoting the change process.

The 2013 review also presented a series of recommendations. NATO should ensure that training on UNSCR 1325 (in particular, on participation, prevention, and protection) occurs both before deployment and on site. This was specifically a strong recommendation to the commanders and individuals holding leadership positions. Another recommendation was to further strengthen and continue to build on the structure of gender advisors. Gender advisors work to ensure that a gender perspective will be taken into account in the analysis, planning, conduct, and evaluation of NATO-led operations and missions, as NATO commanders and staff are not yet themselves skilled in this regard.

One of the best practices identified and already relied on by NATO is the process of external and independent reviews of its progress in achieving the aims set out in the 2014 action plan. This process has been repeated twice, with the latest review not yet available externally. This is a laudable procedure and other organizations should follow suit. The conclusions of the first review stress positive achievements and progress but note that much remains to be done. As time passes and additional reviews are undertaken, the focus on maintaining previous gains and avoiding erosion within the organization will be essential to maintaining organizational momentum.

While almost everyone agrees that gender equality is critical, there is slow progress on the underlying broader gender equality front among most nations, including the NATO alliance and its partners. Change can happen, it has happened, and it is happening. From some viewpoints, the military and security forces have been part of the problem, but they could, and must, be part of the solution. Military and security forces, including NATO forces, should be viewed as role models and as drivers and agents for transformation and change. NATO holds a high status within the global military world, and several nonmember and aspiring-member nations continue to look to what NATO prioritizes. In this regard, NATO is a trailblazer.

The process of change starts with actions and concrete lessons. NATO, as well as other military and security sector actors, has the procedures and skills in place to address and handle (i.e., support prevention and protection) sexual violence and gender-based violence. Positive effects can be achieved by displaying best practices, providing mentorship, and setting a good example for international partners. Additionally, military organizations must support more officers, soldiers, and operators to perform their daily work at all levels based on tactics, techniques, and procedures that respond to and deal with sexual violence and continuously work with an integrated gender perspective. Military personnel, both male and female, should be used more often as agents for change when it comes to capacity building or reform within local security forces.

When implementing UNSCRs on WPS, one of the fundamental principles is that the individuals and groups that are the beneficiaries of greater participation, prevention, and protection must be consulted and have ownership of the process. The approach of women and grassroots activists "nothing about us, without us" is applicable when transforming an organization. It is as applicable to the organization one aims to transform as it is to the WPS agenda, which requires consultation with women and women's organizations as a fundamental component of UNSCR 1325. The notion of "nothing about us, without us" is applicable both to women in conflict or crisis settings and to soldiers and officers within any military organization. This idea highlights again the necessity of a bottom-up approach to a transformational process.

The military has the means to provide close protection for specific groups or individuals, and likewise, decisions and resources can be put in place to provide certain areas or events specific needed protective measures. For example, hostage and rescue operations and negotiations are military capacities that could also be used in relation to prevention and protection from SGBV. Moreover, liaising with other military and security forces and with the local population and representatives from local and international organizations is key. This type of liaison is important from both a situational awareness and a coordination perspective. Monitoring, mapping, and reporting of security threats made to specific individuals and groups and improved security and risk analysis in specific regions and areas of operations could emerge with improved communication both among security actors and between military and civilian/humanitarian organizations. This could serve to increase the awareness regarding threats of sexual violence and to influence and inform the overall security response. Information collection, briefing, and analytical skills are core capabilities within the military profession. If this capacity could also be used to map, analyze, and assess gender-related issues (including SGBV), individuals at risk or affected by this type of violence would be far better supported. Furthermore, these efforts could improve early warning capacity.

In addition, other core capabilities of military organizations, including information/data collection, monitoring trends, data analysis, and reporting, could also be used to support the collection of evidence in order to identify and hold perpetrators accountable.

To use such military capabilities, clear directives are needed throughout the organization. Resources need to be allocated and provided at all levels within NATO and in the national military structures. Presently, the military capacity is not being fully utilized, although it is within reach if effective direction and guidance are issued and implemented accordingly.

Finally, it is problematic to equate gender only with women, excluding men.[44] Men and women are both constructing and constructed within the existing gendered hierarchies. If the gendered structures for men, women, girls, and boys are not taken into consideration and accounted for, security analyses and assessments and ultimately security responses will be flawed and less effective. The key strategy for the military could be to focus on prevention and protection by ensuring that security and safety issues affecting girls and women, as well as men and boys, are addressed before violations take place.[45] This is a security problem not only for individual women and girls but also for society, and one that cannot solely be addressed through the typical responses of law enforcement and the judicial system.

Moreover, the institutionalization and full integration of gender perspectives are still in the initial phase, and appropriate structures and systems are still being developed. NATO is a large and complex organization in which, in general, change is slow. Therefore, achieving a gender perspective has not been realized in all of NATO's preparations for the defense of the alliance's territory or within its crisis management plans. Therefore, optimally ensuring the equal participation and protection of men and women in the event of a crisis is still not fully considered or planned in some situations. These internal weaknesses constitute challenges when the alliance implements the WPS agenda and attempts to address SGBV. Thus, the question remains: How can NATO, with its own internal gender-related challenges, credibly respond to the security problems and the lack of participation by women in its external operations? The short answer is that NATO cannot yet do so, but ambitions are high, the policy framework is strong, and the nations have pledged their commitment, so there is great potential. However, the incoherence between the internal and external aspects of gender and WPS will constitute a challenge, not least when it comes to credibility.

To conclude, while areas still need to be strengthened and previous gains and achievements need to be protected, many of the current global best practices on gender are to be found within NATO. The organization has made tremendous efforts in terms of establishing and institutionalizing appropriate structures, and this work is necessary to ensure effective implementation of the WPS agenda in NATO's internal and external activities. However, much of what has been achieved so far is based on pure gender mainstreaming, which will not make grand headlines or end up in glossy brochures. Subsequently, it is less visible that NATO is actually and directly impacting the lives of people wherever it conducts its activities.

Notes

1. In the Military Guidelines on the Prevention of and Response to Conflict-Related Sexual and Gender-Based Violence, NATO has expanded the UN term with a specific NATO definition.
2. NATO, The North Atlantic Treaty, 1949.
3. Cynthia Enloe, *Bananas, Beaches and Bases: Making Feminist Sense of International Politics*, updated ed. (Berkeley: University of California Press, 2004).
4. NATO, "Strategic Concept for the Defence and Security of the Members of the North Atlantic Treaty Organization," November 19–20, 2010, https://www.nato.int/strategic-concept/pdf/Strat_Concept_web_en.pdf.
5. NATO, "NATO/EAPC Policy for the Implementation of UNSCR 1325 on Women, Peace and Security and Related Resolutions," April 1, 2014, https://www.nato.int/cps/en/natohq/official_texts_109830.htm?selectedLocale=en.
6. NATO, "New Civil Society Advisory Panel on Women, Peace and Security," October 18, 2016, https://www.nato.int/cps/en/natohq/news_136119.htm.
7. Helene Lackenbauer and Richard Langlais, "Review of the Practical Implications of UNSCR 1325 on NATO-Led Operations and Missions," *Leadership* 5 (2013): 92.
8. In ACT the gender portfolio was initially assigned to individuals as an additional task. The position was not formalized in the structure as a full-time gender advisor position until 2012.
9. NATO, Bi-Strategic Command Directive 40-1, September 2009; NATO, Bi-Strategic Command Directive 40-1, August 2012; NATO, Bi-Strategic Command Directive 40-1, October 2017.
10. NATO, Bi-SC Directive 40-1 (2017).
11. Since 2011, strong encouragement is frequently undertaken through letters, bilateral meetings, and force generation conferences.
12. NATO, "2016 Summary of the National Reports of NATO Members and Partner Nations to the NATO Committee on Gender Perspectives," November 15, 2017, https://www.nato.int/nato_static_fl2014/assets/pdf/pdf_2017_11/20171122_2016_Summary_of_NRs_to_NCGP.pdf; NATO, "UNSCR 1325 Reload: An Analysis of Annual National Reports to the NATO Committee on Gender Perspectives from 1999–2013," June 1, 2015, https://www.nato.int/issues/nogp/meeting-records/2015/UNSCR1325-Reload_Report.pdf.
13. NATO, "UNSCR 1325 Reload."
14. Sahana Dharmapuri, *Not Just a Numbers Game: Increasing Women's Participation in UN Peacekeeping*, Providing for Peacekeeping No. 4 (New York: International Peace Institute, July 2013), https://www.ipinst.org/wp-content/uploads/publications/ipi_epub_not_just_a_numbers_game.pdf.
15. Interview with a staff officer from SHAPE, November 6, 2017.
16. Annica Kronsell and Erika Svedberg, *Making Gender, Making War: Violence, Military and Peacekeeping Practices* (London: Routledge, 2011).
17. Ibid.
18. Anthony King, "The Female Combat Soldier," *European Journal of International Relations* 22, no. 1 (2015), https://doi.org/10.1177/1354066115581909.
19. Ibid.; Norbert Elias and John L. Scotson, *The Established and the Outsiders: A Sociological Enquiry into Community Problems*, 2nd ed. (London: SAGE, 1994).

20. King, "Female Combat Soldier."
21. European Union Agency for Fundamental Rights, *Violence against Women: An EU-Wide Survey* (Luxembourg: Publications Office of the European Union, 2015).
22. NATO, "Military Guidelines on the Prevention of, and Response to, Conflict-Related Sexual and Gender-Based Violence," June 1, 2015, https://www.nato.int/issues/women_nato/2015/MCM-0009-2015_ENG_PDP.pdf.
23. United Nations Secretary General, "Note to Correspondents on Voluntary Compact on Preventing and Addressing Sexual Exploitation and Abuse," September 29, 2017, https://www.un.org/sg/en/content/sg/note-correspondents/2017-09-29/note-correspondents-voluntary-compact-preventing-and.
24. "Military Sexual Assault Fact Sheet," Protect Our Defenders, December 9, 2016, http://www.protectourdefenders.com/factsheet/.
25. The Department of Defense says that "about 10,800 males are sexually assaulted every year ... roughly 8,000 women are assaulted." From Jim Garamone, "Experts: Males Are Also Victims of Sexual Assault," DOD News, February 20, 2015, https://www.defense.gov/News/Article/Article/604140/.
26. Charlotte Isaksson, "Slow Justice Is No Justice: Sexual Exploitation in Military and Civilian Operations," *Just Security*, February 9, 2017, https://www.justsecurity.org/37495/slow-justice-justice-sexual-exploitation-military-civilian-operations/.
27. Robert Egnell, Petter Hojem, and Hannes Berts, *Implementing a Gender Perspective in Military Organisations and Operations: The Swedish Armed Forces Model* (Uppsala: Uppsala University, Department of Peace and Conflict Research, 2012).
28. NATO, ACO gender advisor job description, revised 2013.
29. Egnell, Hojem, and Berts, *Implementing a Gender Perspective*.
30. NATO, Bi-Strategic Command Directive 40-1, August 2012; NATO, Bi-Strategic Command Directive 40-1, October 2017.
31. Lackenbauer and Langlais, "Review of the Practical Implications."
32. Elias and Scotson, *Established and the Outsiders*.
33. Maj. Gen. Karl Engelbrektson, interview by the author, February 6, 2018.
34. Planning guidance to the military commanders and planners giving direction and guidance for the end state, expected outcomes, and objectives of any mission or operation.
35. NATO, *Allied Command Operations Gender Functional Planning Guide*, July 24, 2015, https://www.forsvarsmakten.se/siteassets/english/swedint/engelska/swedint/courses/genad/07-aco-gender-functional-planning-guide.pdf.
36. A key future focus will be on analysis in countering violent extremism, etc., in NATO's counterterrorism action plan.
37. NATO/SHAPE, *Comprehensive Crisis Operations Management Handbook*, SH/OPI/CCOMC/15-310491 (July 15, 2015).
38. SAGE is the key directing and guiding instrument regarding education, training, and exercises for ACO.
39. Headquarters located in the UK, the Netherlands, France, Greece, Italy, Turkey, and Spain.
40. NATO standardization programs require that all allied units deployed to foreign operations be compatible primarily in combat tactics, communications, and logistics support. One of these programs, CREVAL, ensures the units will be able to fully cooperate in conducting joint defense or attack operations.
41. Enloe, *Bananas, Beaches and Bases*.

42. King, "Female Combat Soldier."
43. Lackenbauer and Langlais, "Review of the Practical Implications."
44. This is something that NATO itself is highlighting in all three versions of the Bi-Strategic Directive 40-1.
45. Ilya Lozovsky, "A Wake-Up Call for NGOs," *Foreign Policy*, June 5, 2015, https://foreignpolicy.com/2015/06/05/a-wake-up-call-for-ngos-tunisia-arab-spring-oslo-freedom-forum/.

12

Conclusion

Lessons of Comparison and Limits of Generalization

Robert Egnell and Mayesha Alam

Throughout history, women have played varied but very limited roles in military affairs. This started changing in the second half of the twentieth century—although the processes to integrate women fully in military organizations have in most cases been painstakingly slow and constrained. In 2000 this process was aided by the passing of UN Security Council Resolution (UNSCR) 1325, which placed unprecedented international focus on the experiences and roles of women during war and called for their increased participation in resolving and preventing conflicts. But neither 1325 nor the resolutions that have followed it are panaceas to the incorporation of women, and gender mainstreaming more broadly, in peace and security processes. One of the most understudied but critical areas related to the women, peace, and security agenda has been military and stabilization operations.

Military organizations are controversial and complicated in the women, peace, and security agenda. On the one hand, they are viewed by some feminist scholars and activists as the very materialization of the patriarchal order in which power relations are determined and negotiated through violence, as well as the final bastions of male exclusivity and hypermasculine organizational cultures. Military organizations, in this sense, are inherently problematic—something to overcome or dismantle. On the other hand, another branch of feminist perspective accepts that the rule of law and international security are upheld through coercive measures—police and military—and that violence is sometimes necessary to protect society and liberal values. In this view, the military can also be seen as part of "the solution" to, for example, protecting women from sexual and gender-based violence in war or as the instrument through which to maintain order and defend national interests. Regardless of perspective, the military organization is consequential to national and international security, so it should be at the very core of debates on gender equality and the broader women, peace, and security agenda.

This volume has therefore sought to examine how gender perspectives and the presence of women have taken hold and been received in different military organizations. This has been achieved through a comparison of the integration processes in eight countries and the UN and NATO. Not only have several detailed histories of the processes in each case been provided, but the analyses have also zoomed in on common research questions and variables: Where did the pressure and the decisions to change come from? Who, or what department, was put in charge of the process? Was emphasis placed on the integration of women or gender perspectives? Who were the key agents of change? What were the biggest roadblocks? Which processes or decisions turned out to be essential or limiting? Was the aim of the process described as one of increased military effectiveness or gender equality? How does the timing and tempo of change fit into a broader international normative and political context?

In general, there are at least three reasons why armed forces of the world are increasingly opening up to women and applying gender perspectives in operations. First, societal change to advance gender equality is driving change within military organizations' policies toward women. This is, for sure, a tediously slow process that in many places started decades ago with necessity ushering the first women into administrative and support roles within armed forces. Second, UNSCR 1325 is recognized and under some degree of implementation in most countries. This has increased attention to gender equality, women's empowerment, and the salience of gender mainstreaming in operations in a variety of government agencies (including those that may have been unengaged or even hostile to such ideas in the past). Third, operational lessons from the military campaigns of the last two decades—whether we call them stability operations, peacekeeping, state building, or counterinsurgency missions—point to how understanding women's experiences and roles in society is critical to reducing civilian insecurity, gathering accurate and comprehensive intelligence, engaging or interrogating women, and operating with cultural sensitivity. When pursuing the strategic aims of operations—regardless of whether they are defined as military victory, protection of civilians, or stabilization—being able to apply a gendered analysis in operational approaches and to integrate female perspectives and capabilities is increasingly seen as important by both political leaders and those commanding armed forces.

The important question for this final chapter is what conclusions can be drawn from the comparative approach. Are there general lessons to be learned for ongoing and future change processes? To structure that discussion, the following sections return to the research questions and areas of contention that were described in the introductory chapter.

Sources of Change

In trying to increase our understanding of the relative successes and failures of the change processes covered in the book, it has been important to try to understand where the impetus for change has come from and to what extent that has affected the processes.

The first conclusion of the book, something that really stands out, is the uniqueness of the different national implementation processes. Arguably, the most important finding is therefore the historical and cultural contingency of these types of organizational change processes. The chapters in this volume show that there is no singular model or ideal approach for the integration of women or gender perspectives into national militaries. We cannot understand the change processes in South Africa without the political and social context of the apartheid regime and the strategic needs during its border wars. We cannot understand the early integration of women in the Israel Defense Forces (IDF) without understanding the real and perceived existential threats confronting the Israeli state-building project. Similarly, the countries deeply affected by World War II have their particular historical imperatives, and others have general women's rights movements in civilian society that are important to understand within their particular cases. In short, historical, political, cultural, and geographic factors shape how, why, when, and to what extent both gender mainstreaming and gender balancing have been achieved in the different contexts. This finding thereby also highlights the limited utility of standardized blueprints in difficult societal and organizational change processes and the need for deep knowledge and understanding of the environments one is seeking to engage or study.

At the same time, the comparative approach of this volume has produced several interesting findings. There are, for example, two very clear international sources of change that have had a strong impact on almost all the national change processes covered in the volume. First, the success of the women's rights movement in the 1970s and 1980s, nationally and internationally, is evident as an "external" source of change for military organizations. With a couple of notable exceptions, most chapters make strong references to changes in both national and international legislation due to these movements. Internationally, the 1979 UN Convention on Elimination of All Forms of Discrimination against Women (CEDAW) provided an important impetus for reform. This was two decades before UNSCR 1325, which in most cases provided the launching point for the processes to integrate gender perspectives in the conduct of operations. The decisions to include women were in many cases not based on what Samuel Huntington would refer to as the functional imperative (the professional needs related to the nature of warfare) but rather the societal imperative (the ideology and culture of the society).[1] This means that it was not necessarily operational needs, a changing security environment, or arguments of military effectiveness that led to these changes, but rather general societal trends toward increased gender equality and emphasis on women's rights. Thus, the pressure to integrate women came from outside the organization.

The Israeli and South African cases nevertheless stand out as exceptions in several ways. As Hanna Herzog shows in chapter 8, the State of Israel was founded during a military struggle with its neighbors, and the enlistment of women was thought of as part of the nation-building project and as a necessity for the sake of national security given the army's enormous need for personnel. From the very founding of the IDF in 1948, the organization based itself on the principle of universal conscription, whose aim was to include women in the army by means of a law. In chapter 10 Lindy Heinecken highlighted that in South Africa a shortage of white males who could fight for the apartheid regime in the border wars led to the inclusion of women in the armed forces as early as the 1970s—again, on the basis of perceived operational needs rather than societal changes. On the other side of the front line, black women also joined the anti-apartheid guerrilla groups around the same time.

The second overarching international imperative for change came with UNSCR 1325. This time, not only was the process of gender balancing continued, but it was also complemented by efforts to implement gender perspectives in organizations and operations. The change processes after UNSCR 1325 have varied tremendously in the different country cases, but all chapters refer to this landmark resolution as an important moment of development. Sweden and the Netherlands have clearly taken the lead by making substantial efforts to integrate these perspectives in both policy documents and the field of operations. In many ways, an institutionalized gender organization has been created in these countries—one that has worked to mainstream a gender perspective, conduct training, and establish specific gender-related functions such as gender field advisors and gender focal points.

When looking at the catalysts in these two front-runner cases, as well as in the cases of NATO and Australia, it is clear that the change processes have often been driven by particular individuals—strong change agents—and by incidents that require reactions. In Sweden and at NATO, a senior gender advisor has been instrumental in creating organizational change thanks to tremendous tenacity and diplomatic skill. In Australia senior leaders such as Defence Minister Stephen Smith, Sex Discrimination Commissioner Elizabeth Broderick, and Chief of Army David Morrison responded to incidents and challenges in consequential ways. The Australian case highlights the need for buy-in from both senior leadership and insider change agents at lower levels in order to achieve substantial organizational change. As Susan Harris Rimmer concludes in chapter 9, these individual actors have nevertheless often "wrought change" rather than achieved a committed institutional acceptance of the utility of women's integration and gender reform for improved operational effectiveness: "Nevertheless, these actors have successfully introduced several reforms that could provide sustainable change to the ADF institutional framework toward gender equality outcomes." Other countries are only just beginning to come to terms with what a gender perspective would mean within the context of military organizations and operations. Importantly, the general level of gender equality in society is far from the only factor explaining the front-runners. Internal organizational factors and external operational demands and experiences are also important when explaining change processes—good and bad.

Interestingly, or worryingly, the national action plans (NAPs) for the implementation of UNSCR 1325 seem to have limited impact on the change processes within military organizations. The NAPs of, for example, Australia, Canada, the Netherlands, Sweden, and the United States vary greatly from country to country but generally rely on both the rights-based and utilitarian approaches to integrating gender perspectives in military operations. NAPs have from a strategic and international perspective proved to be one of the most important tools for implementing the vision outlined in UNSCR 1325 and subsequent associated resolutions, and many include specific sections focused on the defense sector. NAPs are, however, exactly that—policy guidelines and directives that do not guarantee requisite resources for adequate and prolonged implementation. For NAPs to advance gender mainstreaming and gender balancing in the armed forces, monitoring and evaluation to adjust approaches, meet benchmarks, and adhere to timetables must accompany implementation activities. Otherwise, the usefulness of NAPs for military and stabilization operations—as for other areas of application—is likely to be severely limited.

Effects and Consequences of These Change Processes

Measuring the impact of change in terms of operational output or effectiveness has not been the primary goal of this volume. It is also notoriously difficult to measure the impact of a single variable in something as complex as war fighting or peacekeeping. Instead, what this volume has looked at is the impact in terms of changed organizational culture and behavior (gender integration) and impact on recruitment and retention (gender balance).

The multi-case analysis that this volume provides does not present a success story in any of these categories—although there are kernels of real success in minor areas in several of the country cases. While many national armed forces have at least started a process of integrating more women into missions and applying gender perspectives in operations, the effectiveness and impact of these change processes have been mixed at best. Part of the explanation for the limited successes is found in the existing military organizational cultures, which have traditionally emphasized highly masculinized warrior ideals. The clash between the existing culture and the change process has in many cases led to resistance from the establishment. In other cases, the change processes are making important progress, affecting large parts of the organization and conduct in operations. This volume has obviously covered both extremes and a number of cases in between.

Thus, while progress has certainly been made in several important ways—both in terms of increasing the number of women and integrating a gender perspective in operations—it is clear that much work remains to be done. The number of women in military organizations has certainly increased over the last few decades, along with their access to equal opportunities. However, these numbers have now stalled at very low figures in many countries—even in the most gender-equal cases with the most gender-sensitive armed forces. The Dutch armed forces have only 9 percent women, and the Swedish armed forces still have only 6 percent female officers. It seems the different country cases provide different explanations for these failures, but a common feature is the culture of the military organization. The existing culture simply fails to attract women in large numbers and fails to retain the ones that do try. In terms of the introduction and integration of gender perspectives, most countries are just getting started. In chapter 6 Brenda Oppermann's case study of the US Army 10th Mountain Division's attempts at implementing these perspectives in Afghanistan provides important lessons for similar efforts in the future. As an example, the 10th Mountain Division case clearly highlights that good intentions are not enough and that tools like female engagement teams need to be not only well put together and trained but also overseen by commanders who are trained in how to use them. Another important lesson comes from Sweden, where the gender field advisors operated in many different ways. One takeaway from that case, described by Robert Egnell in chapter 3, was that projects-based operations aimed at women in the local community often had very limited impact, while more internally focused advising within the staff often had more of an impact as it affected the behavior of the entire unit. Gender perspectives in military operations clearly deserve more research in order to increase our understanding of their impact and potential—in terms of both helping military organizations reach their aims and limiting the negative impact on civilians, particularly women, in the area of operations while doing so.

Experiences of Women in the Armed Forces

Does the integration of women and gender perspectives actually represent a substantive change in gender relations or organizational culture? Despite the progress made in recent years to recruit, retain, and promote women in the armed forces, all the national militaries examined in this volume continue to be highly masculinized structures. Stories of sexual abuse and assault within military organizations are constantly reported in media in all countries covered in this volume. Severe problems clearly remain, and change processes for gender equality and mainstreaming, as several of the chapters in this volume highlight, are slow to take hold in military cultures that have been traditionally male-dominated. Dedicated leadership at senior and middle management levels combined with sustained political backing is necessary but not sufficient to achieve gender mainstreaming and balancing. Institutional reforms that institute family-friendly policies, for example, for parental leave, benefit both male and female personnel, whereas incentives for women to join and remain in service, including clear promotion tracks, not only boost morale but also help facilitate diversity in positions of authority. At the same time, creating enabling environments in which male and female members of the armed forces can thrive requires strict policies and accountability mechanisms to thwart sexual harassment, sexual assault, and all forms of gender-based discrimination that may hold back men and women from performing their duties to the best of their abilities. This is not simply about ensuring high human resources standards but also about making sure the soldiers are mentally and physically fit for their work, which is essential to the overall functioning of the military.

In chapter 7 on the British forces, Anthony King provides an important perspective by highlighting that although women have in many cases seemingly been successfully integrated within the organization, it would be wrong to speak of success or to idealize the reformation of gender relations in the British forces. The concept of the "honorary man," central in King's analysis, means that the integration of women does not represent a major transformation of gender norms or concepts. According to King, "On the contrary, it affirms traditional norms, including the slut-bitch binary, because only a few selected individual women are accorded this status. They are included in a substantially unrevised masculine grouping; gendered concepts, language, and practices remain broadly unchanged."

In chapter 2 on the UN case, Sabrina Karim notes that while gender mainstreaming is clearly a more holistic way to ensure that missions adopt a gender perspective, gender balancing has been a more popular route owing to expedience, not least because it is measurable. The UN case nevertheless also highlights serious drawbacks of this approach as female peacekeepers are not able to reach their full potential owing to the gendered structures that exist both in contributing country militaries and also within the peacekeeping mission. Karim writes, "While gender mainstreaming is perhaps a preferable tool, it suffers from inadequate conceptualization and has not been effective because of a pervasive male dominance within peacekeeping culture."

Similarly, Stéfanie von Hlatky's study of the Canadian case highlighted that the few studies that have been published on the experiences of women identify serious professional challenges that are specific to women. Women have reported that they never felt fully integrated into the military and that their ability to be promoted while in the military or their ability to find good jobs after leaving was hindered by the lack of experience brought on by exclusion.[2] The *External Review into Sexual Misconduct and Sexual Harassment in the Canadian Forces* finds that a masculine, and often highly sexualized, organizational culture is evident. Not only is this culture hostile to women and LGBTQ members, it is also considered conducive to more serious incidents of sexual harassment and assault.[3]

Obviously, in many cases there have also existed formal restrictions against women. As an example, the US, British, and Australian armed forces only recently lifted their bans on women's serving in combat roles. Such exclusion has had a severe impact on women's options for pursuing careers on equal terms. The use of force is, after all, the main raison d'être of any military organization, and combat experience, or at least command of combat units, is often a prerequisite for career advancement.

A key takeaway of this discussion is that simply adding women, without serious efforts to change the culture and the legal framework of the organization, may not only limit the results of women's participation. It may even have negative effects for the women involved. Again, the Canadian external review finds that a cultural shift of military organizations is key to improve women's experience in the armed forces: "It is not enough to simply revise policies or to repeat the mantra of 'zero tolerance.' Leaders must acknowledge that sexual misconduct is a real and serious problem for the organization, one that requires their own direct and sustained attention."[4] However, the gender-aware leadership required for such change is difficult to attain in the short term.

Gender Balance or Gender Mainstreaming—Any Lessons?

An important area of contention within the feminist literature is whether gender balancing (increasing female recruitment and representation toward parity) or gender mainstreaming (achieving gender equality by assessing the implications for women and men of any planned action, including legislation, policies, and programs in all areas and at all levels, and adapting approaches accordingly) is the most effective and efficient approach to organizational change.[5]

In relation to this debate, a key finding of the comparative approach of this volume is that the often-expected correlation or causation between the integration of gender perspectives and the inclusion of women has not been found. This is surprising given that one can hypothesize that increasing the number of women in an organization would lead to increased gender awareness and integration of gender perspectives in the conduct of operations. One can also hypothesize that a more gender-sensitive organization would be considered a more welcoming and attractive work environment for women—something that would lead to increased recruitment. As noted, however, the case studies in this volume do not support these hypotheses. On the one side are armed forces that have been able to recruit a substantial number of women—such as the US, South Africa, and Israel—but that have not been very successful in integrating a gender perspective in the organizational culture or in the way they conduct operations. On the other side are countries like Sweden and the Netherlands that have gone through an impressive change process in terms of integrating gender perspectives in the organization but are still failing to recruit women in substantial numbers.

The lack of support for these hypotheses does not, however, mean that they are falsified. A possible explanation for the lacking correlations could be that not enough time has passed since the changes started taking place. This would hold particularly true in the case of gender awareness leading to increased recruitment.

First, these processes started with UNSCR 1325 in the year 2000 and have in many cases only just begun. Changing organizational culture takes time, and the target audiences for recruitment may not even have had a chance to notice the small changes that have been achieved. In essence, it takes time to change the external popular perceptions of an organization to the extent that it affects recruitment. The time factor is more troubling in the other casual direction—increasing the number of women leading to increased gender awareness. Gender-balancing processes were in many cases launched many decades ago, and women have still had very limited impact on the organizational cultures and operational conduct. In most cases, military organizations have shown remarkable resistance to cultural change. The temporal dimension is, however, not the only factor that may have affected the limited results.

A second factor would be scale. The limited number of women in military organizations may have limited the possibility of more substantial shifts in culture or conduct. Plenty of studies highlight the need for reaching a certain "critical mass" before women would have a substantial impact on organizations—especially when the existing culture is not only resistant but also contradictory in its masculine ideals.[6] Thus, it is possible that time is a factor with little importance if the number of women within military organizations has simply not reached the point when it starts having a substantial impact on the organizational culture. Looking at the reversed causality, the amount of organizational change may also be perceived as too limited to have a substantial impact on the recruitment of women. The positive effects on recruitment and retention in some experiments with all-female or at least critical-mass-level integrated units in Norway and Sweden certainly suggest that more substantive change processes can indeed achieve effects on gender balance.[7]

Instrumentalist and Rights-Based Approaches to Change

The introduction highlighted that a central point of contention among scholars and practitioners concerned about gender equality in military and other governing institutions revolves around the aim or rationale for transformation or change. Commonly, both feminist scholars and activists treat gender equality as an end in itself, arguing that women—as persons endowed with equal rights—should be offered the same opportunities and privileges as men irrespective of strategic imperatives. Military organizations should thereby become more gender equal simply because it is "the right thing to do." In other words, this framing of the debate builds off the thrust of women's rights movements and focuses on UNSCR 1325's commitment to increased women's participation and empowerment as inherently good pursuits. From this perspective, we simply do not need any other arguments than women's rights are human rights and women should have equal access.

While such arguments are noble and fair, and their aims may sound compelling to a civilian audience, they unfortunately often fall on deaf ears within military organizations. The extreme tasks—the functional imperative of fighting and winning wars in defense of the nation—remain too strong, and gender equality is therefore not perceived as having anything to do with military operations. On the contrary, such change is often described as detrimental to the fighting power of military organizations, which are by their nature seen to be exceptional and therefore ought to be treated as such.[8]

Instead, the results from several cases, not least Sweden, NATO, and the Netherlands, indicate that a more successful approach, at least initially, is to emphasize that the implementation process serves to strengthen the military in its constant striving for maximized effectiveness in its core tasks—that implementing gender perspectives is actually "the smart thing to do." So in this framing, strategy rather than rights serves as the primary motivator for incorporating women into a diversity of roles and responsibilities and for mainstreaming gender perspectives into operations.

What are the risks of linking the integration of women or a gender perspective to operational effectiveness? Skeptical feminists argue that including women on the basis of their "effectiveness" or "utility" is indeed one of the key problems of UNSCR 1325. The fundamental problem with an "instrumental" approach that stresses operational effectiveness alone is that it may involve a rather superficial remedy that does not explore the transformative potential of a gender perspective. After all, the purpose of UNSCR was not to improve the effectiveness of military organizations but to achieve gender equality and international peace and stability.

Feminists also highlight several other risks involved in the instrumental approach.[9] One such risk is that the instrumentalist argument often involves an essentialist view of women and their competences. If women are recruited as "peacemakers" or for their oft-emphasized compassionate, diplomatic, or communicative skills, they are also most likely to play "character roles" within the organization in which such skills are valued. In other words, within military organizations, women will be used to fill competence gaps (and most often what are perceived as nonessential and peripheral duties) rather than allowed to affect the organization as a whole or to compete with men on equal terms.[10]

Not only does the instrumental approach often entail stereotypical views of women's contributions or qualities—performing women's roles in the organization rather than participating as equal and worthy members. If things go wrong, or if the changes do not live up to the expectations of increased effectiveness, the risk is that women's inclusion or gendered approaches will be thrown out again.[11] Kathleen Jennings, for one, highlights this risk—not least since many of the claims regarding increased military effectiveness justifying women's increased participation in peace operations have limited quantifiable empirical support.[12] Gender-balancing efforts made simply with instrumentalist argument thereby risk doing women a disservice.[13]

Carol Cohn takes the argument further by highlighting that the essentialist notion of "women-as-peacemakers" risks leaving the dominant political and epistemological frameworks of the war system untouched.[14] If Cohn is right that many of the efforts to include women or a gender perspective fail to address the larger structural issues of a "masculine war system," two more risks naturally follow. First, a danger is that feminist efforts are co-opted and used by institutions for purposes that do not reflect the feminist agenda. African American feminist Audre Lorde effectively invoked the language of the US civil rights movement by arguing, "The master's tools will never dismantle the master's house."[15] This risk is particularly obvious when it comes to military organizations in which women can be used simply as tools of violence for the purpose of military victory or oppression rather than peace. Second, if the change processes only nibble at the edges of untouched structural problems, they are unlikely to have much of an impact regardless of whether the aim is the empowerment of women or mere military effectiveness. Sabrina Karim's study of women in UN peacekeeping operations in chapter 2 indeed highlighted that female peacekeepers are inhibited in their ability to reach their full potential because they are working in the context of a male-dominated institution. Thus, the instrumental value that women bring to missions may not be achieved unless there is also transformative cultural change within the mission or organization.

The tension between processes of change for reasons of operational effectiveness on the one side and the more transformative and often rights-based processes on the other nonetheless overlap in substantial ways. The successes in the first phases of implementing a gender perspective in the armed forces of Sweden, the Netherlands, and NATO were to a large extent based on approaching the implementation process as one of instrumental changes to improve operational effectiveness of the existing organization. *Presenting* the implementation process in this limited and instrumental way avoided unmanageable pushback and instead helped build support for the process within the organization. Moreover, while the task was approached in an instrumental fashion, many of the processes that these organizations have successfully completed are also somewhat transformative in nature. A network of people with better understanding of gender perspectives can provide an important platform for further change. The limited instrumental approaches can thereby have ripple effects that create more substantial transformations of gender norms and relations within the organization. The presentation of the choice between instrumental or transformative approaches, or between military effectiveness or women's rights, is therefore often unnecessary and should, for tactical reasons, instead be approached as an issue of narrative or "packaging." While avoiding the language of principled conviction may sometimes be painful, the outcomes should be seen as more important than the conviction that drives the processes.

Final Thoughts

In addition to these key takeaways, this compilation of case studies provides an unprecedented record of experiences to date in a variety of countries. In doing so, the book makes a valuable contribution to scholarship on the subject. We hope this volume will inspire further in-depth research on these cases to examine more closely the implementation, impact, and effectiveness of specific policies and programs mentioned in this book or new initiatives that may be developed in the future.

At the same time, additional research that builds on this project has the potential to shed light on experiences and questions related to other countries, regions, and intergovernmental organizations not covered here. A range of issues warrants further theoretical and empirical engagement. For example, while different chapters in this book have touched on multiple branches of the military, more systematic analysis is necessary to demonstrate how both the integration of women and the incorporation of gender perspectives vary in land, air, and marine forces. Comparisons of this kind should look at variation within cases and across countries. More research is also necessary to reveal the mechanisms and pathways through which the participation of women and gender mainstreaming changes what happens not only in the field but also within institutional structures.

In this book we have tried to highlight how cooperation has worked across some countries and institutions, but this is a promising area of investigation in which, we hope, scholars will come together to provide insights into what makes collaboration effective and why. Relatedly, joint training exercises to advance mutual goals are increasingly common in peace-support operations, regional defense initiatives, and military offensives, but we know very little about how disparities in gender balancing and gender mainstreaming affect outcomes of these trainings. Considering unresolved debates among feminist scholars about the role, relevance, and rightful place of military organizations, it will be critical that those with opposing views engage each other in critical analysis. Finally, as should be abundantly clear from this volume, the many practical and intellectual components of this subject are by their nature interdisciplinary. Therefore, in the future, we look forward to research collaborations that span different paradigms, fields, and methods to tackle the voluminous opportunities and challenges related to gender and women in the military.

Notes

1. Samuel P. Huntington, *The Soldier and the State: The Theory and Politics of Civil-Military Relations* (Cambridge, MA: Harvard University Press, 1957).
2. Donna Winslow and Jason Dunn, "Women in the Canadian Forces: Between Legal and Social Integration," *Current Sociology* 50, no. 5 (2002): 641–67; Nancy Taber, "Learning How to Be a Woman in the Canadian Forces / Unlearning It through Feminism: An Autoethnography of My Learning Journey," *Studies in Continuing Education* 27, no. 3 (2005): 289–301; Canadian Defence Academy, *Women and Leadership in the Canadian Forces: Perspectives and Experience* (Winnipeg: Canadian Defence Academy Press, 2007).
3. Marie Deschamps, *External Review into Sexual Misconduct and Sexual Harassment in the Canadian Armed Forces* (Ottawa, ON: Canada Department of National Defence, 2015), i, http://www.forces.gc.ca/assets/FORCES_Internet/docs/en/caf-community-support-services-harassment/era-final-report-(april-20-2015)-eng.pdf.
4. Ibid.
5. Robert Egnell, "Gender Perspectives and Military Effectiveness," *Prism* 6, no. 1 (2016): 73–89.
6. Drude Dahlerup, "The Story of the Theory of Critical Mass," *Politics and Gender* 2, no. 4 (2006): 511–22.
7. Huntington, *Soldier and the State*.
8. Martin van Creveld, "To Wreck a Military," *Small Wars Journal*, January 28, 2013, http://smallwarsjournal.com/jrnl/art/to-wreck-a-military; Martin van Creveld, "The Great Illusion: Women in the Military," *Millennium* 29, no. 2 (2000): 429–42.
9. See, for example, Dianne Otto, "Power and Danger: Feminist Engagement with International Law through the UN Security Council," *Australian Feminist Law Journal* 32 (June 2010): 97–121; Johanna Valenius, "A Few Kind Women: Gender Essentialism and Nordic Peacekeeping Operations," *International Peacekeeping* 14, no. 4 (2007): 510–23.
10. See Valenius, "Few Kind Women," 510; Kathleen Jennings, *Women's Participation in UN Peacekeeping Operations: Agents of Change or Stranded Symbols* (Oslo: Norwegian Peacebuilding Resource Centre, 2011), 1.
11. Jennings, *Women's Participation*, 1.
12. Ibid.
13. See, for example, Dianne Otto, "The Exile of Inclusion: Reflections on Gender Issues in International Law over the Last Decade," *Melbourne Journal of International Law* 10, no. 1 (2009); Dianne Otto, "Power and Danger: Feminist Engagement with International Law through the UN Security Council," *Australian Feminist Law Journal* 32 (June 2010): 97–121; Carol Cohn, "Mainstreaming Gender in UN Security Policy: A Path to Political Transformation?," in *Global Governance: Feminist Perspectives*, ed. Shirin Rai and Georgina Wayle (Basingstoke: Palgrave Macmillan, 2008).
14. Cohn, "Mainstreaming Gender."
15. Audre Lorde, "The Master's Tools Will Never Dismantle the Master's House," in *Sister Outsider: Essays and Speeches* (Sydney: Cross Press, 1984), 110.

CONTRIBUTORS

Mayesha Alam is a doctoral candidate in political science at Yale University, where her research interests intersect comparative politics and international relations with a focus on violent conflict and its aftermath. She previously served as the associate director of the Georgetown Institute for Women, Peace, and Security and taught at the graduate level at the School of Foreign Service at Georgetown University. Mayesha has also worked with the UN, World Bank, and Organization for Security and Co-operation in Europe (OSCE) in the US and abroad. She is the author of *Women and Transitional Justice: Progress and Persistent Challenges in Retributive and Restorative Processes* (Palgrave Macmillan, 2014) and numerous reports and articles. Originally from Bangladesh, Mayesha was awarded the Soros Fellowship for New Americans. She holds a bachelor's degree from Mount Holyoke College and a master's degree from Georgetown University.

Robert Egnell is a professor of military sociology and the head of the Department for Security, Strategy and Leadership at the Swedish Defence University. He is also a senior fellow with the Security Studies Program and the Institute for Women, Peace and Security at Georgetown University. Previous positions include being a visiting professor and director of teaching in the Security Studies Program at Georgetown, a senior researcher at the Swedish Defence Research Institute (FOI), and an assistant lecturer at the Department of Political Science at the University of Dar es Salaam, Tanzania. His publications include numerous articles in professional and academic peer review journals, as well as four books: *Gender, Military Effectiveness and Organizational Change: The Swedish Model* (Palgrave Macmillan, 2014), *Counterinsurgency in Crisis: Britain and the Challenges of Modern Warfare* (Columbia University Press, 2013), *New Agendas in Statebuilding: Hybridity, Contingency and History* (Routledge, 2013), and *Complex Peace Operations and Civil-Military Relations: Winning the Peace* (Routledge, 2009). Robert has a PhD and an MA in war studies from King's College, London, as well as an MA and a BA from Uppsala University. He is also a captain in the Swedish Army reserves with operational experience from the first Swedish battalion in Kosovo in 1999–2000.

Susan Harris Rimmer is an associate professor and an Australian Research Council Future Fellow in Griffith Law School in Brisbane, Australia. She is also a research associate at the Development Policy Centre in the Crawford School, Australian National University. Her Future Fellow project is called "Trading Women's Rights in Transitions: Designing Diplomatic Interventions in Afghanistan and Myanmar." Susan is the author of *Gender and Transitional Justice: The Women of Timor Leste* (Routledge, 2010) and over forty refereed academic works. She was named in Apolitical's World's 100 Most Influential People in Gender Policy in 2018. She was selected as an expert for the official Australian delegation to the fifty-eighth session of the UN Commission on the Status of Women in New York in March 2014. She has provided policy advice on the UN Security Council, G20, Indian Ocean Rim Association (IORA), and Mexico, Indonesia, South Korea, Turkey, and Australia partnership (MIKTA).

Lindy Heinecken is a professor in the Department of Sociology and Social Anthropology, Stellenbosch University, South Africa. Her research is focused on the armed forces and society, and she has published widely on a range of issues. Her more recent research focuses on gender integration in the military, military recruitment, and peacekeeping. She serves on numerous academic boards, including the Council of the Inter-University Seminar on Armed Forces and Society (IUS) and the International Sociological Association's (ISA) Armed Forces and Conflict Resolution Group (RC01), and she is a National Research Foundation B3-rated researcher.

Hanna Herzog is a professor emerita in the Sociology Department at Tel Aviv University and a former chair of that department. Cofounder of the Women and Gender Studies Program at Tel Aviv University, she served as its head. She is codirector and cofounder of "Shavot" (WIPS)—the Center for Advancement of Women in the Public Sphere, Van Leer Jerusalem Institute. She specializes in political sociology, ethnic relations, sociology of knowledge, generation as a sociological phenomenon, and sociology of gender. She has written numerous articles on the politics of ethnic and racial relations, women in politics and politics of women, Palestinian women citizens of Israel, gender and military, and gender, religion, and politics. Among her books in English are *Gendering Politics: Women in Israel*; *Getting Respect: Responding to Stigma and Discrimination in the United States, Brazil, and Israel* (written with others); and *Gendering Religion and Politics: Untangling Modernities* (coedited).

Stéfanie von Hlatky is an associate professor of political studies at Queen's University. She received her PhD in political science in 2010 from Université de Montréal, where she was also executive director for the Centre for International Peace and Security Studies. Before she joined Queen's, she held positions at Georgetown University, the Woodrow Wilson International Center for Scholars in Washington, DC, Dartmouth College, and ETH Zurich. She has published in the *Canadian Journal of Political Science, Defence Studies, International Journal, European Security, Asian Security,* and the *Journal of Transatlantic Studies,* and she has a book titled *American Allies in Times of War: The Great Asymmetry* (Oxford, 2013) and two edited volumes with Georgetown University Press (2015) and McGill-Queen's University Press (2016).

Charlotte Isaksson is a senior advisor to the principal advisor on gender and WPS in the European External Action Service (EEAS) in Brussels. She has worked primarily with gender in the domain of security and defense, including operations and missions. Between 2011 and 2016, she was gender advisor to SACEUR and Allied Command Operations, NATO, at SHAPE. Before that she served as senior gender advisor within the Directorate of Operations at the Swedish Armed Forces Headquarters and held a position with the Swedish Ministry of Defense. Her work has focused on gender equality and integration of gender perspectives, including implementing UNSCR 1325 on women, peace, and security and its subsequent resolutions on conflict-related sexual violence. She has also served as gender advisor in different international missions and headquarters. As an institutional entrepreneur, she has been the originator and prime mover for several projects, including Genderforce, and she has established and institutionalized structures, such as the function of a military gender advisor and the Nordic Centre for Gender in Military Operations. She has a military background, and besides her higher military education, she holds two academic degrees, in sociology (Lund University) and in international relations (Cambridge University).

Sabrina Karim is an assistant professor in the Department of Government at Cornell University. She is the coauthor of *Equal Opportunity Peacekeeping: Women, Peace, and Security in Post-Conflict Countries* (Oxford, 2017). The book was the winner of the Conflict Research Studies Best Book Prize for 2017. Her work has appeared in *International Organization,* the *British Journal of Political Science,* the *Journal of Peace Research, International Interactions, World Development,* and *International Studies Quarterly.* Her research focuses on conflict and peace processes, particularly state building in the aftermath of civil war. Specifically, she studies international involvement in security assistance to post-conflict states, gender reforms in peacekeeping and domestic security sectors, and the relationship between gender and violence. Born and raised in Colorado, Sabrina earned her PhD from Emory University in 2016. Before her doctorate degree, she received a Fulbright Fellowship and earned her master's degree as a Clarendon Scholar from Oxford University. She has an undergraduate degree from Georgetown University's School of Foreign Service.

Anthony King holds a chair in war studies at Warwick University, specializes in the study of war and the armed forces, and is particularly interested in the question of small-unit cohesion. His most recent publications include *The Combat Soldier: Infantry Tactics and Cohesion in the Twentieth and Twenty-First Centuries* (Oxford, 2013) and *Frontline: Combat and Cohesion in the Twenty-First Century* (editor, Oxford, 2015). He has just completed a monograph on divisional command, supported by a research grant from the Economic and Social Research Council (ESRC). This book, titled *Command: The Twenty-First Century General*, will be published by Cambridge University Press in January 2019. He is currently developing a project on urban warfare.

Yvette Langenhuizen is currently heading the Gender Office in the OSCE Special Monitoring Mission to Ukraine. Before joining the OSCE, she had worked as women, peace, and security advisor in the Office of the NATO Secretary General and as political advisor to the NATO Senior Civilian Representative in Afghanistan. She gained experience on the national level both with the Netherlands Ministry of Defence and the Netherlands Ministry of Foreign Affairs, with a focus on Dutch contributions to peace and security efforts in and around the Horn of Africa. While at the Ministry of Defence, she was also involved in the development of the Netherlands' third national action plan on UN Security Council Resolution 1325.

Brenda Oppermann serves as a senior advisor to military and civilian organizations such as the US Army, US Navy, US Agency for International Development, United Nations, NATO, the Organization for Security and Cooperation in Europe, and various nongovernmental organizations. She has extensive experience working in fragile states and areas of conflict and post-conflict in Africa, Central Asia, Europe, and the Middle East. Her research and expertise include the integration of women and gender considerations into military operations, the role of informal justice in stability operations, the role of women in insurgencies, and the impact of legal pluralism, particularly customary law, on women's status. She holds a JD from Western New England University School of Law, an MA in international relations from Yale University, and a BA in comparative literature from the University of California–Irvine.

INDEX

Tables indicated by a *t* following the page number.

academies, military, integration of American, 113, 114, 118, 139n10
Action Plan Diversity, 97
Afghanistan: Canadian Armed Forces in, 81; NATO in, 244; Netherlands Armed Forces in, 100–101; Swedish Armed Forces in, 43–44, 43–47, 50; United Kingdom in, 141, 142, 145, 147–48; United States in, 114–15, 119, 120, 122–36
Afghan Local Police (ALP), 135
Afghan Peace and Reintegration Programme (APRP), 134
African National Congress (ANC), 81–83, 211
African Union (AU), 215, 233
Africa Standby Force, 215–16
Allied Command Operations (ACO)/ NATO, 228, 235, 236–37
Allied Command Transformation (ACT), 228, 235
Amram-Katz, Sarit, 156
apartheid, 208, 209, 211, 212, 255, 256
Army Field Manual, 125
Army Nurse Corps, 116
Australia: national action plan in, 173, 189, 194–97
Australia, New Zealand, and United States Treaty (ANZUS), 175
Australian and New Zealand Army Corps (ANZAC) Day, 175
Australian Defence Force (ADF): Broderick Review in, 186; combat restrictions in, 192–93; culture in, 180–92;

history of, 174; HMAS *Success* incidents with, 183–84; integration of, 178–93; in major conflicts, 174–75; *Pathway to Change* document in, 186, 187–90, 199; Sexual Misconduct Prevention and Response Office for, 198; Skype incident with, 181–83; Talisman Sabre exercise with, 122, 197; in World War I, 175; in World War II, 200n4
Australian Defence Force Academy (ADFA), 173
Australian Sex Discrimination Act, 5
Azanian People's Liberation Army (APLA), 211

Bangladesh, 32–33
Ban Ki-moon, 31–32
Baranowski, Michelle, 76
Bedouins, 169n1
Beijing+5, 25
Beijing Platform for Action, 25
Ben-Shalom, Uzi, 146
Bi-Strategic Command 40-1, 82, 124, 229, 233, 237–38, 244
Bosnia, 25
Brahimi Report, 24–25
Broderick, Elizabeth, 186, 191, 257
Browne, Kingsley, 84
Brownson, Connie, 144
Burton, Clare, 191
Burundi, 215

Cameron, David, 141

Canadian Armed Forces (CAF): in Afghanistan, 81–83; background on women in, 74–75; chronology of women in, 74–75; female experience in, 77–83; gender balancing in, 76; gender mainstreaming in, 76–77, 80–83; gender perspective and, 73–84, 76t; integration of, 75, 77–78; military culture in, 75–77, 76t, 78; Security Council Resolution 1325 and, 79
Canadian Charter of Rights and Freedoms, 74
Canadian Human Rights Tribunal, 75
Carrier-Sabourin, Krystel, 80
Central African Republic (CAR), 234
change: instrumentalist approaches to, 262–65; organizational, 234–45; rights-based approaches to, 262–65; sources, 255–57
Chapman, Krystel, 80
Charlesworth, Hillary, 175–76
Chavez, Dennis, 139n10
Chief Directorate Equal Opportunities (CDEO), 213
Civil Military Cooperation (CIMIC) Centre of Excellence, 102
Civil War (United States), 115, 138n1
Coalition Forces Land Component Command (CFLCC), 122
cohesion, 146–47
Cohn, Carol, 264
Combat Exclusion Rule, 113
Combat Readiness Evaluation (CREVAL), 242
Combat Related Employment of Women (CREW), 74, 75
Combined Joint Staff Exercise (CJSE), 46
Committee of Women against Mixed Sailing, 90
Committee on Gender Perspectives (NATO), 76
Comprehensive Operational Planning Directive (COPD), 240–41
compulsory service, 153, 169n1
conduct and discipline teams (CDT): peacekeeping operations and, 34–35

conflict-related sexual violence (CRSV): peacekeeping operations and, 27; prevention of, 11. *See also* sexual and gender-based violence (SGBV); sexual exploitation and abuse (SEA)
Congo, 44, 45, 47, 215
Connell, Raewyn W., 154
Convention on the Elimination of All Forms of Discrimination against Women (CEDAW), 5, 89–90, 180, 192–93, 204n73, 214, 256
Convention on the Political Rights of Women, 89
counterinsurgency (COIN), 120, 124, 125
Cox, Eugene E., 139n10
Crimea, 7
Criminal Code Act (Australia), 180
cultural support teams (CSTs), 120, 129
culture. *See* military culture
Cyprus, 27, 33

Darfur, 215
Davis, Karen, 83
De Blaquiere, Dylan, 182
Defence Abuse Allegations Review, 178
Defence Abuse Response Taskforce (DART), 181, 199
Defense Women's Network (Defensie Vrouwen Netwerk, DVN), 91–92
Democratic Republic of the Congo (DRC), 44, 45, 47, 215
Democrats '66, 98
Department of Field Support (DFS), 28, 29–30
Department of Peacekeeping Operations (DPKO), 28
Department of Political Affairs (DPA), 30
Deschamps, Marie, 73, 75, 78, 83
descriptive representation, 159–61
desegregation, of armed forces: in United States, 7
de Vries, Jack, 97
Direct Ground Combat Definition and Assignment Rule, 113, 114, 118–19, 137
discrimination: in Canadian Armed Forces, 74; in Netherlands Armed

Forces, 91, 95; in Swedish Armed Forces, 43–44, 62–64; in United Kingdom military, 142–44
diversity policy: in Netherlands Armed Forces, 96–97
Division for the Advancement of Women, 25
Dutch Labor Party, 98
Dutch Women's Committee (Nederlands Vrouwen Comité), 88, 109n8

effectiveness. *See* military effectiveness
Egnell, Robert, 197
Ellicot, Robert, 192
engagement teams, mixed and female, in Swedish Armed Forces, 49–51
Engelbrektson, Karl, 239
Enloe, Cynthia, 142, 176, 226
equality, gender. *See* gender equality
Equality and Gender Equality Directive (Swedish Armed Forces), 56
Equality Guidance Document (Swedish Armed Forces), 57
essentialism, 9–10
Euro-Atlantic Partnership Council (EAPC), 226–27
European Economic Community (EEC), 89
European Social Fund (ESF), 99
European Union Mission in the Congo (EUFOR RD Congo), 44, 45, 47
Executive Order 13595, 121, 122
experiences, female, in armed forces, 43–44, 62–64, 77–83, 142–44, 259–60

Fahy, Robyn, 173
Fallon, Michael, 141
female characteristics, 9–10
female engagement teams (FETs), 14, 49–51, 54–55, 120, 125–26, 126–27, 130–34
feminism, 89, 142, 145, 155, 159, 167–68, 263
feminist scholarship, 5
Field Manual, 125
First Intifada, 157

First Lebanese War, 157
Fogarty, Gerard, 188
"Forward Looking Gender Strategy (2014–2018)" (Department of Peacekeeping Operations), 28, 29–30
Fourth World Conference on Women in Beijing, 92–93, 121
FPG. *See* Gender Functional Planning Guide (FPG)
fragmentary order (FRAGO), 126
France, 59, 234
Fulton, James G., 139n10
functional imperative, 6

gender: military effectiveness and, 5–12
Gender Action Plan (Netherlands), 93–95
Gender Advisors (GENADs), 81
gender advisors (NATO), 228–29
gender balancing, 13–14, 261–62; in Canadian Armed Forces, 76; military culture and, 75, 76t; in Netherlands Armed Forces, 91; in peacekeeping operations, 28–31, 31–33, 37
gendered approach, to peacekeeping operations, 24–27
gender equality, 3, 230, 235–36, 243; in Australia Defence Force, 174, 189, 191–92, 199–200; gender balancing and, 13–14; gender mainstreaming and, 11; in implementation, 4; in Israel Defense Forces, 160–61; military operations and, 7; in NATO, 234, 240; in South African National Defence Force (SANDF), 174, 212, 213, 215, 219; in Sweden, 57; in Swedish Armed Forces, 52, 56–59, 63; in United States military, 137, 233
Gender Equality Plan (Swedish Armed Forces), 57
gender field adviser (GFA), 41, 43, 45–47, 55
Gender Focal Points, 41, 48–49
Genderforce, 43, 62–63, 99–100, 102, 105
Gender Functional Planning Guide (FPG), 241

gender mainstreaming, 11–12, 261–62; in Canadian Armed Forces, 76–77, 80–83; defined, 29; in Israel Defense Force, 162–67; military culture and, 75–76, 76t; in NATO, 229–30; in peacekeeping operations, 28–31, 33–36, 37–38; in South African National Defence Force, 214–17
Gender Multiparty Initiative, 98
gender perspectives: in military operations, 193–97; NATO and, 229, 240–41
Global Affairs Canada (GAC), 80–81
Goddard, Nichola, 80
Goffman, Erving, 177
Goren, Shlomo, 158
Gyles, Roger, 183–84

Hammarskjöld, Dag, 35
Hammond, Philip, 141
Hennis-Plasschaert, Jeanine, 87, 98
Hernes, Helga Marina, 161
HMAS *Success*, 183–84
HNLMS *Tjerk Hiddes*, 95
"honorary male status," 145–46, 148–49
Hotovely, Tzipi, 165
Houston, Angus, 182
Hurley, David, 187
Hutchinson, Clare, 228

individualism, 6–7
institutions, total, 177
instrumentalist approaches to change, 262–65
"Integrating a Gender Perspective into the Work for the United Nations Military in Peacekeeping Operations" (Department of Peacekeeping Operations), 29
integration: of Australian Defence Force, 178–93; of Canadian Armed Forces, 75, 77–78; of Israel Defense Forces, 154–59, 160–61, 162–67; of NATO, 230–34; of Netherlands Armed Forces, 88–98; of South African Armed Forces, 207–8, 217–18; of Swedish Armed Forces, 55–66; of United Kingdom military, 141, 144–49; of United States military, 113, 114, 117–22; of United States military service academies, 113, 114, 118, 139n10
international security: as purview of men, 1
International Security Assistance Force (ISAF), 44, 80, 81–83, 124, 244
Iraq, 44, 119, 120, 141, 142, 145
Isaksson, Charlotte, 52
Israel: Jewish national religious logic in, 157–59, 170n22; military organizational logic in, 156–57; security logic in, 156; as Western state, 155–56
Israel Defense Forces (IDF): compulsory service in, 153, 169n1; culture of, 153–54; as exception, 256; in First Intifada, 157; in First Lebanese War, 157; gender mainstreaming in, 162–67; integration of, 154–59, 160–61, 162–67; as melting pot, 153; Rabbinate in, 158, 166; reframing de-gendering of, 159–67; Security Service Act and, 155–56, 157–58, 160, 168; Segev Committee and, 163–64, 166; in Six Day War, 157, 158, 159; Women's Corps in, 156–57, 160; in Yom Kippur War, 157, 159

Jennings, Kathleen, 263
Jewish national religious logic, 157–59, 170n22
Joint Defence Facility Pine Gap, 175
Joint Professional Military Education (JPME), 121

Kafer, Bruce, 182
key leader engagements, 127–28
Kier, Elizabeth, 146
Kirkham, Andrew, 182
Korean War, 74, 116, 117
Kosovo Force (KFOR), 239–40, 244
Kronsell, Annica, 14
Kvinna till Kvinna, 43

Liberia, 33, 35, 59
Lioness Program, 120
Lloyd, Libby, 189
Lorber, Judith, 154

MacCoun, Robert, 146
macho culture: in Netherlands Armed Forces, 95–96
male status, honorary, 145–46, 148–49
Mali, 105–6
Marine Air-Ground Task Force, 175
Marine Corps, 119, 123
Marine Vrouwenafdeling (MARVA), 88
masculinity, 1, 147, 153–54, 158–59, 210–11, 264
McChrystal, Stanley A., 124
McDonald, Daniel, 181–83
McKean, Melanie, 184
Military Academy, 118
military capability, 7–8
military culture: in Australian Defence Force, 180–92; in Canadian Armed Forces, 75–77, 76t, 78; internal and external dimensions of, 75–77, 76t; in Israel Defense Forces, 153–54; as macho, 95–96; in NATO, 231; in Netherlands Armed Forces, 95–96; organizational, 133; "slut-bitch" binary in, 143–44; in United States military, 133
military effectiveness: in changing world, 6–10; gender and, 5–12
Military Leadership Diversity Commission, 119
military observation team (MOT), 48
military observation team (MOT) Juliette, 49–50
military observation team (MOT) Y, 50
Miller, Alice, 160, 168
mixed engagement teams (METs), 49–51, 54–55
MK. *See* Umkhonto we Sizwe (MK)
Morrison, David, 176–77, 189, 199
Multidimensional Integrated Stabilization Mission in Mali (MINUSMA), 105–6

NAC Initiating Directive (NID), 240
Namibia Plan of Action on Mainstreaming a Gender Perspective in Multidimensional Peace Support Operations, 25, 27
national action plan(s) (NAP), 2, 10; Australia, 173, 189, 194–97, 195–96;

limited impact of, 257; Netherlands, 101–2; United States, 113, 114, 120–22, 124, 137
NATO Committee on Gender Perspectives (NCGP), 231
Naval Academy, 118
Navy Nurse Corps, 116
Netherlands Armed Forces: in Afghanistan, 100–101; diversity policy in, 96–97; gender action plan in, 93–94; Gender Action Plan in, 93–95; gender advisors in, 104–5; Genderforce and, 99–100, 102, 105; integration of, 88–98; macho culture in, 95–96; in Mali, 105–6; National Action Plan and, 101–2; quality debate in, 97–98; Security Council Resolution 1325 and, 92–93, 99, 101–2
nontraditional security issues, 8–9
Nordic Battle Group, 3
Nordic Centre for Gender in Military Operations, 41, 46, 48, 66, 239
Nordic Defence Cooperation (NORDEFCO), 48
North Atlantic Treaty Organization (NATO), 164; in Afghanistan, 244; Allied Command Operations, 225; Allied Command Transformation, 225; Australian Defence Force and, 173–74; Bi-Strategic Command 40-1 of, 82, 124, 229, 233, 237–38, 244; Canadian Armed Forces and, 76, 77; and Comprehensive Operational Planning Directive, 240–41; data monitoring by, 80; gender advisors, 228–29; gender mainstreaming and, 229–30; gender training sessions by, 121–22; integration of, 230–34; Kosovo Force, 239–40; Nordic Centre for Gender in Military Operations in, 41; organizational change and, 234–45; Security Council Resolution 1325 and, 226–29, 237–38, 243, 244–46; and SHAPE WoMen, 242; women, peace, and security agenda in, 229–30. *See also* International Security Assistance Force (ISAF)
Northwest Rebellion, 74

Norwegian Armed Forces, 48
nurses, 74, 115–17, 207

"office wife," 163
Olsson, Louise, 3
Operation Enduring Freedom (OEF), 83
operations order (OPORD), 123, 126
Oram, Tara, 76
organizational change, 234–45
Organization for Economic Co-operation and Development (OECD), 41
Otto, Dianne, 13

Palestinians, 169n1
Pan African Congress (PAC), 211
Panetta, Leon, 141
parental leave, 57
participation: of women, 10–11
Partij voor de Vrijheid (PVV), 97–98
Pathway to Change, 186, 187–90, 199
Payne, Marise, 173
peacekeeping operations. *See* UN peacekeeping operations
Pearce, Dennis, 184
Police Training Group (PTG), 101
posttraumatic stress disorder (PTSD), 83
Preventing Conflict, Transforming Justice, Securing the Peace: A Global Study on the Implementation of United Nations Security Council Resolution 1325 (UN Women), 30–31
prevention, of conflict-related sexual violence, 11
professional cohesion, 146–47
professionalization, 147–48
protection of women, 11
provincial reconstruction team (PRT), 43–44
Public Law 94-106 (United States), 113, 114, 118, 137
purdah, 130

Rabbinate, 158, 166
race, 57, 149, 208, 214
recruitment: in Netherlands Armed Forces, 91–92; in Swedish Armed Forces, 58–62
Red Cross, 88

representation, descriptive, 159–61
Revolutionary War (United States), 115, 138n1
rights-based approaches to change, 262–65
Robert, Stuart, 187
Roberts-Smith, Len, 181
Royal Canadian Mounted Police (RCMP), 81
Royal Commission on the Status of Women, 74
Rumble, Gary, 184, 190
Russia: Crimea and, 7
Rwanda, 25

SACEUR's Annual Guidance on Education, Training, Exercises and Evaluation (SAGE), 241
Sampson, Deborah, 138n1
Sasson-Levy, Orna, 161, 163, 164
Schuurman, Marriët, 227–28
security. *See* international security; women, peace, and security (WPS)
Security Council. *See* UN Security Council
Security Service Act (Israel), 155–56, 157–58, 160, 168
Segev Committee, 163–64, 166
Servicewomen in Non-Traditional Environments and Roles (SWINTER), 74, 75
Sex Discrimination Act (Australia), 180, 192, 193
sexual and gender-based violence (SGBV), 216–17, 227, 231–32, 233–34, 235, 240
sexual assault: in Swedish Armed Forces, 64–66
sexual exploitation and abuse (SEA), 232–33; peacekeeping operations and, 26, 34–35. *See also* conflict-related sexual violence (CRSV)
sexual harassment: in Swedish Armed Forces, 64–66
sexuality, 142–43
Sexual Misconduct Prevention and Response Office (SeMPRO), 198
SHAPE WoMen, 242
situational awareness, 132

Six Day War, 157, 158
Skåre, Mari, 227
"slut-bitch" binary, 143–44
Smith, Stephen, 180, 187, 190, 191, 199, 257
social cohesion, 146–47
South African Border Wars, 207
South African Defence Force (SADF), 209; as exception, 256
South African National Defence Force (SANDF): gender mainstreaming in, 214–17; integration of, 207–8, 217–18; political context with, 209, 212, 215–16; roles and functions of women in, 213–14, 216–17; security context with, 209, 212, 215–16; in South African Border Wars, 207; in World War I, 207
South African Women's Army College, 210, 212
Southern Cross Fund, 211
Spanish-American War, 115–16
Special Operations Forces, 119
Staal Commission, 95–96
status, honorary male, 145–46, 148–49
Stavridis, James, 228
Sudan, 215
Supreme Allied Commander Europe (SACEUR), 228, 241
Swedish Armed Forces: in Afghanistan, 43–47, 50; antidiscrimination in, 62–64; application of gender perspectives in military operations of, 42–51; in Democratic Republic of the Congo, 44, 45; discrimination in, 43–44, 62–64; female engagement teams in, 49–51; as forerunners, 41; gender field advisers in, 41, 43, 45–47, 55; Genderforce and, 43, 62–63; implementation of gender perspective in, 52–55; integration of women in, 55–66; mixed engagement teams in, 49–51; recruitment for, 58–62; Security Council Resolution 1325 and, 42–43, 45, 54, 56–57; sexual harassment and assault in, 64–66
Swedish Equality Act, 5, 56
Swedish International Development Agency (Sida), 46

tactical behavior: gendered perspectives and, 8–9
tactics, techniques, and procedures (TTPs), 114
Talbot, Steve, 177
Talisman Sabre 2015 (TS15), 122, 197
Task Force Uruzgan (TFU), 100–101
Taylor, Chantelle, 147–48
Tellegen, Marie Anne, 109n8
10th Mountain Division. See US Army 10th Mountain Division
Terry, James, 125, 128
Timor-Leste, 34
Toetsingskader, 103–4
total institutions, 177
Turkey, 242

Ukraine, 7, 67
Umkhonto we Sizwe (MK), 211
UN Department of Peacekeeping Operations, 9, 23
United Kingdom military: in Afghanistan, 141, 142, 145, 147–48; discrimination in, 142–44; integration of, 141, 144–49; in Iraq, 141, 142, 145
United States: Civil War in, 115, 138n1; desegregation of armed forces in, 7; national action plan, 113, 114, 120–22, 124, 137; Revolutionary War in, 115, 138n1; women in armed forces of, 59
United States military: in Afghanistan, 114–15, 119, 120, 122–36; Army Nurse Corps in, 116; and Direct Ground Combat Definition and Assignment Rule, 113, 114, 118–19, 137; integration of, 113, 114, 117–22; in Iraq, 119, 120; in Korean War, 116, 117; Navy Nurse Corps in, 116; and Public Law 94-106, 113, 114, 118, 137; service academies, integration of, 113, 114, 118, 139n10; sexual crimes in, 233; in Spanish-American War, 115–16; in Vietnam War, 116; women as percentage of, 116–17; and Women's Armed Services Integration Act, 113, 114, 117, 137; in World War I, 116; in World War II, 116, 117
UN Mission in Cyprus (UNFICYP), 27, 33

UN Mission in Liberia (UNMIL), 33, 35, 59
UN Mission in Timor-Leste (UNMIT), 34
UN Multidimensional Integrated Stabilization Mission in Mali (MINUSMA), 105–6
UN peacekeeping operations: Brahimi Report and, 24–25; and conduct and discipline teams, 34–35; conflict-related sexual violence and, 27; effects of, 23; gender balancing in, 28–31, 31–33, 37; gendered approach in, evaluation of, 31–36; gendered approach in, evolution of, 24–27; gendered approach in, reasons for, 27–28; gender mainstreaming in, 28–31, 33–36, 37–38; history of, 24–25; Security Council Resolution 1325 and, 24, 25–27, 29, 36; and sexual exploitation and abuse, 26, 34–35; women, peace, and security agenda and, 23, 25–26; women's protection advisers and, 27
UN Security Council: recognition of women by, 1
UN Security Council Resolution 1325, 10, 39n8; adoption of, 1; Canadian Armed Forces and, 79; in framework, 3, 4t; gender mainstreaming and, 11; marginalization of, 5; misrepresentation of, 6; national action plans for, 2; NATO and, 226–29, 237–38, 243, 244–46; Netherlands Armed Forces and, 92–93, 99, 101–2; peacekeeping missions and, 24, 25–27, 29, 36; resistance to, 67; and rights-based approach, 12–13; South African National Defense Force and, 214; Swedish Armed Forces and, 42–43, 45, 54, 56–57
UN Security Council Resolutions (UNSCR): 1820, 10, 26, 194; 1888, 10, 26, 194; 1889, 10, 26, 194; 1960, 10, 26, 194; 2106, 26, 194; 2122, 26, 194–95; 2242, 26, 194
US Agency for International Development, 126

US Army 10th Mountain Division, 114–15, 122–36
US Special Operations Command (USSOCOM), 119

van Creveld, Martin, 164
van der Knaap, Cees, 93, 94, 107
Vietnam War, 116
violence. *See* sexual and gender-based violence (SGBV)
VVHK. *See* Women Auxiliary Corps (Vrijwillig Vrouwen Hulpkorps, VVHK)

Walker, Mary, 138n1
Wall, Peter, 141
warrior mind-set, 6
West Point, 118
Whitecross, Chris, 75
Wilhelmina, Queen of Netherlands, 88
Windhoek Declaration and Namibia Plan of Action on Mainstreaming a Gender Perspective in Multidimensional Peace Support Operations, 25, 27
women, peace, and security (WPS), 10–12; Australian National Action Plan on, 173, 194–97, 195–96; NATO and, 227–28, 229–30; United States National Action Plan on, 113, 114, 120–22, 124, 137; UN peacekeeping operations and, 23, 25–26
Women Auxiliary Corps (Vrijwillig Vrouwen Hulpkorps, VVHK), 88
Women's Armed Services Integration Act, 5, 113, 114, 117, 137
Women's Corps (Israel), 156–57, 160
women's protection advisers (WPAs): peacekeeping operations and, 27
work-life balance, 57
World War I, 116, 175
World War II, 116, 117, 169n6, 175, 200n4

Yom Kippur War, 157, 159

Zionism, 158

www.ingramcontent.com/pod-product-compliance
Lightning Source LLC
Chambersburg PA
CBHW032033300426
44117CB00009B/1042